JANE CAMPION

A Maori woman character from *The Piano* on the beach at Karekare, New Zealand. Courtesy of the Australian National Film and Sound Archive.

Cinema, Nation, Identity

JANE CAMPION

Edited by Hilary Radner, Alistair Fox, and Irène Bessière

 wayne state university press detroit

CONTEMPORARY APPROACHES TO
FILM AND TELEVISION SERIES

A complete listing of the books in this series can be found online at wsupress.wayne.edu

General Editor
Barry Keith Grant
Brock University

Advisory Editors
Patricia B. Erens
School of the Art Institute of Chicago

Lucy Fischer
University of Pittsburgh

Caren J. Deming
University of Arizona

Robert J. Burgoyne
Wayne State University

Tom Gunning
University of Chicago

Anna McCarthy
New York University

Peter X. Feng
University of Delaware

Lisa Parks
University of California–Santa Barbara

13 12 11 10 09   5 4 3 2 1

Library of Congress Cataloging-in-Publication Data

Jane Campion : cinema, nation, identity / edited by Hilary Radner, Alistair Fox, and Irène Bessière.
        p. cm. — (Contemporary approaches to film and television series)
    Includes bibliographical references and index.
    Includes filmography.
    ISBN 978-0-8143-3432-4 (pbk. : alk. paper)
    1. Campion, Jane—Criticism and interpretation. I. Radner, Hilary. II. Fox, Alistair.
III. Bessière, Irène.
    PN1998.3.C3545J36 2009
    791.4302'33092—dc22
    [B]   2008052804

♾

Designed by Maya Rhodes
Typeset by BookComp, Inc.
Composed in Adode Garamond and Bee Three

Contents

CONTENTS

Annabel Cooper

Acknowledgments

The editors wish to acknowledge the generous assistance received from La Fondation Maison des Sciences de l'Homme (Paris) through its director, M. Alain d'Iribarne, and from the University of Otago, New Zealand. Travel grants provided by the former and research grants awarded by the latter made possible the international research colloquium held in Dunedin 6–9 December 2006, upon which this book is based, and the editorial team is grateful for the unfailing support of Professor Geoff White, deputy vice chancellor of research at the University of Otago. Additional resources were also provided by Professor Evelyn Tribble of the Department of English, the Department of Media, Film and Communication Studies, and the Cultures and Identities Research Network at the University of Otago.

Special thanks are due to a number of people who assisted with mounting the Jane Campion colloquium, and with preparing this book: Pam Fossen, Natalie Smith, Olivia Blundell, and Melissa Cirinna, who helped with the colloquium, and Ellen Pullar, who helped with the formatting and proofing of the book. Ellen Pullar also provided invaluable help in procuring and preparing the images that are reproduced in this volume. We would particularly like to thank Sally Bongers for participating in the colloquium, and for her insightful and illuminating interventions throughout its course.

Additionally, the editors would like to thank staff at the Alexander Turnbull Archive and the New Zealand National Film Archive, Wellington, the Australian National Film and Sound Archive, Canberra, and at the Margaret Herrick Library, California, United States, for their friendly guidance concerning research materials, and for making available visual and print materials for the colloquium and this book.

Finally, we would like to record our sincere thanks to Dr. Lisa Marr for her invaluable assistance in checking the proofs.

Introduction

An Antipodean Filmmaker in an International Context

Alistair Fox and Hilary Radner

This book originates from a discussion held in Paris between Alistair Fox, a New Zealand scholar, and Irène Bessière, *Chargée de mission* at La Fondation Maison des Sciences de l'Homme, in April 2004, over ways of developing intellectual ties between France and New Zealand. It was decided on that occasion that a collaborative project on a topic of mutual interest would be an effective way of renewing and extending relationships between international scholars from the two hemispheres. Significantly, the works of the New Zealand–born filmmaker Jane Campion emerged as the most fertile common ground, given the intense interest in her shown by French film scholars and critics, who had been the first to discover her when her early student film *Peel* (1982) was awarded the prize for the best short film at the 1986 Cannes Film Festival. This French discovery of Jane Campion was confirmed subsequently when she gained the distinction of being the first woman director to receive the Palme d'Or at Cannes.

Once Campion had been identified as the subject for a collaborative research project, the logical outcome was an international research colloquium, organized jointly by Hilary Radner and Irène Bessière, co-hosted by the University of Otago and the Maison des Sciences de l'Homme, and held in Dunedin, New Zealand, in December 2006. This colloquium was accompanied by a retrospective of Jane Campion's films and a roundtable involving Sally Bongers, the cinematographer of Campion's early films. The purpose of these events was to bring together scholars, not only from France and New Zealand, but also from a range of other countries, including Australia, Belgium, and the United States. Again, the degree of enthusiasm for this enterprise displayed by all participants was striking—a further indication that Campion's films provide a field in which people from a wide range of cultural backgrounds, approaching the subject from a variety of different disciplinary perspectives, might enter into fruitful dialogue on matters of mutual interest.

Jane Campion: Cinema, Nation, Identity is the result of that productive colloquy. Building upon the earlier work of groundbreaking scholars such as Dana Polan, whose *Jane Campion* (British Film Institute, 2001) gave one of the first synoptic overviews of Jane Campion's work to date, this volume deepens existing insights into Campion by establishing for the first time the extent to which the content and style of her oeuvre are the product of preoccupations that derive from her personal family circumstances, the cultural formation imparted by her New Zealand upbringing, and her own awareness of her place within the world of filmmaking generally and of her status as a woman filmmaker in particular.[1] In exploring these issues, this book also unravels the paradox of how Campion can be a filmmaker whose work is inflected with the traces of a singularly local formation, while nevertheless commanding an appeal that is cross-cultural and international.

In the first section, a number of scholars explore the ways in which subjectivity and identity are created in Campion's films, including that which she constructs for herself. Hilary Radner investigates the extent to which Campion's films may be considered as belonging to the genre of the woman's film, and situates her in relation to other women filmmakers of her generation, showing that even though Campion may not be directly identified with a specifically feminist viewpoint, her cinema is a cinema for women, constructing a distinctively feminine subjectivity, and interpellating a feminine viewer as a member of a body of women spectators who choose to see themselves through the self-fulfillment and self-realization that her films present. Muriel Andrin pursues this theme by showing how Campion uses cinematographic techniques, mise-en-scène, and representation of the body to construct a different language—a "poetic of the inner sense"—that generates a subjective temporality, an interiority, or a space in which the self is "allowed to live." Adopting a different approach, Harriet Margolis, through an analysis of the mother-daughter relationship in Anna Campion's short film *The Audition* (1989), in which Jane Campion and her mother, Edith, play themselves, explores the self-conscious awareness of the Campion women, suggesting the importance of autobiographical elements in the construction of the identity projected to the outside world through Jane Campion's own films. Finally, Chris Holmlund examines the acting style of Harvey Keitel in Campion's *The Piano* (1993) and *Holy Smoke* (1999), and the interaction between Campion and Keitel. Holmlund suggests how the production of the affects and effects for which Campion strives depends, in part, on the nature of the collaborative working relationships she establishes—which is one of the distinguishing characteristics of her practice as an auteur, whether these relationships are formed with actors or with cinematographers.

The second section examines Campion's close relationship with literature, the creative originality that is manifest in her adaptations of literary sources, and explores how the nature of the transformations she achieves attests to an idiosyncratic singularity of vision and purpose that derives from her New Zealand background and her personal mythology. Tracing the successive stages of adaptation from the printed version of Janet Frame's famous *Autobiography*, first to Laura Jones's screenplay and then to the filmed version of *An Angel at My Table* (1990), Lawrence Jones establishes the strong personal significance that Frame's story had for Campion, who, Jones shows, used it as a vehicle for expressing a character suffering from hypersensitivity and seeking liberation from the restrictive puritan social environment in which both Frame and Campion came of age. Picking up on this theme, Alistair Fox demonstrates the importance of puritanism as a force in Campion's formation by tracing the lines of connection between the earlier novel that provided the inspiration for *The Piano*, Jane Mander's *The Story of a New Zealand River*. He shows how, in both the film version and the novelization of *The Piano*, the transgressive eroticism depicted is generated as a reaction against the puritanical repression that dominated New Zealand society during Campion's childhood. Irène Bessière, by comparing Campion's film of Henry James's *The Portrait of a Lady* (1996) with the original novel, delineates the transformation of the central character, Isabel Archer, from a Jamesian heroine into a characteristic Jane Campion woman. In Campion's film, Bessière shows, Isabel comes to embody a contemporary vision of womankind—of the place of women in society, of the relationship between men and women, and of the nature of personal fulfillment—that is distinctly different from that of James. Finally, Kathleen McHugh, through an analysis of a number of Campion's films, focuses on how their extratextual and textual framing assimilates their source texts to the field of Jane Campion's oeuvre and signature. McHugh underlines how the nature of Campion's treatment of source texts causes the films to serve an autobiographical purpose, functioning as a kind of poetic ethnography.

The third group of essays in this volume acknowledges that although Campion devotes considerable attention to the evocation of feminine internal space, she nevertheless exploits the symbolic potential of external physical locations as a means both of registering what is taking place in the inner life of her characters and of setting in motion the psychodynamic processes that attend their search for personal self-fulfillment. Jean Bessière identifies the presence of an international trope in a number of Campion's most important movies, revealed in the movement of a "transfer character" between the Old and the New World, or vice versa, in order to experience a cultural Other that leads to reinscription of a transformed personality. He shows how *The Portrait of a Lady* can, in fact, be read as an archaeology of the two films that preceded it, with the movement of Isabel Archer from the United States to Europe mirroring that of Janet in *An Angel at My Table* and the movement of Ada in *The Piano* from Europe to colonial New Zealand. In contradistinction, Rochelle Simmons identifies Campion's use of suburban settings and the suburban life of Australia as a means of depicting the stifling effects on women of contemporary gender roles from which they seek to escape. At other times, Simmons shows that Campion, especially in her earlier works, also uses suburban backdrops, accompanied by a bizarre style and expressionist cinema techniques, to assert the value of the local as a resistance to the hegemony of Hollywood. Finally, by tracing the trajectory of Campion's own career, Raphaëlle Moine demonstrates the importance of geographical contexts in Campion's own life, showing how Campion's evolution from local antipodean filmmaker to international auteur reflects an articulation of the local, the national, and the international that is one of the significant traits of contemporary international art cinema itself.

A final group of essays presents a number of responses to Campion's films by an array of viewers, attesting to the fact that although Campion is a highly personal and idiosyncratic director, she nonetheless manages to interpellate a wide range of viewers across a broad cultural spectrum in a variety of ways. Through an analysis of the French reception of *An Angel at My Table* and *The Piano,* Simon Sigley reveals an appreciation on the part of French critics for the invigorating vitality and primitive energies of what was perceived as an *art brut,* with Campion's films bearing the alluring marks of both familiarity and alterity, and with New Zealand itself serving as an imaginary signifier for emotional projection. Sue Gillett, on the other hand, taking a psychoanalytic and ficto-critical approach, shows how the powerful emotional experiences that Jane Campion's heroines undergo within the diegesis elicit an equally powerful affective response in the spectator, in a way that unsettles the viewer's adult subjectivity with the purpose of initiating a regression, fragmentation, and reconstruction of the adult subject. Through her examination of the presence of spiritual issues and the representation of spirituality in Campion's films, Ann Hardy demonstrates how these films contain elements that make them susceptible to interpretation through a religious frame of reference. In particular, she provides a reading of *Holy Smoke* as an undogmatic exploration of spirituality—a film that pursues an apprehension of the moral occult that also, inevitably, expresses itself in the exploration of intimate relationships. Finally, to end this section and provide a fitting conclusion to the whole book, Annabel Cooper offers a reading of Jane Campion as an antipodean, from the perspective of an antipodean woman, showing how the quality of being antipodean attaches itself to Jane Campion's films and to Campion herself, in that she draws on the inheritance of "the antipodean feminine" not only in the construction of the adventures her heroines undergo but also for the fashioning of her own public persona. The effect, Cooper argues, is that Campion produces a narrative that, while answering back to the Old World on one hand, generates the impression of an identity that is somewhat mobile and contingent on the other—reflecting Campion's participation in ambiguities that have been both fruitful and troubling.

Taken as a whole, the essays in this book offer a multiplicity of new insights into the role of art and the artist, the nature of sexual relationships, and national and gendered identities. On one level, the essays attest to the ways in which "authorship" continues to be a useful category for the analysis of film—on the model offered by cinema scholars such as Janet Staiger, in which the "author" is considered to function as an agent within the confines of a set of narrative tropes and institutions that constitute the culturally written.[2] In this respect, the sense of authorship that emerges from the essays in this book is much closer to the notion of creative imitation used to describe Shakespeare's adaptation of his sources than to the idea of an artist who forges an original vision ex nihilo. Although the authorship analysis offered in this volume enhances understanding of Campion's oeuvre, the definition of *auteurism* that is used necessarily implies an understanding of the cultural function and production of the filmmaker as auteur within the larger context of cinema as a global industry.

On another level, these essays illuminate the way that Campion, through her art, has been able to tap into a number of discourses that often seem contradictory: feminist, psychoanalytic, nationalistic, and even spiritual. There appear to be many "Jane Campions" as a result, with viewers experiencing a very powerful emotional reaction to whichever "Jane" they detect. The reaction of the audience when *Sweetie* was screened at Cannes suggests the spectrum of possibilities: a large number of viewers booed the movie and left, while the remainder of the audience cheered. This demonstrates the power of Campion's art to polarize spectators, often in a passionate way— as illustrated by Adrian Martin's disparaging dismissal of her or the outrage of indigenous scholars at the way she depicted Maori in *The Piano*—but it seldom leaves them feeling indifferent, which is a supreme testimony to her significance as a filmmaker.[3]

These essays as a group show why Campion occupies an unusual place as an auteur who is singular in her antipodean exoticism but who nevertheless has a global appeal. Being both inside and outside European and Western culture, she can offer a perspective that is critical, yet not dismissive, reflecting a stance that is both apart from and a part of the material she addresses. Because of her particular history and the set of relations to cinematic institutions that this implies, Campion occupies a singular place in the world of cinema, with her films constituting a body of work that is distinctive—stylistically, generically, and in terms of the personal vision that they embody.

Notes

1. See also Ellen Cheshire, *The Pocket Essential Jane Campion* (Harpenden: Pocket Essentials, 2000).

2. See, e.g., Janet Staiger, "Authorship Studies and Gus Van Sant," *Film Criticism* 29:1 (Fall 2004): 1–22.

3. Adrian Martin, "Losing the Way: The Decline of Jane Campion," *Landfall* 200 (2000): 88–102; Leonie Pihama, "Ebony and Ivory: Constructions of Maori in *The Piano*," in *Jane Campion's* The Piano, ed. Harriet Margolis (New York: Cambridge University Press, 2000), 114–34.

Part I
Subjectivities and the Construction of Identity in Jane Campion's Films

Jane Campion on the set of *The Portrait of a Lady*. Courtesy of the Academy of Motion Picture Arts and Sciences.

"In extremis"
Jane Campion and the Woman's Film

The Woman's Film and the Auteur Director

In 1986, during that same period in which Jane Campion came of age as a filmmaker, Charlotte Brunsdon, the feminist media scholar, introduced her edited volume *Films for Women* with the following statement: "Within commercial film production there have always been movies made specially for female audiences, often showcasing women's fashion and featuring women's stars." She continues: "These films for women were usually stories of love, loss, longing, and sacrifice."[1] For Brunsdon, what defines a film as "for women" is what she calls a "notion of gendered address" that can be translated into a set of viewer expectations tied to certain genres, which may be confirmed or disappointed and which are often reinforced through marketing.[2] Brunsdon's introduction highlights why it was that Rick Altman, as well as a generation of genre critics following in his wake, such as Raphaëlle Moine, have underlined the woman's film as an example of a genre constituted by viewers and viewing practices, in particular feminist critics, rather than by producers.[3] While Altman specifically saw the woman's film as emerging out of feminist concerns, the spate of recent guides for women in search of "chick flicks" highlights the validity of the concept beyond academia.[4]

Writers of these guides, such as Kim Adelman in *The Ultimate Guide to Chick Flicks: The Romance, the Glamour, the Tears, and More,* tend to justify the films that they select along lines very similar to those proposed by Brunsdon, that is, in terms of how these films address a feminine viewer. Adelman explains: "By definition these films are specifically created to appeal to females—our emotions, our issues, our fantasies, our fears."[5] In *Chick Flicks: A Movie Lover's Guide to the Movies Women Love,* Jami Bernard places Jane Campion's *The Piano* in the category "Emotional Rescue" with *The Bodyguard* (1992), *Gaslight* (1944), *Someone to Watch Over Me* (1987), and *Summertime* (1955), locating Campion within a certain genealogy that moves across genres, periods, and directors, unified by the way these films gratify certain kinds of expectations on the part of women viewers.[6] Not surprisingly, again Bernard's definition of the "chick flick" echoes Brunsdon: "In today's parlance, a Chick Flick is much more than a melodrama. It is any movie that makes a special connection with a female audience. It can be defined by the qualities it has that usually attract women—female stars, familiar situations, cute guys, emotional catharsis."[7]

While these popular viewing guides testify to the way in which women have embraced the movies as an integral part of feminine culture, and continue to do so, the feminist reaction to cinema is more varied, characterized by peripatetic turns. Writers like Marjorie Rosen and Molly Haskell in the 1970s saw cinema, and in particular the woman's film, in a largely negative light. In *Popcorn Venus: Movies and the American Dream,* Rosen describes films of the 1930s as offering "a belated distortion of the truth of woman's social role."[8] Haskell is equally critical, imputing to cinema the role of reinforcing the "lie" of "women's inferiority."[9] Nonetheless, feminist film theorists, such as Sue Thornham, attribute to Haskell the beginnings of a different kind of analysis, which recognizes that though cinema, and the woman's film in particular, supports the status quo, it also is "resistant to ideologies of femininity."[10] Thornham's position reflects the manner in which certain Hollywood films popular with the "femmes" (in *Variety*'s terms) were reclaimed by feminist scholars who assessed them, not as the instrument of patriarchal oppression, but as proto-feminist expressions of women's concerns in a world that was largely indifferent to their lot.[11] Jeanine Basinger propounds, for example, that "seeds of unrest, even rebellion, were planted in female minds by the evidence that they saw on screen, despite the conventional endings that turn a story into a cautionary tale."[12]

While feminist scholars reevaluated the woman's film of the past, women directors, feminist and nonfeminist, entered increasingly the world of mainstream narrative cinema.[13] As Thornham comments:

If we look at the films of Sally Potter, who with *Orlando* (1993) has made a similar move, or Jane Campion (*The Piano,* 1993), it would be difficult to maintain that these films do not manifest the concerns central to feminist theory: the relationship of women to language, and to public and private histories; sexual difference and its relationship to other forms of difference; the limits and the possibilities of desire; the relationship between women—in particular between mothers and daughters. At the same time, they fully engage—if subversively—with the conventions of popular film: in this case, with costume melodrama and the "woman's film."[14]

Thornham points to certain films (including those by Campion) as representing perhaps a new form of the woman's film, produced by "auteur" directors, emerging out of what was frequently called a "counter cinema," while engaging with the traditional concerns of the genre. Significantly, Campion exemplifies a director whose work successfully straddles the various concerns of the feminist critic and the feminine viewer, in particular through her film *The Piano* (also routinely taken up by chick flick guides). Her hybrid status as an auteur director of women's films raises significant questions about the role of the woman's film today, and about its shift from the matinee feature of movie palaces to the art house theater and festival circuit.

Scholars like Basinger paid little attention to the director or notions of "authorship"; in contrast, recent discussions of contemporary women's cinema by scholars such as Alison Butler and Christina Lane privilege the woman director.[15] For these younger scholars, these films are women's films precisely because they are films by women—that is to say, defined in terms of authorship.[16] The focus on authorship echoes certain changes within the film world itself: in an era in which the public no longer exclusively relies on specific formulas to define a film, media industries have produced parallel sets of distribution and viewing strategies in which the mark of the individual directors on specific films is a significant factor in terms of marketing and reception. Because Campion's work clearly addresses women viewers while also being the product of an auteur, it offers a fertile context in which to explore these two competing definitions of women's cinema—as a cinema for women or a cinema by women.

Gendered Address and the Cinema of Jane Campion

According to scholars like Brunsdon and Basinger, Hollywood produced a cinema for women by addressing women through films that elaborated upon certain thematic issues within a narrative organization that was character-driven, focusing on a woman as both the subject (the organizing sensibility) and the object (the topic) of the story. At first glance, Campion's films — almost inevitably organized around a single female protagonist who is often ambivalent, torn in her desires and aspirations—recall those features that Basinger sees as defining the woman's film of classical Hollywood, which offered a "consistently inconsistent purpose and attitude" that both challenged and reaffirmed the traditional woman's role while serving "to place a woman as the center of the story universe." In other words, "I am woman and I am important."[17] The centrality of the woman and her concerns was accompanied by the idea that love is the single most important legitimating function of the woman, and in fact "love" is what makes her a woman.[18] Finally, "a temporary visual liberation of some sort," which at times Basinger refers to as the "happy interlude," emphasized the crucial function of the woman's desire as something that was by its nature transitory, the property of cinema rather than life. In Basinger's words, this "happy interlude" is "an escape into a purely romantic love, into sexual awareness, into luxury, or into the rejection of the female role that might only come in some form of questioning."[19]

In keeping with Basinger's definition, Campion's films construct a subjectivity that posits the heroine as the primary narrative vehicle for the film's story. In this sense, she, the heroine, is at the center of her universe. This subjectivity is, however, fragile, its integrity threatened by the intrusion of other points of view—those of other (competing) subjectivities in the form of friends, sisters, and lovers. These others may, on the one hand, be threatening, as in the case of Dawn in *Sweetie* (1989) and Malloy in *In the Cut* (2003), or they may, on the other hand, perform the function of a double whose sacrifice preserves the subjectivity of the heroine and her place in the story as more or less intact, as in the case of Pauline in *In the Cut*. Most important, these others can perform a redemptive function (e.g., Baines in *The Piano*, P. J. Waters in *Holy Smoke*); however, this redemption is always costly and accompanied by a violation of that initial subjectivity. Ada in *The Piano* suffers assault and mutilation; Ruth in *Holy Smoke* is imprisoned by her family, stripped of her clothing, psychologically and physically isolated, and tormented and humiliated to the point of fleeing alone into the outback. In both cases, there are brutal and irrevocable consequences for the heroine, who will be forever changed and chastened through these experiences.

The extreme nature of the heroine's dilemma in her confrontation with the other and its consequence (often death for her double, as with Dawn in *Sweetie* and Pauline in *In the Cut*) moves the woman's film out of the arena of domestic melodrama or romantic comedy into other genres—the gothic romance (*The Piano*) or the erotic thriller (*In the Cut*).[20] Thus the mise-en-scène echoes the potentially fragmented and violated subjectivity of the heroine, whose universe is never completely whole.[21] In this sense, Campion offers a contemporary version of the woman's film that foregrounds the problem of contradiction and of film's inability to reconcile that contradiction—because the adult world requires the acceptance of loss (within the cinema of Campion). In the case of Kay in *Sweetie*, she loses her sister; for Ada in *The*

Kay and Dawn, competing subjectivities in *Sweetie*. Photo by Regis Lansac. Courtesy of the New Zealand National Film Archive.

Piano, it is the piano itself and what it signifies that must be relinquished.[22] Isabel in *The Portrait of a Lady* (1996) remains (literally) on the threshold of her decision, a decision by which she stands to lose, whatever the outcome, having already lost that which she held most dear, her innocent enthusiasm for a universe of infinite possibility.

Ultimately, it is not the point of view of the secondary characters that poses the most consistent threat to the story world of the film: it is the film-maker herself who, as an auteur, asserts her dominance over the narrative within the film through the use of stylistic devices that disrupt the story, such as the surreal animated sequences inserted into *Sweetie, The Piano, The Portrait of a Lady, Holy Smoke,* and *In the Cut;* the reverse chronology employed in *Two Friends;* and the controversial contemporary-documentary-style sequence that introduces *The Portrait of a Lady,* to name a few.[23] The nature of these ruptures is not stylistically consistent; it is the act of rupture, the drawing attention to the film as such and to its "createdness" and hence its creator, the auteur, that is sustained, if not always in the same manner.

Colin MacCabe, in an oft-quoted article, argues that certain films in the post-Hollywood era used such strategies of interruption (or to use Brecht's term, "alienation") to undermine the realism of the cinematic narrative and thus effect a kind of political commentary on cinema as a narrative institution.[24] While this might have been the case for certain directors of the 1960s and 1970s, Campion's interventions, her constant reminders of her authorial presence—she goes so far as to appear in certain of her films, for example, a dance sequence in *In the Cut*—have a different function.[25] They remind the viewer that this is a woman's narrative, written by a woman with a very specific view. As such, these interventions lend authenticity to the narrative. Rather than detracting from the realism of the story, Campion's presence encourages the viewer to find a kind of emotional fidelity to the woman's perspective that lends credence to the experiences that her films invoke.

Should her authorial interventions prove insufficient, Campion is careful to reiterate her position in numerous interviews.[26] She does not allow the viewer to forget that these are her stories or her story articulated as a palimpsest of visual and thematic strands maintained and developed from film to film beginning with her earliest works.[27] These recurring narrative themes and devices, evident even in Campion's student films, include (but certainly are not limited to) an emphasis on the double and the pair as a visual motif, the reworking of what Sigmund Freud calls the family romance, the persistence of the mother/daughter dyad, the theme of artistic and erotic self-realization (often intertwined), and mise-en-scène as the externalization of the heroine's state of mind.[28]

Doubles and the Female Pair:
From A Girl's Own Story to In the Cut

Mishaps: Seduction and Conquest (1981), Campion's earliest film available for public viewing, recounts the tale of two brothers, establishing a pattern in terms of doubling and the use of familial relations to set the terms of the doubled pair. Similarly, *Peel: An Exercise in Discipline* (1982) focuses on the interactions within a familial triangle, where the aunt takes the position usually accorded the mother, creating a family romance at one remove in which brother and sister, child and woman, father and son are alternately paired and separated. Sister doubles brother, while son doubles father in an endless permutation of formal compositions and emotional alliances.[29] More significant in terms of Campion's development as a woman auteur director is *A Girl's Own Story* (1984). This film, the final and most mature work to come out of Campion's film school years, recounts the story of one young girl, her

Frannie and Pauline, the themes of the double and family romance in *In the Cut*. Courtesy of the Academy of Motion Picture Arts and Sciences.

"own" story, by positioning her story against that of a number of other young girls (one in particular) whose resemblance is underlined by their school uniforms. A girl's story can only be told through the proliferation and doubling of girls; a single girl is never enough to represent the complexities of girlhood, a strategy echoed in *Two Friends* (1986), which cements Campion's position as a director who tells women's (and girls') stories.

While Campion's early films as a group were significant—establishing her status as an auteur director, in particular *Peel*, for which she won the Palme d'Or in 1986—*A Girl's Own Story*, which Kathleen McHugh describes as "Campion's first sustained narrative," plays a singularly crucial role in establishing the scope and distinctiveness of Campion as a director who makes films for and about women, as underlined by the title.[30] Although the film was made in the 1980s in Australia, New Zealanders born in the late 1940s and 1950s frequently report that the film conveys what it meant to grow up female in New Zealand, citing trivial details such as the girls' uniforms, the ubiquitous electric heaters (which reappear in *An Angel at My Table*), as well as social issues, such as the treatment of unwed mothers and the general sexual repressiveness of the late 1950s and 1960s.[31] Thematically and visually, then, this film offers a narrative matrix through which the viewer can come to identify a set of films as being by Campion. Kathleen McHugh, for example, highlights the relationship between *A Girl's Own Story* and the more recent *In the Cut,* underlining how Campion, through the way that she revises the original novel by Susanna Moore, enlarges "the theme of the double . . . all intertwined in the family romance added to the film."[32] Similarly, McHugh comments on the film's opening dream sequence: "The black, white, sepia, and red film stock of the dream sequence pointedly revisits the cinematography of *Mishaps: Seduction and Conquest,* while the ice skates and leather glove reanimate traumatic images from *A Girl's Own Story.*"[33]

This accumulation of invested images and devices evokes the ways in which Campion's films facilitate the interpellation of a feminine viewer, as a member of a body of women spectators who choose to see themselves through Campion's films and for whom this accumulation signals a kind of ownership and belonging, echoing many of the concerns of both the woman's film and feminist film theory as adumbrated by Thornham.[34]

Campion's Image

Campion's own relationship with her image (the proliferation of photographs that alternate between girlishness and glamour) and her oeuvre (her films are often accompanied by novelizations, copious radio interviews, etc.) serve to posit her as the star of her own productions. Symptomatic of the position that she occupies is the controversy surrounding her national identity: is she a New Zealand director or an Australian director?[35] Or, more properly, does her work fall into the category of art cinema produced for a nomadic and global intellectual class (into which she herself falls)?[36] Perhaps, as the heroine of her own work, she occupies a position that she imagines as outside history, in which "the woman herself" constitutes the pivotal instance of identity, an identity defined like that of her heroines through self-fulfillment and self-realization within the confines of a universe in which she is the center.

Feeding into Campion's personal mythology is the mythology surrounding her family within New Zealand. McHugh comments that "her parents were both prominent figures in New Zealand theater and she grew up in an environment saturated with theater, performance, and film" and, further, that her father, Richard Campion, was "described by historians as a 'giant of New Zealand theater.'"[37] The Campion family photographs are housed in the Alexander Turnbull Library, one of the major New Zealand national archives. The catalog includes the following description:

Jane in her mother's house at Otaki, from the Edith Campion Collection. Courtesy of the Alexander Turnbull Library, Wellington, New Zealand. (Reference number PAColl-5872–077.)

These photographs are part of a larger collection comprising a voluminous correspondence, along with notes, drafts, newspaper cuttings and other papers relating to Edith Campion, a former director of R Hannah Ltd, an actor and a writer of short stories and poetry. Included in the correspondence are many letters, scripts and film treatments from her daughters Jane and Anna Campion, who are both involved in the film industry. The papers as a whole reflect in detail the life and problems of a talented upper middle-class family in the dying years of the twentieth century.[38]

The catalog description positions the family as paradigmatic of a larger category, "a talented upper middle-class family in the dying years of the twentieth century," evoking a larger history that has defined the Campions, but in which they are also actors and performers. The Campions, then, as both exceptional and ordinary, like the heroines of the woman's film, produce a collection of photographs that provide a social document, contributing to the position that Campion holds as the heroine of her own life in the public's eye—certainly, at the very least, within New Zealand. That these photographs found their way to the Turnbull available for public viewing implies a self-consciousness on the part of the Campion family as it performed itself. This self-consciousness, as well as the biographical connections between Jane Campion's life and cinema, is underlined by *The Audition* (1989), a film directed by her older sister, Anna Campion. In the film Anna directs Edith Campion and Jane in a reenactment of Edith's audition for the part that she plays in *Angel at My Table*.[39]

Typical of the collection in the Turnbull Library is a picture of Jane Campion as a youngish woman (dated 1980s–90s).[40] In an uncontrived snapshot, Campion looks straight into the camera, her lips forming a tentative smile, her hair pulled back severely, and a black jersey draped casually over her shoulders. Behind her are a collection of photographs, tacked almost haphazardly on the wall, of herself, her sister, and her mother. This collection in this same arrangement, in fact, appears in *The Audition,* thus identifying this image as a photograph of Jane taken in her mother's home in the late 1980s, possibly by her mother herself. The photographs displayed behind Jane contribute to an understanding of the way in which identity as a process of construction and performance underlines the family's own sense of self—and more important, Jane's conception of herself as a woman defined primarily through relations with other women—and with herself as she once was, as she anticipates she might become.

The most prominent photograph is one of Jane herself, probably taken during the period in which she appeared in New Zealand director Barry Barclay's short film *All That We Need* (1966) as an allegorical figure, the Flower Girl, representing nature and its virtues. Also featured are images of Anna Campion, of Jane and Anna, of Jane and her mother, and of a cat. Many of these images, such as the picture of Jane and her mother, are included in the folio housed in the Turnbull. In these collections of photographs (both on the wall and those in the Turnbull collection more generally), we find echoes of the visual tropes that mark Campion's oeuvre: the young girl, the female pair, often two sisters but perhaps two friends, the mother/daughter dyad, the cat. Male figures are present in this collection, in particular in earlier family photographs; however, the Campion women dominate, including Campion's young daughter. Campion's films might be said to generate a similar album of images (images that recall those in her mother's family album), which produce the heroine's universe and position her as the center of that universe but which also refer us back to the director herself.

Art, Life, and the "Happy Interlude"

The resonance that Campion's teasing out of these relations through film evokes in an international audience can be tied to specific influences that created the context in which she emerged as a filmmaker—one which encouraged her to see film as a mechanism whereby the relations of the self to the self might be explored, and to consider the fears and desires of women as deeply important and significant. In this sense, it is the film itself that provides the equivalent of the "happy interlude" ascribed to the classical woman's film by Basinger. Campion's films invite the viewer to share within the space of the cinema itself the experience of a happy interlude that might be termed the experience of art itself. This is to say that this interlude allows the female viewer to experience her concerns as significant, not at a remove through the creation of a fictional fantasy world, but through a conversation with a highly regarded woman director who authorizes and legitimates these concerns by presenting them through the medium of art. For example, Campion explains her relationship to the heroine Isabel Archer of *The Portrait of a Lady*: "Isabel was like myself—a romantic addict when I was young and falling in love. I did a con-job on myself, occasionally with very unsuitable people, and it was a great revelation to me that I knew her on such a close and personal basis that I felt such permission to get in there and play with her and to be involved in James' story."[41] Similarly, in the documentary *Portrait: Jane Campion and* The Portrait of a Lady (1997), about the making of *The Portrait of a Lady*, Campion herself comments: "I'm not really living my life, I'm living my film"—recalling the invitation to at least temporarily "live my film" that she offers cinema spectators.[42]

Campion's heroines often struggle over the choice of life or art. In *An Angel at My Table*, the protagonist, Janet Frame, is portrayed as finding redemption through her writing and her solitary status as a woman artist. Dana Polan describes Frame at the film's conclusion: "Solitude has now become the site of her self-affirmation. Aesthetic creation has become her life."[43] In *The Piano*, Ada's art, her piano, is sacrificed so that she can find fulfillment through ordinary speech. While these controversies indicate certain problems at the heart of women's experiences, the films themselves as an experience resolve the conflict between life and art by presenting the two simultaneously, as an opportunity to "live my art."

Two significant influences encouraged this double focus on Campion's own inward experiences and their relations to women's experiences more generally as the subject of her art. First, the Australian Film and Television

School fostered a climate that was favorable to the development of an auteurist approach, in particular one influenced by the work of French director François Truffaut, in which the director often looked to his or her own
life for inspiration.[44] While Campion tended to minimize the influence that
film school had on her work—portraying herself as a rebel—the outsider
status that she accords herself is belied by the way she is featured (with Sally
Bongers, her cinematographer for *A Girl's Own Story* and *Sweetie*) in the
1982–83 Australian Film, Television, and Radio School (AFTRS) Report,
for example, implying that the school recognized and fostered certain kinds
of talent.[45] McHugh explains: "Campion's technical training took place in an
institution nominally committed to an art, rather than a trade, orientation
to the cinema."[46]

A second significant influence was Second Wave Feminism. As Kathleen
McHugh asserts, "Campion fortuitously came of age in an era and national
industry transformed by femininism."[47] Indeed, in Australia in the 1970s, the
role of women in the media was a national concern, resulting in highly favorable conditions for aspiring women filmmakers in the 1980s, and McHugh
concludes that "in many ways, she [Campion] was at the right place at the
right time and was exactly the right kind of student for AFTRS in the early
1980s."[48] Campion appeared at a moment when hard battles had been won—a
moment that was especially encouraging of women who wished to reflect upon
their status and identity rather than fight political battles. Campion herself
commented in a 1993 television broadcast: "I feel as a filmmaker I grew up in
Australia and am very much the recipient of a very generous attitude towards
film education particularly for women, which is unique in the world."[49]

At the Center of Her Universe

Not coincidentally, Campion's development as a director coincides with other
developments in feminine culture, such as the academic explosion in the area
of feminist criticism, feminist theory, women's studies, and, later, gender
studies. Women felt free to question the terms of femininity both within
and without academia without necessarily seeing themselves as making a
political statement. And though Campion often questions the parameters
and capacities of women, she rarely seems to question their status as women.
Her gaze is directed inward toward the kinds of concerns that scholars such
as Jeanine Basinger have identified with classical Hollywood's woman's film.
Campion explains why she went into film as a medium: "I decided I wanted
to do work about things I was thinking about and involved in, which were
generally relationships and love . . . and sex!"[50]

These are the themes that Basinger identifies with the woman's film; however, the kinds of operations that Campion performs upon these themes have as much in common with feminist film theory as with the classical Hollywood film, as noted by scholars such as Sue Thornham and Dana Polan. Within Campion's corpus, the woman's film pushes the conventions of the genre in order to make certain kinds of extreme statements about the ways in which a woman figures her identity and her desire. In a 1992 interview, Campion explained that she wants to let women know that she has an "understanding of women as different from men." She sees herself as "attracted to the . . . sensitivity and the complexity of women." She thinks that "women are privileged" by "our society being allowed to be developed . . . in a more whimsical way than men are." She concedes that "I've come to like men more . . . not to see them as the enemy. . . . Men are just as emotional as women naturally, there's more pressure on them to suppress it."[51] Nonetheless, the basis of her understanding, her point of departure, is "woman," and she ensures that we look with women as much as at them in her films. Film scholar Stella Bruzzi goes so far as to claim that "*The Piano,* enforcing a simple inversion of the normative process, addresses the question of what happens when the agent of the gaze is female and its object is the male body."[52]

The controversy that surrounds Campion's work derives at least in part from the way in which she repeatedly positions these women, who are of European origin and whose gaze is "white" within the context of a certain political extremity.[53] For example, in *The Piano,* Ada's personal drama unfolds against a political backdrop of the rape of a country, which Campion portrays without sentimentality, emphasis, or comment. In *Holy Smoke,* Ruth—for whose family India can only be imagined as a touristic interlude or the source of a terrible unspeakable threat—seems to deviate from her obsession with her own salvation by the film's conclusion. We leave her working among the poor (albeit for animal rights), but without any statement that might indicate a shift in point of view—whether her point of view or the vision of the world offered by the film itself, which though not entirely coinciding with that of Ruth or her family, is not independent of their assumptions. The film offers a world in which the primary investments of the characters are in themselves and those within their intimate circle. Similarly, in *In the Cut,* notwithstanding Frannie's dedication as a teacher, she seems oblivious to the political realities of her students' world, that of the African American youth in a deeply racist society.

These geographies appear to have as their primary function to portray the extremity of the heroine's psychic condition—in the case of Ruth, for

15

example, her desperate need to escape the alternatingly claustrophobic and agoraphobic aridity of Australian family life, and in the case of Frannie, her inability to reconcile her romantic imagination with erotic reality. This focus on the heroine has been a source of controversy, not only in terms of Campion's films, but also in terms of the genre of the woman's film as a whole; nonetheless, the woman's film remains relentlessly self-absorbed.[54]

The fissured subjectivity that Campion develops might be said to work against this self-absorption, for like many heroines of the woman's film, Campion's heroines are punished for their inability to consider the Other. It is difficult, however, to consider this rupture in the narcissistic universe of the female protagonist as politically motivated. On the contrary, the force that enables Campion's heroine to achieve closure, to live as an integrated self in a world haunted by fragmentation, is usually good old-fashioned heterosexuality. Kay loses her sister but appears to regain sense of self with Louie. Ada finds, if not happiness, at least peace with Baines. Isabel Archer is unusual because she finds herself alone at the film's conclusion. She is alone but also somehow psychically whole because of the lessons that she has learned, if at great cost, through heterosexuality. In Campion's cinema the only alternative to heterosexuality is the family romance, in which maternal and sibling relations prevent the imagining of other erotic possibilities—or finally, as in the case of Janet Frame, art and solitude.

In the last analysis, Campion's feature films, beginning with *Sweetie,* are "safe," in spite of the extreme situations in which the heroines find themselves—like the women's films of classical Hollywood. Thus, while the heroine of Susanna Moore's novel *In the Cut* dies, her murder concluding the novel, in the film, Frannie triumphs over her aggressor and escapes into the arms of her awaiting lover.[55] True, there is a kind of atmosphere of dreariness and pain that surrounds this reunion; this is a chastened couple, expelled from Eden, yet alive and animated by hope, one that preserves the possibility of heterosexual femininity as a mode of identity.

It is probably the case that Campion's appeal lies in the fact that she does not stand completely apart from the last twenty years of feminine culture, which has tried to preserve the conventions of femininity while interrogating its norms, living through feminism without necessarily either taking up the banner or rejecting its rhetoric. She becomes, then, a filmmaker who is difficult to classify because, though on the one hand she certainly pushes the limits of the "chick flick," on the other she never entirely escapes from its confines. Campion's work emerges out of feminism as part of a movement that might be termed "After Feminism," which, rightly or wrongly, assumes that the category "woman" offers a figure of the human that transcends boundaries (national, ethnic, religious, class). Her films testify not only to the limitations of this perspective but also to the necessity of imagining these unifying human figures that offer the promise, if only in mythic form, of an understanding that respects the individual subject while embracing something that might be called the universal.

A "Feminist Orbit"

Campion's films, then, if not overtly "feminist," usually fall within what Christine Gledhill calls "the feminist orbit."[56] They are films that, in Christine Lane's words, "centrally engage with feminist issues," though not necessarily feminist in intent or design.[57] Within this context, Campion (b. 1954) often appears alongside a generation of directors like Susan Seidelman (b. 1952), Martha Coolidge (b. 1946), Kathryn Bigelow (b. 1950), and Lizzie Borden (b. 1958), who came of age in a period marked by what Kathleen McHugh calls "Global Feminism" and whose early films might be considered a form of "counter cinema," their later films moving increasingly into mainstream production.[58] In comparison to their male counterparts, these women have directed relatively few films and their films have received a proportionally greater amount of attention from women, academic women in particular. Among this group, Campion is notable for being a New Zealander and for maintaining a regular, if not especially prolific, output of films, retaining her position as an insider/outsider within the film industry. In contrast, director Susan Seidelman—who, like Campion, attended film school; whose first feature production *Smithereens* (1982) was also presented at Cannes; and whose later film *Desperately Seeking Susan,* like *The Piano,* enjoyed a certain iconic status within both feminine culture and feminist criticism—has focused on television in recent years, pointing to the way that Campion as a New Zealander/Australian may have enjoyed a greater autonomy than her American and perhaps even her European counterparts.[59]

Campion's work might also be productively compared to that of a generation of Francophone directors such as Catherine Breillat and Clair Denis. Institutions such as the International Festival of Women's Film held in Créteil created an environment that encouraged a cinema that fell within a feminist orbit, albeit with a more restricted distribution, confined to the Francophone world. Indeed the 1999 festival featured one of the first retrospectives of Campion's work. Similarly, there are significant parallels to be drawn between Campion's career and that of the Canadian filmmaker Patricia Rozema as well as the Indian expatriate Mira Nair. The wide spectrum of women auteur directors that might be included within a feminist orbit testifies to the validity of Kathleen McHugh's concept of a global feminism, albeit within a relatively restricted world of affluent social groups.[60]

Developments in the film industry during the 1980s facilitated the growth of films within the "feminist orbit." Independent filmmakers, including women filmmakers, benefited from changes in the economics of film production. In the late 1980s and 1990s, film production moved in two opposing directions—one toward an emphasis on event films, blockbusters that appealed to the broadest possible audience, and the other toward niche films, often low-budget (and thus low risk) films by first-time directors that took advantage of the "market fragmentation" resulting from the large number of high-concept films. Independent niche companies, such as Miramax and New Line in particular, profited from savvy or lucky target marketing, successfully challenging the studio oligarchy while exploiting the need for product arising out of new technologies, VCRs, satellite, cable, and, later, DVDs.[61] Christina Lane in her 2000 study of independent women directors in Hollywood comments: "In the early 1990s, 'major independents' were dependent on studios in many ways; however, they were often able to foster a degree of autonomy because their films did not seem, on the surface, to threaten studio product."[62] The result from Lane's perspective was that "the line between counter cinema and commercial cinema was beyond blurry—it was practically moot."[63] The development of a body of films that might be understood as falling with the feminist orbit while retaining a purchase on feminine culture arose out of a cultural milieu, as Thornham notes, but also in response to favorable economic conditions in which certain niche or even counter cinema perspectives were deemed to be "good business." This blurring of distinctions, then, is a quality that defines the new woman's film across a number of areas, including production and distribution.

Campion's career (like that of Seidelman and others of her generation) was determined by these shifts and the new perceived demand for narrow-cast films—initially manifested, in Campion's case, through the support of French-based companies (who, with government subventions, also sought to exploit the demand for niche Anglophone films) like CiBy 2000 (which produced *The Piano*) and Polygram (which produced *The Portrait of a Lady*) but also the major American independent Miramax (which produced *Holy Smoke*).[64] Campion's more recent film *In the Cut* (2003), again in English but produced by Pathé, relied on European funds, while seeking to appeal to a primarily Anglophone female audience. With its high profile stars, Meg Ryan and Mark Ruffalo, the film falls somewhere between mainstream entertainment and art house fare, both in terms of its production values and its address to a specific kind of woman's audience—literate, able to recognize references to Virginia Woolf without being radical.[65]

Campion's French connections enabled her to keep her distance from Hollywood and exert greater control over her productions while exploiting an Anglophone niche audience of women viewers who sought to see women's issues portrayed on screen but who also wanted more serious fare than offered by the likes of Nancy Meyers or Nora Ephron, Hollywood directors who made films for women that were clearly commercial in their orientation. This niche within a niche reflected the increased interest in women as a significant film-consuming demographic in the cinema industry as a whole, and Hollywood in particular—as an audience that was distinct and could be differentiated from the more event-oriented audience to whom blockbusters were usually targeted. This new niche also emphasized a growing gap between the art world, which continued to support a more overtly feminist strand of production that extended the concerns of the initial feminist film theorists, and the world of independent cinema, which reached a broader if not necessarily a mass audience.

Campion's films, then, operate across a range of fields as "for women"—for popular women viewers and for women viewers and scholars focusing on feminist concerns. This reception revolves around the place of feminism and femininity in contemporary culture—and as such reflects the heterogeneous nature of the woman's film of classical Hollywood as defined by Jeanine Basinger. This heterogeneity is also, I would argue, a reflection, on the one hand, of the fragmented definitions of feminism today and, on the other, of the ambivalent yet pervasive legacy of Second Wave Feminism. Seidelman, for example, is described as "never backing down from her feminist roots" while claiming "she wasn't a political filmmaker, averring that she was really interested in sociology in her filmmaking."[66] Similarly, Patricia Rozema, a Canadian filmmaker from the same generation, asserts, "I'm not a polemicist or a moralist. I don't promote certain behaviors. I look and write in reaction."[67] Campion is described as occupying a parallel position by feminist authors Judith Redding and Victoria Brown. These women directors, then, are united through the fact that though their films are inevitably judged by the variable yardsticks of feminisms, their own relations to politics are ambivalent. They see themselves as observers rather than activists, which tends to distinguish them from the more experimental and more overtly political artists such as Dara Birnbaum, Trinh T. Min-ha, or the younger Salla Tykkä coming out of a tradition established by theorists and artists such as Laura Mulvey and Martha Rosler in the 1970s.[68] The division, then, seems to exist not so much between a counter cinema and a commercial cinema for women as between the theoretically marked museum- and gallery-based work—often installation pieces and often neo-formalist in inspiration—and the more observational and narrative films that cross over into mainstream distribution.

The production, distribution, and reception of Campion's work, and thus finally her success, depends upon significant generic encodings that situate her work as part of a body of films directed toward women, within a feminist orbit without having a specific feminist agenda, that occupies an ambiguous position between counter cinema and commercial cinema—a position dependent upon the manner in which she is recognized as an auteur, working in a vexed and complicated milieu in which individuality and agency survive only with difficulty. Lizzie Borden, another filmmaker from the same generation, comments: "Jane Campion is the ultimate auteur. Even though *The Piano* was a collaborative effort, Campion leaves an indelible stamp and a series of memorable moments that stay with you long after you leave the theatre."[69]

As the "ultimate auteur," Campion's career represents the paradoxical legacy of Second Wave Feminism, which encouraged women of Campion's generation to achieve a singularity of vision while simultaneously promoting a theoretical model that undermined the validity of such achievements, viewing them as potentially anti-feminist. Perhaps Jane Campion's genius lies in the ways in which she was able to embody these contradictions within a rich and significant oeuvre that animates a certain kind of conversation about woman and her concerns, neither falling into dogmatism nor offering apologies or excuses for her failings.

Notes

1. Charlotte Brunsdon, *Films for Women* (London: British Film Institute, 1986), 1.
2. Ibid., 3.
3. Rick Altman, *Film/Genre* (London: British Film Institute, 1999), 72–77; Raphaëlle Moine, *Les genres du cinéma* (Paris: Nathan, 2002), 99–100.
4. Examples of such guides include Kim Adelman, *The Ultimate Guide to Chick Flicks: The Romance, the Glamour, the Tears, and More* (New York: Broadway Books, 2005); Jami Bernard, *Chick Flicks: A Movie Lover's Guide to the Movies Women Love* (Secaucus, NJ: Carol Publishing Group, 1996); and Jo Berry and Angie Errigo, *Chick Flicks: Movies Women Love* (London: Orion, 2004).
5. Adelman, *Ultimate Guide to Chick Flicks,* 1.
6. Bernard, *Chick Flicks,* 17–30.
7. Ibid., xii.

8. Marjorie Rosen, *Popcorn Venus: Movies and the American Dream* (New York: Coward, 1973), 140.

9. Molly Haskell, *From Reverence to Rape: The Treatment of Women in the Movies* (Baltimore: Penguin, 1974), 1–2.

10. Sue Thornham, *Passionate Detachments: An Introduction to Feminist Film Theory* (London: Arnold, 1997), 19.

11. *Variety,* 31 December 1947, 10.

12. Jeanine Basinger, *A Woman's View: How Hollywood Spoke to Women, 1930–1960* (New York: Knopf, 1993), 11.

13. Thornham, *Passionate Detachments,* xii.

14. Ibid.

15. This shift should not be understood as a complete change in perspective within feminist film scholarship. The approach defined by Brunsdon and others in the 1980s continues to be explored by scholars such as Roberta Garrett. See Roberta Garrett, *Postmodern Chick Flicks: The Return of the Woman's Film* (New York: Palgrave Macmillan, 2007).

16. Alison Butler, *Women's Cinema: The Contested Screen,* Short Cuts 14 (London: Wallflower, 2002); Christina Lane, *Feminist Hollywood: From* Born in Flames *to* Point Break, Contemporary Film and Television Series (Detroit: Wayne State University Press, 2000).

17. Basinger, *A Woman's View,* 13.

18. Ibid.

19. Ibid.

20. Dana Polan points out that Campion's films draw upon a number of different genres, describing them variously as women's cinema, romantic cinema, fatal melodrama, the woman's gothic, costume films, satire, art films, and screwball comedy, suggesting the importance of traditional narrative forms in her work as well as the degree of hybridization (as a sign of her authorial intervention) to which her films are subjected. See Dana Polan, *Jane Campion,* World Directors Series (London: British Film Institute, 2001), 26, 34, 35, 45, 68, 102, 105, 149.

21. Butler describes this phenomenon in *The Piano* as "the film's representation of female subjectivity *in extremis.*" Butler, *Women's Cinema,* 105.

22. E.g., Tania Modleski points out that *The Piano* documents how "violence against the mother . . . becomes crucial to the separation of the daughter from her mother and the daughter's emergence as a sexual being." See Tania Modleski, *Old Wives' Tales, and Other Women's Stories* (New York: New York University Press, 1998), 32.

23. Dana Polan refers to these markers as "the weird style of these films," "the David Lynchian aspect," and "quirkiness." See Polan, *Jane Campion,* 12, 145.

24. Colin MacCabe, "Realism and the Cinema: Notes on Some Brechtian Themes," in *Tracking the Signifier: Theoretical Essays: Film, Linguistics, Literature* (Minneapolis: University of Minnesota Press, 1985), 33–57.

25. Kathleen Anne McHugh, *Jane Campion,* Contemporary Film Directors (Urbana: University of Illinois Press, 2007), 138–39. Dana Polan situates Campion's films, *The Piano* in particular, as part of a "re-fashioning of the art film for the 1990s,"

which he, citing Thomas Elsaesser, sees as moving away "from the probing positing of questions." Polan, *Jane Campion*, 17.

26. See Virginia Wright Wexman, ed., *Jane Campion: Interviews*, Conversations with Filmmakers Series (Jackson: University Press of Mississippi, 1999).

27. E.g., Tania Modleski comments on how Campion, in her interviews, brings back the issue of the mother/daughter relationship in *The Piano* to a discussion of her own mother, to whom she dedicates the film. See Modleski, *Old Wives' Tales*, 42.

28. See McHugh, *Jane Campion*, for a detailed discussion of thematic and visual consistency in Campion's films.

29. *Passionless Moments* (1983) does not fit the patterns established in Campion's other films; however, it is also a coauthored work with her then partner, Gerard Lee.

30. McHugh, *Jane Campion*, 130.

31. Private conversation with Alistair Fox and Annabel Cooper during the research colloquium "Jane Campion: Cinema, Nation, Identity," held at the University of Otago, December 2006. See Alistair Fox in this volume for a fuller discussion of the sustained significance of sexual repression in Jane Campion's work.

32. McHugh, *Jane Campion*, 126.

33. Ibid., 130. In style, this sequence, which is repeated throughout the film at several junctures, also recalls the travelogue sequence inserted in *The Portrait of a Lady*, recounting Isabel's Grand Tour in the period between Osmond's proposal and their marriage.

34. Dana Polan notes in the context of *The Piano* that "for some commentators, the film becomes a positive embodiment of a 'Mulveyan' filmmaker," referring to the 1970s writing of widely cited film theorist Laura Mulvey. Polan, *Jane Campion*, 45.

35. See Annabel Cooper in this volume for a fuller discussion of Campion's status as a New Zealand director.

36. See Raphaëlle Moine in this volume for an extended discussion of Campion's films in an international context.

37. McHugh, *Jane Campion*, 3.

38. PAColl-5840, Alexander Turnbull Library Catalogue, Alexander Turnbull Library, Wellington, New Zealand. I would like to thank Ellen Pullar for drawing my attention to this collection.

39. Edith Campion plays the role of Janet Frame's formidable and inspiring high school literature teacher, Miss Lindsay, in *An Angel at My Table*. For a full discussion of *The Audition*, see Harriet Margolis in this volume.

40. PAColl-5872–077, Jane Campion (1954–), [ca. 1980s–1990s], Edith Campion Collection, Dye Coupler Print, 8.8 × 12.7 cm, Alexander Turnbull Library, Wellington, New Zealand.

41. Jane Campion, "Director's Commentary," *The Portrait of a Lady*, DVD, Universal Studios, 2001.

42. For a discussion of Jane Campion's version of Isabel Archer in *The Portrait of a Lady*, see Irène Bessière in this volume.

43. Polan, *Jane Campion*, 167.

44. See, e.g., Jerzy Toeplitz, *History of the French Cinema*, Jerzy Toeplitz, ISBN 0 6 42 92497x. Housed at the Australian National Film and Sound Archive, Can-

berra, Australia. Toeplitz was the director from 1974 to 1979 of the Australian Film, Television, and Radio School (AFTRS) and set the terms of its curriculum (Campion attended in 1981–84). For a discussion of the role of autobiography in the films of François Truffaut, see Antoine de Baecque and Serge Toubiana, *Truffaut* (New York: Knopf, 1999).

45. 1982–83 AFTRS Report, Australian National Film and Sound Archive, Canberra, Australia.

46. McHugh, *Jane Campion,* 13.

47. Ibid., 16.

48. Ibid., 13. See *The Professional Participation of Women in the Media,* UNESCO Seminar, May 1976, at which Professor Jerzy Toeplitz, then director of AFTRS, gave the keynote address. See also *Report on Women in Australian Film Production* (Ryan, Eliot, Appleton), sponsored by the Woman's Film Fund and the Australian Film and Television School, and *On the Job Training Scheme,* 1984, sponsored by the AFTRS. All documents housed at the Australian National Film and Sound Archive, Canberra, Australia.

49. Episode No. 228537, broadcast 25 May 1993, *Seven Nightly News,* TVW7 (Perth, W.A.), Australian National Film and Sound Archive, Canberra, Australia.

50. Wexman, *Jane Campion,* xiii.

51. Episode No. 254081, "Jane Campion: Interviewed by Peter Castaldi: Oral History," 1992, Australian National Film and Sound Archive, Canberra, Australia.

52. Stella Bruzzi, "Tempestuous Petticoats: Costume and Desire in *The Piano,*" *Screen* 36, no. 3 (Autumn 1995): 261.

53. For a discussion of this position, see Lynda Dyson, "The Return of the Repressed? Whiteness, Femininity, and Colonialism in *The Piano,*" *Screen* 36, no. 3 (Autumn 1995): 267–76. See also Mark Reid, "A Few Black Keys and Maori Tattoos: Re-Reading Jane Campion's *The Piano* in Post-Negritude Time," *Quarterly Review of Film and Video* 17, no. 2 (June 2000): 107–16.

54. For a broadly based discussion of these issues, see bell hooks, *Black Looks: Race and Representation* (Boston: South End Press, 1992).

55. Susanna Moore, *In the Cut* (New York: Knopf: 1995).

56. Qtd. in Lane, *Feminist Hollywood,* 26.

57. Ibid., 27.

58. Internet Movie Database, http://www.imdb.com, accessed 18 August 2007; McHugh, *Jane Campion,* 13, 16.

59. A significant number of the women directors on whom Lane focuses have moved into television as their careers developed. Examples include Lizzie Borden, who directed an episode of *Red Shoes Diaries* (1996); Seidelman and Coolidge, episodes of *Sex and the City* (1998); Seidelman, *Now and Again* (1999); Coolidge, *CSI: Crime Scene Investigation* (2006–7); Bigelow, episodes of *Homicide: Life on the Streets* (1998–99); Claudia Weill, *My So-Called Life* (1994) and episodes of *Once and Again* (1999–2000). Finally, Amy Heckerling took her critical and popular success *Clueless* (1995) to the small screen (1996–99). Campion tried her hand at television early in her career with *Two Friends* (1986) and *Dancing Daze* (1985). Internet Movie Database, http://www.imdb.com, accessed 18 August 2007.

60. For a discussion of the woman's film within a global context, see Alison Butler, *Women's Cinema*.

61. Lane, *Feminist Hollywood*, 29–40.

62. Ibid., 32.

63. Ibid., 33.

64. Internet Movie Database, http://www.imdb.com, accessed 18 August 2007.

65. For a discussion of Campion's literary references, see McHugh, *Jane Campion*, and Kathleen McHugh's article in this volume.

66. Qtd. in Judith M. Redding and Victoria A. Brownworth, *Film Fatales: Independent Women Directors* (Seattle: Seal Press, 1997), 151.

67. Ibid., 211.

68. I am indebted to Catherine Fowler for drawing my attention to this new generation of feminist artists.

69. Lane, *Feminist Hollywood*, 281.

Pauline in the opening sequence of *In the Cut*. Courtesy of the Academy of Motion Picture Arts and Sciences.

Her-land: Jane Campion's Cinema, or Another Poetic of the Inner Sense

> One day we who live at the edge of the alphabet will find our speech.
>
> —Janet Frame, *The Edge of the Alphabet*

In the title *To the Is-land,* the first volume of her autobiographical trilogy, Janet Frame questions, indeed overturns, a traditional system of symbolic linguistic organization by inserting a simple hyphen while leaving the word apparently intact. It is not only words that are involved in this revisitation; the construction of phrases and stories, their punctuation, and the relation of characters to language are also affected. In Frame's works, one finds the repudiation of a language that she considers ossified, along with a compulsive need to defy its conventions and the restraints that are inherent in it, and to create a revolution. As Gina Mercer puts it,

[Frame] subverts current patterns again and again, by making up new languages in novels like *A State of Siege* [1966] and *The Rainbirds* [1967], even removing language altogether in an apocalyptic rainstorm in *The Carpathians* [1988] where letters and punctuation marks deluge down from the sky, washing away all "logical thought . . . [causing] the natural destruction of known language . . . [opening the way for] a new language, a new people, a new world."[1]

Frame, however, promotes her revolution through maintaining the coexistence of two states—in other words, by generating new variations on the semantic significations of language that exists rather than by attempting to create a new language that is entirely separated from conventional language. Patrick Evans aptly describes this two-fold impulse that informs Frame's conception of *The Edge of the Alphabet* (among other of her novels): "That is the fundamental division of Frame's artistic vision—between the boredom and regulation of the alphabet world and the world at the edge of the alphabet with its lush growths of language that heal and make whole."[2] What Frame succeeds in doing microcosmically with a hyphen, in her attempt to reinvent her feminine identity through a new mode of expression—which parallels what she does at a macrocosmic level in the whole body of her poetic and prose works—Jane Campion achieves through her cinematic works and their mise-en-scènes from her early short films to her more recent projects. Her idea of a different language did not merely eventuate out of the blue; it was formulated in reaction to the dominant classical conception of cinematic representation. Campion, like Frame, generally works within the notion of a permanent coexistence between the two forms. Accordingly, whereas Germaine Dulac's *La souriante Madame Beudet* or Chantal Akerman's *Jeanne Dielman,* two attempts to create a "nouveau language," are usually viewed as experimental efforts, Campion's films offer instead a classical narrative structure within which narrative "breathing spaces" are naturally able to be inserted.[3] As with Frame, these breathing spaces manifest themselves in different guises and through a range of extremely complex variations, which are achieved through such devices as the way shots are composed, and through the handling of time.

In fact, these breathing-spaces turn out to be fundamentally linked to the conception of time. As Herbert Read has argued with respect to the works of Cézanne, Campion, as with other directors, "endeavors to detach the perception of the meaning of linguistic and rational elements from reality so that it becomes possible to apprehend an original reality."[4] Instead of ordinary time, which depends on preestablished temporal strata consisting of days, hours, minutes, and seconds, a subjective form of temporality is substituted, which is constructed out of synaesthesic experience, and out of a phenomenological time that is lived "free from constraints that oblige one to conform to time as regulated by the physical world."[5] Linearity and "protension" (the main characteristic of cinema according to Roland Barthes) are maintained, while being interspersed with moments of stasis that impart a different rhythm to the narrative progression—often making it "strange" (in the Freudian sense of a defamiliarization that is generated with respect to the known object). Campion seems to have extended and transformed the hypothesis of Laura Mulvey, who maintained that "the presence of woman is an indispensable element of spectacle in normal narrative film, yet her visual presence tends to work against the development of a story line, to freeze the flow of action in moments of erotic contemplation."[6]

The series of short segments in Campion's *Passionless Moments* is an ironic example of this idea in which image-action has been replaced by moments in which "nothing happens." In his commentary on *Two Friends,* Dana Polan expresses surprise at observing a structuring scheme that begins in medias res and "leaves causes and effects of individual narrative developments unexplained even if one can sort out their place in the overall temporal order."[7] Then again, Campion's cinema is associated with the writing of Virginia Woolf and her stream of consciousness—as is made evident by the reference to Woolf in *In the Cut* (2003), in which Frannie makes the class she is teaching study Woolf's *To the Lighthouse.*

The conception of duration, according to Henri Bergson, would seem to provide some essential keys to an understanding of this handling of time. When he defines duration as such, Bergson envisages it as a succession of our states of consciousness when our subjective self allows itself to live and refrains from establishing a separation between the present state and previous states. Thus, duration is essentially a continuation of "that which is no longer in that which is."[8] For Bergson, it is the experience of duration that matters, not duration as a concept. Campion's manner of filming seems to reflect a desire to work and render this idea of interior duration in accordance with a Bergsonian philosophy that conceives "of the self and of consciousness as interiority—with the primacy of interiority being, in fact, the condition without which no experience of duration is possible," and with this interiority being also independent of any space involving sociality.[9]

The opening sequence of *In the Cut* showing Pauline (Jennifer Jason Leigh) strolling under a shower of golden petals, accompanied by a gentle rendering of "Que Sera Sera," or that in which Frannie (Meg Ryan) discovers the severed head of her sister and clutches it for an abnormally long time in her lap—what strikes one above all about these sequences is both the atemporality, the removal from any social or contextual given (which distinguishes them from the films of Akerman or of Agnès Varda), and also the duration (in its literal sense), indeed the exhaustiveness of the lived experiences. Just at the point where the sequence would generally stop in the frame of the image-action, it is naturally pursued and prolonged here. While it is their duration (or length) in the common sense of the word that most immediately strikes one at first sight, it is actually the representation of an interiority, of a continuation of "that which is no longer in that which is" that is articulated here, in a space in which the self is "allowed to live": the happy childhood with one's mother and sister.

But the length of the shots does not explain everything. Understanding of this other temporality is also generated by filmed elements that condition our perception of the relationship between past and present and, in the same movement, since they are practically indissociable, by cinematographic techniques that bring these elements into being. Analyses of the films of Dulac, Maya Deren, and Akerman have systematically underlined the importance of the access they provide to the mental world of the characters (even if with Akerman this access is realized through a filmic referentiality that seems to run counter to subjectivity). It is undeniably the case that the desire of these filmmakers to provide access to this mental world dictates the formal aspect of the representation. However, it is the body that is placed in the mise-en-scène, and it is the body that evolves in the filmic space. The primordial aspect of the body seems obvious, but no one has yet investigated the value of the body in filmic composition apart from Gilles Deleuze in *L'Image-temps:* "Female auteurs, female directors, do not owe their prominence to a militant feminism. What is more important are the innovative ways in which they have presented the body in the cinema, as if women had to conquer the source of their own attitudes and the temporality that corresponds to them as an individual or collective *gestus.*"[10] And what happens if it is not mental space, the feminine imaginary, but indeed the body, conceived of as both an external envelope and an internal substance, that determines the structuring of time and filmic matter? It is a question here—outside of any simplistic consideration that would aim to reformulate the nature/culture dichotomy under another guise—of understanding how the body, not only in its corporeal being, but also in its evolution and its metamorphoses, enables the creation of another cinematic temporality.

To generate this new temporality, in which the symbolic temporarily gives way to the imaginary, work on language is of paramount importance. The idea of giving access to another form of language is systematically present, whether in an intradiegetic or extradiegetic manner. The characters Campion places before the camera all have a particular relationship, indeed a transgressive one, to language. Consequently, they suffer linguistic "disorders." Janet Frame tries to create her own poetic language and in this way to escape from a masculine form of writing that does not allow her to describe what she feels (*An Angel at My Table*). Ruth, who is supposed to be "deprogrammed" after a mystical experience in India, engages in a play of language with her "healer" in which words are turned against him (*Holy Smoke*). Other characters, however, are still more radical in their behavior—for example, Sweetie, who adopts nonverbal communication as a sign that she has rejected the symbolic order of language. In protest against her father, she barks and makes as if she is going to bite him.

The Campion character who is closest to the heroines of Janet Frame is undoubtedly Ada (*The Piano*). Like Daphne Withers (*Owls Do Cry*, 1957), Istina Mavet (*Faces in the Water*, 1961), and Very Glace (*Scented Gardens for the Blind*, 1963), Ada, confronted by Stewart and the world, rejects society and refuses to speak. Her silence exhibits a refusal to open up a dialogue with masculine imprisonment and a determination to create an exclusive feminine space that she occupies with her daughter. Ada generates a new form of language through multiple voices: her own internal voice, which commences the narration; her daughter, who translates her feelings and requests; her notes; Baines; and also, first and foremost, her piano and her music. Her language does not take a single, unique form but rather several forms that are fragmented, multiple, as well as drawing on the sensory imagination. The main character of *In the Cut*, Frannie, is a professor of literature who conducts research into poetry and slang words. In her first dialogue with her sister, she explains that words like "broccoli" and "virginia" designate sexual attributes in slang, underlining the sexual and violent potential of this other form of language. In the metro, she lets her thoughts roam in response to the poetic phrases that she encounters there.

This singular relationship to a language that is diverted, atrophied, or rejected engenders a natural focalization on the body and the way it is placed in space. The body of the characters becomes the dominant element in the representation—all forms of communication pass through it. Deleuze, again in *L'Image-temps*, had already underlined the role of the body, in what he calls its "attitudes and postures," as a means of accessing the mind: "It is through the body (and no longer through the body's intermediary) that cinema binds its marriage with the mind, with thought."[11] Even if it is always shown in its everyday functions, the body is not simply a social body or a body opening toward the imaginary. It reveals itself above all in all its carnal quality—living matter that one uncovers, cuts, for the sake of better exposing both the exterior and the interior. Its (r)evolutions are numerous. Pleasures rub shoulders with traumatic experiences, even to the point of often making way for them, as in the case of the electro-shock treatments suffered by Janet Frame in *An Angel at My Table*.[12]

If, in the case of the characters of Madame Beudet (in Dulac's film) or of Jeanne Dielman (in Akerman's film), the body is defined mainly through its confinement in claustrophobic interiors, the body takes on another signification in the films of Campion. The marginality of Frame's characters is articulated through a certain form of language, but in this instance it is stylistic compositions that underscore this state. The manner in which Campion places her characters in the shot has been described as one of her signature

31

stylistic characteristics. In *Sweetie,* the character is placed in a corner of the frame, allowing the rest of the free space to be invested with the landscape, with the effect that the character is enclosed within her own prison (body or mind). In other films, such as *The Piano* or *The Portrait of a Lady,* even when the characters are centered within the frame, Campion often films her actresses with their back turned toward the camera, blocking access to their face, so that the psychological tension of the character is conveyed entirely through their body and the conduct of their movements, or through their immobility.

But Campion does not rely solely on the composition to achieve her effect. Sue Gillett emphasizes the way that Campion elects to represent her actresses (even the most beautiful, such as Nicole Kidman). They are shown with their imperfections, their vulnerability in uncompromising and extremely realistic close-up shots.[13] The most trivial of everyday actions (such as urinating, defecating, etc.) are integrated into the narrative, revealing the aesthetic of the female body from an entirely different perspective: the "full," plump beauty of Kate Winslet (*Holy Smoke*), the oily hair of Holly Hunter (*The Piano*), the naked body of Genevieve Lemon smeared with excrement (*Sweetie*), the wrinkles of Barbara Hershey (*The Portrait of a Lady*). The body also becomes that which allows a link to be established between different spaces, that which makes and creates meaning in a universe whose dimensions collide with one another. With the body becoming the place not only for the communication link but also for interiority, the sensations experienced are the motor for this representation, as much at the level of the story as in the relationship of the film to the spectator. For Bergson, "when we speak of sensation as an interior state, we mean to say that it arises in our body."[14]

Synaesthesic cinematic-sensation was already evident in Dulac's films as a result of her use of cinematographic devices that seek to render the physical experience of the characters and convey it to the viewer through blurred focus, accelerated episodes, slow motion sequences, double exposures, and so on. From then on, temporality obeyed the laws of feeling, rather than depending upon an objective relationship with time, as illustrated by the reduction of real time to a minimum in the diegesis of a film like *La souriante Madame Beudet.* Sensation, which is recurrently evoked, is similarly one of the principle elements in Campion's cinema. Laleen Jayamanne aptly describes this return of synaesthesic cinema:

The way in which the piano is performed both by Ada and by the film's mise-en-scène activates visual, tactile, kinaesthetic, auditory, and even olfactory memory traces for the characters (the piano tuner smells the sea on it). It is therefore a multi-sensory object, and for Ada, a prosthetic extension of her body, so to speak. There are many examples of this link that people have noted, but the one I find most memorable is the two-shot of Ada gazing from a high cliff at her abandoned piano lying far below on the beach (seen in extreme long shot). A fragile (out of focus) and yet insistent jagged febrile Gothic line created by the fluttering ribbon of her bonnet seems to touch the piano (across a vast space) creating a tactile link between her body and the object of desire, enchantment, and longing.[15]

The close-up is the determining filmic device here, as it removes the shot from all spatio-temporal frames of reference, while participating in the flow of the other shots among which it is inscribed. It is what allows the bodily relationships that a character has with his or her surroundings to be most effectively revealed through an array of tactile emotions.[16] It is not so much faces that are targeted but rather fragmented portions of the body—in particular, hands (or feet) and whatever they are touching—to render this tactile sensation that inheres not only in everyday actions (in what appears to be a respectful imitation of Jeanne Dielman's gestures) but also in dreamlike wandering: the feet of Pauline in the dewy grass of the garden, Frannie's hands gripping the severed head, Ada's hands, half-covered with mittens, caressing the water of the ocean before ordering her piano to be thrown into it. Bodies are not envisaged in their totality but rather in their capacity to exist in the form of quasi-autonomous elements. Cutting is ubiquitous, in the shot and on its surface, indeed, even in the soundtrack. Similarly, ideas of fragmentation and blood are manifest in the title of *In the Cut,* the severed head of the sister, and Frannie's symbolic nightmare in which she imagines her father slicing the neck of her mother with the blades of his ice-skates.

If the characters in the mise-en-scène are bodies that are engaged in the experience of feeling, it is equally the case for the spectators. In this regard, Vivian Sobchack has identified the importance of a cinematic experience that directly and literally activates sensations in the viewer. She describes her experience of watching *The Piano* as "a relatively rare instance of narrative cinema in which the cultural hegemony of vision is overthrown, an instance in which my eyes did not 'see' anything meaningful and experienced almost blindness at the same time that my tactile sense of being in the world through my fingers grasped the image's sense in a way that my forestalled or baffled vision could not."[17]

The effect here comes from being confronted with an "objective" shot that arouses a tactile comprehension in the spectator. To return to Bergson on this matter, we are not simply involved in the perception of exterior objects but also caught up in sensation, in the experience of affect—"that which we mingle from the interior of our body with the image of exterior bodies; it is what we need to extract from perception first of all in order to discover the purity of the image."[18]

It is therefore the body that seems to dictate its time in the film, as if skin and flesh were imposing a structure on the temporal progression and articulation of the filmic montage. The central role accorded to the body and sensations, then, imposes a temporality of feeling, of an experience that is not susceptible to rational articulation, and which must be represented through a duration that is linked with the present to be transmitted and communicated to the spectator. According to Bergson, "My present is, then, sensation and movement; and since my present forms an indivisible whole, this movement has to be attached to this sensation, and to prolong it in action; my present is, in essence, sensory-motor."[19]

One arrives here at a certain form of derealization, even though it is very different from that derived from the prolonged shots of Akerman. A postulate of realism, as if the film's function were to document reality, no longer exists, and the worlds that are represented anchor themselves directly in a distinctive subjectivity, indeed, a plastic abstraction. In Campion's films, the treatment of the fragmentation of bodies extends even to the way the film itself is handled, as if by a natural extension, allowing for a distinctive kind of derealization that is achieved through the technique of postmodern collage. This is seen in the use of silent film to represent Isabel's exotic journey, in the dreamlike erotic fantasy in which she imagines herself being caressed by her suitors in *The Portrait of a Lady,* or again in the credit sequence with the contemporary young women discussing their first kiss and their hopes for their romantic future, in the ice-skating sequence where the parents meet in *In the Cut,* in the story of Ada's earlier life in *The Piano,* and in the fantastic colored images in the style of Pierre and Gilles in *Holy Smoke* in which Ruth appears to P. J. Waters as a goddess with multiple arms.[20] Film lends itself to these unusual breathing spaces and to this new form of language that is as unpredictable as it is fascinating.

"This is the story of Janet Frame." This phrase, which opens *An Angel at My Table* straight after the subheading "To the Is-land," resonates like an echo in this study. The central and most important preoccupation in the film is with identity; while Frame's distinctiveness resides in her physical appearance and her "uncontrollable frizzy hair," it can also be read in her sex and the story that starts with the loss of a twin two weeks after her birth. She is the *other* in all things—a character "relegated to the 'farthest' rim, to the outside."[21] Writing is her way of (re)defining herself, a new way of viewing the world, in accordance with a new subjectivity that is closely tied to her vision (as is evident in several sequences, such as the one in the train in which she creates a frame with her hands in order to see the world "through a mask"). Her way forward, just like that of Campion or that of the real-life Frame, will be that of a mistress of symbolic language who refashions it to serve the purposes of her own poetic. Having returned from her European journey, now being acclaimed as an incomparable writer, Frame can at last try on the shoes of her father, articulating language as her own, confronting her own image in the mirror—that which she has created.

Notes

Translation from the French by Alistair Fox. Unless otherwise noted, passages quoted from French texts are also translated by Alistair Fox.

1. Gina Mercer, *Janet Frame: Subversive Fictions* (Dunedin: University of Otago Press), 3.
2. Patrick Evans, "At the Edge of the Alphabet," in *The Ring of Fire: Essays on Janet Frame,* ed. Jeanne Delbaere (Sydney: Dangaroo Press, 1992), 84.
3. Sandy Flitterman-Lewis had already noted the presence of these kinds of moments in the films of Agnès Varda, notably in *Sans toit ni loi,* in the form of the twelve musical interludes filmed with a mobile camera that followed Mona before ending up focused on elements in the landscape. "*Sans toit ni loi*—le 'portrait impossible' de la féminité," *CinémAction* 67 (1993): 171–76. We should note that in this specific case, the theorist adheres to the notion of an intentional distancing that is imposed on the spectator—which is emphatically not the case with the examples considered here.
4. Herbert Read, *Le sens de l'art* (Paris: éditions Sylvie Messinger, 1984), 8.
5. Paul Ricoeur, *Temps et récit, Tome III Le temps raconté* (Paris: Seuil, 1985), 230.
6. Laura Mulvey, "Visual Pleasure and Narrative Cinema," in *Issues in Feminist Film Criticism,* ed. Patricia Erens (Bloomington: Indiana University Press, 1990), 28–40.
7. Dana Polan, *Jane Campion* (London: British Film Institute, 2001), 86.
8. Henri Bergson, *Durée et simultanéité* (Paris: Quadrige/Presses Universitaires de France, 1968), 55.
9. Jean-Louis Vieillard-Baron, "L'intuition de la durée, expérience intérieure, et fécondité doctrinale," in *Bergson—la durée et la nature* (Paris: Presses Universitaires de France, 2004), 45.
10. Gilles Deleuze, *L'image-temps* (Paris: Editions de Minuit, 1985), 256.
11. Ibid., 246.
12. This idea has not only been expressed by Campion in contemporary cinema; other female directors following her, such as Julie Taymor, Claire Denis, and Marina De Van, have exposed the body not only as a surface but also as an interior space that can be fragmented, cut, opened, and explored.

13. Sue Gillett, "A Pleasure to Watch: Jane Campion's Narrative Cinema," Screening the Past, http://www.latrobe.edu.au/screeningthepast/firstrelease/fr0301/sgfr12a.htm, paragraph 12 (accessed 21 October 2008).

14. Henri Bergson, *Matière et mémoire* (Paris: Presses Universitaires de France, 1939), 58–59.

15. Qtd. in Polan, *Jane Campion,* 86.

16. One could equally focus on the olfactory dimension of Campion's films, as in the scenes in *Holy Smoke* in which Ruth's mother, having arrived to reclaim her daughter in the first sequences of the film, experiences India as a sensory assault.

17. Vivian Sobchak, *Carnal Thoughts: Embodiment and Moving Image Culture* (Berkeley: University of California Press, 2004), 53–84.

18. Bergson, *Matière et mémoire*, 59–60.

19. Ibid.

20. *Pierre et Gilles* is the signature used by the French artists Pierre Commoy, a photographer, and Gilles Blanchard, a painter. They are known for the hand-tinted photographs they produced together after meeting in 1976.

21. Mercer, *Janet Frame,* 8.

Jane Campion with her mother, Edith, as Miss Lindsay on the set of *An Angel at My Table*. Courtesy of the Alexander Turnbull Library, Wellington, New Zealand. (Reference number PAColl-5872–102.)

The Campions Indulge in *The Audition*

An Angel at My Table (1990) does not shirk the inevitable representation of influences on a young artist's life, and one of the most memorable of these acknowledgments is a short scene about twenty-five minutes into the film in which a teacher brings a bit of poetry to vivid life in high school student Janet Frame's eyes and mind. A black-gowned teacher marches menacingly down a hallway, enters a classroom full of dully uniformed young women, and launches into a vibrant recital of Arthurian legendry. As her arm swings to suggest a sword's arc through the air, Janet's head jerks to follow the movement, seeing—for real—what the teacher has painted in words. The scene, a characteristically auteurist intrusion of realized fantasy amid the dominant realist narrative, is simultaneously a testament to the teacher's power, the student's imagination, Edith Campion's acting ability, and Jane Campion's respect for her mother.

It is also the McGuffin for Anna Campion's short student film *The Audition* (1989), which features Edith and Jane bickering over Edith's participation in *Angel*—and anything else they find to pick apart. While Anna gets credit for the film as its director, *The Audition* seems really to be as much Edith's and Jane's film, since they are the subjects and actors of the film. Certainly Jane, for reasons that will be made clear, deserves some credit for much of the film's cinematic style. What is *The Audition*: a documentary, a parody, a home movie, a melodrama? Depending on one's point of view, the correct answer is all of these.

Edith's cameo in *An Angel at My Table* is framed, so to speak, on the one side by a scene in which Janet Frame and an older, more sophisticated sister do a bit of Hollywood-style posing, and on the other side by a scene involving a sort of town freak, whose identification of herself as Other includes questions of identity, even without her asking the New Zealand girls gawping in front of her that classic Kiwi question: "Whaddarya?" While in the one scene Janet and her sister imitate Hollywood language and refer to "the studio," in the other scene the girl they see after school standing behind a white picket fence does not wear a school uniform. "I'm really Spanish, of course," she tells them, "*and* I'm Roman Catholic. What are you?" *Angel* is to some extent about Janet Frame's journey toward understanding what she is, and an acceptance of who she is without the contempt "whaddarya" implies.[1] On a much smaller scale and especially for those who read it as a documentary, *The Audition* suggests that the Campion women, far more self-consciously than in Janet Frame's case, are aware of who they are, and Jane and Edith are particularly aware of who they are in relation to each other.

Near the end of *The Audition,* Jane gives Edith her motivation for the scene Edith plays in *Angel.* This is also the first time in *The Audition* that Edith makes it completely through the poetic passage she enacts. While Edith has been reciting her lines, Jane has been mouthing them along with her. Her pleasure in watching her mother's performance is evident, and if we do not see the shining sword itself, we can see a director's satisfaction with what she expects to capture on film.

An Angel at My Table was made after Jane Campion's three student films, the Sydney Women's Film Unit–commissioned *After Hours* (1984), some short Australian television work, the Australian telefeature *Two Friends* (1986), and *Sweetie* (1989). Campion's career, in other words, was doing well at this point, based on the international attention her student films attracted, despite the fact that her film school teachers were not particularly thrilled by them.[2] They thought her films were not commercial enough to help her into a filmmaking career, but by then Campion had a passion to tell stories through films, and the Australian Film, Television, and Radio School had enabled her to pick up technical skills and to make as many short films as she could.[3] As Campion says of this phase of her life, "I was very motivated, because I wanted to tell my stories."[4]

So it was reasonable, from an objective point of view, for her to recommend film school as an option to her older sister, Anna (b. 1952). Anna had earned an undergraduate degree in London after a five-year stint as a professional actor.[5] Anna's *The Audition,* which is distributed by Women Make Movies, is a student piece made for film school in England. In a melodramatic way, it captures the process of auditioning Edith Campion for her small part in *An Angel at My Table,* although it never announces the fact, and indeed takes steps to hide the participants' identity. Janet Maslin of the *New York Times* somewhat unkindly wrote of *The Audition* that "the story's mother-daughter dynamics are of much greater interest than Ms. Campion's stilted, uncertain directorial technique."[6] I think one can safely say that *The*

Audition has received most of its international attention because of Jane Campion's success. Funded in part by the New Zealand Film Commission, Television New Zealand, and what is now Creative New Zealand but what was then the Queen Elizabeth II Arts Council of New Zealand (an unusual package of support under the circumstances), *The Audition* was produced by the Royal College of Art Film Department and won a BBC Student Drama Prize in 1989.[7] Despite Maslin's comments, *The Audition* has some excellent camerawork by New Zealand cinematographer Waka Attewell (who appears in the film briefly), and it is edited by Jamie Selkirk (now best known for his work with Peter Jackson's films). It is simply not a typical or run-of-the-mill student film.

Anna's second short film, *Broken Skin* (1991), was nominated for the Golden Palm at the 1991 Cannes Film Festival.[8] *Loaded* (1994), a feature made in Britain with financial support from, among others, the British Film Institute, Miramax, and the New Zealand Film Commission (and with special effects by Weta Digital), has not led to further feature films, although it won a special mention at the Directors' Week awards for Fantasporto in 1995 and was nominated for the Bronze Horse at the 1994 Stockholm Film Festival. Despite the lukewarm reception *Loaded* had from both the public and reviewers, Anna's career did not entirely collapse, for she collaborated with Jane on *Holy Smoke* (1999). While Jane's career has been on hold while she raises her daughter, Anna's career does not seem to have prospered.

What of Edith Campion, née Hannah (a well-to-do and well-known New Zealand family of the time)? Edith was born in Wellington in 1923, orphaned at an early age, and married in 1945 to Richard Campion.[9] An heiress, Edith, with Richard, was able to found the New Zealand Players in 1953, a brave endeavor that foundered on the realities of the costs of touring high-art theater in a country so large and so sparsely populated as New Zealand. As noted New Zealand playwright Bruce Mason wrote in 1963, the New Zealand Players were in competition with more mainstream—and grassroots—theatrical efforts around the country.[10] While Richard continued teaching and directing, Edith's theatrical career was largely ended by the Players' collapse, then the birth of her three children, and finally by surgery in 1972 that affected her mobility.[11] (When Edith marches down the hallway in *Angel*, she is wearing a brace on her right leg.) Edith turned to creative writing, and in 1977 she published *A Place to Pass Through*, a collection of short stories. In 1979 her novella *The Chain* was published along with the well-established Frank Sargeson's novella *En Route* in a volume titled *Tandem*. (Local publisher Reed Press published both of Edith's books, and Sargeson, of course, played a role in Janet Frame's career, as *Angel* shows.)

Reviews of Edith's work in the New Zealand arts journals *Landfall* and *Islands* were mixed. Sargeson referred to "the author's technical ease" and "the original and excellent writing" with regard to the short stories, which he summarizes as being about "the private agonies of the solitary individual made hopelessly lonely and depressed by entanglement in the day-to-day trappings of contemporary urbanised life."[12] The *Islands* review refers to "competence" in a mixture of faint praise and quibbling about the writing; the stories themselves are praised for their "versatility" in providing "a compendium of states of life in which middle-class characters of all ages may find themselves: a frustrated spinster, an asthmatic child, a hypochondriac matron, a schizophrenic boy, the victim of a small-town abortionist, parasitic alternative lifers, disillusioned lovers, a bickering married couple, isolated old people, a New Zealand girl abroad."[13] The reviewer takes pains to say that Edith avoids the sort of blatant labeling this summary suggests, and praises her "exactly seeing eye."

In contrast, the *Landfall* review of *The Chain* (the only review of these four written by a woman) is harsh: "The novel disappoints in the quality of the writing. It is often precious. . . . There is an uneasy balance between prose and poetry which merely appears self-conscious."[14] Again, though, the *Islands* review is complimentary ("Campion writes as if this were her umpteenth book"); the review also notes that a recent University of Canterbury dissertation by Heather Roberts suggests that "our women writers often tend towards an inner spaciousness of the imagination that compensates for their characters' unwilling physical fixity," a description fully appropriate to Edith's morbid subject—that is, the slow movement toward death of a man who wakes up to find himself inexplicably chained to a tree in an unfrequented forest.[15] The reviewer notes,

Unlike most males in our fiction [Edith's protagonist] is obliged to spend much [of what's left of his life] inside his head—a New Zealand woman writer's revenge, you might say, on the unreflective, free-roaming male of New Zealand fiction. . . . Proving Yourself [as Edith's protagonist must do] is a version of what man and more specifically men have been doing in natural New Zealand for the last 140 years, and one of the principal functions of *The Chain* seems to be the exposure of the wrongness of this attitude.[16]

(While there are no obvious, direct connections for us to draw between Edith's theatrical and literary endeavors and Jane's film work, the references to a good eye, an interest in the interior experiences of her characters, and the perception of a criticism of the national male character developed since earliest colonial days are worth considering, if we want to look for influences on Jane's take on the world. However, that is not precisely the path I want to follow at the moment.)

Jane's references to her mother in early interviews credit Edith with introducing her to international films, particularly those by Luis Buñuel, and to fashion, since her mother had at least one Chanel suit, thus giving Jane a more sophisticated view of the world than she would otherwise have had.[17] The extraordinary thing about this exposure is that it came in a country notorious at that time for its provincial qualities and, most especially, its demand for conformity.[18] Jane expressed her discomfort with the nonconformity of her parents' lifestyle in various ways.[19] Among other things, she opted for anthropology rather than drama when she studied at university.

Jane's somewhat mixed feelings about her mother appear in interviews that refer to Edith's romanticism as well as her debilitating depression. As for the romanticism, Jane says, "Love was a mysterious force that [Edith] would coach us about. So you became aware that the object of that was my father, and therefore he seemed very powerful in terms of our happiness."[20] Most extraordinarily, Jane has referred to a moment "in her teens [when] her mother was affected so badly by depression [that Jane] offered to help her die."[21] In response, Jane says,

I had to get away, I couldn't breathe, I couldn't see for myself my own optimism any more. . . . And her [way of] [*sic*] looking at the world seemed almost contagious. . . . [But Edith] said to me, "I don't want to die, . . . I want to feel good about things," and that was the real turning point for me. I realised that my job was not to sort of see her in darkness, but say, "Oh, it's going to be better, you're going to get better."[22]

So when, in *The Audition,* we hear Jane discussing self-help books and Edith complaining about and parodying the expensive neurolinguistic programming workshop she attended at Jane's instigation, when we hear Jane exhorting her mother to approach things differently and Edith responding that Jane is more confident in herself and cares less about other people, it is awfully tempting to read this material as a sort of reality TV show before its time. Consider, for example, this IMDb user description of *The Audition:* "A quirky and ultimately moving short film that gives fans of Campion an invaluable peek into her own personality and her relationship with her mother, Edith."[23]

How valuable is the information we might glean from *The Audition?* Wellington, despite its population of around four hundred thousand and its status as national capital, is really still a small town in the way informa-tion circulates. While researching this essay, I learned that my friendly A/V librarian had been a student with Anna Campion. He volunteered that Anna and Jane hated each other when they were young, Anna being particularly annoyed by Jane's greater popularity with men.

Indeed, the first time I saw *The Audition*, the person presenting it spoke of it as Anna's slightly naughty, unflattering picture of Jane. The subterfuge of identifying Edith as Edith Armstrong and Jane as Jane Wright in the film's credits was cited as an attempt to distance the material somewhat from its grounding in reality.[24] And my understanding was that, at that time at least, the film was not meant to be available for screenings in New Zealand (de-spite the financial support from various New Zealand funding agencies).

Yet, watching this film again for the first time since that somewhat clan-destine viewing in the mid 1990s, and after of course growing far more familiar with Jane Campion's films and background, I am struck this time by how it supports Sam Neill's remark that he "would have played the third Maori from the left for Jane."[25] Jane's patience with her mother's fidgets in front of the camera and her constant praise and reassurance for Edith sup-port the comments from various actors who have worked with her about what a safe environment Jane provides for her actors. In other words, while the film cheekily and repeatedly shows Jane as the bully that Edith calls her, it also provides evidence of Jane's good professional qualities.

But wait. Am I taking the same false path that I have suggested the IMDb user has done in accepting *The Audition* at face value? Let us look together at some of what I think of as the key scenes in *The Audition*, noting the relation between the dialogue and the images.

We begin with the second sequence of the film, just after the title, which moves physically en route from collecting Jane at the airport through Wel-lington's Mount Victoria Tunnel up the Kapiti coast to Edith's home and conversationally through such topics as how to drive, how beneficial self-help books can be, how to drive, self-help books, Jane's latest film, memories of family car trips, and Edith's current preference for swimming in the river rather than the ocean.

From this point Jane and Edith engage in a dialogue that is comically at cross-purposes, as the following sample indicates:

Jane: I read one of those books I sent you. It really helped me. . . . It . . . calmed
    me down.
Edith: There is a speed limit, you know. A hundred.
Jane: Well, did you read one of them?

Edith: Yes, yes. It was good.
[Beat]
What was it about again?

Jane starts her reply, but her mother's attention drifts out the window and she interrupts Jane to ask, "How did the film go? The new one." Edith interrupts again as Jane starts to answer, and soon they switch to discussing the road and a family memory of traveling along it. By now, windows are open and the soundtrack carries traffic noises, the air rushing by, and a multitude of cicadas. One might think it almost portentous—some sort of classical allusion to Furies—when Edith says, "Listen to the cicadas," if it weren't for the ever more insistent visual references to Jane's *Peel* (1982) and the scene's final joke. Jane asks Edith, "Have you been for any swims this year?" Edith answers, "Yeah, but I like the river best. I've never been happy in the sea since I saw *Jaws.*"

There is the stand-up comedian's humor, of course, of ending this sequence with the joke about *Jaws,* along with the parodic humor of quoting shots from *Peel.* There is also the humor of dialogue spoken by a couple largely at cross-purposes. In addition, for many of us there is the echo of our own past experience of driving with a parent in the car, and for some of us there is the echo of attempts to improve one's mother by giving her the benefit of our own educational epiphanies (a pattern hinted at in some of the films described by Lucy Fischer in *Cinematernity* when she deals with mother/daughter stories told from the daughter's point of view).[26] From a psychological point of view, Anna's film already suggests perhaps some difficulty in separation, or some form of narcissism, between both the mother and the daughter, on the one hand, and at least *one* of the sisters with the other.

The film is once again full of portentous possibilities but overwhelming humor. After wandering aimlessly around her house, Edith enters Jane's bedroom. She sits down on Jane's bed and begins a conversation with "I feel anxious in the morning. Do you? . . . I supposed I cared about my marriage too much," followed by a list of things that make her unhappy. Jane takes a breath from an inhaler as she listens, asks "helpful" questions, but ultimately shows no sympathy, lecturing Edith on her "attitude." Edith, in keeping with her behavior in the scene previously discussed, changes the subject, this time in a move designed, like much of the scene's visual content, to call attention to Jane's body, saying, "You really should have done something about that mole on your neck."

Here the humor lies in the bit of tit for tat with which the scene ends. If Jane has been a bad daughter, then Edith can be a bad mother—and they

Edith and Jane Campion in the bedroom scene in *The Audition*. Courtesy of Anna Campion.

both end up looking childish. Meanwhile, Anna's camera follows its fascination with Jane's body (here with the apparently nude Jane in bed, on Jane's lips in the audition scenes, and again on Jane's body in the film's penultimate scenes when Jane "tak[es] some sort of exercise," as Edith puts it). With its reference to the absent father, this scene implicitly puts the family together in one room, perhaps significantly the bedroom, suggesting in its way something of the family's problematic qualities. However, while incest occurs in both *A Girl's Own Story* and *Sweetie,* Jane specifies that "incest was not a personal experience."[27]

Since we later learn that Edith suffered from asthma as a child, the physical connection between mother and daughter suggests a psychological connection based in their vulnerability. In a sense, *The Audition* is a film about the extent to which mother and daughter are alike rather than having separate personalities. When finally the definitive difference between these two is clearly stated in the last staged dialogue between them, that difference is almost lost, having been outweighed throughout the film by representations of their similarities.

To understand this last staged dialogue, though, we need the context Anna has created for our perception of Jane and Edith's interactions. The opening scene is one of a number of examples of Jane's casual rudeness to her mother, in this case, as seen from Edith's perspective, leading to Edith's

Edith Campion before the camera in the sound check scene in *The Audition*.
Courtesy of Anna Campion.

diminishment. This scene exemplifies Anna's repeated presentation of Jane in an unflattering—diminishing—way.

After a shot of cinematographer Waka Attewell describing the lighting, we move to a close-up of Jane peering through the camera and agreeing with his set-up. She then calls her mother into the room for "just a sound check," but apparently Edith does not understand the process. Jane asks how she is doing with the passage, and Edith expresses uncertainty about both the learning process and what is happening at that moment in front of the camera. Having asked whether she should start and getting the go-ahead, Edith no sooner begins than Jane stops her, saying, "that's good" with reference to the sound test. Not until the film's end will Edith make it through the passage, in the future stopping herself, until the moment, previously referred to, when Jane gives her actor her motivation.

Anna successfully plays the sound test scene for laughs, emphasizing the timing of the interruption and the lack of communication between mother and daughter. While the laugh seems at first to come at Edith's expense, it also sets up Jane as insensitive and unobservant, careless of how her behavior affects her mother. Because we see the sound test largely from Edith's perspective, the situation's technical requirements fade away in consideration of the rudeness they cause along with her diminishment. Later, in the penultimate scene, Edith finally expresses her point of view and calls Jane a "bully."

Lest we have any doubts about how self-reflexive this film is, here is the opening shot as the most confrontational scene between mother and daughter begins:

Jane: You never say what you mean. It's always so bloody complicated with you.
Edith: You bully me, you bully other people. . . .
Jane: OK, Mum, what shall we do? Shall we just sit here and contemplate how meaningless life is? That'd be fun, wouldn't it? Shall we do that?
Edith: I can't help finding life meaningless.
Jane: I mean it, Mum. It's that fat negativity of yours. You're always giving it something to eat.
Edith: But you feel good inside yourself. I don't. I feel scared and frightened.

Here, as throughout *The Audition,* I hear echoes of dialogue from *Sweetie* in some of Jane's intonations and even words and phrases, which raises the question of how much of *Sweetie* we should take as autobiographical. That, of course, brings us to territory that makes me, as an alien resident of what is essentially Jane's hometown, rather nervous, in the same way that talking about *A Girl's Own Story* as autobiographical does.

And yet, people do. *Sweetie* of course prompted comments about what Jane's relationship with her sister must be like. In 1993 Jane told an interviewer that she and Anna are "passionate about each other. We were passionate as children, too, except that it was in the opposite way. We hated each other. It's one of the greatest turnarounds in a relationship that I've ever had."[28] Noting that "family life has been the butt of some very dark humour in [her] films," one interviewer asks Jane what inspired the "bizarre behaviour by both parents and siblings." "Not my family," she says firmly. "If my family was really weird, I think I'd have found it very hard to do stories that reveal what can go wrong with the family unit."[29]

Jane has included her family in dedications and credits on her major films, from the dedication to Edith at the end of *The Piano* through the robust thanks to her father in more than one film's credits to the pathetic dedication of *The Portrait of a Lady* to her dead son.[30] She dedicated *Sweetie* to Anna, in part as acknowledgment, she has said, for the fact that she couldn't have made it had not Anna been available to help with Edith during a health crisis.[31] And, of course, she has helped Anna's career in various ways. In everything that Jane Campion has ever told people about herself, she has made it clear that she likes to be amid friends and family, that she dislikes being isolated and alone.

What has this little exploration of a bit of obscure history revealed, so far as we have gone with it? Summarizing some of the psychological literature behind her analysis of *East Lynne* in *Motherhood and Representation*, E. Ann Kaplan writes that "female jealousy, possessiveness, and competition are the product of woman's 'incompleteness,' her positioning in patriarchy as object, not subject."[32] I'm not willing to speculate on the extent to which this assertion describes the relationships among Edith, Anna, and Jane, but I do find *The Audition*'s objectification of Jane curious.

It would be helpful, of course, to know to what extent Jane was involved in developing ideas for *The Audition*. It might be helpful as well to know what Anna's brief was for her assignment. But clearly *The Audition* is not a documentary; it is a crafted presentation of a mother/daughter relationship, one that plays with the reality of two relatively well known lives—well known at least by some people, who would get the joke. Craft, Jane Campion has made clear throughout those early interviews, interested her. She had stories to tell, stories inflected by her training as an anthropologist, her identification with young women, and her fascination with the physicality of sex. She practiced telling these stories in different media until she found what worked for her, and then she mastered the craft.

The one bit of personal information I think we *can* take from *The Audition* that can be applied to readings of Jane's films—especially since it has been confirmed by Jane in interviews—is that, unlike Edith, Jane is by nature an optimist. Over the years I have heard assertions that the "happy" ending of *The Piano* was imposed on Campion by Harvey Weinstein—something I have never seen confirmed by any remotely reliable source, despite hearing repeatedly that there were two versions of the ending. I am sure that in Campion's various drafts of the screenplay there were many versions of the ending, but I am increasingly inclined to think that people who expect dark endings from Campion are wrong. It is obvious to me that it was Campion's choice to change the novelist's ending of *In the Cut;* certainly Susanna Moore's version is grim, grim, grim.[33] In 1993 Campion told an interviewer that she does not consciously "resist unhappy endings": "But I like to get the audience back on their feet. Give them something to get them out of the cinema, so they can walk back home."[34]

Finally, to try in my own way to end on a happy note, I'm amused by the apparently unintentional irony of Janet Maslin's criticism of Anna's direction, since to criticize Anna is indirectly to criticize Jane, given how much *The Audition* quotes and parodies Jane's films. In addition to the visual quotation from *Peel,* there are echoes of *Sweetie* in Jane's conversations with Edith. Additionally, one particular sequence from *The Audition* imitates moments in both *After Hours* and *Sweetie*. These are shots in each film that, without establishing shots or other forms of set-up, show individuals outdoors, doing mundane things in a back garden; eventually we realize that someone is watching them from inside.

First we see Edith placing a water sprinkler. Then we realize that our point of view is from inside the house (although the angle is "wrong," given that Edith will soon step directly from the garden into the room where her observer sits). Meanwhile, on the soundtrack the noise of a typewriter has been fading up, and we realize that Jane has been working, only to be interrupted by the noise of the sprinkler hitting the window where she sits. "Mum," she calls, "Turn it off," while rapping on the windowpane. Edith has not quite heard Jane, so she comes into the house. She props herself on the edge of the table where Jane is working, but Jane asks her to be careful of some books she is working with. Then Edith begins talking about how uncomfortable she is about the screen test she and Jane worked on earlier in the day. She wonders whether she was any good, she recalls having enjoyed acting on stage, and she says she does not feel right about the work Jane is offering her. After fulsome praise for Edith's abilities, Jane finally says, "I'd really love to have you in it [her film]. It'd mean a lot to me." Then, without missing a beat, she concludes, "Could you move that sprinkler while you're at it, though, Mum? It really is incredibly annoying."

Like some sort of enfant terrible, as selfish as Sweetie herself, Jane Campion appears in her sister's "fiction" film, letting Anna set her up as the bully Edith says she is. Meanwhile, Edith engages in a caricature of her own position. Carol Jacobs notes that "the humor of *The Piano,* in fact, is often produced by a theater of doubling."[35] The Campions do seem to have made a theater of their lives that doubles their films—or is it the reverse?

Referring to Jane's emotional response to Edith's rendition of a passage from *Juno and the Paycock,* Alistair Fox writes:

It was moving and full of pathos, in a way that suggested to me a deep compassion for Edith on Jane's part (and, implicitly, on Anna's part) that accompanies their efforts to defend themselves against her very despairing and fearful sense of the world. I intuit that this relates in some way to the complicity one senses between the three of them. At the very least, it reveals something important about Jane in terms of her relationship with her mother.[36]

That's the tricky thing about this film. It so clearly is not a documentary in the sense of a genre characterized by a search for factual truth. Yet so much of this film is nonetheless grounded in the Campions' lives: the house and other locations, the theatrical career, the failed marriage, the movies in progress, the fascination with self-help.

One can imagine how much fun all three women had taking the piss out of themselves and their family history while making this movie, in a sort of game of sailing dangerously close to the wind of truth. Like the IMDb user, I think *The Audition* is really quite revealing, but not necessarily in the way he understands it. To paraphrase a sentiment from the 1960s, how do you know she's kidding when she *doesn't* say she's kidding?

Notes

1. David McGill, *Up the Boohai Shooting Pukakas: A Dictionary of Kiwi Slang* (Lower Hutt, New Zealand: Mills Publications, 1988), 122.

2. Mark Stiles, "Jane Campion," in *Jane Campion: Interviews,* ed. Virginia Wright Wexman (Jackson: University Press of Mississippi, 1999), 5.

3. Michel Ciment, "Two Interviews with Jane Campion," in *Second Take: Australian Film-Makers Talk,* ed. Raffaele Caputo and Geoff Burton (Saint Leonards NSW, Australia: Allen and Unwin, 1999), 52.

4. Ibid., 50.

5. L. H. Wong, "Biography for Anna Campion," Internet Movie Database, http://www.imdb.com/name/nm0133044/bio (accessed 27 November 2006).

6. Janet Maslin, "Future In-Laws Meet and Eat and Eat and Eat," *New York Times,* 28 March 1991, C12.

7. Wong, "Biography for Anna Campion."

8. "Awards for *Broken Skin,*" Internet Movie Database, http://www.imdb.com/title/tt0101511/awards (accessed 30 November 2006).

9. Cover copy for Edith Campion, *A Place to Pass Through and Other Stories* (Wellington: A. H. and A. W. Reed, 1977); Mary Cantwell, "Jane Campion's Lunatic Women," *New York Times Magazine,* 19 September 1993, 41.

10. Bruce Mason, "Towards a Professional Theatre," *Landfall* 65 (1963): 74.

11. Cover copy for Campion, *A Place to Pass Through;* Cantwell, "Jane Campion's Lunatic Women," 41.

12. Frank Sargeson, "Review," *Landfall* 125 (1978): 90–91.

13. Dennis McEldowney, "Short Stories," *Islands* 7, no. 3 (1979): 316.

14. Kristina McVeigh, review of *The Chain,* by Edith Campion, *Landfall* 132 (1979): 392.

15. Patrick Evans, "Coat, Strides: A Happy Ride," *Islands* 7, no. 5 (1979): 558.

16. Ibid.

17. Miro Bilbrough, "Different Complexions: Jane Campion, An Interview," in *Film in Aotearoa New Zealand,* ed. Jonathan Dennis and Jan Bieringa (Wellington: Victoria University Press, 1992), 95; Rachel Abramowitz, "Jane Campion," in Wexman, *Jane Campion,* 189.

18. Abramowitz, "Jane Campion," 189.

19. Bilbrough, "Different Complexions," 95; Kristin Williamson, "The New Filmmakers," in Wexman, *Jane Campion,* 6.

20. Bilbrough, "Different Complexions," 96.

21. Sue Williams, "A Light on the Dark Secrets of Depression," in Wexman, *Jane Campion,* 175.

22. Ibid.

23. Nicholas Davis, "A Quirky and Ultimately Moving Short Film—Invaluable to Campion Fans," user comment on *The Audition,* Internet Movie Database, http://www.imdb.com/title/tt0096849/#comment (accessed 27 November 2006).

24. The names may or may not be worth exploring for hidden meaning.

25. Brian D. Johnson, "Rain Forest Rhapsody: *The Piano* Is a Work of Passion and Beauty," in *Jane Campion's* The Piano, ed. Harriet Margolis (New York: Cambridge University Press, 2000), 173.

26. Lucy Fischer, *Cinematernity: Film, Motherhood, Genre* (Princeton: Princeton University Press, 1996).

27. Ciment, "Two Interviews," 51.

28. Sandra Hall, "The Arts/Film," in Wexman, *Jane Campion,* 166.

29. Ibid.

30. Miro Bilbrough, "The Piano," in Wexman, *Jane Campion,* 123.

31. Ciment, "Two Interviews," 61; Myra Forsberg, qtd. in Margolis, *Jane Campion's* The Piano, 34n12.

32. E. Ann Kaplan, *Motherhood and Representation: The Mother in Popular Culture and Melodrama* (London: Routledge, 1992), 81.

33. Sue Gillett, hearing this at the colloquium, confirmed that Jane Campion herself acknowledged changing the ending from the original when she fronted the Australian premiere of *In the Cut.*

34. Hall, "The Arts/Film," 167.

35. Carol Jacobs, "Playing Jane Campion's Piano: Politically," *MLN* 109, no. 5 (1991): 782n8.

36. Alistair Fox, e-mail message to author, 11 May 2007.

Harvey Keitel as P. J. in *Holy Smoke.* Courtesy of the Academy of Motion Picture Arts and Sciences.

Campion-Keitel Connections,
a.k.a. "We are the piano"

"From the marines to the Method and beyond"

Jane Campion often speaks of her respect for Harvey Keitel as an actor, emphasizing how much he contributed to *The Piano* (1993) and *Holy Smoke* (1999). Of *The Piano,* she comments: "I didn't find anyone who had the presence of Harvey. [He] was linked to strong memories of cinema that I had when I was very young. . . . His work is tender and masculine. . . . It's the depth of his inquiry into life that makes Harvey so interesting."[1] Elsewhere she continues: "He's now looking at all his softer, more personal emotional sides."[2] Keitel returns the compliments, referring to Campion as "a goddess . . . mystical . . . a little girl . . . a friend . . . with all the qualities of being a great guy."[3]

The blended attributes each uses to describe the other say much about the fluidity of their collaborations. To date, however, there has been no thorough exploration of how Campion's encouragement and direction helped Keitel to create "George Baines" and "P. J. Waters" as (anti)heroes and counter forces together with actresses of strikingly different physiques and acting styles. Most academic critics still approach film characters as if they were freestanding beings or puppets controlled by a director's strings without acknowledging how vital an actor's input is.

Why do so few studies appraise performance? The short answer, summarizing Sharon Carnicke, is that analysis of acting is thought to be both too hard and too subjective.[4] Nevertheless, as Carnicke and others demonstrate, by drawing on acting theories that provide the basis for actor training and supplying detailed observations of movement it is possible to develop a "professional terminology for analysis."[5]

Keitel's performances are unquestionably responsible for the fact that academics view the characters he plays in *The Piano* and *Holy Smoke* as, in Patricia Mellencamp's words, "figures of hybridity and reciprocity."[6] Having studied with Stella Adler, Frank Corsaro, Lee Strasberg, and others, Keitel is adept at bridging the gaps between self and "other." Always also he taps into his experiences as a marine, confronting fear, exploring the unknown, relying on his fellows and superiors.[7]

The better to show how Keitel crafts Baines and P. J., I preface my assessment of his partnerships with Campion and her leading ladies by a brief discussion of his acting training and evolution. I then zero in on his work in *The Piano* and *Holy Smoke,* analyzing four key sequences from each film. With each, following Paul McDonald's lead, I carefully attend to those "fragmentary moments when the actions and gestures of the performer" . . . "impart significant meanings about the relationships of the character to the narrative circumstances."[8] Although in both films one finds "an actor who slips into his role's clothes, environment and attitude without any distractions of actorish business," his performances are strikingly different.[9] *The Piano* is more realist and naturalist, and *Holy Smoke* more hybrid, verging at moments on heightened theater thanks to Campion's surrealist leanings and Keitel's immersion in Method-informed approaches.[10] Add to these differences the fact that Keitel's costar in *The Piano* plays a mute, while *Holy Smoke* is wound around dialogue. In each case, of course, the final choice of actors rested with Campion.

I conclude by enlisting other directors' opinions about Keitel's performances in their films and glossing Keitel's evolution as actor and arts activist. Last, I return to Keitel's and Campion's own assessments of their collaborations. Because for Keitel as well as Campion teamwork is paramount, per a maxim of Constantin Stanislavsky, I title this last section "We are the piano."

"Take the titty . . . suck the titty": Keitel on Acting

Talking about the child he was helping raise with Lorraine Bracco, then his partner, Keitel tells the following anecdote:

When my oldest girl was maybe around four and a half . . . and we were playing "Baby and Mommy," I was cradling her in bed. And she said "Okay, Baby"—I was the Baby—"Take the titty." And I took her titty. Then she said, "Okay, I'll be the Baby and you be the Mommy." And I was struck, I thought for a moment, I wasn't certain what to do, and I said to her, "I can't, because I'm a Daddy." And she said, "It's just *pretend.*" And I said, "Okay, it's just pretend. Fine. Suck the titty." And I learned something in that moment which continues to nourish me greatly.[11]

Stanislavsky developed similar exercises—devised in his case with his six-year-old niece—for his acting classes. Both Keitel and he understand that a child's games can prompt an actor's concentration and imagination.[12] Like many Method-trained actors, however, Keitel is evasive when asked to talk about his work: "I feel I'm teaching outside my competence."[13] He says, "It's not that I can't share [things], because I do, but they have to be shared in another way—through the work." He does not want to betray the "mystery" that underpins good performance.[14]

So how to divine what he understands as "good performance"? The task is complicated by the fact that, like most actors working today, Keitel draws on many approaches as he creates his characters. Nonetheless, in interviews he *does* most frequently invoke Adler. For him as for her, therefore, I would imagine that "good performance" entails three things: (1) meticulous study of the text, (2) resolute probing into oneself, and (3) profound commitment to one's director and fellow actors. From studying Keitel's work with Campion and with other directors, it is obvious that he begins by situating his character's actions within the text's action as a whole. Like a detective, he subdivides and analyzes the script, striving to discover the ruling idea behind his character in relation to the screenplay's "given circumstances" and structure of actions.[15] Following Adler and Stanislavsky, he's confident that "the truth in art is the truth of your circumstances."[16] He emphasizes that "about 90% of [acting] is homework and the other 10% is bringing your ideas to life in a rehearsal. . . . It's always a painful process."[17]

Keitel combines a passion for character work with an expansive sense of self, believing that under any habitual daily self one can find an endless multiplicity of possible selves. Adler taught that to create a character actors needed to become "actor anthropologists," to read widely, study architecture, painting, and more.[18] Keitel would agree. He does *lots* of research before he undertakes a role, and he reads voraciously. Corsaro, Strasberg, Adler, and Penny Allen all taught him to be "interested in humanity, in expression, in change, in enlightenment, in art."[19]

He tries to choose projects that are personally challenging, that permit him to learn from and with others. "For the most part I've been lucky. . . . [M]ostly I've worked with profound people," he says.[20] Yet he admits that "there have been a few instances when directors wanted to push me around to satisfy their egos, so I became difficult. They weren't interested in any sort of a collaboration. . . . [Those films] always stunk."[21]

Keitel loved working with Campion because she encourages participation. And all *The Piano*'s actors benefited from the time for rehearsal and exploration that Campion made possible. As his work together with his costars and supporting actors in *The Piano* and *Holy Smoke* shows, he excels at conveying distinct emotional moments, and at times he even portrays passive states "actively," much as Stanislavsky would have wished.[22]

"I have never done a nude scene"

Keitel has said that "an actor tells a story the way his conscience dictates is best to tell it. Actors do not do nude scenes. They play events in the story. Whether they're dressed or undressed is up to their conscience and their artistic sense. I want to be clear about this point. Is it clear that I'm not actually doing nude scenes?"[23]

What, then, to make of the fact that, of all the sequences featuring Keitel in *The Piano,* the one that has received the most attention is the one where he moves naked around the piano, dusting it with his shirt as the camera plays hide and seek with his penis? And he's naked twice more too: first, when throwing aside the red curtain that divides his bed from the rest of the cabin, he reveals himself to Ada (Holly Hunter), insisting that he wants to "lie" together (she acquiesces, stripping as well); second, when she comes to his house after he has returned her piano, and they make passionate love. Many viewers, moreover, remember Keitel's bare "bod" in *Who's That Knocking at My Door?* (dir. Martin Scorsese, 1968), *Fingers* (dir. James Toback, 1978), *Bad Lieutenant* (dir. Abel Ferraro, 1992), and *Holy Smoke.* So how on earth can he claim that he has never done a nude scene? Easily, if one evaluates his gestures, stance, and movements in the piano dusting scene and elsewhere in light of what he and other actors do throughout *The Piano.*

Campion knew what she wanted in casting Keitel, fixing on him for the role of Baines early on because she found no one who possessed as much "presence" as he did: "I thought that he was interested in different things, experimental things. People told me his age could be a problem. So I watched one of his latest films, *The Two Jakes,* and I thought that he . . . seemed young."[24] Keitel in turn was intrigued by the script she sent: "That script had one ingredient that almost every script I read does not have: a vast dimension of things being unexplained to the audience or even to the characters themselves—and that's just a real haunting part of the story, very, very haunting."[25] According to Campion, he "wanted to act in a film that spoke of the relationships between men and women, rather than another story of cops and robbers. He had not often been given the opportunity to express certain qualities of tenderness that he possesses."[26]

As usual, Keitel prepared extensively for his part, "dig[ging] into [the script] to discover where the character is coming from, . . . analyzing what the author had in mind," even learning to speak some Maori.[27] Watching the film it is obvious that he has calibrated the ways Baines's gestures, facial expressions, and delivery shift within and between scenes. That some were shot out of order makes no difference: his preparation helps ensure continuity.

At times the relatively short (5'7") Keitel seems to loom over the diminutive (5'2") Hunter. Much is made of their contrasting skin tones: where she is pale-skinned and slight, he is ruddy, with a "tree-trunk body, . . . knotted chest, gnarled face, and insistent frown."[28] Both highly trained actors with excellent technique, the two worked closely together, looking, in Hunter's words, "for the unspoken mystery that enveloped every scene. . . . I don't think Harvey has to work hard to have access to that. I think Harvey is just a really tender guy."[29] Thanks to director of photography Stuart Dryburgh's framing, even before Baines, Ada, and Stewart (Sam Neill) meet, they are "inextricably linked."[30] When Baines, Stewart, and a handful of Maori arrive on the beach to bring Ada, Flora (Anna Paquin), and their possessions back to Stewart's house, Keitel communicates Baines's concern for Ada both nonverbally and verbally. Wearing a slight frown and clenching his jaw in concentration, standing next to Neill, Keitel appraises her, then murmurs, "She looks tired." Twice he can be seen gazing at her, holding first his left hand, then his right hand, near his heart.

Four sequences from the second act demonstrate just how carefully Keitel creates Baines together with Hunter, Paquin, Neill, Campion, and Dryburgh. In the first, Ada knocks on Baines's door and hands him a note asking him to bring her piano up from the beach. In extreme close-up we see Keitel's dirt-rimmed fingers take the note. He tilts his head apologetically, a bit defiantly, a half-smile in his eyes, and confesses in a vaguely Scottish accent: "I'm not able ta read." Moving back and forth in indecision, he mutters kindly, "I'm sorry. I can't do that. I don't have the time. Bye." He shuts the door in their hopeful faces, but his body language has sent mixed messages. They wait. He emerges, walking purposefully, mouth set. He looks at them and again insists, "I can't take ya there, can't do it!" Yet he saddles his horse as, in unison, their bonneted heads tilt sideways and they smile.[31] Almost imperceptibly, a smile creeps into Keitel's eyes too.

That Keitel uses an accent is highly unusual. In almost every other film, even when playing a French, Californian, or Hebrew character, he retains his native Brighton Beach Brooklyn-ese. Here, however, the rolled r's, broad vowels, and slight lilt he affects soften his thin tenor, helping to make him believable as a loner in tune with nature and open to love. As always, his ability to convey emotion through facial gestures—furrowing his brow, narrowing or half-opening his lips, breaking out into a sudden smile—is impressive, and it is crucial to a film where close-ups on faces and hands are paramount.

The next sequence, where the three are back on the beach with the piano, showcases New Zealand's northern seashore and Campion's and Dryburgh's placement of the actors' bodies within it. In extreme long shot we see Keitel, wide-brimmed black hat planted on his head, follow Hunter and Paquin at some distance as Paquin runs and Hunter walks quickly toward the piano. In medium shot the camera pans right to show Hunter's hands and torso at the piano and Keitel's legs moving (out of focus) at the side. Flora runs up and hugs her mother, then runs off. As Hunter plays, Keitel walks past in offbeat counterpoint, then looks thoughtfully back at her from under his hat. In reverse shot, she smiles happily at the piano, then at Paquin, who dances and turns cartwheels in the sand in delight as (out of focus) Keitel paces in front. Hunter closes her eyes in bliss. As she launches into a restatement of the theme, replete with rolling bass arpeggios, Keitel turns back twice more to look at her, his hands now clasped behind his back, mouth partly open, obviously touched by what he is hearing and seeing. The corset Hunter wears accentuates her slim waist, making her look fragile but tough. Keitel's layers of colorful clothing—vest, jacket, shirt, thick belt, checked pants—make him seem broader. Significantly, of all the performers, only Hunter will later echo this meditative, yearning posture, walking out of Stewart's house after her piano has been returned, body tipped forward, left hand clasping the right behind her back, gazing off into the bush.

As Ada and Flora play a slower, duet variation on the theme, Baines moves behind and to the left of the piano, gathering up boards and carefully leaning them on the piano body. The camera pulls back gradually. Finally, a high angle extreme long shot from the cliff above discovers Flora putting the finishing touches on a giant sea horse made of shells. A pan reveals Keitel waiting patiently on the left. Hunter walks past, looking back briefly. Paquin trots up to join her. Keitel follows in their footsteps at a third and slower gait, arms swinging. The contrasting but complementary beats of the movements are haunting, especially since set amidst the remote stretch of seascape.

Keitel's stance and gaze throughout the sequence express attentiveness, interest, and respect. Like Strasberg, Estelle Parsons, and Stanislavsky, he knows that active listening and group work are essential: a good actor must

Keitel makes Baines's fascination and longing visible without words, through a combination of attentive stance and contemplative expression.

constantly react. Many instructors teach the value of focusing on an "object of attention"—usually the actor's partner, but material objects as well—as a way to "direct the viewer's eye to the character's priorities."[32]

In the piano sequence (i.e., in the first of the three notorious "not-nude" scenes), the piano clearly stands in for Ada as "object of attention." The sequence begins with Baines lying on his bed half hidden behind a curtain, watching and listening to Ada as she plays. Keitel's left hand cradles his head; with his right, he draws the curtain aside. The music continues briefly as we see only the piano, two shafts of light surrounding it: Ada has gone. In silence and medium shot, Keitel slowly removes his shirt and stands, naked, in front of it. He wipes the top and closed lid, bends to dust a leg, then moves slowly from right to left around and behind the grand, gently massaging it with his shirt. His movements recapitulate the direction he took around Hunter and the piano on the beach, but now his body brushes up against the instrument periodically. He ends in front of the keyboard, stroking the piano with his left hand as dust motes hover in the air. His aging is poignantly obvious: he bulges a bit around the middle, although his muscular arms, sinewy legs, and taut torso still communicate a sense of considerable physical power. Baines's nudity is clearly symbolic here, a signal of his longing, receptivity, and openness. Worth noting too is that Paquin/Flora later performs the same dusting movements when Baines returns the piano to Stewart's house. In

Baines lovingly tends the piano, an object of attention that here clearly stands in for Ada in her absence. There is no "nudity" here, only vulnerability and openness.

fact, she even moves around the piano in the same direction as Keitel does here, emphasizing that in this film dusting is never just dusting, but always also expresses caring, concern, and love.

Stanislavsky often had his actors perform exercises built around sight, hearing, touch, smell, or taste, seeing in such drills a way for the actor to develop a sense of her or himself through concentration, imagination, and communication. He found improvisations on silent moments particularly valuable, because they enable actors to express emotion and communicate plot points differently than they could through dialogue. Keitel's ability to be silent *and* complexly, richly expressive suggests how compatible Baines and Ada are. As Laleen Jayamanne observes, Baines can read the correspondences among language, objects, and bodies. When in the third act Ada sends Baines a white piano key, an "A," on which she has burned the message "George Baines you have my heart. Ada McGrath," she does so knowing that Baines cannot read but will intuit what she means, "because he is 'Harvey Keitel.'"[33]

Keitel's gestures and posture consistently convey the shifts in Baines's moods. A key transformation is evident in a fourth sequence involving Baines and Stewart.[34] The scene begins with Baines lying on his side in bed, his dejection obvious. He has just sent Ada away and returned her piano, because, in his words, "the arrangement is making you a whore and me wretched. I want you to care for me, but you can't." Hair plastered to his head, breathing heavily, Stewart thrusts open the cloth that covers one of the small windows in Baines's cabin. He has run up hill to learn why Baines has returned the piano; he wants to be sure he will not have to give back the eighty acres of land he exchanged for it and Baines's lessons. That Neill is shot in close-up and Keitel in medium-long shot scene gives Keitel more space in which to work. He rolls over, exposing his stomach, one hand shielding his face, the other held at chest level, the fingers curled as if helpless. He grunts in response to Stewart's query, "don't want ta learn," then sighs and sits up. In profile, he resignedly strokes his hair back with both hands. From the window, Stewart nervously twitters, "I can't afford the piano if you need me to pay." "No, no payment. I have given it back," says Baines heavily. He sits down by the fire, back curbed in misery. Relieved, Stewart responds, "I'm not sure that I want it myself." Keitel eyes him narrowly. Then half-swallowing his final line so that the last part comes out only in a mumble, he replies: "'Twas more to your wife that I gave it."

The register, pitch, and pace of Keitel's exchanges in response to Neill vary more than do those with Hunter and Paquin. His halting, dampened speech here stands at one end of the spectrum of his vocal performances; at the other, find his animal-like scream and cry of anger, "I'll crush his skull!" when he receives Ada's chopped off finger. He consistently looks more grounded than the six-foot Neill, clad in too-tight clothes and too-small top hat, ever can.[35] Often he hunkers down, communicating nonverbally his connections with the earth and/or, as here, his sorrow. Hand gestures are similarly telling, whether he defensively holds up his hands or listens to Ada play, legs apart in welcome, one hand on his knee, the other cupping his chin in reflection and absorption. And he strokes, grabs, or gently touches Ada, Flora, and the piano; he never pats them.

Following Campion's script and directions, in tandem with his fellow actors and Dryburgh, Keitel uses posture, gestures, facial expressions, and movement throughout *The Piano* to write variations on seduction, loss, and love. Campion had encouraged Keitel to explore aspects of his masculinity he had worked on in rehearsal but never had had the chance to perform. Thinking him cast against type, critics and audiences were stunned by how well he plays a romantic lead. Keitel was surprised by their surprise: he had rehearsed and played many love scenes before in his acting classes.

"[I'm] interested in the condition of the world"

Keitel was fifty-three when *The Piano* was released. Six years later, working with Campion, Kate Winslet, Pam Grier, and director of photography Dion

Beebe on *Holy Smoke,* Keitel created an equally memorable male character, P. J. Waters. In May 2000, one year after *Holy Smoke* was released, he spoke about aging, calling sixty "a frightening age. My body . . . [is] going to die. But in terms of my self—with a capital *S*—I am no age, and I do not feel any age. I just feel rich and privileged to be alive and to do the work I have. . . . My body dying and what I feel as a human being, to me, are two different things."[36] He turns to art because for him it is ageless, about universals like "love, shame, sex, friendship, survival, goodness." He is intent on studying and representing "the condition of the world."[37]

With a December/May relationship at its core, age and aging are front and center in *Holy Smoke.* Per producer Jan Chapman, Campion had Keitel in mind for the "rather mythic role of P. J. since the very inception." To cast Ruth, in contrast, Campion first tested several hundred Australian actresses to see whether an unknown might be more appropriate. She settled on Winslet only after screen-testing her with Keitel. As Chapman put it, "We hadn't met anyone else who had that kind of power and intensity. [Kate] and Harvey were equals in the kind of energy they create."[38] Grier was also cast for her acting ability, in recognition that to many she has become an icon.[39]

Working with a script full of tonal shifts, Keitel portrays P. J. as a character who develops coherently, if at times absurdly, over the course of the narrative. A tragicomic figure, P. J. is, as he tells Ruth, just "a regular person, and you know it!" He is neither the devil she at one point sees him as (though in one sequence I will discuss he looks very much like a devil) nor her savior (for all he assumes a Pietà-like stance, cradled in her arms, in the penultimate scene).

P. J. first appears at the beginning of the second act, eighteen minutes into the film. Brought from the United States to cure Ruth of her attachment to a spiritual leader she has found in India, the titles introduce him as a "cult exiter." By P. J.'s own (offscreen) count, Ruth is "Case 190." Thinner than in *The Piano,* sporting a mustache and a little goatee, Keitel, from the moment he makes his entrance wearing tight blue jeans, black shirt and jacket, dark glasses, and high-heeled, glistening, snakeskin cowboy boots, turns heads, especially female heads. Striding through the Sydney airport toward the baggage claim, Neil Diamond's kitschy "I Am . . . I Say" blasting on the soundtrack, Keitel makes P. J. look and act like a macho Marlboro man whose grizzled neck, lined forehead, and dyed black hair betray his aging. Confidently, he marches up to a row of luggage carts. Five taller, younger men and one woman are striving, stupidly, to pull carts from the middle of the pile. Effortlessly, Keitel dislodges the last one, twirling it into the hands of a grateful older woman, then sends a second shooting off as well. Finally, he grabs a third away from a younger and more muscled man who, like him, is chewing gum, but less ferociously so.

Outside on the tarmac P. J. meets Ruth's family. He clearly sees himself as cock of the roost, bowing over the hand of Ruth's simpering sister-in-law, Yvonne (Sophie Lee) ("that's Yvonne, with a Y"), steering the tallest and oldest man, Stan (Austen Tayshus), away from the rest of the group, one hand firmly on his elbow, cautioning him in a rush in Keitel's legendary Brooklynese: "I can't begin this work without-a-properly-experienced-assistant. Those are the RULES." For emphasis, Keitel's head moves forward on the last word. In profile, he gestures with his right hand, fingers spread, a move designed, since he is a small man, to take up more space, to be imposing. At the same time, that Beebe shoots most of the family scenes in a "wide, almost naturalistic style, often using a steadicam so the dynamic of the family [is] spontaneous," brings out the family's zaniness, making the pompous P. J. by comparison more normal.[40]

Offbeat humor continues in the second sequence involving Keitel as well. Again, his movements and delivery establish P. J.'s authority while simultaneously revealing his narcissism. Clad in a leopard-print bikini, Yvonne is called in from poolside to attend a briefing. Inside Keitel paces back and forth. Adoringly crouching on her knees or standing behind him, Yvonne is all eyes and ears as P. J. pontificates about the "basic three-step system" he uses. Yvonne's husband, Robbie (Dan Wylie), Stan, and a third man are more interested in eating pizza and checking their cell phones than in listening. P. J. continues unfazed, detailing how he plans, in three days, to "steer the subject toward a breakthrough, a breakdown, whatever you care to call it." For punctuation, Keitel puts his left hand in his pocket. "Step one. Isolate her. Get her attention and respect. When she's listening, well, I start to push. The heat goes on." He adds, as if in afterthought, "It's very traumatic to the subject." Walking back left, now gesturing with both hands, he breaks off momentarily to refuse an offer of pizza, then, arms and hands waving in parallel motion, continues: "Step two—I remove all her props. Her books. Her sari if she's wearing one. Is she wearing one?" He concludes with a flourish, arms raised high, again in parallel motion: "Finally, the clouds of her unreason burst upon the earth. There's tears, sobs, hugs with the family and . . . it's over for me. But. Just beginning for you." Parallel movements are acting staples, designed to convey intention.

Reversing direction, Keitel struts back right, combing his hair as he boasts that he only has a 3 percent recidivist rate. When Yvonne asks if he has a wife or a lady friend, he replies flirtatiously, "Why do you ask?" takes the lid off a pillbox, and pops a pill. "I imagine you could persuade any woman to do anything," she coos.

She is, of course, wrong: P. J. is about to meet his match. An abrupt cut takes us away to the desert, where mountains loom high between orange soil and a blue sky dotted with orange clouds. A car speeds across the frame. Heading for the Halfway Hut, Ruth is singing Alanis Morissette's in-your-face, I'm-over-you song "You Oughtta Know" at the top of her lungs: "And I'm here to remind you / Of the mess you left when you went away. . . ." From here on, P. J. and Ruth are locked in a veritable battle of the sexes that ends only when both are exhausted and each acknowledges how much he/she appreciates, even loves, the other. As Kathleen McHugh underlines, "the battle that transpires between Ruth and P. J. is less a matter of their calculation than of their 'acting out'—in seductions, transgressions, and violations whose consequences dramatically shift the balance of power back and forth between them."[41]

A third exemplary sequence occurs after P. J. succumbs to his attraction to Ruth and sleeps with her under the guise of "comforting" her. De rigueur, Keitel has appeared "not-nude," although Winslet's is the more audacious performance (she pees as she advances on him) and Keitel is only seen in bed with her in long shot. Act three thus opens as P. J.'s carefully laid "exiting" plans have gone awry: "Day three, oh shit!" Yvonne and Ruth's gay brother and his lover descend on the Halfway Hut and spirit the eager Ruth and the reluctant P. J. away for an evening of dancing and drinking. Atypically for *Holy Smoke,* there is very little dialogue; instead music and movement tell the story.

In contrast to the family scenes, Beebe uses a more intimate style of shot construction and composition. Working primarily in medium shot and close-up, Keitel is extraordinarily generous as an actor, often keeping focus on Winslet when the two are in frame by acting with his back three-quarters to the camera. The close shots reveal Winslet's little double chin, round cheeks, and mobile features; she is obviously younger than Keitel and, at 5'8", an inch taller. Keitel subtly varies his expressions as he watches Ruth dance provocatively with another woman to "I Put a Spell on You." Beebe's camera dollies in to an extreme close-up on Keitel looking up darkly from underneath his eyebrows, forehead deeply creased, eyes unblinking, intense, registering anger, jealousy, and distress. Green-blue lava lights and shadows surround him, making him look truly fiendish. Suddenly, unable to watch any longer, P. J. tries to retaliate by dancing with Yvonne, his back to Ruth and her "girlfriend," which means he misses Ruth's exit from the pub. Panicked, fearing she has disappeared, he rushes out to find two young blokes plying her with liquor and pawing her. "You her dad or something?" asks one. Incensed, protective, Keitel clocks him, chases both away, then gingerly pulls Ruth's sweater down from around her neck, and helps her away.

A less experienced performer than Keitel, Winslet has a demanding role: often her character must display a range of emotions within a single scene. The same is not true of Grier's much smaller part as P. J.'s assistant, Carol. Yet Grier also matches Keitel move for move, bringing decades of experience with her to the role. Campion and Chapman found Grier to be, in Chapman's words, "an absolutely brilliant human being. She's someone who has a sense of what life is about quite beyond the everyday."[42]

P. J.'s and Carol's most revelatory sequence begins the day after the pub trip. Blithely ignorant of the fact that Carol has flown to Australia to find out what's happening, P. J. is showering outside the Halfway Hut. An abrupt cut from his point of view to Carol's lime green high-heeled sandals shows his surprise. To cover his discomfiture, he waves her close for a kiss, then—oh so lovingly—towels off the water he leaves behind on her face. Furrowing her brow, Carol asks, "Did you disconnect the phone?" Apologetically P. J. invents an excuse and protests, "I was going to call you." "When?" "When I finished." The bright lighting and medium shots disclose the gray hairs on his chest. Never has he looked as old, and from his halting delivery of explanations it is clear he is telling lies. Fed up, Carol says, "You're incredible! I can't believe what I'm seeing!" She walks away indignantly, waving towards the hut, and raises her voice, even though she knows and we see that Robbie and his kids are waiting around the corner in their station wagon. "She's on the couch! NEKKED! Are you fucking her for instance? What's going on?" "Nouoooo." Defensively, Keitel adds a diphthong to the vowel. Grier retaliates with feminist righteousness: "You could damage this girl!"

Unlike his performance as Baines in *The Piano,* never in this film does Keitel curb his back. Even in the last shot of this sequence he stands defiantly erect, ignoring Grier's parting threats of "One more day! One more day!" as she holds up a long lime green fingernail in warning. The camera dollies back with her, leaving him standing defiantly on a little platform, hands on hips, towel wrapped around his middle, cross stripes accentuating his waist. Near the film's end P. J. chases Ruth through the desert, arms outstretched, ridiculous in the red dress he has agreed to wear at her bequest. Finally, exhausted, he collapses, but here too Keitel keeps his body straight, making P. J. look toppled by love.

Quoting Stanislavsky, Estelle Parsons often said, "A good actor acts for the audience. A great actor acts with the other actors for the audience."[43] Campion worked closely with all her actors, envisioning P. J. as someone with "a deep need for challenge, maybe even an experience of surrender," maintaining that "Ruth meets with one of her own in P. J.: an explorer, but one who has been wounded by the experience."[44] She admires Keitel's performance immensely: "The guy is unbelievably courageous and exciting as a man. . . . [He]'s as macho and as masculine as any man I have ever encountered, perhaps more so, and in that position he's now looking at all his softer, more personal, emotional sides. And he can embrace them. And it just makes him completely beautiful, fascinating to me. I mean it's not easy. He's not perfect. There's parts that haven't made the crossover, for all of us."[45]

Most critics, however, did not share her enthusiasm. Review titles like "Sex Shack Shocker" and "Sects Appeal" testify to unfortunate marketing strategies. Yet Keitel has no complaints. He enjoyed bringing P. J. to life: "There's no crying over spilled milk here," he says.[46] For him, Campion's *Holy Smoke* offered him a stellar opportunity to explore anew "the condition of the world."

"We are the piano"

Most directors Keitel has worked with respect him. Abel Ferrara finds that "in addition to having incredible technique, he immerses himself in his work with a great deal of courage."[47] For Quentin Tarantino, because "Harvey has . . . toughness in his back pocket, it frees him to do other things and to nuance the role in surprising ways."[48] James Toback also sings Keitel's praises:

I was watching *Fingers* for the thousandth time when suddenly Harvey Keitel "playing" a scene with Marian Seldes, his mother in the film, came through to me with uncanny force. It was not just that he became a character (a transference that had happened long before); it was that I myself had only partial existence without the character he had become, so profound was my own notion of who I was now anchored in it. . . . Excitement, terror, confusion, love, most of all gratitude to Harvey for the miracle of having given flesh, rhythm, voice, life to an idea, a presence, trapped in mind, flattened on a page.[49]

Julian Schnabel commends Keitel's performances as well: "You have a very odd sense of delivery. I notice that your timing seems very studied, not self-conscious to where it would seem academic, but it's almost as if you can slow all of your facial expressions down, as well as your whole body, until it's like a freeze-frame of every emotion. All of a sudden everything is noticeable."[50]

Keitel is motivated by a strong conviction of what cinema could be, should be: "I think we have too many films that are fun. Cinema has the power to have a profound effect on the thinking of the citizenry, same way the Greek theater began. . . . That is a role I'd love to see cinema take again . . . providing a deeper truth, . . . making something that will feed us, help us deal with the feeling of being lost in the world."[51] He dreams of having the wealthy pay for tickets for people who do not have enough money to go to see good films, as in the days of the early Greek theater.[52] With Ellen Burstyn and Al Pacino, he now heads the Actors Studio; all donate their services. He has become a beacon for young independent filmmakers. "Thank goodness technology has evolved to the video camera, and so young talents can get together with their friends, actors, writers, directors, cinematographers, set designers, cost designers and make their own films. And get them seen," he says. "If I were to sacrifice the quality of film stock, of one film, to do ten personal stories on video, I would do the ten."[53]

Bottom line, what makes both *The Piano* and *Holy Smoke* so extraordinarily intriguing is the extent of collaboration among Campion, Keitel, Hunter, Neill, Winslet, and Grier. For Campion, Keitel was an ideal partner: "I had always admired him, his curious work and curious choices, that interesting intensity. I wasn't intimidated by the screen Keitel, his tough guys with crimson cocks. . . . What I found was a very sharp mind and a very sophisticated person, interested in the politics of relationships."[54] Again and again she salutes his "commitment to acting," explaining that "his philosophy about [acting] is absolutely staunch and excited. For me, he brought a whole alertness and awareness of the acting tradition, he's one of those people that really live it."[55] Of their work together on *The Piano* she says: "[We] were in agreement from the start. . . . I remember ringing him up and saying, 'One of my concerns, Harvey, is that you've had so much more experience than me. . . . [But] I still want to be able to direct you. What do you think?' And he said, 'Well, Jane, let me tell you something. All actors are very scared, very anxious. All we want to really do is please the director. So why don't we do this: you allow me to do a thing the way I want to do it first of all, and then I'll promise you I will try anything you ask me.' . . . He was able to recreate and repeat with new and interesting nuances quite easily."[56] With *Holy Smoke* she goes further: "I think that [Harvey] is somebody who feels things deeply. Who is exposed to life in a real way and has suffered and has found benefit in going deeply into himself and thinking about it and working it out. He's on the path, you know, to waking up and to finding some journey to his heart and invention and approach to removing fear."[57]

Keitel is, as usual, more terse. He loves *The Piano*: "Which is why I never saw it again. Every wish I had to be in a great film and in an important story was fulfilled."[58] He says, "What is it that I have to offer in an interview? I don't think it is to explain the character. The film speaks for itself. Jane wrote the text. Jane directed it. I think what I have to offer . . . concerns Jane's writing that story to begin with."[59] *Holy Smoke* is special too because here Campion allowed him to play with his classic tough guy character. Following Stanislavsky, he reminds us: "Actors are their own instruments. Their emotions, their physical beings are the instrument. There is no pen, no paper, no piano, no keys. We are the piano. . . . And directors help by supplying the environment. The trust."[60]

Yet if actors' bodies are "the piano," then surely all actors are also "pianists," and their directors are therefore pianists, improvisers, composers too. What better way, in fact, to conceptualize the multiple, collaborative, achievements of filmmakers and actors like Campion and Keitel than to imagine that, through these films they are *both* saying, "We are the piano?"

Notes

1. Campion is referring to Keitel's performances in *The Duellists* (dir. Ridley Scott, 1977) and *Bad Timing* (dir. Nicolas Roeg, 1980). Campion, Thomas Bourguignon, and Michel Ciment, "Interview with Jane Campion: More Barbarian than Aesthete," in *Jane Campion: Interviews,* ed. Virginia Wright Wexman (Jackson: University Press of Mississippi, 1999), 107.

2. Nancy Kapitanoff, "Cult of Campion," *Pulse!* February 2000, 36.

3. Marshall Fine, *Harvey Keitel: The Art of Darkness* (New York: Fromm International, 1998), 209. Keitel frequently calls Campion a "goddess." See, e.g., his comments in interviews with Lawrence Grobel, "The *Playboy* Interview: Harvey Keitel," *Playboy,* November 1995, 59; Georgina Howell, "The Gospel According to Harvey," *Vogue,* December 1993, 290; and Kristine McKenna, "Leaps of Faith," *Los Angeles Times,* 18 October 1992, calendar, 7.

4. See Sharon Carnicke, "The Material Poetry of Acting: 'Objects of Attention,' Performance Style, and Gender in *The Shining* and *Eyes Wide Shut,*" *Journal of Film and Video* 58, nos. 1–2 (2006): 21–30.

5. Ibid., 21. Studies on acting include Cynthia Baron, Diane Carson, and Frank P. Tomasulo, eds., *More Than a Method* (Detroit: Wayne State University Press, 2004); Alan Lovell and Peter Krämer eds., *Screen Acting* (New York: Routledge, 1999); Paul McDonald, "Film Acting," in *Oxford Guide to Film Studies,* ed. John Hill and Pamela Church Gibson, 30–35 (New York: Oxford University Press, 1998); Paul McDonald, "Why Study Film Acting? Some Opening Reflections," in Baron, Carson, and Tomasulo, *More Than a Method,* 23–41; James Naremore, *Acting in the Cinema* (Berkeley: University of California Press, 1988); and Pamela Robertson Wojcik, ed., *Movie Acting: The Film Reader* (London: Routledge, 2004).

6. Patricia Mellencamp, *A Fine Romance: Five Ages of Film Feminism* (Philadelphia: Temple University Press, 1995), 182.

7. See Oren Moverman, "To-Hell-and-Back Harvey," *Interview*, May 1999, 60, 130.

8. McDonald, "Why Study Film Acting?" 32.

9. David Thompson, "Harvey Keitel: Staying Power," *Sight and Sound* 3, no. 1 (1993): 22.

10. In discussing the Method, it is important to recognize two things: (1) "the" Method is not singular and (2) Method techniques can be and are used in all kinds of performances. Originally developed and modified by Stanislavsky, Strasberg, Adler, Sanford Meisner, Maria Ouspenskaya, and others variously translated Stanislavsky's teachings as "Method acting" in the United States. See, e.g., Sharon Carnicke, *Stanislavsky in Focus* (Amsterdam: Harwood Academic Publishers, 1998), and David Krasner, "Strasberg, Adler, and Meisner: Method Acting," in *Twentieth Century Actor Training*, ed. Alison Hodge, 129–50 (London: Routledge, 2000).

11. David Morgan, "Actor: Harvey Keitel," *Wide Angle/Close Up*, http://members .aol.com/morgands1/closeup/text/keitel.htm (accessed 31 July 2006).

12. Carnicke, *Stanislavsky in Focus*, 148. See also Sharon Carnicke, "Stanislavsky's System: Pathways for the Actor," in *Twentieth Century Actor Training*, ed. Alison Hodge, 11–54.

13. Howell, "Gospel According to Harvey," 290.

14. Moverman, "To Hell-and-Back Harvey," 60.

15. Speaking about his performance in Spike Lee's *Clockers* (1995), Keitel says: "I have to divide the elements up in my own mind. I've heard it said about detectives by detectives that they're great actors, that by the nature of their profession they have to be. To get information, you often have to put on a pretty good show. And the ones that are great detectives are in a sense great actors." John Anderson, "Welcome to His Neighborhood," *Los Angeles Times*, 17 September 1995, 28.

16. Stella Adler, *The Technique of Acting* (Toronto: Bantam Books, 1988), 31.

17. Pete Hamill, "Keitel on a Roll," *Vanity Fair*, April 1986, 122.

18. Krasner, "Strasberg, Adler, and Meisner," 140.

19. Grobel, "*Playboy* Interview," 56.

20. Thompson, "Staying Power," 24.

21. Grobel, "*Playboy* Interview," 52, 56.

22. See Carnicke, *Stanislavsky in Focus*, 154–55.

23. Grobel, "*Playboy* Interview," 51. Interviewed in *Premiere*, he says much the same thing: "I've done no nudity in my career. An actor doesn't do nude scenes. An actor plays an event and tells a story. . . . It's not about nudity, it's about revelation. So if anyone wants to discuss nudity with me, they can forget about it because it's not relevant." Jason Matloff, "Who's Afraid of Harvey?" *Premiere*, March 2005, 118.

24. Bourguignon and Ciment, "Interview," 107.

25. Qtd. in press kit for *The Piano*, n.p. Press materials available at the Margaret Herrick Library of the Academy of Motion Picture Arts and Sciences, Los Angeles, California.

26. Bourguignon and Ciment, "Interview," 107.

27. Keitel qtd. in *Actors on Acting for the Screen,* ed. Doug Tomlinson (New York: Garland, 1994), 303; see Bourguignon and Ciment, "Interview," 104.

28. Karen Schoemer, "Harvey Keitel Tries a Little Tenderness," *New York Times,* 7 November 1993, section H, 24.

29. Ibid.

30. Erin McGlothlin, "Speaking the 'Mind's Voice': Double Discursivity in Jane Campion's *The Piano,*" *Post Script* 23, no. 2 (2004): 28.

31. The nine-year-old Paquin and Hunter adored each other from the start, so it was natural that Paquin "would use all Hunter's mannerisms of performance." Campion, qtd. in press kit for *The Piano.*

32. Carnicke, "Material Poetry," 25.

33. Laleen Jayamanne, *Toward Cinema and Its Double: Cross-Cultural Mimesis* (Bloomington: Indiana University Press, 2001), 35.

34. I choose this moment rather than, say, the climactic love scene between Ada and Baines because, as Campion underlines, *The Piano* is "a study of men and women. . . . The men are just as important as Ada. . . . It's a film about relationships." Marli Feldvoss, "Jane Campion: Making Friends by Directing Films," *EPD Film,* August 1993; reprinted in Wexman, *Jane Campion,* 98.

35. As Campion points out, Neill does not have the same training or command of technique as Keitel. Bourguignon and Ciment, "Interview," 108. Neill describes Stewart as an erratic character: "I lurch from indifference to jealousy to love to anger to trying to find a way to cut through it." Graham Fuller, "Interview with Sam Neill," *Interview,* June 1993, 44.

36. Even Weiner, "The Rap on Harvey Keitel," *Detour,* May 2000, 74.

37. Ibid., 73.

38. Qtd. in press kit for *Holy Smoke,* 23. Press materials available at the Margaret Herrick Library of the Academy of Motion Picture Arts and Sciences, Los Angeles, California.

39. Ibid., 22–24.

40. "Dion Beebe," *Daily Variety,* 18 January 2000, n.p.

41. Kathleen Anne McHugh, *Jane Campion* (Urbana: University of Illinois Press, 2007), 116.

42. Qtd. in press kit for *Holy Smoke,* 24.

43. Qtd. in Carnicke, "Material Poetry," 25.

44. Qtd. in press kit for *Holy Smoke,* 21.

45. Kapitanoff, "Cult of Campion," 36.

46. Wiener, "Rap on Harvey Keitel," 73.

47. McKenna, "Leaps of Faith," 33.

48. Ibid.

49. Michael Fox, "Harvey Keitel," 1996 San Francisco Film Festival handout, 78.

50. Julian Schnabel, "Harvey Keitel," *Interview,* August 1990, 86.

51. Brian Case, "Dark Star," *Time Out,* 30 December 1992, 17.

52. See Elisa Leonelli, "Harvey Keitel's Journey," *Venice,* May 1996, n.p.

53. *Hollywood Reporter,* 4 April 2000, n.p.

54. Ritts, "Gospel According to Harvey," 289.

55. Qtd. in press kit for *The Piano*.

56. Miro Bilbrough, "*The Piano,*" *Cinema Papers* (Melbourne), May 1993; reprinted in Wexman, *Jane Campion,* 120.

57. Kapitanoff, "Cult of Campion," 36.

58. Eve Ensler, "Harvey Keitel: Movie Profile," *Interview,* March 2005, 112.

59. Schoemer, "Harvey Keitel Tries a Little Tenderness," 24.

60. Hamill, "Keitel on a Roll," 122.

Part II
Jane Campion and Her Sources

The four Janets. Janet Frame with the actresses who played her in *An Angel at My Table: (seated left to right)* Alexia Keogh (as Janet Frame as an adolescent), Karen Fergusson (as Janet Frame as a child), Kerry Fox (as Janet Frame). Courtesy of the New Zealand Film Archive and Hibiscus Films.

"I can really see myself in her story"
Jane Campion's Adaptation of Janet Frame's *Autobiography*

As Jane Campion stated in 1990, the first volume of Janet Frame's *Autobiography, To the Is-land,* and the two volumes that followed, *An Angel at My Table* (1984) and *The Envoy from Mirror City* (1985), had a strong personal influence on her. Looking back on the experience of filming *An Angel at My Table,* she commented on the strong personal significance Frame's story had for her and suggested that what had touched her deeply was also felt by others: "I can really see myself in her story. That makes it attractive and personal for me. I feel other people will see a part of themselves that they hadn't valued before, because what Janet suggests is all the vulnerability and shyness that exists in people."[1] That confluence of the personal and the universal perhaps explains why *An Angel at My Table* can be seen at the same time as a faithful adaptation of Frame's very personal story and yet as a distinctly "Campion" film, expressing her idiosyncratic imagination and her thematic preoccupations. It can also be seen as an explanation for the great popular success of what began as a modest television series, a success that influenced the work and public images both of the young filmmaker at the beginning of her career and the older novelist nearing the end of hers. The story of the development of the film from Campion's initial response to the first volume of Frame's autobiography in 1983 through the making of the screenplay and film to the public response to the film and its effect on Campion's career and on Frame's later life is a complex and moving one. This account will focus especially on the adaptation of Frame's books in Laura Jones's screenplay and on Campion's adaptation of that screenplay into the finished film, with some attention to the origins and the afterlife of the project.

77

Origins of the Project

Campion read Frame's *To the Is-land* soon after it was published in New Zealand and Australia in 1983, while she was still in film school in Australia. By March 1984 she and Bridget Ikin had written to Frame seeking television rights to make a three-part television series of the book. From the first they were aiming high "because we both consider the work to be a classic of New Zealand literature, we are both insistent that if the project is to be done at all, it should be . . . conceived with the highest standards of quality and commitment, with the aim of making it, too, a classic."[2] Frame replied that she was interested but preferred the idea of one film for each book (for there were two more volumes to come) to a television series, and referred them to her agent, Tim Curnow, in Sydney. When Ikin and Campion met with Curnow the next month, he indicated that Frame would not agree to any assignment of film or television rights until all three of the volumes had been published but promised not to option the rights elsewhere in the meantime and to send them a typescript of the third volume when it was ready at the end of the year. Frame was impressed with the serious intentions of the two young women, but Curnow wrote to her that he thought they were "a couple of dreamers" and that nothing would come from their proposal.[3] Campion visited Frame in December 1984, and they got on well, with Campion explaining to Frame why she thought that a television series would suit the autobiography better than a cinematic film. *An Angel at My Table,* the second volume in the autobiography, had appeared in May of that year, and the third volume, *The Envoy from Mirror City,* was due for publication in June 1985; Frame again asked Campion to wait until all three volumes were published, but promised to give the Campion-Ikin proposal priority consideration then. She wrote to Curnow after the meeting: "I'd be interested in any proposal she has for making a film from the three volumes."[4] Negotiations were carried out from September 1985, and an agreement was signed in January 1986 for the making of up to six films from the books (although Campion and Ikin thought three would be more likely), Frame having the right to approve the scripts and to be consulted about casting. Campion and Ikin promised "a quality television series, designed to create a wider market for the autobiographies (and by implication the other works of Janet Frame), and to appeal to those already familiar with the books."[5]

Ikin has recounted that during these negotiations when she asked Frame if she had any photos that could help them to visualize the Southland and Otago world of her childhood, she brought out a whole box of family photos. When they asked why these photos had not appeared in the autobiographies, Frame replied, "No one asked whether I had any." Perhaps because of Campion's and Ikin's response to the photos (Ikin said, "They became much-loved references for us in the writing and making of the film"), Frame went on to include a selection from the photos in the one-volume edition of her autobiography that appeared in 1989 (just before the release of the film *An Angel at My Table*).[6]

The two young "dreamers" had persisted in their proposal and had won the opportunity to make their television series and perhaps even at that stage had some effect on the republication of the autobiography itself. Their next step was to seek financing for the project. Ikin has said that "although Frame is well known in literary circles, it was simply the appeal of a great story which attracted overseas buyers." In terms similar to Campion's she described the nature of that appeal: "It's a very personal growing-up story. . . . It's about coming to grips with who you are and being free to be that person and trying to free yourself from the constraints that other people put on your personality . . . a vulnerable story about growing up and finding out who you are." Ikin thought that although the story had a particular New Zealand resonance, its basic appeal was universal.[7] That New Zealand resonance was important for the New Zealand Film Commission, which became the primary financer of the project. According to Lindsay Shelton, the commission's marketing manager, "The commission didn't want to finance a television series. But it did want to support a New Zealand project by Jane Campion," and that possibility won them over: "Jane's desire to direct a New Zealand film presented another chance for the commission to enable a talented expatriate to return home. And the story of how Janet Frame overcame personal disasters and illness to become New Zealand's most celebrated author was one that seemed ideally matched to the director's talent."[8] With the New Zealand Film Commission's support, Campion and Ikin could confidently move ahead in the process of adapting Frame's three volumes into a three-part television series. The first requirement for the adaptation was a screenplay.

Laura Jones and the Screenplay

Campion had already approached Laura Jones as a possible writer of a screenplay and had sent her *To the Is-land* to read. Jones had not at that time read the book but knew Frame's work from having previously read *Owls Do Cry, Faces in the Water,* and *Living in the Maniototo*. Jones's response to the book was immediate and positive and in the same vein as Campion's and Ikin's, as she later told Marion McLeod: "It opened our feelings about our own lives and ourselves. We all loved the book and wanted to make an equal film experience, to be true to the tone of the books."[9] As the project gathered momentum, Jones devoted all of 1987 to writing the screenplay. She first outlined a scene breakdown, then discussed it with Campion and Ikin and modified it. That became the basis of a first draft, which she discussed with Campion and Ikin before she wrote a second draft, which she also discussed with Frame. Campion has said that she and Jones worked closely in the making of the screenplay, with Frame's books working as "a mediator" between them, and Jones has said that Campion's "guiding words" for her that she kept in mind throughout the process were "tenderness (without sentimentality) and strength (without sensationalism)."[10] It was clear to Jones that this adaptation was different from the adaptation of a novel. With a novel she felt "responsible to the novel," but with the autobiography she felt "responsible to the *author*. . . . My responsibility was to Janet's version of her life, to what she calls the 'fiction' of her life."[11] Frame, according to Jones, "*loved* the script—not just liked it but *loved* it."[12] Frame wrote to Ikin early in 1988 that she found the script "quite luminously beautiful."[13] To Curnow ten days earlier she had written more temperately that she had found the script "clever and faithful" but that she preferred "to make as little comment as possible," for she was clear that it was not her script, "and the whole must belong to the person writing it." She had gone on to say that she would "like music and sky (in various countries) and the quality of light and death to be 'characters' which continue with [her] throughout the series," for to be a "true picture of [her] life among people, it needs to include the rich 'other' life."[14] She also made this suggestion directly to Campion and Ikin: "I'd like to stress the importance of all kinds of music, haunting songs and so forth, and the accompanying sky as a feature, almost a character in my life."[15]

The one aspect of Jones's script that bothered Frame was the hospital scenes derived from *Faces in the Water,* about which she had had doubts from the first and to which she had only reluctantly agreed in the preliminary negotiations. In *An Angel at My Table,* Frame had referred the reader to *Faces in the Water* for full descriptions of "the memorable family" of the other patients in the hospitals and for an account, through the character of Istina Mavet, of her sense of hopelessness and her fear that she would be held in "forced submission to custodial capture" for the rest of her life.[16] The implication is that the hospital experience required a whole book. Instead of trying to give a condensed account of it in the autobiography, Frame named the people who had helped her, gave one sample scene of abusive "care" (the enforced public toileting scene that is included in the film), and moved on to the now famous story of her reprieve from a planned leucotomy and her subsequent discharge from the hospital. Her feelings about covering the hospital years in the film were similar. She wrote to Curnow in late January 1988 that the hospital time is "a film in itself and ought to be portrayed as a period of years and years rather than a 'dipping into' to get a taste . . . a time of the seemingly everlasting nightmare . . . which still haunts me."[17] She eventually arrived at an agreement with Ikin and Jones about what could be used. She also made suggestions about idiom, costuming, and furniture, especially for the childhood scenes, and sent them a tape of her version of the rhymes and songs that she remembered from childhood.

The adaptation of the books for a television miniseries presented Jones with expected problems. The most obvious one was length: the 428 pages of the autobiography needed to be reduced to about 80 pages of screenplay. She told McLeod, "As always you have to lose so much. The thing is to cut and cut and yet still keep the spirit of the book."[18] Frame was well aware of this difficulty and saw it as analogous to her own in writing the book, as she told an Italian journalist in a telephone interview: "I realise the immense choice that is made in creating an autobiography—not only the material but also the method of recording it. The film's scriptwriter and director are faced with a similar choice—to choose from so much material. I limited my life with my choice of words; the screenwriter had to choose again, with further limits." Thus, she said, in a sense "a film is new creation."[19] Ikin, speaking of Frame's visit to the "studio" when they were shooting the film in Auckland, spells out how the attitudes of Frame, herself, Campion, and Jones were congruent: "We'd always viewed the autobiographies as Janet's personal fiction, her mythology—as much fiction as any of the novels. I think that the process of adaptation appealed to Janet's fascination with the transmutation of reality into fiction. We were busy converting her fiction into our fiction, casting actors as 'little Janet,' 'teenage Janet,' and 'Janet,' finding or making Eden Street and Willowglen—even making her rooms in Ibiza—in an Auckland warehouse."[20]

The treatment of Frame's family background and early childhood is indicative of the kind of choices that Jones had to make. She omitted the accounts of the Frame and Godfrey ancestors and of the pasts of Frame's father and mother. Of the Southland early childhood, she retained only a few brief images. The Frame and Godfrey grandmothers and Frame's Aunt Maggie are omitted entirely, and the role of Lottie Frame is much reduced, including her writing of poetry. As Maria Wikse has noted, "there is nothing in the film of Lottie Frame's great interest in poetry, her publications in the local newspaper, or her dream of publishing her work more widely."[21] Most of the songs and rhymes that Frame remembered were omitted, as well as most of the anecdotes showing her fascination with language.

On the other hand, the episodes and sequences that Frame had developed more as dramatic scenes with social interaction and dialogue are presented fully: the stealing of her father's money, the handing out of the gum she bought with it to her classmates, and the resultant public punishment; the sequences concerning Janet's friendships with Marjorie ("Poppy") and Marguerite. For some of the less socially interactive developments, such as Janet's admiration and imitation of the "imaginative, dreamy" Shirley, Jones found effective visual means of presentation—Janet watching Shirley, Janet imitating her in the mirror (as Sue Gillett has commented, the film consistently presents Frame as watcher as well as one being watched, not simply the conventional cinematic female recipient of the male gaze).[22] The scenes that Jones did choose to present have not been selected simply for their dramatic potential but also for their thematic resonance. Jones has said that, much as Frame had done, she chose not to try to impose a strict plot line but to use an episodic structure held together by some thematic kind of organization. Thus, the stolen money/gum episode relates to other scenes having to do with "truth and its consequences," especially in the sequence leading to the loss of Poppy as a friend. This episodic-thematic mode Jones thought to be especially suitable for a television series, while "a feature film needs a stronger shape or form."[23] Campion approached this episodic structural concept from a different angle when she said that she was attempting "to find a new way of representing the workings of memory" so that the childhood scenes in part 1 act as "a kind of mental photograph album"—"the very first memories are just like flashes, not stories at all, just a scene," whereas in the second part there is more plot coherence to express the more developed consciousness of Janet, and it is "very much a drama about a woman who is struggling for her life."[24]

A subtler problem that Jones faced is raised by McLeod: "How to translate a work about words, about writing—where language is the main character—into a visual medium."[25] Jones attempted as much as possible to include scenes having to do with Janet writing or reading or thinking about and learning about language (but many of these did not survive the final cut of the film). In the screenplay for the years of childhood and adolescence, there is Janet telling her hawk and bogie story to her sisters; there is Janet shown reading a children's reader entitled *To the Island* and later discussing the pronunciation of "island" with Myrtle; there is Janet writing her school essay about her "adventure" while she is shown experiencing it (all of these were cut in the film, although the second was included in the television version); there is Janet arguing with Myrtle about her choice of words in a poem and then presenting the poem to the class with her own word reinstated; there is

Myrtle reciting Walter de la Mare's "The Prince of Sleep," first to her sisters in the graveyard and then over the radio as Janet eagerly listens and mouths the words along with her; there is Janet picking out books at the Athenaeum and then distributing them to the family; there is Janet reading her poem on Dot's Page for Little Folk in the *Otago Daily* Times (modified in the film); there is Janet listening enthralled and visualizing the sword as Miss Lindsay reads aloud the passage about Excalibur from Tennyson's *Idylls of the King;* there is Janet reading aloud to her sisters from Whitman's "The Lost Mate" after the death of Myrtle; there is Janet listening to the adolescent Poppy recite from Keats's "Ode to a Nightingale"; there is Janet writing to the imaginary Mr. Ardenue and reading Arnold's "The Scholar Gypsy" or reading to herself from George Borrow's *Lavengro* as she walks to school.

The themes of literature, words, and writing are fully represented in the screenplay. Yet, necessarily, much of the book's subtle development of these themes is lost. The screenplay omits most of the book's complex attitude toward the Romantic poetry that the young Janet, her sisters, her mother, and her teachers loved—the attitude that the poetry speaks of "all the unspoken feeling that moved alive beneath the surface of each day and night" and enriches them, but that, especially in its more sentimental later practitioners such as Rupert Brooke or Alfred Noyes, it subjects them to what Frame calls "the corruption of literature," the imposition of simple stock responses on the complexity of experience in poems written in conventional poetic diction, poems that encouraged her in such things as "the shallow acceptance of glorifying the war dead."[26] Even in some of the included scenes, nuances are necessarily lost. In the "hungry generations" scene with Poppy, the screenplay brings out well (and the film itself brings out even better) the sense of the girls being puzzled by a gap that has been forced between them. But it omits what is communicated in the book by the report of Janet's thought and the commentary of the narrator, that the poem's reference to the "hungry generations" speaks for Poppy's panic concerning her own future but that the young Janet does not yet see the relevance to her own life that the mature Janet as narrator is aware of, though the young Janet does sense that something significant is going on—all of this implication underlined by the chapter title, "The Hungry Generations."

For the writing years of the young adult and the woman the treatment of the themes of language, writing, and literature is similar. The screenplay shows us key indicative scenes: Janet being coached by June as to signing the author's copies of *The Lagoon;* Janet despairing when she reads a bad review of the book (not included in the film); Janet writing words of poetry on the wall of her solitary confinement room at Seacliff (Coleridge in the screenplay, Shakespeare in the film); Janet reading a rejection letter from Charles Brasch at *Landfall* (not included in the film); her literary mentor Frank Sargeson criticizing her prose and introducing Janet to the writing of Proust (not included in the film); Janet responding eagerly both to the reader and to the poem when the young writer Karl Stead reads aloud from the later poems of Yeats; Sargeson and Janet sending off the manuscript of her first novel, *Owls Do Cry*, and later responding in different ways to the letter of acceptance; Janet shyly talking of her two published books to the would-be writers in London; Janet suffering Bernard's terrible taste in poetry, including his own, in order to receive his sexual attention; Janet talking of her writing with her psychiatrist, R. H. Cawley, with her publisher, Mark Goulden, and with fellow writer Alan Sillitoe; and finally, Janet typing in the small caravan in the garden of her younger sister, June, and her husband, Wilson Gordon.

Again, much concerning the themes is necessarily omitted: Janet's excitement at discovering the New Zealand literature of the Allen Curnow–Sargeson generation; her hesitant, unsure relationship with Brasch; Sargeson's attitude toward women and women's writing and Janet's feelings about this; Janet allowing herself to be pushed into the false roles of "writer in a country cottage" and "writer of bestsellers in the West End"; the Mirror City metaphor and her realization that Mirror City was her "true home."[27] Jones was especially aware of the last of these, telling McLeod that "a difficult decision had to be made about the material dealing with the envoy." She would have liked to have had the time and space to use "some sort of surreal expression for the abstract idea," but as it was she had to "let Frame's life tell the story."[28] As for the richly metaphorical metacommentary about memory, writing, and fiction, including some of the most memorable passages in the books, Jones attempted to incorporate some as voiceovers: the one-paragraph opening chapter (not included in the film); the description of the receiving of ECT as "equivalent in [degree of] fear to an execution"; the passage about the unique point of view brought back from the "territory of loneliness" that for the returnees is "a nightmare, a treasure, and a lifelong possession" (not included in the film).[29] But most of the great passages of commentary and metacommentary are omitted. In the predominantly visual medium of film they probably would have been felt as verbally oriented intrusions, as Campion presumably felt the ones she cut to be. In trying to include some of the metacommentary in the screenplay, Jones was perhaps attempting to retain something of the books' felt presence of the older narrator mediating the reader's response to the younger character, but Campion in her selections and excisions for the film, as Maria Wikse notes, "avoids mediated narration" and instead "invites

Janet with Frank Sargeson and Karl and Kay Stead in *An Angel at My Table*. Courtesy of the New Zealand Film Archive and Hibiscus Films.

us to align with [Janet's] experiences as they unfold rather than having them retold from a temporal and spatial distance."[30]

Jones's screenplay, then, is a sensitive and creative adaptation of verbal structures for a visual medium, one that probably within the limits imposed by the medium and by the length available could not have expressed the complexity, subtlety, and relative completeness of the books but that captured well their narrative and thematic shape and their tone. It gave Campion, who had been involved in its creation, the necessary material with which to work in completing the translation from a verbal to a verbal-visual medium.

From Screenplay to Film

Campion, as we have seen, felt that the personal appeal to her feelings of Frame's autobiography was related to a more universal appeal to people's sense of their own emotional vulnerability. Looking back on the film, she said in 1991, "Rather than insanity, I wanted to speak of hypersensitivity, vulnerability."[31] Because her response was first of all personal, she found that she put a lot of herself into the finished work: "In the beginning I wanted to be of service to Janet Frame and her vision with this film. There is certainly more of me in the final result than I was conscious of when I started. My goal was to bring to the screen the emotions I had felt while reading the book."[32] She knew that Frame did not expect an "objective" approach: "She knew that I would add my view and interpretation." To be "of service to Janet Frame and her vision" and to be true to her own response to the book meant not that she was trying to present in the film the "real" Janet Frame but that she was trying to present her sense of the "Janet Frame" that was a construct existing in the pages of the autobiography, analogous to a character in a novel: "I am not interested in the real Janet Frame but only in the literary character which she made of herself. The latter is what I had to do justice to."[33] In focusing on "Janet Frame" as a literary character, Campion felt she was in a sense being true to Frame's own method and assumptions, revealed in her response to Jones's screenplay, for "She is a very mature woman who knows that this story of her life is also fiction."[34] At the same time Campion was aware that it would have been impossible to catch all the nuances of the books in a film; she told Hunter Cordaiy that "I get more enjoyment out of novels than I do at cinema now," and confessed that she would like to write a novel herself, an ambition she probably at least partially accomplished in the novelization of *Holy Smoke* with her sister, Anna, with its use of shifting points of view and varied "documents" and its nonchronological sequencing.[35]

In setting out to realize her vision of Frame's vision, Campion very early on had made some basic decisions. Central was the decision to aim for a television miniseries as more suited to the material than a feature film. Related to that choice was her sense that she was not working within the conventions of the biopic of the artist; this was not to be "The Janet Frame Story." She was following her own inclination in choosing a female rather than a male artist, not for feminist reasons, but rather because, as she said, "I am a woman. So it seems totally natural that I have female protagonists."[36] In choosing Frame's "Janet Frame" as her subject, she was, as in her other films, running counter to the tradition of seeing women as glamorous figures subject to the male gaze. Rather, she said, she wanted to show "vulnerability and . . . character traits that are not very glamorous."[37] In this respect, her artistic preferences and the material that Frame's books offered came together well. One shudders to think what a Hollywood version of "The Janet Frame Story" might have been, while it is indicative of the compatibility of the filmmaker and the writer that the one "typical" episode from the Seacliff years that Frame chose to dramatize, that of the enforced public toileting, fits right in with Campion's concern in her films, both before and after *An Angel at My Table,* to show the female body not as a glamorous artifact to entice males but rather as a natural organism that pisses (as *Sweetie* had shown dramatically, possibly one source of the rejection of that film by segments of the audience at Cannes).

Jones's screenplay was consonant with Campion's vision, but Campion has said that she did not follow it rigidly, and comparison of the published screenplay with the finished film shows she made considerable changes, both cuts and rewritings.[38] Some of these changes had to do with length restrictions: in order to fit three parts of the screenplay into approximately fifty-minute segments she had to make cuts, reducing about eighty pages of screenplay to about the equivalent of sixty-five pages. The changes also were often in the interest of narrative simplicity—to have fewer changes of place and time. But there are other cuts and sometimes rewritings of scenes that seem to be primarily for emphasis—to reduce Lottie Frame's role in Janet's life, to accentuate Janet's aloneness and the threat hanging over her, and to emphasize the importance of her eventual sexual liberation from a restrictive puritan social environment.

We can see these factors clearly in the severe modifications of the opening sequences. Jones opened the screenplay with sixteen brief scenes (taking up only four pages), eight of them without dialogue, to give brief impressions from Janet's first six years. Campion cut out twelve of these, leaving only the first three of the baby's first steps (and the third of those is reduced to a fleeting image) and an expanded version of the fifth—the now famous image of Janet walking alone down a country road. Some of the scenes seemed to have been cut for narrative continuity: the railway sheds at Edendale (no. 7), the railway house at Wyndham (no. 10) (with the places identified by lettering against a black screen); the children in one of the sheds listening to the "rats" in the wall and to their father playing the bagpipes (no. 8); Janet's discovery of worms in her feces (nos. 11–13); Janet observing the sheep's expression and imitating it for her father (nos. 14–15).

The other cuts and transformations in the opening sequence have important consequences for character and theme. The transformation and expansion of Jones's fifth scene is especially important as it introduces the sense of Janet's aloneness and her fears. Jones's screenplay version derives from a passage in the autobiography in which Frame describes standing by the gate in Outram, listening to the wind in the telegraph wires and having her "first conscious feeling of outside sadness. . . . In listening to the wind and its sad song, I knew I was listening to a sadness that had no relation to me, which belonged to the world."[39] It is one of the most effective passages concerning childhood, and Jones tried to remain true to its details in the screenplay—the gate, the "white dusty road," the swamp on the other side of the road, the telegraph wires above, which "travel down the road to a vanishing point. The sound of the wind in the wires is accentuated, keening, unrelieved. Janet, small and alone, feels the outside world's sadness."[40] Jones uses poetic, emotional language to suggest the desired visual and aural images (as well as the child's facial expression and possibly body language). But the scene in the film is very different: the road is not white and dusty; there is no swamp or gate; there are no telegraph wires; the only "keening" is from Don McGlashan's musical background; and Janet is in motion rather than still, walking toward the camera, stopping while a voiceover (not in the screenplay) gives her name and birthdate, and then running away as if in fear when the voiceover tells of the death of her twin at birth. The red hair of the young Janet contrasts vividly with the green of the fields on either side of the road, an effect that Campion has said she consciously aimed for in that and other scenes photographed in New Zealand, where the "New Zealand light" brings out the colors.[41] The scene is visually stunning and, as Wikse comments, anticipates "the tragic sibling deaths in Janet's life" and "also hints that from the very first, as her unnamed twin died at birth, Janet is always looking for someone (a mirror self) who is missing."[42]

Equally significant are the other cuts from Jones's screenplay in this sequence—three scenes involving Lottie Frame with the children (nos. 4, 6, 9). In the first of these, Lottie shows the children a stone and holds it up to Janet—"a small, mysterious planet; treasure," and Janet soundlessly mouths the word "stone." In the second she encourages Janet to tell her "Bird, Hawk, Bogie" story to her siblings (one of the most quoted passages in the book), and in the third she points out the direction of the South Pole to the children, "the sky lit from Antarctica," and Janet again soundlessly mouths the words.[43] All three scenes focus on the language theme and on Lottie's role as an encourager of Janet's love of language. The language theme also figures in the deleted final scene of Jones's sequence, the "smell the pretty pink towel" scene at the dentist's. In the book this is a significant scene because of links to the other scenes in which Janet learns about the deceptiveness of language, but Jones had not been able to use the other related motifs (such as "permanent" waves that were not permanent) so that the scene is isolated and not very effective in the screenplay. Campion seems to have found that the subtleties of the language and poetry themes were simply not suitable for filming because of their totally verbal, nonvisual nature.

Campion's other major changes in the screenplay for part 1 are mostly in the sequences immediately following and are partly consequential upon the changes in the opening scenes. Because she had cut all reference to the family's living in Edendale and Wyndham but she wanted to retain the theft and gum sequence, which was set in Wyndham, Campion had to shift that sequence to Oamaru, placing it after the scene in which the family goes by rail to Oamaru, and Janet sees for the first time the "loonies" on the station platform as they pass through Seacliff. This scene was not in the autobiography, and Jones probably drew it from *Faces in the Water,* where in both chapters 1 and 8 Istina remembers how at Cliffhaven "the train stops for twenty minutes to give the travelers a free look at the loonies gathered about, gaping and absorbed."[44] Frame's only Seacliff station scene in the autobiography was in the first chapter of the second part when Janet is on her way south to Dunedin to begin training college (Jones includes that scene also in the screenplay and the television version, but Campion cut it from the film). Placed this early in the film, with the camera lingering on the image of the distressed patient that Janet sees through the train window (framed by her mother's blocking hands), the scene is portentous. Since the theft and gum episode marks in the film the beginning of the time in Oamaru, Jones's introductory scene of Janet wondering at the flush toilet in the new house is cut (but it was retained in the television version). Campion also cut the first full Oamaru sequence in the screenplay—Janet's "adventure" as she reads *To the Island* at school, reads another adventure story at home, and "writes" in her head the story of her own adventure of exploring Oamaru (nos. 27–34). Again, it was the sequence dealing with language and writing that Campion cut. Campion has said she would have liked to have included more of Janet writing, but it would appear that when she had to make cuts for length she tended to cut those scenes that were much more verbal than visual, which included some of the scenes about writing, just as she cut most verbal signs and voiceovers.[45]

A similar pattern prevails in the rather more severe cuts from the screenplay in part 2. Campion is clearly simplifying the narrative, but she is also changing some of the emphases, continuing to omit scenes and sequences that focus primarily on language and writing and very much reducing the role of Lottie Frame. Changes primarily to reduce length and simplify narrative probably include the cuts of the stay with June and Wilson Gordon in Auckland before Janet goes into Avondale and of the verbal cues of place names against a black screen indicating geographic shifts (nos. 60–64), thus combining several different hospital experiences into one. Campion also cut all of the Caversham boarding house sequence (nos. 77–85), with its dramatization of Janet's social fear and timidity and its relationship with her beginning to write seriously. While this cut could be justified in terms of narrative simplification, it again was at the expense of the themes of writing and language, as was also the omission of the scenes of Sargeson's advice about prose style and Proust and Janet's response to it (nos. 95–96). However, the crucial scenes concerning the writing of *Owls Do Cry* and the acceptance of it for publication were retained (nos. 99, 103–4).

The cuts hardest to defend on grounds of length or narrative simplicity are those of scenes concerning Lottie Frame. Brief and yet emotionally important, they include Janet's attempting to get her mother to go with her out under the pine trees "in the cool of the evening" (no. 86) and the sequence of the news of Lottie's death and Sargeson's and Janet's response to it (nos. 100–102). When these cuts are considered along with the cuts of the positive scenes with Lottie in part 1, we can see why Wikse commented that "the film adaptation blanks out Frame's mother as a literary influence. Indeed, the mother's virtual disappearance is interesting in light of her resurrection in the autobiographies."[46] The "virtual disappearance" began with Jones's screenplay, which omitted references to Lottie's own dedication to writing poetry, but Jones had included the scenes showing Lottie's formative influence and Janet's love and concern for her that Campion cut. In contrast, Campion retained the scenes showing Janet's father in a positive light in relation to her—his giving the young Janet the railway notebook in which to enter her poems and his making the bookshelves for her when she returns the first time from hospital, telling her he does not want her to leave home again—while she has cut one of the negative scenes, the one in which he plays on Isabel's fears with his song about the mine and cruelly mocks Janet (part 1, no. 69). In the screenplay, the final meeting with him and the departure for Europe (as in the autobiography) are from Wellington, but in Campion's film version he comes to Auckland. He cannot understand Sargeson but supports her in his own way, so that the scene, as Wikse has noted, places her between her biological colonial father and her literary postcolonial one. This different emphasis, with the mother's part minimized and the father's made significant, fits in with Campion's other work, especially *Sweetie* and *Holy Smoke,* where the mother figures are less important than the fathers.

In *Sweetie* the most significant family relationship is between the sisters, and while Campion has cut out some of the significant mother-daughter scenes from Jones's screenplay, she has retained almost all of those in the first two parts that focus on the relationship between sisters. This emphasis on sororal relationship is one that Campion shares with Frame and Jones: the strongest scenes between the sisters in the autobiography have been included by Jones in the screenplay and emphasized by Campion in the film.

The literary theme is retained when it can be dramatized in the relationship between sisters, so that we see Janet admiring Myrtle's recitation of poetry and mouthing the words along with her when she listens to her sister's radio broadcast but also keeping her poetic independence by retaining her own phrase in her school poem, despite Myrtle's demand that she use a more "poetic" noun. We see Janet admiring and envying Myrtle's confidence, self-assertion, and her nascent sexuality. We see the sisters bonding as they turn over in bed in unison, read *Grimms' Fairy Tales* together and dance out "The Blue Light" at night in the pine plantations, or playact together with Marguerite on their camping holiday. And we see Janet and Isabel devastated by Myrtle's death. In part 2 we see Janet, June, and Isabel reading the clouds together; we see Janet and Isabel "testing" Aunt Isy's prize chocolates together; but we also see the growing rift between them as Isabel cannot understand Janet's desire to be a writer, not a teacher. And there is Janet's lonely despair at Isabel's death. In the film for Janet her sisters are, as Eve Rueschmann shows, "attachment figures and objects of fantasy and desire," as well as allies against social humiliation and figures against whom she sometimes must define herself.[47]

In the third part, Campion made extensive cuts in the interest of reducing length and increasing narrative continuity and simplicity: in the Ibiza sequences, several substantial scenes involving Janet's relationship with Catalina and Francesca; all of the Andorra sequence, including the miscarriage and the relationship with El Vici (with the miscarriage postponed until the return to London); and in the second London stay, some of the scenes with the Morgans and the only scene with Millicent the librarian. More significant are the modifications of Jones's scenes to emphasize more fully the theme of sexual liberation. That thematic emphasis was set up in parts 1 and 2, with the contrasting themes of puritan repression of all things sexual and of adolescent revolt against it. The theme of repression is first powerfully established in part 1 with the Poppy sequence, culminating in Dad's violent punishment of Myrtle (one of the few occasions in the film when he is shown in a bad light). Janet is shown to be excited by Poppy's shared knowledge about sex but utterly surprised at the adult response to her announcement that "Myrtle and Ted did it in the plannies this afternoon." Myrtle's revolt against the repression takes the symbolic form of slacks and cigarettes. The last sight Janet has of her is her imitation Hollywood bump and grind as she goes off to the swimming baths and her death. The connection is not made explicit, but Janet's guilty shame at her first menstruation later is perhaps related to Myrtle's death, which Janet may have felt almost as a punishment for her sexuality and revolt. In part 2, it is the younger Isabel who is the representative of sexual revolt, with her boyfriend who wants her "to go all the way" and with her suggestion that she and Janet should eat Aunt Isy's prize chocolates. As Rueschmann points out, in the film "candy and sweets are consistently metonymically linked to illicit pleasure and sublimated female sexuality," and the girls avidly consume the forbidden sweets as they speculate about Aunt Isy's and Uncle George's sex life.[48] And, as Myrtle's death might have been read by Janet as punishment for her sexuality, so Isabel's death might have been similarly interpreted.

Most of the scenes dealing with sexuality and repression in parts 1 and 2 are played in the film pretty much as Jones wrote them in the screenplay. Campion makes a few minor changes, as when she introduces Janet's hesitant sexuality into the scene in which she reenacts John Forrest's praise of her "talent for writing" by having her finger her underwear strap as she gazes into the mirror repeating Forrest's words so that she becomes both Forrest giving out praise and, in the mirror image, Janet responding sexually to it. It is in part 3, in the sequence concerning Janet's affair with Bernard, that Campion moves beyond the screenplay to emphasize Janet's awakening sexuality. The change that sets up the emphasis is in the scene where Janet watches Dora going upstairs to meet Edwin, her lover, and envies her. The scene is silent in the screenplay with almost a stage direction to indicate the feelings that the actress is to communicate silently: "Janet feels as sexless as a block of wood."[49] Jones's simile is drawn from Frame's franker and fuller account in the autobiography: "I longed wistfully to be as full of secrets as she seemed to be, that would prompt a man to discover them, but for so long I had blocked all exits and entrances that I knew or felt that I was as sexless as a block of wood. I had smoothed myself away with a veneer of protection."[50] In the film, Campion uses a slightly shortened version of the first sentence as a voiceover that, with Kerry Fox's vocal expressiveness, communicates well Janet's envy and frustration, and her recognition of her sexual self-repression.

The scenes with Bernard carry out more explicitly than in the book or the screenplay the freeing of Janet's repressed sexuality. In the book, Frame had dealt fully and frankly with Bernard's "practiced hands" seeking "the 'right' places" in her and with the first occasion of their making love, when Janet stares at Bernard's "large erected penis," which Frame as retrospective narrator bizarrely describes as "the red-roofed dovecote full of white doves ready to fly into the sky and never return." After that there are references to making love frequently, but there are no further particularized occasions until the final one, except for the brief mention of having "savored the feeling of transgressing" when in bed with Bernard eating the tinned corned beef that Patrick Reilly had mailed to her. On that final occasion (which may have been the cause of her pregnancy), it is not the sexual activity that is particularized but rather the way that Bernard had "effectively destroyed" their "perfect love" by saying it would be terrible if she had a baby. The sense of freeing herself from sexual repression is an important element in the sequence, but in the account of the courtship and the love affair it is counterpointed by her uncomfortable awareness of herself and Bernard: her own implicit lies in pretending to have experience she had not had, his crassness of speech and poetry and actions (carrying condoms about "like indigestion tablets"), and the two of them enacting clichés from *True Romance*. The affair is followed by her admission to herself that she had been engaged in a "deliberate engineering of [her] feelings."[51]

In the screenplay, Jones follows the initial lovemaking scene with a brief, wordless scene of the two swimming together and a scene of the two with other Americans playing a Maori stick game, with a voiceover in which Janet says she had become Bernard's "woman" (nos. 46–47). She omits the final lovemaking scene from the book and instead has Bernard shocking Janet as they are reading together by casually announcing that it is his last week in Ibiza (no. 50). In the film Campion expands and further sexualizes the swimming scene by having Janet swim naked as Bernard admires her movements and comments from his perch on a rock above the water. She considerably expands the stick game scene while omitting the generalizing voiceover and adds a further scene of semi-nudity and sexual caressing on the rock above the bay. Both the screenplay and the film show Janet embarrassed by Bernard's taste in poetry and by his own feeble attempt at a poem ("quoted" more fully than in the book) but otherwise do not emphasize as strongly as the book Janet's ironic awareness of him, and the *True Romance* motif comes in only in a voiceover quoting a summary passage from the book: "*True romance* indeed! So much for poetry and music! I was beginning to suspect that I might be pregnant." The changes from book to screenplay and from screenplay to film are not large, but the end result is that the theme of sexual liberation is emphasized much more in the film than in the book, and Janet's ironic double awareness is played down. Campion's implication is that although the man was unworthy and Janet herself had been aware of this, Janet's sexual experience itself is necessary and liberating. In that respect, the film fits in with Campion's other cinematic explorations of female sexual liberation.

The scene in part 3 that differs most markedly from both the book and the screenplay is the final one. In the book Frame moves gracefully from an account of returning to the Gordons' Northcote house and her caravan in their garden with "a heap of apparent rubbish" after an expedition to Willowglen to retrieve family mementos, through an account of Pamela Gordon using some of Janet's rescued "treasures" in her playhouse, to a meditation on her own carrying of "treasures" into her "playhouse, Mirror City," ending with a conversation in the narrative present with the Envoy from Mirror City about the proper initial use of the treasures of her more recent experience being in fiction rather than in autobiography. In the screenplay Jones has a sequence of brief vignettes: two of Janet typing in the caravan, bracketing one of Janet walking through and lying in the grass on the hill above the Northcote street while a voiceover summarizes where she has arrived: "Now that writing was my only occupation, regardless of the critical and financial outcome, I felt that I had found 'my place' at a deeper level than any landscape, of any country, would provide."[52] In the film the hill scene and voiceover summary are omitted, while the final vignette, which Jones has as Janet typing in the caravan in June Gordon's garden, wearing earmuffs to shut out the noise of the Gordon children playing, becomes a more complex scene: outside the caravan in the evening, Pamela Gordon is dancing to "Let's Do the Twist" and turns up the music louder in the caravan, while Janet is attempting to type; June comes out, turns down the music, offers coffee to Janet, which is refused, and goes in the house with her daughter; the lights in the house go out, Janet comes out of the caravan as the music still plays softly, dances a few half-hearted steps, then is moved to go back in the caravan and write a few words in a notebook, then returns to the typewriter composing what looks like *A State of Siege,* reads aloud a phrase that especially pleases her, and smiles with a quiet pleasure. It is a wonderfully suggestive conclusion, showing a more mature Janet who can step a bit to the social dance but chooses not to, because she is first of all her own unique person, confidently and happily engaging in the defining activity of her life, writing.

Campion, then, made some changes in the film from Jones's screenplay, but the screenplay generally gave her a good framework on which to build the film. The result was a work that might have had, as she said, "more of [her] than [she] was conscious of when [she] started," but at the same time was certainly "of service to Janet Frame and her vision." Its basic narrative line is Frame's, and Frame's essential themes are present in it. However, its emphases are Campion's own, and it fits well within her oeuvre. Frame's themes of language, literature, and writing are there (and are the endpoint), but they are subsumed within the larger theme of personal growth, becoming one's own woman in a restrictive, conformist social environment, with a special emphasis on liberation from the internalized sexual repression of New Zealand puritanism. It is central to the book that Janet finally establish

94

herself as a citizen of Mirror City, and that is where it ends. It is central to the film that she become her own person, and writing is the way that she does it.

Campion's personal style was also necessarily expressed in the uniquely cinematic means of expression over which she as director had final control and which were not contained in the books and mostly not contained in the screenplay: the casting and emotional interpretation of the parts, the imagery, the music. The famous photograph of the actual Frame posing with the three Janets of the film implies the successfulness of the casting, as does the use of stills of one or more of the film Janets for the covers of some of the editions (especially the translated editions) of the autobiography after 1990. The choice of Kerry Fox to play the young adult and adult Janet turned out to be an especially inspired one. Fox has said that she learned much about playing the part of Janet (acting a part, not carrying out an impersonation, she insisted) by reading and re-reading the autobiography and some Frame poems, getting "the underlying essence of the words, what words could do and how they could fire the imagination," but also from Campion's direction, her urging Fox to "shed another skin," make herself appear more vulnerable.[53]

Jones, who herself has been a visual artist as well as a poet, has said, "I was keen to discover a visual language, which is why I like working with Jane. Her images carry meanings."[54] Those images, created by Campion and Stuart Dryburgh, the cinematographer, often from Jones's suggestions in the screenplay, are of crucial importance in carrying the emotional weight of the film. Frame's stated wish for images of the sky Campion and Dryburgh vividly realized, sometimes in images not given in the screenplay, such as the recurring one of the sunset sky with the silhouette of the train seen against it (an image that Dryburgh said in the commentary to the Criterion DVD had come from stock New Zealand railways footage). Other such images included those of Janet seen against a bright blue sky taking Scrapers to be milked or outlined against the sky as she trudges to Willowglen. At the other extreme from the sky shots, and even more frequent and more effective, are the close-ups of Janet, especially when she watches and/or listens to something or somebody she admires or she is moved by: Janet watching Shirley as she sings, with the camera looking back and forth between Janet's envious gaze and Shirley's studied soulfulness; Janet gazing at Miss Lindsay as she recites the Excalibur passage until she "sees" the sword; Janet gazing longingly at Karl and Kay Stead as Karl reads Yeats aloud. At crucial moments, the close-up is held through a long silence, as when Isabel returns home after Myrtle's death, with the focus on her shocked face and with Janet's suffering face gradually coming into focus in the background, or the long painful silence as we watch Janet's face paralyzed with fear when she faces the school inspector. These shots are certainly suited to the "intimacy" of the television screen, as Campion and Ikin thought, but they also work well on the cinema screen.

At times the visual quality of the scenes is complemented by music (sometimes within them, sometimes in the background), most of which is not found in the screenplay or in the tunes that Frame supplied, but which is utterly appropriate. There is the recurrent association of Myrtle with "Somebody Stole My Gal": when Myrtle is preparing to go out in her new slacks to meet a (pretend?) boyfriend (the boyfriend is not in the screenplay) while Janet admires her, the radio is playing that tune; the last time Janet sees Myrtle alive, when Myrtle attempts to persuade her to come to the swimming baths with her and Marguerite and Isabel, the background music of ragtime piano segues into the chorus of "Somebody Stole My Gal" as Janet watches Myrtle lead the girls in a musical exit developed from the screenplay's call for "an exaggerated sashaying walk"; finally, when Janet kneels down beside the dead Myrtle's dress on her bed, the ragtime piano chorus of the tune slowly rises in the background.[55] Music is used suggestively again in the chocolate-stealing scenes, this time as an aural image of puritan repression, for as Janet and Isabel eagerly consume the chocolates, Uncle George's radio in the background is playing "Onward Christian Soldiers" in one scene and another hymn in the other. Later, as Wikse points out, the theme music for Janet is not present in any of the hospital scenes except the one where she is writing poetry on the "cell" wall, but it picks up again and rises in volume when she leaves the hospital, "indicating that after the silence of hospitalisation Janet regains her voice—including her emotional indicator, her music soundtrack."[56] In the Ibiza sequence, Spanish guitar music is used suggestively, especially for the love scenes, and then the travel theme that had been played triumphantly at the beginning of part 3 is played slowly and ironically when the love affair has ended.

All of these elements go into the making up of a film that is indeed a "classic," and recognizably a Campion one. At the same time it is a film doing Frame a service, one that in its success as film strongly contributed to her becoming an international figure and a national icon, as her story and the film's came together after 1990.

The Afterlife of the Film

Frame had wished for three films rather than for a television miniseries, but Campion and Ikin had been consistent in opting for television, with showings of the 16-millimeter original version of the three television episodes only at film festivals except in New Zealand. It was tested first at the Sydney and Melbourne film festivals and was a huge success, being voted the most popular film at the Sydney festival. This success was repeated in showings at the Wellington, Auckland, Christchurch, and Dunedin festivals. By then Campion, at the urging of Shelton of the Film Commission, had agreed to convert the episodes to a 35-millimeter single feature film for general showing. Shelton had shown the videotapes to a few distributors and had had offers he had had to refuse because of the Campion-Ikin ban on theatrical distribution. He took the tapes to the 1990 Cannes Film Festival, showed them privately to distributors, had more offers, and finally persuaded Campion to go along. Only in 2001 did she tell him that the main reasons she had been opposed to theatrical distribution were that she did not want to repeat the painful experience she had with *Sweetie* at Cannes when the theatrical audience had been deeply and noisily divided about the film and, rather contradictorily, that she was also afraid that after her early films it would appear too tame. The conversion to a feature film was not radical: Campion cut out the separate opening and closing credits for parts 2 and 3 and deleted a few brief scenes, cutting only six minutes all told. The only difficulty was in the "blowing-up" process of going from 16- to 35-millimeter, which caused some trouble with the opening sequence.

The feature film version became an immediate success. It won several standing ovations and swept eight awards, including the Silver Lion and a Special Jury Prize, at the Venice Film Festival in 1990; won awards for best film and best direction, cinematography, screenplay, female performer, and supporting actor at the New Zealand Film Awards the same year; and was the first New Zealand film ever selected for the New York Film Festival and won a standing ovation for Campion, Ikin, and Fox in September 1990. After that, it went on to take awards at many other festivals, including Toronto and Berlin. It had long theatrical runs in Australia, New Zealand, the United States, the United Kingdom, and Italy, among others.

For Frame the immediate result was increased (or renewed) sales of the autobiography, including the first American paperback, and more reprints and additional sales of her fiction. Although the autobiography itself had been the cause of the initial breakthrough in this regard in the 1980s in the English-speaking world, in non-English-speaking countries the pattern was different: most translations of the autobiography itself appeared only after the film. Curnow commented that after the theatrical and television release of the film interest in Frame's work in non-English-speaking countries increased dramatically, the autobiography was translated into eight languages, and there were many more translations of some of the works of fiction.[57]

Certainly the international impression of Campion's film was one factor in which in the last fourteen years of her life (1990–2004) Frame, although she published no new work, became a national icon in New Zealand, awarded all of the honors her country had to give. The influence of the Campion film on that development is symbolized by the drawing that appeared in the *Otago Daily Times* at the time of her death in early 2004: an empty chair at a plain table with the caption "An Angel Leaves the Table." There was an identification, "Janet Frame 1924–2004," but the reader was expected to recognize the allusion to the second volume of Frame's autobiography and to Campion's film.

That confluence of the personal and the universal in the appeal of Frame's autobiography to Campion resulted in a film that served both the filmmaker and her subject well.

Notes

1. Hunter Cordaiy, "Jane Campion Interviewed," *Cinema Papers,* December 1990; reprinted in *Jane Campion: Interviews,* ed. Virginia Wright Wexman (Jackson: University Press of Mississippi, 1999), 74.

2. Campion and Ikin to Frame, 26 March 1984, qtd. in Michael King, *Wrestling with the Angel: A Life of Janet Frame* (Auckland: Viking, 2000), 460.

3. Curnow to Frame, 13 April 1984, qtd. in King, *Wrestling with the Angel,* 460.

4. Frame to Curnow, qtd. in Tim Curnow, "Connections," in *The Inward Sun: Celebrating the Life and Works of Janet Frame,* ed. Elizabeth Alley (Wellington: Daphne Brasell Associates Press, 1994), 32.

5. Agreement between Janet Clutha and Hibiscus Films, 16 January 1986; Ikin to Curnow, 1 September 1985, qtd. in King, *Wrestling with the Angel,* 473.

6. Bridget Ikin, "An Assemblage of Janets," in Alley, *Inward Sun,* 141–42.

7. Qtd. and paraphrased in Shelley Clement, "Frame to Screen," *Onfilm* 6, no. 6 (1989): 13–14.

8. Lindsay Shelton, *The Selling of New Zealand Movies* (Wellington: Awa Press, 2005), 104.

9. Marion McLeod, "The Language of the Is-land," *NZ Listener,* 8 October 1990, 102.

10. Michel Ciment, "The Red Wigs of Autobiography," in Wexman, *Jane Campion,* 64; McLeod, "Language of the Is-land," 102.

11. Ibid.

12. Ibid.

13. Frame to Ikin, 7 January 1988, qtd. in King, *Wrestling with the Angel,* 484.

14. Frame to Curnow, 28 December 1987, qtd. in King, *Wrestling with the Angel,* 484.

15. Frame to Ikin and Campion, qtd. in Ikin, "Assemblage of Janets," 142.

16. Janet Frame, *An Autobiography* (Auckland: Vintage, 2004), 221.

17. Frame to Curnow, 30 January 1988, qtd. in King, *Wrestling with the Angel,* 484.

18. McLeod, "Language of the Is-land," 102.

19. Qtd. in Shelton, *Selling of New Zealand Movies,* 114.

20. Ikin, "Assemblage of Janets," 142–43.

21. Maria Wikse, *Materialisations of a Woman Writer: Investigating Janet Frame's Biographical Legend* (Oxford: Peter Laing, 2006), 177.

22. See Sue Gillett, "View from Beyond the Mirror: The Films of Jane Campion," *The Moving Image* 7 (2004): 32–37.

23. McLeod, "Language of the Is-land," 102.

24. Lyndon Barber, "Angel with an Eccentric Eye," in Wexman, *Jane Campion,* 60.

25. McLeod, "Language of the Is-land," 102.

26. Frame, *Autobiography,* 74, 79, 123.

27. Ibid., 425.

28. McLeod, "Language of the Is-land," 102.

29. Frame, *Autobiography,* 213–14, 224; and Laura Jones, *An Angel at My Table: The Screenplay from the Three-Volume autobiography of Janet Frame* (London: Pandora, 1990), 48, 51.

30. Wikse, *Materialisations,* 178.

31. Yves Alion, "Interview with Jane Campion: In the Country of the Hypersensitive," *Revue du Cinema,* April 1991; reprinted in Wexman, *Jane Campion,* 84.

32. Ciment, "Red Wigs of Autobiography," 67.

33. Heike-Melba Fendal, "How Women Live Their Lives," *EPD Film,* April 1991; reprinted in Wexman, *Jane Campion,* 84.

34. Ciment, "Red Wigs of Autobiography," 67.

35. Cordaiy, "Jane Campion Interviewed," 78.

36. Ibid., 88.

37. Fendel, "How Women Live," 87.

38. Cordaiy, "Jane Campion Interviewed," 76–77.

39. Frame, *Autobiography,* 12–13.

40. Jones, *Angel at My Table,* 1.

41. Ciment, "Red Wigs of Autobiography," 67–68.

42. Wikse, *Materialisations,* 179.

43. Jones, *Angel at My Table,* 1, 2.

44. Janet Frame, *Faces in the Water* and *The Edge of the Alphabet* (Auckland: Vintage, 2005), 15.

45. Cordaiy, "Jane Campion Interviewed," 80.

46. Wikse, *Materialisations,* 173.

47. Eva Rueschmann, *Sisters on Screen: Siblings in Contemporary Cinema* (Philadelphia: Temple University Press, 2000), 36–50.

48. Ibid., 44.

49. Jones, *Angel at My Table,* 76.

50. Frame, *Autobiography,* 342–43.

51. Ibid., 345–53.

52. Jones, *Angel at My Table,* 93.

53. See Miro Bilbrough, "Being Janet," *Listener,* 8 October 1990, 103; Alison Carter, "Kerry's Janet Moves Cinema-goers to Tears," *New Zealand Women's Weekly,* 6 August 1990, 8–9; and Philip Wakefield, "Finding the Angel Within," *Evening Post* (Wellington), 4 October 1990, 12.

54. McLeod, "Language of the Is-land," 103.

55. Jones, *Angel at My Table,* 22.

56. Wikse, *Materialisations,* 200.

57. Curnow, "Connections," 33.

Shedding repression: Baines and Ada in *The Piano*. Courtesy of Photofest.

Puritanism and the Erotics of Transgression
The New Zealand Influence in
Jane Campion's Thematic Imaginary

"Where is New Zealand in The Piano*?"*

Writing on Jane Campion's most famous film in 1999, the Australian scholar Ken Gelder asks the question: "Where is New Zealand in *The Piano*?"[1] Even though Campion herself has frequently admitted the influence that New Zealand and being a New Zealander has had on her, there have been very few attempts to explain the nature of this influence. At best, commentators point to her use of the New Zealand landscape to suggest what is elemental and primitive, or the presentation of the indigenous Maori people as "indexes of the exotic and ineffable mystery."[2] There have been few (if any) attempts, however, to account for how the distinctive social configuration and value system of New Zealand society—both in its colonial form and its postcolonial legacy—may have helped to determine the way Campion views the world that she constructs in her films.

This is surprising, given Campion's many comments in interviews about the importance of her native country to her cinematic imaginary. She has confessed that when she read the first volume of Janet Frame's autobiography she felt as if she were discovering her own childhood again—"feeling the specialness of that New Zealand childhood."[3] As early as 1984, nearly a decade before *The Piano,* she signaled a desire to make a film dealing with "everything [she] felt about being a New Zealander in New Zealand."[4] On another occasion, noting "the Puritan side of the colonists" and the fact that New Zealand is "a Presbyterian work ethic country," Campion confessed her curiosity about who her ancestors were, and how New Zealand "must have been a very puritanical society for them"—especially as far as the repression of sexuality is concerned.[5] She has also acknowledged the lasting influence of the New Zealand landscape in terms of furnishing symbols that convey "a lingering effect of the unconscious," so that it is able to function "more like an emotional scenery."[6] As she commented in the notes accompanying the published screenplay of *The Piano*, "The bush has got an enchanted, complex, even frightening quality to it, unlike anything that you see anywhere else."[7] Specifically, the New Zealand landscape gave Campion images that she could use to evoke interior psychological conditions and states of feeling arising from the experience of repression. This is revealed in her description of the New Zealand bush as "claustrophobic, impenetrable . . . like swimming under water"—a subjective feeling that is reinforced in *The Piano* by Campion's instruction to Stuart Dryburgh, her cinematographer, to shoot the scenes in the bush with a blue autochrome to suggest an underwater world that correlates symbolically with Ada's subjective sense of entrapment and emotional claustrophobia.[8] Apart from this sinister side, the New Zealand bush also had a positive aspect for Campion. She saw it as having "a kind of enchantment about it" that made it fit for serving as the symbolic backdrop for an archetypal psychological journey: "It's kind of fairy-tale-ish, you know, how people go into the woods. It's rite-of-passage type of landscape. The journey these people take is towards a kind of awakening of their sexual passions."[9] This association is particularly marked in the scene in which Flora and a number of other youngsters embrace the trees in imitation of the sexual activity Flora has witnessed between Ada and Baines.

More generally, the contrast between the "very wild beaches, especially the black sands of the west coast beaches around Auckland and New Plymouth, and the very private, secretive and extraordinary world of the bush" allowed Campion to develop a contrast between civilization and primitivism, and between passion and repression.[10] Both in terms of her thematic preoccupations and her symbolic system, then, the New Zealand landscape has, by Campion's own admission, exerted a powerful influence on the formation of her imaginary.

There is an even more powerful New Zealand influence, however, that has not yet been specifically identified by critics—Campion's sensitivity to the crippling effects on New Zealanders of her generation of the puritanism brought originally to this country by the British settlers, subsequently developing into a cultural pattern that dominated New Zealand society during the mid-twentieth century, persisting through the 1960s. Puritanism as understood in the discourse of New Zealand identity refers not only to the religious movement deriving from Calvinism but also to a secularized version of it, based on a tyrannical work ethic and a distrust of mere pleasure that is enforced by a highly repressive code of behavior. Central to this code was a requirement that propriety (linguistic, behavioral, and social) should be observed at all times. There were also severe restrictions on sexual behavior, accompanied by an avoidance of the expression of emotion, and of any reference to what were considered to be the "animal" functions of the body. The code itself, as Lawrence Jones has noted, was "enforced by the external mechanisms of public shaming and punishment and by the internal mechanism of guilt."[11]

By Campion's own account, the influence of puritanism was evident in her own family. In one interview, confessing her youthful dislike of the theatrical social life of her parents, Campion noted that it was "no wonder they were like that": "They were so repressed that they must have sought every theatrical or overly exuberant person out and just included them in their social life. Which is what I wound up doing."[12]

Indeed, Campion's lifelong preoccupation as a filmmaker with sexuality and eroticism may be viewed as a response to, and a reaction against, the puritanical repression that dominated New Zealand society during her childhood. Most, if not all, of her films depict actions and circumstances that array themselves somewhere on the continuum of responses to puritanism that Bill Pearson identified in his classic essay on the New Zealand character, "Fretful Sleepers," written in 1951, three years before Campion's birth:

Puritanism runs in a spiral: first its religious context is lost and with it the justification of the restrictions on enjoyment of the senses, it hardens into habit: second, a younger generation rebels and seeks what was forbidden, the thrill of the chase spiked with a sense of guilt. What they hunt is symbolized in the sex act: but since the pleasure, if isolated, is momentary and the more it's sought the less it can be found, they are tracking down a mirage . . . everyone is after it [sex] but there's nothing in it. A new austere puritanism grows which is a contempt for love, a sour spit, a denial of life itself.[13]

As just such a member of a younger generation rebelling against puritan strictures, Campion admitted that as a young filmmaker she was indeed drawn to seek what was forbidden, being "particularly committed to what was nasty, what isn't spoken about in life."[14] This impulse to address the forbidden or repressed was evident during her time at art school when, by her account, "I started doing these crude, pornographic paintings, kind of funny as well as being pretty awful, *but nobody told me off.*"[15] Similarly, her early short films deal with "concealment" or dysfunction in families—what Campion has described as "the tragic underbelly" of family life that often expresses itself in perverse or forbidden sexual behavior (including incest and child molestation).[16] Her subsequent feature-length films continue these preoccupations.

Sweetie (1989) presents two sisters, one (Kay) who embodies repression, and the other (Dawn, a.k.a. "Sweetie") who represents its anarchic opposite—the Jungian "shadow" of what is repressed in Kay. The film itself explores not only how Kay's search for happiness is subverted by her inner fears but also how Sweetie's abandonment of restraint is ultimately self-destructive, betraying an ambiguity in Campion's vision that reminds one of the disillusionment with the rebellious solution that Pearson identifies.

One of Campion's professed reasons for making her next film, *An Angel at My Table,* was the fact that she found Frame's "intimacy and openness" liberating: "It's sort of like you're coming clean . . . the sort of sense of not hiding anything from anybody."[17] Many of the scenes she adapted from Frame's autobiography depict Janet experimenting with transgression, as when she steals money from her father's coat pocket, or when she spies on her sister engaged in sexual intercourse, and then shocks her family by using the forbidden "F word" at the dinner table.

In fact, the prime motivation across Campion's whole oeuvre seems to be either a desire to achieve liberation from the self-containment and concealment enforced by the codes of puritanism or else a desire to explore or comprehend the implications of the transgressive rebellions that puritanism provokes. This is seen in *Holy Smoke,* when Ruth first abandons spirituality and holiness for sex, and then finds herself the victim of a self-punishing masochism—a theme that is taken up and elaborated in Campion's film *In the Cut.* It is also seen in *The Portrait of a Lady* in what Campion describes as Isabel Archer's "voyage towards darkness and underground regions" when she is irresistibly drawn to Osmond because of his dangerous sexuality.[18] The underlying dynamic for Campion's exploration of these themes, I would argue, derives from her experience of the intensely repressive moral and social codes in the land of her birth that had reached their apotheosis in the decades of the mid-twentieth century.

Jane Mander as Jane Campion's "Inspiration"

The specifically New Zealand origins of Campion's preoccupation with puritan repression, together with a search for some kind of liberation from it, have not been fully appreciated hitherto because of a general lack of awareness of Campion's debt to an earlier New Zealand source—Jane Mander's 1920 novel *The Story of a New Zealand River.* In this novel, which is set during colonial times, Alice, a Scottish woman, arrives in New Zealand with her piano, accompanied by her illegitimate daughter, marries a man whom she does not love, and goes to join him in a remote location. Subsequently, she forms a relationship with a neighboring bushman, David Bruce, whom she visits in his shanty to escape the confines of her loveless marriage, and is discovered there with her lover by her husband. Following the death of her husband, Tom Roland, Alice enters a union with Bruce, a fully masculine but sensitive man, with whom she is able to find a happiness that transcends sex. From the parallels in the storyline alone, it is clear that Campion's film has a close relationship with this novel.

While a small number of scholars, notably Mary Paul, Hillary Frey, Ann Hardy, and Diane Long Hoeveler, have drawn attention to Campion's debt to Mander, most commentators remain unaware of it, or, rather, unaware of its significance.[19] Indeed, faced with allegations that she had plagiarized *The Story of a New Zealand River* in writing *The Piano,* leading to calls for her to return the Oscar she had won for Best Screenplay, Campion and her camp felt obliged to downplay it.[20] Her use of Mander, however, is now well attested. In 1985 the holders of the film rights to *The Story of a New Zealand River,* Bridget Ikin and John Maynard—who would soon produce Campion's film of *An Angel at My Table*—asked Campion to direct a film version of Mander's novel. Campion, however, was not happy with the screenplay that had been developed for this film, which was to have been called *The River,* and indicated that there would need to be substantial changes before she would be interested.[21] In one letter, Campion informed them that she had been working on "*The Piano Lesson,* my inspiration from Jane Mander's melodrama and you will see there is precious little of the original, but the inspiration was still there."[22] The opening of the story outline for *The Piano Lesson* reads: "New Zealand's first piano was left abandoned on a beach. Alice's husband could not see the use for it. However, Alice's attachment to her piano was unique, for she was mute. Her passion and love of her piano went well beyond the bounds of simple use; it was through the piano that she felt herself to speak."[23] Campion's use of the names of the characters in Mander's novel proves that its influence was direct and explicit. In another letter written during 1985, Campion also refers to "our David Bruce," who is "not much convinced by the piano, but is very taken by Alice and her prowess."[24] However far beyond her source Campion may have developed her version of the story, these allusions to *The Story of a New Zealand River* put her knowledge and use of Mander's novel beyond doubt.[25]

Why was Campion drawn to develop a story outline, and subsequently a feature-length film, that had Mander's novel as its "inspiration"? The answer can be inferred by looking at those details of *The Story of a New Zealand River* that Campion retained, together with the changes that she added from her own invention. From this it will emerge that she recognized in Mander's work the outline of a paradigmatic story that held the potential for symbolic elaboration for the purpose of exploring both the nature of repression and the role of eroticism in its "cure."

The similarities between *The Piano* and *The Story of a New Zealand River* are obvious, and far from "superficial" as has sometimes been claimed.[26] Long Hoeveler has suggested that "the four central characters of Campion's film were broadly sketched on the canvas already created by Mander, and supplemented by readings in nineteenth-century British literary classics and contemporary feminist short stories. . . . [T]he shape of their personalities, their situations, and their attitudes are identifiably similar."[27] This strikes me as correct, with the exception that Campion's Alisdair Stewart, the husband, is a very different kind of man from Mander's Tom Roland, the latter being a promiscuous womanizer, whereas the former is as puritanically repressed as his wife initially is.

At the most general level, the novel and the film share the same story of a repressed woman who travels to the Antipodes to escape the shame of an unmarried pregnancy, eventually finding liberation from her entrapment through a relationship with a man who provides the sensitivity and understanding that her husband lacks. Asia, the eight-year-old daughter who accompanies Alice, has a mischievous character, a delight at wild nature, a sense of the dramatic, and a vivid imagination that provides a contrast with her mother's repressed dourness—just as the vivacity of Flora, the nine-year-old daughter who accompanies Campion's Ada, contrasts with her mother's rigid self-containment. In both cases, the bond between mother and daughter is unusually close. Alice also brings with her a piano packed in a heavy case, and we are told that she, like Ada, plays "to a world of her own, to something in herself that had no other means of expression."[28] This "something within her" consists of Alice's own natural impulses: "She was secretly afraid of her impulses. She could not understand why any one who hated them as much as she did should have them so violently. She had been taught and she still believed that impulses were monstrous inventions of evil to be fought and suppressed."[29] Through her playing of the piano, Alice reveals a "capacity for feeling" that otherwise lies deeply repressed, to the extent that those who hear her believe that her playing is "the result of more than natural gifts"—anticipating the consternation that Aunt Morag experiences in *The Piano* on hearing Ada's passionate playing, which contrasts with her own playing, described by Nessie as "plain and true."[30]

The parallels between the novel and the film extend into the presentation of the attempted remedy for what Mander describes as the "awful disease" of puritanism.[31] Both Alice and Ada seek rescue through an extramarital relationship with a fully masculine man who is nonetheless sensitized to their emotional and erotic needs. Serving as a compensation for the lack of satisfaction both women derive from their marriages, these relationships not only provide "food for . . . starved emotionalism" but also release an intense sexual hunger, the gratification of which is deferred out of a sense of honor in Alice's case until after the death of her husband, and is only slowly released in the case of Ada.[32] Significantly, when Alice is finally free to marry David Bruce after the death of her husband, she finds that "the sex relation had no longer for her that glamour of mystery that so stirs and fires the feelings and imaginations of youth."[33] Similarly, after her intense erotic experimentation with George Baines, Ada's attempted suicide near the end of *The Piano* suggests a waning of the satisfaction that she might have believed eroticism could hold out to her. Campion appears to have absorbed from Mander the insight that eroticism, insofar as it is fueled by a self-protective fantasy process, loses its driving motive once the barriers to gratification are removed—a theme to which Campion would return repeatedly in her later films.

Beyond these general similarities, the parallels between *The Story of a New Zealand River* and *The Piano* extend into many specific details that suggest the restricting of spontaneity: for example, the hard black hat that Alice is wearing when she is first described, and her coils of chestnut hair; the Maori children and women she encounters on the beach whose easygoing ways contrast with the propriety of the Pakeha; her icy manner "that would freeze hell"; her frigidity toward her husband; and the idea that the characters are like "puppets in a show."[34] These similarities show not only that Campion drew upon Mander, whether or not she was conscious of doing so, but also that Campion's interest in her predecessor's novel lay primarily in the latter's assault on puritanism, manifest both in the repressive codes enforced by patriarchal authority and also in its psychologically claustrophobic and suffocating consequences for women.

In the film version of *The Piano,* Campion's awareness of puritanical repression as a force against which the heroine has to struggle is emphasized in a number of ways—especially by the presence and comments of the Maori characters who do not share it, as when they refer to Stewart as "old dry balls" or tease Baines that his sexual member should not "lie asleep" on his belly at night. It is also seen in her use of color to provide a psychological map of contrasting interior states, with scenes filmed in a somber blue autochrome to suggest the suffocating effects of repression set in stark contrast with scenes bathed in a golden light to suggest the release from repression experienced by characters when they escape from the confines of puritanical restraint (as when Ada and Flora are shown inside the tent made from Ada's

An icy manner "that would freeze hell." Holly Hunter as Ada, doubled by her daughter, manifests the demeanor attributed by Jane Mander to Alice, her prototype. Courtesy of Photofest.

petticoat, communing without words to one another, or in the scene where the naked Baines caresses Ada's piano or when the two lovers are engaged in lovemaking). Perhaps one of the most striking imagistic contrasts between repression and its opposite occurs in the juxtaposed scenes where Flora first embraces the trees in a simulation of lovemaking and is then forced by Stewart to scrub their trunks to cleanse away the "filth" of that action.

Sources and Effects of Repression: *The Novelization of* The Piano

This anchoring of *The Piano* in the aesthetic and moral rebellion against New Zealand puritanism evident in Mander's *The Story of a New Zealand River* is even more apparent in the novelized version of *The Piano* that Campion subsequently wrote with the assistance of Kate Pullinger. Campion's declared purpose in writing the novel was to fill in some of the narrative gaps that had characterized the film, "because she continued to be haunted by her characters."[35] She has gone on record as saying that she actually prefers novels to films, "since they illuminate things much more patiently and deeply," and the novelized version shows her attempting to do just that.[36]

In her elaboration of the story of *The Piano*, Campion develops certain aspects of the story that had been only obliquely hinted at in the film version. Both Alice and Ada suffer from the effects of shame and the need to maintain propriety. In *The Story of a New Zealand River*, the unmarried Alice "nearly died of horror" when she discovered she was pregnant, fleeing to Australia for the birth of her daughter, then to New Zealand, where she pretended to be a widow. Thereafter, she lives in terror of being found out.[37] Ada too, we learn from the novelization of *The Piano*, is sent to the Antipodes by her father to avoid the shame of being an unwed mother in Scotland. Moreover, as the novelization makes clear, Ada's muteness itself is triggered as a response to shame.[38] We learn that when she was six the young Ada was literally struck dumb by shame when her father chastised her in front of her aunts for a minor transgression at the dinner table.[39] This retreat into herself is deepened when, at the age of eighteen, Ada finds herself pregnant and betrayed by her young piano tutor, Delwar Haussler, causing her to invoke the same resolve with which she had "willed herself not to speak at the age of six."[40] In both instances, her retreat into self is motivated by Ada's need to protect herself against the trauma of emotional desertion, first by her father and then by her lover, reinforced by a determination of will that is activated by her resentment at the betrayals she experiences by the two men who were most important in her life.

This need to maintain a self-protective defense against the trauma of shame and fear of abandonment leads to the sense of entrapment that both Ada and Alice suffer. They each marry out of a need to maintain propriety, not out of love, which leaves them deprived of both emotional and sexual satisfaction. Alice feels "like a child in the dark" who "crave[s] for the light" and suffers from the destructive effects of her own mind, feeling that everything hurts her.[41] Ada similarly feels that even the bush is in a conspiracy with her unloved husband, perceiving the thick supplejack vines as being "like many arms that reached out to bind her, gray snakes coiling around her, a terrible web in league with the man who had brought her to this place." She eventually finds herself, literally and metaphorically, trapped in a boarded-up hut.[42]

The state of emotional deprivation in which both Mander's and Campion's heroines find themselves leads them to seek displaced means of expressing their feelings and deriving satisfaction. In both cases, as we have seen, their piano-playing provides an outlet for the release of repressed affect, as does each woman's relationship with her daughter. In the case of Ada and Flora, this relationship is described as a "kind of symbiosis" that leaves Stewart "irritated at his inability to participate in their intimacy."[43] In the case of Alice and Asia, the relationship is represented as one that allows Alice's "suppressed emotionalism" to find "vent in the affection between them," creating a bond that is "more than human."[44]

One can see, then, on the basis of Campion's further elaboration of the material she borrowed from Mander's novel, the extent of the influence of her antipodean source.

Campion's Transformative Originality

Having established Campion's debt to her earlier compatriot, however, it is important to acknowledge that Campion possesses an originality that makes the resulting film a creative imitation that is truly her own, rather than merely a derivative adaptation. One can understand Campion's indignation at being accused of plagiarism.[45] The Piano stands in the same kind of relationship to The Story of a New Zealand River as any number of Shakespeare's plays do to the original versions of the stories upon which they were based—for example, Romeo and Juliet, The Merchant of Venice, or Othello, to name just a few.[46] In Campion's case, as with Shakespeare, the original source material is transformed in such a way that the new work that emerges from the creative imitation is more profound than the work upon which it was based.[47] Through a brilliant process of condensation, symbolism, intensification, visualization, and dramatization, Campion intensifies the archetypal potentialities inherent in Mander's narrative and turns it into a vehicle for exploring a number of her own concerns—in particular, the role of shame enforced by patriarchy and puritanism in inducing repression and the need for the female subject to be released from fear of that shame through a transformed masculinity that allows for a return of the desire that is disallowed and repressed. The new elements Campion added greatly extended Mander's insights into the origins of the "awful disease" of puritan repression, as well as providing new insights into the status of a liberated eroticism as its imagined cure.

One of those new elements was the gothic tone and feeling that Campion found in Emily Brontë's Wuthering Heights—which she describes as "a powerful poem about the romance of the soul" that "seems to strike a basic and strong chord in so many people." Its influence is plain to see: in The Piano's tragic tonality, its endorsement of "the right for people to decide to follow their passions," and its "very harsh and extreme" "gothic exploration of the romantic impulse"—to use Campion's own words.[48] It seems clear too that the figure of Ada is based partly upon Brontë herself, whom Campion describes as someone who "barely spoke a word when she went out."[49] At one stage she had even thought of filming an adaptation of *Wuthering Heights* but quickly realized that it would not work: "I'm not English. I belong to a colonial culture and I had to invent my own fiction. I wanted to speak of the relationship between men and women, of the complex character of love and of eroticism, but also of the repression of sexuality."[50] To do this, she felt she had to be "free of the social constraints of Brontë's time, and thus far more sexual; 'a lot more investigative of eroticism—which can add another dimension.'"[51] Nevertheless, she could well imagine the intensity of passion to be found in the novels of the Brontë sisters in the New Zealand landscapes, and her express purpose in *The Piano* was, by showing the encounter of civilization with primitivism, to explore how characters approach love, sex, and eroticism naively, for the first time, and how, in "a raw situation," attraction grows, develops, becomes eroticized, sexual, and then transcends these more elementary responses in order to become "something more spiritual."[52] Eroticism, therefore, of a far more explicit kind than anything she found in Mander or the Brontës, was a further element that Campion introduced into her fiction.

She also made a series of changes that would transform the elementary paradigm she found in Mander into something much more psychologically complex and profound. The first major change Campion made to the source was to make Ada mute. As well as having a powerful symbolic function—suggesting both her voicelessness in the face of a tyrannical patriarchy and simultaneously her defiance of that patriarchal power—Ada's muteness is invested with a complex psychological motivation that serves to link repression with Oedipal family dynamics, in Campion's view of things.

The link, which is only implicit in the film, is made explicit in the novelization and involves the role of Wyston McGrath, Ada's father, in precipitating her willed silence. Prior to the episode at the dinner table, the relationship between father and daughter had been one of mutual adoration, with Ada being "his favored pet."[53] When Wyston punishes her—out of a puritanical desire to maintain propriety in the eyes of the two aunts—the young child not only suffers acute shame but also experiences an equally powerful resentment of her father for his betrayal of the bond between them. Subsequently, when Wyston attempts to repair the breach ("I have punished you and now this last week you have punished me. . . . Are we even?"), Ada finds that she is unable to reciprocate: "Ada heard her father's kind voice and looked into the face she loved so dearly, the face she had called 'Beast,' and despite her enormous love for him, and his utter devotion to her, she could not contradict the edict of her own small iron will. She, as firm as a window grille, would not speak."[54] The deeper reason for Ada's willed silence is made apparent in the novelization: "Soon daughter and father became even tighter, he in his mocking, admiring tolerance, she in her tiny child firmness."[55] Her muteness, in other words, is presented as Ada's unconscious means of binding her father to her through a negative cathexis, grounded in the activation of his remorse, that is, designed to forestall any recurrence of the potential loss of him.

The intensity of this cross-generational bond between Ada and her father is shown in the novelization to be deepened by Ada's failed love affair with Delwar Haussler, her piano tutor. This relationship is presented as one that tempts Ada to relinquish her withdrawal into self-containment because of the seductive emotional communion that she and Delwar are able to share through their playing of the duets he brings her. At first, she resists him, as "she did not want to lose herself to a situation where control might not be regained," having "always enjoyed the solipsism the piano afforded."[56] Soon, however, her resolve disappears, and being transported "into another world where everything had the texture of silk and all was warmth and small rooms made cozy by hearthfires at night," Ada allows Delwar to make love to her out of a "longing for something she could not have expressed."[57] Having relinquished her self-protective control under the influence of Delwar's seduction-through-music, Ada finds his abandonment of her all the more soul-destroying. The effect is to make her "even more forbidding and aloof than she had seemed previously," and she remains as adamantly silent on the identity of the father of her child as she had been literally silent following her chastisement by her father.[58]

Strangely, however, the effect on Wyston McGrath is to draw him even closer to his daughter, whom he treats "with increasing tenderness"—to the extent that some in the town "insinuated with shameful whispers that perhaps it was Wyston himself who had fathered the child." The staff in the house, on the other hand, maintain that "there were times when he confused his daughter with his dead wife, slipping back through the years to when Cecilia had carried Ada."[59] Once again, Campion draws attention to the idea that a complicated relationship with her father underpins Ada's self-containment and her difficulty in relating to other men. On one hand, she yearns for the perpetuation of a closeness in which she herself can occupy the place of her mother in her father's eyes, while on the other hand, she fears being in such a relationship, especially when it is transferred to another man, because of the possibility that the affection of the male Other might be withdrawn.

This fear is presented in the novel as a major cause of Ada's frigidity toward Alisdair Stewart, the husband Wyston McGrath finds for his daughter by advertising in the colonial press. We are told that on the voyage out, "Ada often dreamt of her husband, Alisdair Stewart, whom she had not yet met, and her piano teacher, Delwar Haussler, whom she had not seen long since, and in her dreams the two men became one."[60] This unconscious conflation suggests how the fears arising from her betrayal, first by her father, then by Delwar, become projected on to Stewart as the embodiment of all that she fears about the patriarchy. It is, Campion shows, a fear that derives as much from need, as from resentment.

This additional material in the novelization of *The Piano* is far more than mere backstory. What the novelization presents, in fact, is a sense of the psychic economy motivating the characters that must have lain dormant in Campion's imagination while she was making the film, even though it was not made explicit in the resulting representation.

Campion made other significant changes to the source material she found in Mander. Whereas the husband of Mander's Alice, Tom Roland, is a womanizing figure of macho vitality, Campion turns Ada's husband, Alisdair Stewart, into a repressed male version of Ada herself, thus allowing for a deeper exploration of the sexual repression from which Ada eventually frees herself. In the novelization, as in the film, Stewart is a man who, as a puritan, is at war with "the wanton regrowth of all manner of vine and fern" in the bush.[61] Symbolically, this stands for his subservience to the Presbyterian imperatives of the Scottish society from which he descends. Later, in Campion's vision, he has an opportunity to break free from the constraints of this restrictive puritan morality when he spies on Ada and Baines making love, which arouses his own sexual desire. He corrupts this impulse, however, by translating it into terms of patriarchal dominance and power when he attempts to rape Ada. Later, when she approaches him in bed and caresses him sexually, he is unable to respond and draws up his bedclothes. Campion has gone on record to say that in her imaginative realization of this scene Ada is "searching for herself," which ends up in her treating Stewart as a sexual object in the way that many men treat women.[62] What the scene also acknowledges, however, is the vulnerability of men who, like Stewart, need to be "loved and protected" as much as women do—to use Campion's words.[63] The fact that Stewart draws up his bedclothing to protect himself against the desire aroused by Ada's caresses indicates that his resentment at being used as a sex object is greater than his inclination to achieve the sexual conquest that he had earlier believed he desired. His inability to surrender to Ada's erotic invitation despite his desire also suggests the psychic pressures that will lead him subsequently to chop off Ada's finger in a violent attempt to punish in her the desire he forcibly restrains in himself—through an act of displaced castration, in which the finger represents not only the means by which Ada expresses her passion in music but also the agent of the offending erotic caress. This episode between Stewart and Ada reveals that Campion, in her imaginative treatment of the relational difficulties she descries as existing between the sexes, is as sympathetically compassionate toward the men as she is toward the women, despite exposing their conflicted brutality. Mander also in her novel ended up with a comparable compassion toward Tom Roland, Alice's husband, but Campion's imaginative understanding of this complex seems, to me, to reach far deeper.

Another major modification to Campion's New Zealand source is her introduction of a bartering agreement between Ada and Baines whereby she will let him "do things" to her in exchange for his relinquishing of the piano back into her ownership—key by key. This represents a major updating of Mander, reflecting, as it does, a late-twentieth-century feminist view of the power relations that exist between the sexes. In Campion's vision, however, success in this bartering system cannot in itself supply the totality of what her heroine(s) are looking for: that is, the full appreciation of them as a fully sexualized woman by a man who is himself fully masculine in his sexualized being, while being sufficiently sensitized to a woman's emotional needs to be prepared to relinquish the patriarchal power that his society ordinarily affords him. This, for Campion, is the major corrective needed for the puritanism of her New Zealand tradition as reflected in the source story that inspired *The Piano*. One of her major creative innovations in the film is to show Baines, at first an unlikely appearing candidate, undergoing just such a transformation—out of a desire to share the emotional experience into which Ada is able to enter when she releases her repressed inner being while playing the piano. In this respect, Campion realizes in contemporary terms a potentiality that was only dormant in the imaginative suggestions of her source. Most significantly, the system of barter—representing Campion's sense of the social contract between men and women—is eventually discarded by Baines in favor of an unconditional commitment to the woman he desires. This too reflects an ideal propounded in contemporary popular culture even though the possibility of realizing this ideal is consistently put in doubt.[64]

Finally, a significant change can be seen in Campion's presentation of Ada herself. Whereas Mander's Alice, after many years of self-denial, in which she restrains herself from surrendering to her desire for her lover, is then rewarded by an unequivocal, liberated happiness following the accidental death of her husband, Campion's Ada undergoes an experience that is more complex, even more damaging, and far more equivocal in its outcomes—involving Ada in despair, mutilation, and a flirtation with suicide. Despite the happy ending, which has struck some viewers as somewhat contrived—an earlier version of the screenplay had ended with the drowning of Ada and the killing of Stewart by Baines—the film allows for an ambiguity to persist as to whether Ada will be able to commit herself to a relationship with a man that requires a surrender of the self-imposed protections with which she has surrounded her self.[65] While Ada, Baines, and Flora at the end of the film marvel "at the grace that had delivered them," the sound of the consonants Ada is now able to speak is "still so bad [that] she was ashamed." Symbolically, this might imply that the circumstances in which Ada finds herself have still not allowed her, confidently, to "find her voice." Such a suggestion is reinforced by the final image of Ada floating above her drowned piano—which seems designed to activate an awareness of a catastrophic possibility that only the contrived happy ending of a romantic melodrama has been able to avert.

Repression, Transgression, and Eroticism as Thematic Continuities

Once the formative influence of Jane Campion's New Zealand background and her New Zealand source material on *The Piano* has been acknowledged, it becomes possible to see how the archetypal fable she developed out of hints from Mander's *The Story of a New Zealand River* was able to subsume and adumbrate most of the themes she had initiated in her earlier films, as well as those she would pursue in her subsequent ones. The constraining discipline that Alisdair Stewart tries to impose on Ada is foreshadowed in *Peel* (1982) in the father's attempt to constrain his son, and then the attempt of both father and son to constrain the sister/aunt. This is paralleled in the alliance of Flora and Stewart, who seek to prevent Ada's escape from the commitment to the domestic scene that is required under the ethos of puritanism. In *Peel*, as in *A Girl's Own Story* (1984) and *Sweetie* (1989), the disequilibrium of power caused by excessive patriarchal dominance is shown to result in dysfunction within the family, as is evident in the depression of the respective mothers, the presence of incestuous boundary-crossing (between brother and sister and between father and daughter), and in sexual frigidity—signaled symbolically in the image of ice skating in *A Girl's Own Story*, as well as in the sung refrain, "I feel the cold." It is also depicted explicitly in the contrasting experiences of Kay and Dawn in *Sweetie*, illustrated most graphically in the scene of Dawn reaching between her father's legs in the bath, followed immediately by the scene where Kay draws her bedsheet up to her face—suggesting surrender to an incestuous fantasy on the part of the former and a fear of such a surrender in the latter that is directly linked to her sexual frigidity. Similarly, the patriarchal shaming of the young Ada is foreshadowed by the repeated shaming of Janet in *An Angel at My Table*, as when she is disciplined by her teacher for stealing money from her father's pocket, or when she incurs her father's rage by alluding to forbidden sexual activity in which she has witnessed her sister engaged. Just as Ada is shown to be trapped within the confines of a conflicted relationship with her father grounded in a combination of attachment and resentment resulting from his enforcement of puritanical codes, so too does Janet in *An Angel at My Table* suffer the lingering effects of a similar kind of attachment. This is depicted metaphorically in the image near the end of the film of the socially with-drawn and isolated Janet standing in her dead father's boots.

The thematic relationship between *The Piano* and the movies that followed is just as close. Ada's attempt to find an antidote to her psychic oppression through transgressive eroticism is repeated in the similar attempt by Ruth in *Holy Smoke* to trade "sex for soul." This occurs when she tries to deaden the despair arising from her awareness that her father and brother are "cunt men" who have emotionally abandoned her by seeking to seduce and gain mastery over an older man who reminds her of her father. Finally, the element of masochism and self-destructive recklessness that attends Ada's experimentation with eroticism is picked up and taken to a near-fatal extreme in *In the Cut,* when Frannie Avery pursues a sexual adventure with a man she suspects may be a murderer, and nearly falls victim to a psycho-sexually perverted serial killer as a result.

One can conclude, then, that Dana Polan was wrong in claiming that "Campion's career bears no unity of theme and style but is marked rather by shifts of direction and changes of emphasis."[66] Her oeuvre does have a thematic unity and coherence that allies her with other contemporary New Zealand literary and cinematic artists, such as Maurice Gee or Stevan Eldred-Grigg, who have been exploring the lingering effects of puritanical repression. This unity in her work, I have argued, arises from her experience of, and response to, the puritanical value system and set of social codes pertaining to the New Zealand society within which she was raised.

Notes

1. See Ken Gelder, "Jane Campion and the Limits of Literary Cinema," in *Adaptations: From Text to Screen, Screen to Text,* ed. Deborah Cartmell and Imelda Whelehan (London: Routledge, 1999), 160.

2. Dana Polan, *Jane Campion* (London: British Film Institute, 2001), 3.

3. Bridget Ikin and Tiara Lowndes, *The Making of* An Angel at My Table, 2002, included in *An Angel at My Table: A Film by Jane Campion,* DVD, The Criterion Collection, 2005.

4. Mark Stiles, "Jane Campion," *Cinema Papers,* December 1984; reprinted in *Jane Campion Interviews,* ed. Virginia Wright Wexman (Jackson: University Press of Mississippi Press), 8.

5. See Campion's interviews with Katherine Tulich, "Jane's Film Career Takes Wing," *The Daily Telegraph* (Sydney), September 1990, reprinted in Wexman, *Jane Campion,* 73; with Thomas Bourguignon and Michel Ciment, "Interview with Jane Campion: More Barbarian Than Aesthete," *Positif,* June 1993, reprinted in Wexman, *Jane Campion,* 104; and with Lynden Barber, "Playing It Low-Key," *The Sydney Morning Herald,* 3 August 1993, reprinted in Wexman, *Jane Campion,* 143.

6. Marli Feldross, "Jane Campion: Making Friends by Directing Films," *EPD Film,* August 1993, reprinted in Wexman, *Jane Campion,* 99; interview with Helen Barlow, Universitetet I Oslo, http://www.fys.uio.no/-magnushj/Piano/campion.html (accessed 10 December 2006).

7. Jane Campion, *The Piano* [screenplay] (London: Bloomsbury, 1993), 139.

8. Mary Cantwell, "Jane Campion's Lunatic Women," *The New York Times Magazine,* 19 September 1993; reprinted in Wexman, *Jane Campion,* 161. See also Dryburgh's comments in Campion, *The Piano*: "Part of the director's brief was that we would echo the film's element of underwater in the bush. 'Bottom of the fish tank' was the description we used for ourselves to help define what we were looking for. So we played it murky blue-green and let the skin tones sit down in amongst it" (141).

9. Jay Carr, "Jane Campion, the Classical Romantic," *The Boston Globe,* 14 November 1993; reprinted in Wexman, *Jane Campion,* 169.

10. Miro Bilbrough, "The Piano," *Cinema Papers,* May 1993; reprinted in Wexman, *Jane Campion,* 115.

11. See Lawrence Jones, "Puritanism," in *The Oxford Companion to New Zealand Literature,* ed. Roger Robinson and Nelson Wattie, 455–56 (Oxford: Oxford University Press, 1998).

12. Carr, "Jane Campion," 170.

13. Bill Pearson, "Fretful Sleepers: A Sketch of New Zealand Behaviour and Its Implications for the Artist" (1952; revised 1974); reprinted in *Great New Zealand Argument: Ideas about Ourselves,* ed. Russell Brown, 88–89 (Auckland: Activity Press, 2005).

14. Kristin Williamson, "The New Filmmakers," *National Times,* 20 June 1985; reprinted in Wexman, *Jane Campion,* 9.

15. Stiles, "Jane Campion," 7 (my italics).

16. See Ruth Hessey, "Campion Goes Out on a Limb—Again," *Sydney Morning Herald,* 5 July 1989; reprinted in Wexman, *Jane Campion,* 28.

17. Ikin and Lowndes, *The Making of* An Angel at My Table.

18. Michel Ciment, "A Voyage to Discover Herself," *Positif,* December 1996; reprinted in Wexman, *Jane Campion,* 177.

19. See Mary Paul, *Her Side of the Story: Readings of Mander, Mansfield, and Hyde* (Dunedin: University of Otago Press, 1999), 75–101; Hillary Frey, "The Purloined Piano?" *Lingua Franca* 10, no. 6 (2000): 8–10; Ann Hardy, "The Last Patriarch," *Illusions* 23 (1994): 6–13, reprinted in Harriet Margolis, ed., *Jane Campion's* The Piano, 59–85 (Cambridge: Cambridge University Press, 2000); Polan, *Jane Campion*, 174; and Diane Long Hoeveler, "Silence, Sex, and Feminism: An Examination of *The Piano's* Unacknowledged Sources," *Literature/Film Quarterly* 26, no. 2 (1998): 109.

20. See "Fight-back over Piano Claims," *The Dominion*, 8 April 2000, 31.

21. See Rae McGregor, *The Story of a New Zealand Writer: Jane Mander* (Dunedin: University of Otago Press, 1998), 125–27.

22. See Robert Macklin, "Campion's Award-winning Screenplay 'Inspired' by Novel," *The Canberra Times*, 8 April 2000.

23. Ibid.

24. Ibid.

25. Ibid. See also Robert Macklin, "Creative Effort Went into Film," *The Canberra Times*, 11 April 2000. It is also now known that Campion paid "compensation" of $2,000 to the Mander estate in a confidential agreement prior to *The Piano's* production for "lost opportunity" to publish a film edition of Mander's novel to accompany the release of a proposed film, *The River*, based on *The Story of a New Zealand River*.

26. The New Zealand film critic Sam Edwards, in a piece written for the *Waikato Times*, asserts this view. (See also "Fight-back over Piano Claims," *The Dominion*, 8 April 2000, 31.)

27. Long Hoeveler, "Silence, Sex, and Feminism," 109.

28. Jane Mander, *The Story of a New Zealand River* (Auckland: Vintage, 1999), 39.

29. Ibid., 54.

30. Ibid., 39–40; Campion, *The Piano*, scene 106, 92.

31. Mander, *Story of a New Zealand River*, 30.

32. Ibid., 139.

33. Ibid., 337.

34. Ibid., 13, 209, 227, 240, 299.

35. Jane Campion and Kate Pullinger, *The Piano: A Novel* (London: Bloomsbury, 1994), frontispiece.

36. Andreas Furler, "Structure Is Essential/Absolutely Crucial/One of the Most Important Things," *Filmbulletin*, February 1993; reprinted in Wexman, *Jane Campion*, 91.

37. Mander, *Story of a New Zealand River*, 268–69.

38. Campion and Pullinger, *The Piano*, 209.

39. Ibid., 18.

40. Ibid., 205.

41. Mander, *Story of a New Zealand River*, 111, 123, 128.

42. Campion and Pullinger, *The Piano*, 159, 161.

43. Ibid., 50.

44. Mander, *Story of a New Zealand River*, 80.

45. A major row broke out when the *Oxford Companion to Australian Film* listed *The Piano* as having been "based on the novel *The Story of a New Zealand River* by

Jane Mander; uncredited." When the *Canberra Times* took up the argument, Campion, through her lawyers, issued the following statement:

- Our client's (Jane Campion) script is an original work.
- Our client was aware of Jane Mander's book.
- Any issues concerning the book were dealt with years ago, prior to the production of the film and as part of the ordinary process of reviewing and confirming copyright claim of title to the financing of the film.
- As part of this process, nine years ago, the book, the final screenplay, story outlines, and other materials were subject to a comprehensive legal opinion by Queen's Counsel, who concluded very clearly that there was no foundation for any suggestion of copyright infringement and that any similarities were superficial.
- Importantly, the legal agent of the owner of copyright in the Mander book confirmed in writing that it had no claims of any kind in connection with the book or our client's screenplay or film.

The debate about the copying of Jane Mander's book hits a reef when it comes up against fact and copyright law. I am distressed that uninformed speculation continues in the press.

I am currently seeking an apology from Oxford University Press for its defamatory error. . . .

The Canberra Times has also received a letter from my lawyer demanding an apology and retraction as the article was prepared recklessly and without regards for my rights or the truth. . . .

My lawyer will also be contacting other self-appointed commentators who have, for some reason, found it necessary to push their opinions.

Signed: Jane Campion

While the Oxford University Press published a retraction, the *Canberra Times* never withdrew its allegations. As the debate heated up, the film critic for the *New Zealand Herald,* Peter Calder, went as far as suggesting that Campion should be stripped of her Oscar for Best Original Screenplay in 1994. For detailed accounts of this bitter wrangle, see "Fight-back Over Piano Claims," 312; and "Campion Puts Her Case," *The Dominion,* 8 April 2000, 31. The dispute was also the subject of a TV New Zealand documentary.

46. For a discussion of the process of Shakespeare's creative transformation of his Italian sources, see Alistair Fox, *The English Renaissance: Identity and Representation in Elizabethan England* (Oxford: Basil Blackwell, 1997), 181–217.

47. Mary Paul, in *Her Side of the Story,* has described Mander's novel as a "palimpsest" upon which Campion reinscribed her own version of the basic story (77).

48. Bilbrough, "The Piano," 114; Hessey, "Campion Goes Out on a Limb," 29; Andrew L. Urban, "Piano's Good Companions," *The Australian,* 6 August 1993; reprinted in Wexman, *Jane Campion,* 146.

49. Furler, "Structure Is Essential," 91.

50. Bourguignon and Ciment, "Interview," 105.

51. Urban, "Piano's Good Companions," 146.

52. Furler, "Structure Is Essential," 91; Bourguignon and Ciment, "Interview," 101; Bilbrough, "The Piano," 118.

53. Campion and Pullinger, *The Piano,* 18.

54. Ibid., 19–20.

55. Ibid., 20.

56. Ibid., 165, 168.

57. Ibid., 171.

58. Ibid., 206.

59. Ibid., 207.

60. Ibid., 6–7.

61. Ibid., 21.

62. Bourguignon and Ciment, "Interview," 108.

63. Ibid.

64. I am thinking of the ironic ambivalencies at the end of *Pretty Woman* (1989) or of *13 Going On 30* (2004).

65. See Carol Jacobs, "Playing Jane Campion's *Piano:* Politically," *MLN* 109, no. 5 (1994): 757–85, esp. 775, which cites comments made by Campion at a New York Film Festival press conference; and Bourguignon and Ciment, "Interview," 102.

66. Polan, *Jane Campion,* 160.

Nicole Kidman as Isabel Archer in *The Portrait of a Lady.* Courtesy of the Academy of Motion Picture Arts and Sciences.

Portraits of a Woman

Jane Campion and Henry James

Jane Campion's interactions with literature are profound, original, always interesting, and display an exceptional finesse, whether she is dealing with a literary oeuvre and its author, as in *An Angel at My Table,* which depicts Janet Frame and her writings, or whether she is adapting a classic novel for the screen, such as Henry James's *The Portrait of a Lady.* One should note that Campion's film is the only existing film adaptation of the James novel, which had been considered impossible to adapt to the cinema. In this essay, however, I will not be focusing on the issue of the filmic adaptation of a novel, nor on the remarkable work accomplished by Campion and her screenwriter, Laura Jones, in opening up a text as dense and complex as James's novel to convert it from one medium to the other. Rather, I am more concerned to show how Campion, taking James's novel as her point of departure, develops and deepens her vision of womankind, of the place of women in society, of the relationship between a man and a woman, and, beyond that, how a woman may represent herself to the world in her quest for individual identity. All of these issues are expressed through the portrait that the filmmaker offers of Isabel Archer, as seen from an angle and a point of view that is slightly, but significantly, different than that adopted by James. Through what subtle or more obvious changes does James's heroine become a heroine of Campion—and does she in fact become one? What kind of changes are they—psychological, narrative, or changes involving dimensions that were nonexistent, or barely suggested, in the novel, such as feminine sexuality? Do they impart a feminist flavor to the inherently tragic story of Isabel Archer?

Why would a contemporary filmmaker use a narrative that is more than a century old to speak about a woman and the feminine condition? Campion read, and reread, James's novel from the time she was twenty years old, declaring on a number of occasions that it was one of her favorite books, that she identified herself with Isabel Archer, and that, for her, this story was both timeless and universal. As Sophie Menoux puts it, "According to Jane, the story of Isabel Archer, in *The Portrait of a Lady*, could be the story of any young woman the same age."[1]

Is Isabel Archer truly our contemporary? I shall return to this topic later in this essay, but what is indisputable is that "woman" as a subject is at the center of all Campion's movies. Portraits of women (with both terms in the plural) are without doubt one of the fundamental characteristics and constitute a constant given across Campion's entire cinematographic oeuvre.

Isabel as She Is at the Beginning:
Her Character as Viewed from the Outside

Isabel appears for the first time on the screen just after the contemporary prologue to the film, in a head shot, then in a medium shot, obviously distressed, with tears in her eyes that start to roll down her cheeks. She is dressed in black, which may serve as a way of announcing and affirming her will to achieve independence. She is positioned under a tree in a stately English garden—a tree that fulfills a symbolic function as a shelter and a refuge for her. (I shall return to the role of this tree, which is again present in the final scene of the film.) We are presented with a contrast between the splendor of nature and the serenity of the summer and Isabel's anguish. And what is the reason for such distress? Lord Warburton, a friend of Isabel's uncle Mr. Touchett and of her cousin Ralph Touchett, has just asked for her hand in marriage. He is a rather seductive and very rich man, and therefore his proposal, one imagines, should potentially sweep Isabel off her feet—but this is not the case. She explains why in a conversation with her uncle: she intends never to get married, because she wants to fulfill the potentialities of her soul and her spirit, to "discover life," and is therefore looking to detect the presence of an answering "flame" in the man whom she will eventually choose. She wishes for a life that is more expansive than that which is possible for a married couple. For her, Europe is a veritable promised land, a land that she wants to learn how to get to know. Isabel strikes us as an optimistic young woman who is proud, intelligent, and independent, a little arrogant on account of the image that she has formed of herself, fairly naive, and she does not hesitate to thrust herself into the world in an attempt to live in the way she desires. She is also thirsty for knowledge. When she decides to leave for London (after her uncle's death leaves her an unexpected inheritance that gives her the freedom for which she longs), we see her putting her things away and fixing several notes on the wall on which are written erudite terms such as "nihilism," "aberration," "abnegation," and so on. Is this meant to remind her to search for their meaning? Or is it just to remind her to use them?

Her independence and the fact that she belongs to a different culture (American) situate her outside and above the mores of British society: for example, she does not understand why she cannot leave for London accompanied only by her friend Henrietta or why her cousin Ralph must accompany her as a chaperone. It becomes clear from the beginning of the movie that Isabel expects a lot from her life, and that she possesses a potential—because of her personality, her character, her intelligence, and her strength of will—that could allow her to achieve the kind of blossoming and life that she has always wished for and dreamed of. It is also clear that one of the keys to an understanding of Isabel's character, both in the novel and the film, is to be found in her own image of herself, in her philosophy of life, and in her conception of happiness. She has a positive and elevated idea of herself, asserted with a degree of stubbornness, and longs for (and probably deserves, as she thinks) a life that is different than that of other women of her time. As she declares to Ralph, she does not want to be "another sheep in the flock." For Isabel, happiness and a successful life is to be totally free (and in this she seems to confuse freedom with an absence of constraints) to discover and understand the Europe of myth, to be initiated into it, to meet interesting people, and not to miss any opportunity.

While Isabel knows exactly what she does not want, she is less able to define what she really wants and, above all, does not know how to obtain it. It is a journey into the unknown that she is undertaking, with two aims: first, to discover a world that is completely unfamiliar to her, Europe, and, through that, the meaning of human relationships; and, second, to discover who she really is. Isabel does not consciously set out in search for herself, but it is evident that she does not really know who she is, that she lacks a certain kind of awareness, and that she does not realize the degree of her own innocence and naivety.

Campion literally skips the first hundred pages of the novel in which Isabel's life in the United States, at Albany, is depicted. In the movie, she launches the character on a double journey: on the one hand, it is a geographical, external, physical voyage; on the other hand, it is an interior one. What interests the filmmaker is the confrontation between Isabel and the European world, between Isabel and the various encounters that are going to shape her life story, deepen her character, and lead her to experience a fairly radical evolution—to a much greater extent in the film than in the novel.

Isabel, the World, and Others

From her uncle's Gardencourt property in London, then to Florence and Rome, and back again to England, Isabel explores a part of Europe, its society, its museums, and experiences many decisive encounters. Each of these encounters alters Isabel and leads to a new stage of development in her story. In saying this, I do not mean that all characters have only this function, but paradoxically the way that certain scenes are developed or simply created places Isabel at the center of the narrative, just as she is often in the center of the visual frame. Four men surround Isabel, playing a large role in her evolution and her life: Lord Warburton, Caspar Goodwood, Ralph Touchett, and Gilbert Osmond, the man she will marry. Lord Warburton asks her to marry him, but she refuses. He retains a certain fondness for her and will witness all the changes in Isabel's life, painfully pointing them out when he sees what her marriage has done to her. Goodwood is an American who is in love with Isabel, his only dream being to share her life. He is the only character in the movie who does not change at all. The two men who play a crucial role in determining Isabel's destiny are Ralph and Osmond.

Ralph is in love with his cousin, but he does not press his suit because he is incurably ill. He is the one who respects Isabel the most, and who gives her the means to achieve her freedom by convincing his father to leave her a legacy. Being an heiress has dire consequences for Isabel, because it is what allows her to explore Europe and enter into very destructive encounters with Madame Merle and Osmond. Ralph's character thus becomes a kind of narrative catalyst, being more developed in the film than in the novel. He is sympathetic to Isabel's desire to see the world and is very curious to see what will happen to a young woman who has refused the hand of Lord Warburton. He understands Isabel, but he will, despite himself, become one of the agents of her misery, even though he tries to warn her that Osmond would be a disastrous choice. It is interesting to note that, because of his illness and his fear of expressing his love for Isabel, he remains in the background and plays the role of a slightly voyeuristic observer.

Osmond approaches Isabel at the instigation of his friend and accomplice Madame Merle: Isabel would seem to match his expectations because she is rich and beautiful. Osmond is the absolute villain of the story, but he seduces Isabel through his refined and exquisite taste for works of art, through his personality, which appears to be genuine, and especially through his adroitness. Isabel had been under the impression that the men who wanted to marry her would want to confine her to a narrow, conventional existence. Osmond's brilliant strategy is that of not asking her to marry

Osmond seduces Isabel. Courtesy of the Academy of Motion Picture Arts and Sciences.

him. In an extraordinarily well constructed romantic scene foreshadowing Isabel's future misery (the scene takes place in a mausoleum, in a sort of crypt), in which there is a ceaseless alternation between shadow and light brought about by the play with Isabel's umbrella, he simply declares his love without seeking to constrain her, leaving Isabel that which is most important to her, the freedom to choose: "I am not a suitable person to marry, but I have to tell you I'm absolutely in love with you." Osmond represents both the archetype of the patriarchal hero who wants to dominate women at the risk of destroying them (he draws Isabel into a "house of darkness"), and also a kind of romantic hero. Because of her sentimental idealism, Isabel perceives him only as a romantic type, refined, marginal, and original. Moreover, she is disturbed by her sensual attraction to him. Campion conveys how difficult it is for a woman to escape from convention and social rules, and how it is nearly impossible for her to express and fulfill her sexuality in the Victorian world.

Sexuality is absent in James's novel, and the two scenes with sexual connotations in the film have provoked a lot of indignation. The first of these shows Isabel lying on her bed surrounded by three men, Lord Warburton, Ralph, and Goodwood, being caressed by them. This scene is actually a dream that Isabel has after a visit from Goodwood, in London, who gently caressed her face before leaving, which is what stimulates Isabel's reaction. The second scene takes the form of a short silent film, blending the style of a home movie with that of a film with Valentino, vaguely oriental, in which Isabel arouses the desire of several men, including Osmond. Shot in black and white, it could be considered a psychic journey.

These scenes are equally important because they reveal the psychology of Isabel's character not through words but through images, and because they bring Isabel and her story closer to the contemporary spectator. In Campion's film there are also portraits of other women: Madame Merle, Pansy (the daughter of Osmond and Madame Merle), the Countess of Gimini, Osmond's sister, Henrietta, Isabel's American friend who succeeds in leading the life of a liberated and independent woman, and Mrs. Touchett, Isabel's aunt. All these portraits are developed to a degree and are given a relative importance that does not disturb the equilibrium of the film. Campion considerably extended the character of Serena Merle, investing her with a tragic dimension, and in so doing makes her one of the most interesting characters in the movie. In actual fact, she is by far the best constructed character in the film, and probably the most striking. The character of Madame Merle fulfills several functions in the film with respect to Isabel, who, from their first meeting, looks up to her as a model and displays a profound admiration of her. However, we know, though Isabel does not, that Madame Merle has been the lover and the longtime accomplice of Osmond in his villainy, and it is she who arranges for Osmond to meet and ensnare Isabel. In Isabel's eyes, Madame Merle epitomizes European culture and refinement as a free and independent woman. However, to the contrary, she represents what can happen to an intelligent, talented, and ambitious woman when she meets a man like Osmond and falls under his spell, and, in this respect, she is the exact negative image of Isabel: "the dark lady," as Laura Jones puts it.[2] Nevertheless, she is much more ambiguous than Osmond. She does not detest Isabel and even has some sort of respect for her; she is very much aware of what she has become, and of the place of women in society. As she says to Isabel, "A woman, it seems to me, has no natural place anywhere."

I have reflected on these characters because they exert a certain force in determining the routes and detours that the course of Isabel's life will take, and because, together, they help to delineate her portrait.

There has been much criticism of the place of the secondary plot revolving around the story of Osmond's daughter, Pansy, and of the way Campion develops it. As usual, she focuses on certain facts and structures in the story to intensify them and make them still darker. It seems to me that Pansy has a double role in the film. She portrays a daughter who is completely submissive to her father, formed—I should say, "formatted"—to please and obey him in all circumstances. She declares to Isabel that after having thought about it a great deal, she realizes that she must never disobey or displease her father. But it is her unhappy love story with Rosier, a man who is not rich enough for her father, that will open Isabel's eyes, leading the latter to understand her life, and helping her to find herself.

Isabel passes from light into darkness, and from paradise to the hell of her marriage. Campion wonderfully illustrates this through the play of shadow and light, through somberness, sadness, and the almost morbid ambiance of Isabel and Osmond's house, despite the beauty of its decorations. The garden that provides the setting for the first scene in which Isabel appears in the film is depicted as a place of exceptional beauty, almost fairylike. At the end of the movie, this same garden is covered with ice, stripped of its flowers and leaves. It now represents the space in which Isabel rediscovers her own self, and, to a certain extent, discovers what she has become: "I cannot believe that she is so cold," says Lord Warburton to Ralph. During the entire film, Isabel is always shown within a frame: frames formed of doors, wrought-iron gates, mirrors, narrow streets, and frequently vertical or horizontal bars that symbolize the point at which Isabel's life has become a prison, and how she has become trapped. The movie is both darker and more poignant than the novel, and

Isabel literally and symbolically in the grip of Osmond. Courtesy of the Academy of Motion Picture Arts and Sciences.

Isabel is presented as perhaps even more of a victim, even though she makes her own choices, which all prove to be bad ones. In fact, the Isabel of the film is singularly lacking in the ability to see things clearly, and the revelations that take place in the course of the movie—the fact that Osmond's daughter is also Madame Merle's daughter and that her unexpected inheritance is due to Ralph's generosity—all come from without. In Campion's version, it is always another character who clarifies things, whereas in the novel, Isabel discovers the truth by herself. Her final strength of will comes from the fact that she has found herself at last, and once she has abandoned the more or less romantic illusion and sentimental idealism that was obscuring her view of the world and of others.

A Few Possible Interpretations

Isabel's journey moves from her desire to assert her independence (she refuses to marry Lord Warburton)—which can be attributed to her anticonformism—to the social, psychological, and physical entrapment represented by her marriage with Osmond and ends with an affirmation of self-awareness that is expressed in an open ending: what is Isabel going to do, what is she going to *decide*?

One of the major changes that Campion made to James's novel resides in the ending of Isabel's story. In the novel, Isabel returns to Rome, to rejoin her husband in an act of courage and responsibility. In the film, the end is more open and less clean-cut. Isabel is now a different woman. Even if she were to decide to go back to Rome, nothing would be the same, because she now knows the truth about her life and herself. Despite the general tonality of the film, which is darker and tougher than that of the novel, often being coupled with a deliberately slowed-down rhythm, which has the effect of making the movie seem almost abstract and bold—critics have gone as far as identifying a "gothic" atmosphere (an adjective often used in talking about this filmmaker) and a narrative invested with "psychological horror" in this film—the ending is slightly more optimistic than that of the novel.[3]

The scene in which Henrietta urges Goodwood to be patient even if Isabel rejects him and leaves to join her husband was also deleted. In an interview with Sophie Menoux, Campion explained that, for her, these scenes would not have added anything to the ending of the film, nor to an understanding of the character of Isabel.[4] Moreover, they would have diminished the sought-after effect of concluding the film with exactly the same tree that was there in the beginning.

The tree, whose function is primarily symbolic, is the sign that Isabel has (re)discovered herself, and represents a refuge and a shelter for her, because it belongs to the natural world as opposed to the European social world that is deceptive and artificial. Showing the same tree again, but in a different season, in a different situation, when everything has changed, is one of the ways Campion indicates the passage of time in the story. The tree also belongs to the domain of the sacred and, in this sense, relates to the prologue in which contemporary young women seem to celebrate some kind of nature worship.

The music accompanying the final scene of Isabel's march toward the door of the house, filmed in slow motion, is neither sad nor ponderous, making it possible for us to think that Isabel might construct a life more suited to her personality and aspirations. This is exactly what her final glance expresses when she turns around to face into the lens of the camera: Isabel will no longer take flight, neither geographically nor in illusions.

In considering *The Portrait of a Lady*, many critics have underlined the feminist reading of the novel by the director and her obvious critique of a patriarchal society through the character of Osmond, and of the fate reserved for women, but few have acknowledged that the film is much more complex, and that one could just as easily find in it a restrained, but insistently present, critique of romanticism. In fact, it is concerned with a critique of the discourse of romanticism and the belief in ideal love. Indeed, Isabel is a young woman who wants to fall in love as much as she wishes to experience her freedom fully. Her sentimental and romantic idealism makes her fall into the worst of traps and leads to disaster. Campion thus depicts the dark side of the romantic tradition. Isabel is indeed the victim of the manipulation of Osmond and Madame Merle, but she is equally a victim of this tradition and the illusions that it engenders. Romanticism seems to open the way to freedom, but it actually opens the way merely to the illusion of freedom and a blooming that is illusory.

Although it is not my main purpose here, it seems difficult to speak about Isabel Archer without mentioning that this is the story of a young American woman arriving in Europe, or without thinking of one of the essential themes of James—namely, the confrontation between American innocence and European experience. James himself regarded Europe as a snake pit for naïve Americans who were susceptible to the intrigues of more devious cultures. If his view is justified, this is a harsh and definitive judgment. This is a harsh and definitive judgment, if the assertion is true. The insistence with which Henrietta begs Isabel to marry an American and not a European can appear amusing, even childish, but relates to this recurrent theme in James. In this regard, I would like to make two observations.

The first is that the tension between America and Europe was no longer topical when Campion shot her film. However, Campion found in it a personal and contemporary echo. She says, as she revealed to Michel Ciment, that she felt exactly in the same situation as young American women of the nineteenth century the first time she arrived in Europe.[5] For her, young Australian women today are similar to the American characters in James's novels: innocent, vulnerable, and brave.

The second is that Isabel is not a victim of a conspiracy of Europeans but of "false and wicked Europeans," as Madame Merle says, and in wanting to see the world and know all about it, Isabel ends up imprisoning herself in the closed circle of expatriate Americans. That seems to me to be a subtle game of mirrors.

I will not retrace the differences between the novel and the film already mentioned in this essay, nor the differences in the portrait of Isabel herself. I would like simply to emphasize that Campion's approach to the story is much more complex, and, because of that, more ambiguous than it might appear. It is not a question here of making a simple identification between the filmmaker and the character of Isabel, or of identifying a single feminist perspective on the condition of women in society and the unhappy and tragic story of Isabel, but a question of a multiplicity of points of view, among which are certainly included the feminist and feminine ones. It is also a question (perhaps the most important one) of a painful initiation and apprenticeship that takes place following several trials undergone by the main character. Campion emphasizes in her interview with Ciment that this story deals with what is an essential theme for her: the journey of a young woman that is also an initiation and a quest for feminine identity.[6] A story she believes, moreover, to be universal and timeless. The prologue of the film, shot in black and white and set in the contemporary era, has disconcerted many spectators and critics. It has often been viewed as a declaration by Campion that the film would embody a contemporary feminine reading of James. The film commences with some young women's voices, light and graceful, talking of kisses, of sensations, and of love, whilst the first lines of the credits roll. Then, progressively, we see contemporary young girls appear, at first lying languorously in the grass, then dancing to music in a sort of homage to the Earth goddess, speaking at the same time of the man they love, a man who is a "loyal and clear mirror." Then, the title of the film appears written on the hand of one of the girls, and the story of Isabel begins. This prologue, invested with the atmosphere of a dream, of a pagan rite, and of beauty conveys a double impression:

- The film touches on both romanticism and intimacy; this means that the story will become almost timeless, universally relevant, and concern us.
- The contemporary prologue is going to investigate the story Isabel situated in the past in order to reconstitute it in the present.

By Way of a Conclusion

Isabel Archer is, beyond doubt, the heroine of Campion's who possesses the most potential at the beginning: beauty, personality, an inheritance that makes her completely free to lead the life that suits her, or which she thinks suits her, an authentic curiosity about the world and others, and so on. However, everything that she undertakes and all her choices lead her exactly to where she did not wish to go. We have seen why and how.

Critics have found it somewhat difficult to relate Isabel to the two preceding heroines of *An Angel at My Table* and *The Piano,* Janet Frame and Ada McGrath. It seems to me, however, that there are certain similarities connecting the journeys of these three female characters, pertaining not so much to the storyline as to the essence of their experience: each of the three leaves her country, discovers another world, and eventually finds herself. All three embark on an individual quest for identity and find their place in the world because they come to understand who they are. I think that, in a certain way, Campion's heroines are survivors who end up liberating themselves from what society and others want to impose on them. For all three of them—Janet Frame, Ada, and Isabel—it is a matter of manifesting and revealing a slow, long process of transformation and maturation.

Peter Keough, who took part in the Campion film retrospective organized in 1999 at Harvard University, sees *Portrait* as little more than a film that does justice to James and to the directing talent of Campion: "In her [Campion's] passionate sensibility which grasps that of James without always understanding it, Campion's *Portrait* is almost worthy of both artists. See it as a learning exercise for the next opus: *Holy Smoke*."[7]

Such a view, as in the case of the three heroines, reflects a failure to see the unusual degree of continuity and the coherence that constitute one of the essential features of Campion's oeuvre. It is also to underestimate the interest, the complexity, and the richness arising from the intersection of the views of a novelist and a director on the same character, Isabel. Each of her portraits looks at, and responds to, the other, despite a cultural and historical distance, and despite perspectives on the character that are, in several respects, rather different.

Notes

Translation from the French by Alistair Fox.

1. Sophie Menoux, "'We Are All Isabel Archers': A 'Bonne Femme' Conversation with Jane Campion and Laura Jones," *ALIZES* 16 (1998). http://laboratoires .univ-reunion.fr/oracle/documents/260.html (accessed 21 October 2008).

2. Ibid.

3. See, e.g., Dana Polan. *Jane Campion* (London: British Film Institute, 2001), 137.

4. Menoux, "We Are All Isabel Archers."

5. Michel Ciment, "Un voyage à la découverte d'elle-même: Entretien avec Jane Campion," *Positif* 430 (1996); translated and reprinted in Virginia Wexman, ed., *Jane Campion: Interviews* (Jackson: University Press of Mississippi, 1999), 177–81.

6. Ibid.

7. Peter Keough, "Piano Lessons: Jane Campion Composes Herself," *The Boston Phoenix*, 28 January–4 February 1999, http://www.thephoenix.com (accessed 16 September 2007).

Young antipodean women in a circle from *The Portrait of a Lady*.

Jane Campion
Adaptation, Signature, Autobiography

Jane Campion is an internationally recognized contemporary director known for her distinctive cinematic style and vision and for her *narrative* focus on women. As half of her theatrically released features have been adaptations, a substantial part of her artistic reputation rests on her (re)visions of other writers' work. This essay addresses how both the extratextual (choice, promotion, and reception) and textual framing of these adaptations assimilate their source texts to the field of Jane Campion's oeuvre and signature. In the first instance, an insistent emphasis on Campion's similarity to or identification with the source texts' protagonists results in these films functioning autobiographically.[1] In the second, Campion's placement of her literal signature within cinematic sequences that theorize the logic of the subsequent adaptation effectively appropriates and signs their imaginative work as her own. As a result, it is precisely the mediation of the authorship and signature of *others* in her adaptations that operates to render these films the ones in which her signature and auteurist identity most clearly and forcefully emerges.

Adaptation

Alternating with the three theatrically released features that she has written either on her own or in collaboration with others, Campion has made three film adaptations to date: *An Angel at My Table* (1990), a rendition of fellow New Zealander Janet Frame's *An Autobiography*, the three volumes of which were published in the 1980s; *The Portrait of a Lady* (1996), the hotly anticipated follow-up to *The Piano*, which adapted Henry James's 1908 novel (revised from its original publication in 1881); and *In the Cut* (2003), a vision of Susanna Moore's dark, prize-winning thriller published in 1995. Seemingly, these source texts could not be more different. They cover very

139

different genres (autobiography, turn-of-the-century modernist literature, contemporary thriller) and audiences (national, literary, popular); they draw from disparate periods and locations (early- to mid-twentieth-century New Zealand, Europe in the latter half of the nineteenth century, and New York in the 1990s) and from authors whose styles and sensibilities are directed to very different purpose in their respective texts. Famed New Zealand author Janet Frame's autobiography recounts her childhood, her adolescent struggles with poverty, a tragic misdiagnosis that resulted in multiple stays in mental hospitals, and finally, her adult attainment of her vocation as a writer. Literary modernist Henry James's acute verbal portrait of nineteenth-century American heroine Isabel Archer and her milieu details her quest to Europe for self-discovery. A surprising bequest of fortune ironically hampers that quest, and Isabel ends up making exactly the kind of marriage and life situation she had set out to avoid. Finally, contemporary U.S. author Susanna Moore's first-person thriller details the thoughts and somewhat desolate existence of New Yorker Frannie Avery (actually a contemporary Isabel Archer character) whose defenses and desires propel her toward a horrific death.[2]

Yet despite the incontrovertible differences among these texts, when collected together by the signature "Jane Campion," similarities emerge. All three source texts feature a female protagonist struggling for some kind of self-expression or realization while subject to emotional, physical, and/or institutional duress. This fundamental conflict between the heroine and her environment is mediated by each text's crucial concern with narrating its heroine's imagination and interiority. While Henry James's focus on the interior life of Isabel Archer and her determination to make "enlightened" use of her independence renders her consciousness paradoxically accessible and inscrutable, both Frame and Moore access their protagonists' imagination through their use of autobiographical and fictional first-person narration respectively. Janet Frame has said that she wrote her autobiographies out of "the desire really to make myself a first person," to transcend the "third person" she had been as a child, and as an "oppressed minority," a woman categorized and institutionalized as mentally ill.[3] Moore's narrator/heroine recounts her research, her rapturous engagements with poetry, and her fantasies in a text that in its brutal end suspends its first-person narration and silences Frannie in the third person. Finally, in all three works, the protagonist's interpretation of her world and circumstances is tragically at odds with what the respective writers ultimately portray those circumstances to be.[4]

Beyond their similar focus on their protagonists' interiority and difficult life situations, these works also have compelled Campion's explicit identification with their protagonists.[5] The director references those identifications in press materials on each film such that her choice to adapt these texts chronicles an autobiographically inflected trajectory that traces her own development as a filmmaker and an auteur. The contours of this trajectory emerge from interviews in which Campion has discussed what these works and these women (Janet Frame, Isabel Archer, and Frannie Avery) mean to her, from the films' reception indicated in film reviews, and from the films themselves.

An Angel at My Table narrates the childhood and life of a woman who grew up to be a nationally recognized artist in New Zealand. Campion has said in interviews that she initiated the process of adapting Frame's autobiography while still in film school, after having read the first book, *To the Is-land,* of the three-volume *An Autobiography.* She saw it as "an essay on childhood in New Zealand."[6] From the beginning, she envisioned the adaptation as an "intimate" work, suitable for television, not film, and she secured funding for it from the Australian Broadcasting Company (ABC).[7] Throughout the promotional materials for *Angel,* Campion reiterated that she had to be persuaded to release it as a theatrical feature and only did so after its success at a number of film festivals.[8]

Coupled with her insistence that *Angel* was designed for domestic reception (television), Campion also emphasized the local, "domestic" relevance of the source text and author as being from and primarily known in New Zealand. She underscored her identification with Frame in national and familial terms, telling interviewers that the writer's *An Autobiography* illuminated things about her own New Zealand childhood that she had never understood before.[9] She indicated that she had adapted Frame's autobiography (initially as a television miniseries) to introduce international film viewers to Frame and to the powerful emotions Frame's novels had elicited in her.[10] Though she and Frame came from different class backgrounds, Frame's career coincided with the careers of Campion's parents; all three were important figures in the national arts in New Zealand. In addition to her national and familial identification with Frame, Campion also suggestively linked her own autobiography with the narration of Frame's by casting her own mother, Edith Campion, in a small part in the film (a casting choice documented by her sister, Anna Campion, in her film *The Audition*).[11]

Critically very well received, *An Angel at My Table* received numerous awards and earned twice as much as it cost to produce. Reviewers noted the Campion touch, finding it "instantly recognizable" as her work.[12] Thus, Campion's "portrait of the (New Zealand) artist" becoming a "first person" within the visual medium of film operated as an allegory of her own development as a filmmaker. The promotion, reception, and financial success of the film certified that the director of *Sweetie* (1989) was not a one-hit wonder, but an up-and-coming director, a "first person" and nascent New Zealand auteur with a recognizable vision and aesthetic sensibility all her own.

By the time Campion released her second adaptation, *The Portrait of a Lady*, six years later, the success of her previous feature, *The Piano* (1993), had catapulted her to international commercial and critical fame. For *Portrait*, she had industry backing, the largest budget she had had for a film, and renowned actors, especially women, lining up to work with her.[13] Straddling what was then a fashion in both industry and feminist independent cinema—adaptations of nineteenth-century, usually British, novels[14]—she perversely chose to adapt what Rebecca Gordon aptly described as "the notoriously unfilmable" Henry James's *The Portrait of a Lady*.[15] Campion explicitly endorsed this judgment in interviews, speaking not only of the difficulty of adapting James's novel but of the unpopularity of her choice. She told Rachel Abramowitz around the time of the film's release that she did not think that many people would approve of her "following up the much-loved *The Piano* with a rendition of James's masterpiece." Asserting her identity as an art cinema auteur in the face of her newfound popularity and industry funding, she told Abramowitz, "But I did this [film] for myself."[16] Thus Campion represented her choice in making the film as similar to the choice made by the heroine of James's *Portrait*, in that each woman makes a significantly perverse choice in the face of economic bounty.[17]

That choice turned on the force of her signature. If *Angel* made a name for Campion, that name then enabled her to make *Portrait*. Campion put up her name, and its value as a successful and highly publicized industry brand name, as collateral on her risky endeavor. The promotion and reception of *Portrait* turned on her viability as a commercially successful director up to the task of transforming James's difficult masterpiece into a crossover moneymaker like *The Piano*. The film was framed as a test of her ability to live up to James (for the art cinema/literary crowd); to live up to her own name and reputation generated by her previous film; and to live up to her investors' commercial expectations.

In this context, Campion represented herself as knowingly setting out to make a difficult film, an art cinema film, for herself and in accord with her vision, with the industry's money and imprimatur, just as Isabel willfully chooses a difficult marriage, ironically made possible by a fortune given to her because of her impressive independence of mind and spirit. In another 1996 interview, Campion directly compared herself to Isabel, finding in her aesthetic priorities an analogous conflict to that which assails *Portrait*'s heroine. When Michel Ciment observed that "Isabel is close to your other heroines," Campion responded:

She is courageous and looking for truth; it's what pushes her forward. Personally I feel in myself two principle forces that guide me: the excitement of discovering the truth of things and beings, where it's found, and the desire to be loved. They are two companions that are difficult to reconcile. If, for example, one of my films becomes very popular, I begin to ask myself questions about the degree of truth that it contains, and wonder if that truth isn't too easy to accept![18]

Here, Campion aligns herself with Isabel and her bad choices as she eschews popular favor as a successful filmmaker for the excitement of difficult truths and perverse or singular choices, the marks of an auteur.

The promotion of *Portrait* by Campion and others that aligned the director with Isabel Archer also implicitly represented the film as an autobiographical allegory of its director's aesthetic motivations and aspirations at the time of the film's release.[19] Interestingly, the narrative openings of *Angel* and *Portrait* gesture to markedly different developmental moments. *Angel* suggestively infers Campion's development as an artist through Frame's chronicle of becoming one, and opens with images of an infant and then a toddler taking "baby steps"; it ends with a mature writer busy at her craft. By contrast, the narrative proper of *Portrait* opens on a fully grown young woman, Isabel Archer (Nicole Kidman), "affronting her destiny" as she makes a very difficult choice (to refuse Lord Warburton's hand in marriage). It ends with a freeze frame, a "still" portrait of Isabel, trapped within the consequences of her choice. The gravitas of Campion's choice to adapt James, the master and his masterpiece, and the risk of failure is registered throughout the promotional materials and the reception of the film, with one writer going so far as to comment on the "failed reproduction" thematized within the film reflecting the failed reproduction of the adaptation itself.[20] Finally, the difficulty of Campion's aesthetic endeavor registered not only in Isabel's narrative but in the highly stylized and difficult character of the film itself noted throughout the film reviews.[21]

Campion's adaptation of Susanna Moore's *In the Cut* confronts very different issues and difficulties than those posed by *Portrait*. The film represents her first foray into clear-cut genre filmmaking and, as such, responds to and adapts the source genre as well as the specific source text. Moore's novel itself was formulated as a gendered response to genre. After reading many thrillers, she wondered "if a woman [author] could really do it rough and dirty, and not write that kind of tame, Sue Grafton stuff. And when I read *Vox* and *Damage* I thought, People think *this* is sex, *this* is sexy and erotic?"[22] Moore articulated her challenge to the thriller genre along typical postfeminist lines, striving to outdo the feminists on the one hand by

143

avoiding a tame appropriation, and striving to outdo the boys, on the other, by infusing the genre with real eroticism. In the first instance, her aim to "really do it rough" produced a novel whose savage ending Campion herself declared "unfilmable."

In adapting this novel, Campion set out to articulate a woman's point of view, her imagination, and her desire in a genre whose pleasures generally depend upon a woman's vulnerability and death. She sought to wrest this articulation from her *dis*articulation of the source text and genre, working with and against this generic legacy. She compounds the source text's popular fiction legacy with another—the seventies New Hollywood thriller, some of the most prominent examples of which were fashioned as protofeminist texts. Campion herself mentioned inspirations ranging from *Klute* (1971) to *Chinatown* (1974) to *Taxi Driver* (1976); and film reviewers were as inclined to cite these films (as well as *Looking for Mr. Goodbar* [1977]) as they were to mention Moore's novel.

In her promotional interviews for the film, Campion stressed her identification both with the film's subject and its protagonist, Frannie, embedding these identifications within commentary that indicated the innovations and challenges to the thriller she intended her film to enact. With regards to the film's themes, she said, "A lot of thrillers are just about fear, whereas this is about characters and relationships first. It's a serious modern love story with a character dealing with problems I myself wonder about: sex, shame, lust—you know, things that don't behave in an orderly way."[23]

Campion uses her identification with the problems the film engages to stress their generic appeal, an appeal linked to the text's thrilling treatment of sex and love first and fear second. Her vision of the thriller's plot intertwines it with, and thereby underscores the dangers of, conventional romance for women. Speaking to a reporter at *The Village Voice*, Campion indicated that she "identified strongly with this woman [Frannie Avery] who studies violent and sexual slang, yet uses her intellect as a shield."[24] This comment maps the director's identification with Frannie onto precisely those interests that challenged Moore to engage with the thriller—could she, as a woman writer, be "rough and dirty" enough for the genre. Campion's comments locate her engagement with Moore's story and the thriller within a somewhat different question—whether her remake of this story, featuring a killer who romances and disarticulates women, could in turn disarticulate romantic myths and their dangers to women. In this sense, she uses the thriller autobiographically to investigate questions of her own creative labor in relation to art.[25]

Her interviews also marked a different developmental moment than those of her other adaptations. She wondered,

Could I be Frannie? I don't know if I could, really. But as an artist I'm attracted to subjects I feel I have to grow into. I had a reluctance and a willingness—which I guess is Frannie. . . . She has been disappointed by romance and by the hopes she'd had as a younger woman, but her safeness now was crippling, a kind of deadening. I've had big chapters in my life where I've felt like that—you just wake up and you go, "Why?"[26]

The pessimism and world weariness that reviewers ascribed to *In the Cut*'s female characters ("The bloom is off these roses") also pervaded Campion's commentary about the film.[27] But here this pessimism is, once again, attached to choices. The film proper begins with a door opening, and two women, Pauline (Jennifer Jason Leigh) and Frannie, walking out of it and into the narrative. Midway through the film, Pauline, a hopeless romantic, falls victim to her fantasies and the serial killer who exploits them. The film ends with Frannie, who has made different choices, closing that same door behind her as the screen goes to black.

Signature

Stylistically, Campion seals the transfer of ownership that implicitly subtends any film adaptation by beginning each of these films with a sequence that signs its imaginative work as her own. In each case, she teases out something already implicit in the source text or draws from the author's overall work to craft her own signature in the filmic version. In all three, but particularly the latter two films, Campion signs the film as her *reading*, her appropriation of the source text to address her own narrative, thematic, and stylistic concerns. In the latter two films, this appropriation takes the form of a preface or prologue that contains material not present in the source texts, and it is in these sequences that Campion embeds her literal signature ("directed by Jane Campion"). As I have written extensively on these sequences in *An Angel at My Table* and *In the Cut* in another publication, I will focus on the signature sequence in *The Portrait of a Lady*.[28]

Portrait was neither a popular nor a critical success. Though it opened on 2,614 screens, more than three times as many as for the release of *In the Cut* and five times as many as for the release of *The Piano*, the film lost close to $12 million, much more than either of Campion's other two features that lost money at the box office, *Holy Smoke* ($1.5 million) and *In the Cut* ($3.5 million).[29] Nevertheless, the film presents a rigorous and courageous experiment in film adaptation, while it also extends Campion's career-long investigation into the difficult truths of violence, sexuality, and the perverse conundrums of romantic love, especially for women. Reviewers noted the darker visual and thematic tones of *Portrait* compared to its predecessor, and many used some variant of the word "masochism" to describe its protagonist or its ethos. Whereas the brutality in James inheres in the ironic structure, narration, and inexorable repetitions of his novel, in Campion, it emerges from her wielding of cinematic equivalents to these drawn from pictorial values of portraiture, from her own repertoire of visual idioms, and from her highly self-conscious uses of cinematography. She attempts, through the plastics of the cinematic image, to apprehend the philosophical and stylistic elements of James. But to do so, she must fill in his aporias, his sense of what is unspeakable, with the bodies of her actors. If Campion's cinema makes Isabel a masochist, it does so by concretizing the relationship between idealism and suffering at the heart of James's novel.

Campion's *The Portrait of a Lady* (1996) does not open, as James's novel does, on the lawn of Gardencourt at tea time or on any other scene from its narrative. Rather, the director emulates the structure of James's 1908 New York edition of the novel, the edition used as the basis for the screenplay, and opens with a preface. Notably separating sound and image, Campion's preface begins with a black screen, on which we see the opening credits. In voiceover, we hear contemporary women from Australia and New Zealand discussing erotic attraction, love, and coupling, including the exquisite moment before being kissed, the first erotic touch, an addiction to being entwined with another, practices of mystery to entice the beloved, romantic fate, and the lover as "the most loyal mirror" who reflects the speaker's own love back to her. When the voices finish, we see black-and-white visuals, which shift to color and back again; they depict a diverse group of fifteen or so young women in the woods—black, white, Maori, South Asian, mixed race—as the film's musical motif plays and the opening credits continue to fade in and out. Initially the women, in their teens to early twenties, form a circle, lying on the ground with the camera overhead, making an empty frame in which the text "A Film by Jane Campion" appears. The camera then renders portraits of them, individually or in small groups, poised, posed, looking directly into the camera, smiling, dancing, pensive, enigmatic. The sequence ends as the camera pans down a woman's extended arm, her left palm open to us, her middle finger bearing the inscription "The Portrait of a Lady." Cut to the first shot of the narrative, a close-up of Nicole Kidman's blue eyes.

This nonfiction preface carefully details, through voiceover and image, the logic of Campion's adaptation of James's text and her relation to the narrative that follows. In so doing, the filmmaker takes up several of the points stressed by James in his 1908 preface to *Portrait* concerning the worth of a subject for fiction.[30] For him, its value derives from an affirmative answer to the question "Is it valid . . . is it genuine . . . the result of some direct impression or perception of life?"[31] In Campion's cinematic preface, she addresses the problem of an artist's genuine relation to a creative text adapted from that of another author: how, in other words, to evoke in her film the "moral" sense of the art work articulated in this passage from James:

There is, I think, no more nutritive or suggestive truth in this connexion than that of the perfect dependence of the "moral" sense of a work of art on the amount of felt life concerned in producing it. The question comes back thus, obviously, to the kind and the degree of the artist's prime sensibility, which is the soil out of which his subject springs. That element is but another name for the more or less close connexion of the subject with some mark made on the intelligence, with some sincere experience.[32]

Through the voiceover and the visuals of young women in the woods, Campion attempts to signify "the kind and the degree" of her sensibilities and the "felt life" from which her reading, her vision of *Portrait* emerges. That felt life includes multiple levels and types of experience, from her own historical existence and knowledge of femininity, courtship, and sexuality to her experience as a reader of James and her aesthetic sensibilities and concerns as a filmmaker.

Campion's preface can be seen, in the first instance, as a kind of poetic ethnography that captures the accents, concerns, and appearance of her own ethnotype. The women we hear and see are all marked by geography, race, and historical moment. The accents of the women speaking in voiceover signal that they, like Campion, are from Australia or New Zealand.[33] Unlike the character James identifies in his preface as instigating his fiction and shaping his access to it, that of "a particular engaging young woman," Campion signals here that her fiction originates with a highly diverse group of contemporary antipodean women (see the frontispiece to this chapter). Visually, these young women literally form the frame, or as James would say, the "aperture," of Campion's fiction, her opening onto "the human scene" initially depicted by him. He observes:

The house of fiction has in short not one window, but a million . . . every one of which has been pierced . . . by the need of the individual vision and by the pressure of the individual will. These apertures, of dissimilar shape and size, hang so, all together, over the human scene . . . they have this mark of their own that at each of them stands a figure with a pair of eyes, or at least with a field-glass, which forms, again and again, for observation, a unique instrument, insuring to the person making use of it an impression distinct from every other.[34]

The artist's figure, vehicle for observation, stands at an aperture, possessed of "a pair of eyes" or a "field-glass," and forms a unique instrument. Of the artist's consciousness, the watcher at the window, James remarks: "Tell me what the artist is, and I will tell you of what he has *been* conscious."[35] Campion's preface seems to respond quite directly to this passage as it articulates clearly of what *she* has been conscious, visualizing it, articulating it in the medium of cinema.

Campion's use of soft black-and-white cinematography to render the idyll in the woods, evocative of a pastoral tableau, cultivates a visual nostalgia that both infuses the scene and contrasts with the young women's contemporary clothing, movements, and portable Sony Walkmans. This confused temporality visually apprehends the character and process of Campion's adaptation. While her adaptation of *An Angel at My Table* sought to introduce viewers to Janet Frame and to the affect Frame had provoked in her, Henry James needs no introduction. Campion's preface instead orients the film that follows as her *reading* of the novel, her hand pointing to what she "loves" in it, what she takes from it, what she adds. The voices that open the film apprehend all of these elements. They engage a number of topics: kissing, addiction, eroticism, romantic fate, the electricity of touch, and the narcissism of desire. All of these topics are things left pointedly unsaid in James, elements that nevertheless have force in his novel.[36] These subjects constitute not only what Campion loves in James, however unspoken, but also those about which she has had much to say throughout her previous films. In her own rendering of a "certain young woman affronting her destiny," Campion's sensibility brings the cinema as a medium—as well as the body, female bodies, youth, and desire—to bear on the tale.

Though many critics of this film have seen its opening as a sentimental paean to a "feel-good New Agey feminine community," such a reading does not account for its anachronistic visual representation of contemporary young women, one that anticipates Campion's infusion of *Portrait* with contemporary representations of sexuality.[37] What this anticipation signifies can be gleaned from a close listen to the voices that open the film. Almost without exception, these women articulate their relation to sexuality and sexual expression in a passive sense; they are overpowered by it, addicted to it, whether "it is positive, which it was at the beginning, or negative." The last voice we hear, the one that introduces the first visuals in the film, says: "It

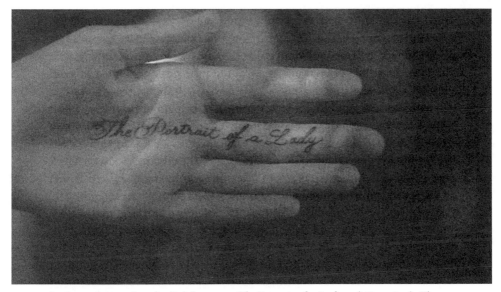

An image suggesting the link between *The Portrait of a Lady* and Campion's *The Piano.*

means finding a mirror, the clearest mirror, the most loyal mirror, so when I love that person I know that they are going to shine that love back to me." A more apt description of Isabel's narcissistically deluded love for Osmond could hardly be found.[38] Campion is not, I hasten to add, judgmental of these voices and what they have to say. Rather, she uses them to make the point that erotic desire, by its very nature, will always in some way confound choice and freedom. If, as Rebecca Gordon argues, "at the heart of James's novel there resonates a question about the very definition of the term 'independence' for a woman," then Campion reframes that question, both for Isabel Archer and for her contemporary counterparts, as one that must take account of sexuality.[39] Her highly ironic preface, therefore, underscores the connection between Isabel Archer and the young women who face her camera, as the screenplay notes, "full of theories" and "independent, impatient, unacquainted with pain."[40]

Campion's preface ends by putting James's title on it, specifically on her extradiegetic finger, that finger not only guiding us to the fiction that follows but also reminding us of her previous film, *The Piano.* It too opens with fingers, and, in its most traumatic moment, its protagonist, Ada, loses one of hers. As *The Piano* catapulted Campion to international fame, her reference to it here implicitly affirms her auteurist status, while also making a knowing gesture to her fans, who had been anxiously awaiting her follow-up to the earlier film. Campion thereby inscribes James's title on a body, on her body, on the body of her work, as the finger is the most recognizable element of her oeuvre. The image suggests we read the film we are about to see not only in relation to James's novel but also in relation to *The Piano*. In that respect, the finger pointedly connects Campion's imagination with James's. In *The Portrait of a Lady*, Isabel Archer establishes her singularity when she declines the economic security and social distinction inherent in the highly attractive marriage proposal of Lord Warburton. To register both Isabel's own sense of the value of what she is refusing and the force of her ideal of independence, the narrator comments that Isabel would have given "her little finger" to have been able to override that refusal, that ideal. Narratively and thematically, Ada and Isabel therefore mirror one another, albeit inversely, in their fingers and acts of refusal: if Ada gave up her literal finger rather than to sacrifice her desire, Isabel would have given her figurative finger in order to feel it.[41]

In inscribing its title on a finger, the film also astutely represents the relation of its adapted text to its forbear. Adapting the literary portrait of Isabel to cinema requires an engagement precisely in the difference between literal fingers and figures (fingers) of speech. The desiring body, so absent in James, so present, tactile, and visceral in Campion, marks the point at which the cultural/historical and formal differences (film and literature) between their *Portrait*s converge. If Campion's film registers the differences between her and James's felt experience and cultural moments through the use of historical anachronisms and the spectacle of Isabel's desiring body, it simultaneously and self-consciously highlights the different media and formal structures within which these social/cultural differences are expressed. Campion's preface, the "travel film" within the narrative, and the liberties she takes with representations of sexuality were disliked by many critics, some outraged at her "disloyalty" to James.[42] Indeed, these experiments clearly defied the conventions of commercially successful film adaptations of nineteenth-century novels, which typically exclude any nonfiction prefatory material and stress "authenticity" in period detail. Yet Campion, in including a preface that introduces her relationship to her subject, to James, and to their respective moments and media, is perhaps more faithful to her literary source and James's philosophical bent than to the *conventions* of her own medium and industry.

The preface and the subsequent fiction make use of what Vivian Sobchack elegantly calls "the carnal foundations of cinematic intelligibility" to animate and embody the same issues that James considers in his 1908 text.[43] In other words, Campion explores the cinema's capacity to think, to theorize, to articulate its own process with the means of intelligibility available to it.

For James, his process involved a key determination in the "architecture" of his novel, a "deep difficulty braved" in its construction, that he should "place the centre of the subject in the young woman's own consciousness."[44] In adapting James's elaborate and difficult verbal architecture to the medium of cinema, Campion took on her own "deep difficulty braved" and confronted it by making use of the formal and pictorial values of portraiture, setting them in tension with the cinema's capacity to represent movement. From within this formally generated tension, she attempts to depict the tragedy of Isabel Archer in specifically cinematic as well as narrative terms. Even as the plot propels the character to her genteel doom, its visuals depict her vitality, her sensuality, her movements increasingly contained, constricted, slowed down, and finally arrested, the film's final image transforming the flesh and idealism of its heroine into a still, a frozen portrait of a lady.

Autobiography

The name "Jane Campion" conjures a wealth of associations generated by the films released under that signature, the promotional materials used to market them, the reviewers, spectators, and academic critics (myself included) who celebrate, decry, or analyze them, and the woman who has signed them. Throughout her career, Campion has used interviews to advertise the logic of her adaptation projects in ways reflected in film reviews and theorized in the films themselves, particularly in their highly self-conscious beginnings and endings. These films mark Campion's appropriation of their source texts in pointed mobilizations of her signature within the sequences that accomplish this theorization. This self-conscious aesthetic theorizing, coupled with Campion's overtly articulated identification with these film's protagonists, produces a distinct autobiographical inflection that progresses through these adaptations. If "a body of work linked by an authorial signature encourages viewers to read each film as a chapter of an oeuvre," Campion's adaptations form an arc somewhat distinct from the rest of her oeuvre.[45] From *An Angel at My Table* to *The Portrait of a Lady* and *In the Cut,* the extratextual and textual framing of these adaptations have functioned as a developmental portrait of Campion as a woman and an artist, carefully imagining the implications of gender, craft, and aesthetic engagement at different moments in her career.

Notes

1. This autobiographical impulse is evident in the films Campion has scripted as well.

2. In my book *Jane Campion* (Urbana: University of Illinois Press, 2007), I discuss the biographical details Frannie Avery shares with Isabel Archer—*In the Cut* is in some way a thriller homage to James's *Portrait*. See pp. 126–27.

3. Elizabeth Alley, "Janet Frame/Interviewed by Elizabeth Alley," in *In the Same Room: Conversations with New Zealand Writers,* ed. Elizabeth Alley and Mark Williams (Auckland: Auckland University Press, 1992), 10.

4. These source texts also pose similar challenges to adaptation—how to convey both a sense of the protagonists' interior lives and the disjuncture between their perceptions and their circumstances cinematically. Campion's interest and skill in mobilizing and blurring the lines between subjective and objective cinematic narration—evident from her short student films on—perhaps inclined her to each of these projects. See McHugh, *Jane Campion,* 18–47. In fact, the blurring between objective and subjective points of view becomes more noticeable across these three films, finding its most insistent realization in *In the Cut.*

5. Kaja Silverman's article "The Female Authorial Voice," in *Film and Authorship,* ed. Virginia Wright Wexman (New Brunswick, NJ: Rutgers University Press, 2003), suggests that the female authorial voice can be discerned, particularly in industry films, through the director's identification with a fictional character that "stands in" for him or her and thereby mobilizes "authorial subjectivity" within the film text itself. In the case of Campion's films, the director consciously articulates this relationship as part of the promotional framing of these works.

6. Michel Ciment, "The Red Wigs of Autobiography: Interview with Jane Campion," in *Jane Campion: Interviews,* ed. Virginia Wright Wexman (Jackson: University Press of Mississippi, 1999), 62–63.

7. Carrie Rickey, "A Director Strikes an Intimate Chord," in Wexman, *Jane Campion,* 52.

8. The film won the Silver Lion and the Grand Jury Prize at the Venice Film Festival, Most Popular Film at the Sydney Film Festival, Best Foreign Film from Australian Film Critics Circle, as well as numerous acting, directing, and screenplay awards. See Wexman, *Jane Campion,* xxv–xxvi. The film cost $2,710,000 to make and grossed $4,784,670. See Kagan World Media, "Film Review and Cost Estimate Report" (FRCE), Baseline, http://www.hollywood.com, *The Piano* (1993); *The Portrait of a Lady* (1996); *In the Cut* (2003).

9. Frame entered Campion's imagination when she was thirteen and read Frame's first novel, *Owls Do Cry.* Upon reading it, Campion said she realized that some ideas could not be expressed through narrative; they needed more poetic expression. Hearing that Frame had spent time in mental hospitals, young Campion wondered about her, about where she had been institutionalized. "She grew to have a mythic proportion to me, her life seemed to sum up the tragic/sad artist. When her autobiographies came out, I was incredibly eager to find out what the story was and I was shocked to find out how normal she was." Lynden Barber, "Angel with an Eccentric Eye," in Wexman, *Jane Campion,* 60.

10. Ciment, "Red Wigs of Autobiography," 67.

11. See Harriet Margolis's fascinating essay on *The Audition* in this volume, chapter 3.

12. Barber, "Angel with an Eccentric Eye," 59. Other reviewers who noted Campion's distinctive touch in the film include Jay Carr, "Campion Focuses on Women's Hidden Voices," *The Boston Globe,* 3 February 1999, D4; Vincent Canby, "Three Novels Are Adapted for *Angel at My Table,*" *The New York Times,* 21 May 1991, C15; Pam Cook, "An Angel at My Table," *Monthly Film Bulletin* 57 (1990): 314–15; Elizabeth Drucker, "An Angel at My Table," *American Film: A Journal of the Film and Television Arts* 16, no. 7 (1991): 52–53; Stanley Kauffmann, "A Woman's Life," *The New Republic* 204, no. 22 (1991): 28–29; Peter Rainer, "*Angel* Has Jane Campion's Stamp on It," *Los Angeles Times,* 14 June 1991, 15; and Terrence Rafferty, "Outlaw Princesses," *The New Yorker,* 3 June 1991, 86–88.

13. Her total budget for this film, including production and advertising costs, was $36,791,000, $13 million more than her second most expensive film, *In the Cut,* and three times the budget of the third, *The Piano.* See Kagan World Media, "Film Review and Cost Estimate Report" (FRCE), http://www.hollywood.com.

14. Industry examples include *A Room with a View* (1985), *Howard's End* (1992), *Emma* (1996), *and Sense and Sensibility* (1995). Feminist independent titles are Sally Potter's *Orlando* (1993) and Patricia Rozema's *Mansfield Park* (1999). Amy Heckerling's witty adaptation of Austen's *Emma, Clueless* (1995), is an example of that rare anomaly, a feminist industry film.

15. Rebecca Gordon, "Portraits Perversely Framed: Jane Campion and Henry James," *Film Quarterly* 56, no. 2 (2003): 14.

16. Rachel Abramowitz, "Jane Campion," in Wexman, *Jane Campion,* 186.

17. Campion said explicitly that she "felt a personal connection to" Isabel Archer. See Douglas Rowe, "Jane Campion Hides Her Passion," *Associated Press,* 17 January 1997.

18. Hunter Cordaiy, "Jane Campion Interviewed," in Wexman, *Jane Campion,* 79.

19. E.g., see Kathleen Murphy, "Jane Campion's Shining Portrait of a Director," *Film Comment* 32, no. 6 (1996): 28–32.

20. See Dale Bauer, "Jane Campion's Symbolic *Portrait,*" *The Henry James Review* 18, no. 2 (1997): 194–97.

21. The following reviewers have all noted the film's difficulty: Murphy, "Jane Campion's Shining Portrait," 28–32; Geoff Andrew, "The Portrait of a Lady," *Time Out,* January 1996; Brian MacFarlane, "The Portrait of a Lady," *Cinema Papers,* April 1997, 35–37; and Patricia Dobson, "Portrait of a Lady," *Screen International* 1075 (13 September 1996), 25.

22. Hal Espen, "Femme Fatale," *The New Yorker,* 21 August 1995, 124–26.

23. Josh Rottenberg, "In the Cut," *Premiere* online, http://www.premiere.com/previews/846/in-the-cut.html (accessed March 2007).

24. Joy Press, "Making the Cut," *Village Voice,* 22–28 October 2003, 52.

25. In *Jane Campion,* I discuss how the opening of *In the Cut* contains pointed references to all of Campion's earlier work, both her feature and her student films; the film thereby functions as a looking back, a review of her visual and thematic priorities and questions, that are then worked out through the different fates of her two protagonists, Frannie and Pauline (Jennifer Jason Leigh). See pages 123–40.

26. Press, "Making the Cut," 52.

27. Graham Fuller, "Sex and Self-Danger," *Sight and Sound* 13, no. 11 (2003): 18.

28. See the sections on these two films in McHugh, *Jane Campion.*

29. Kagan World Media, "Film Review and Cost Estimate Report" (FRCE), http://www.hollywood.com.

30. See Gordon's discussion of Campion and screenwriter Laura Jones's references to James's novel, prefaces, and literary criticism in this film's promotional materials in Gordon, "Portraits Perversely Framed," 15.

31. Henry James, *The Portrait of a Lady,* ed. Robert D. Bamberg, Norton Critical Edition (2nd ed.) (New York: Norton, 1995), 6.

32. Ibid.

33. Alan Nadel, "The Search for Cinematic Identity and a Good Man: Jane Campion's Appropriation of James' *Portrait," The Henry James Review* 18, no. 2 (1997): 181; and Priscilla L. Walton, "Jane and James Go to the Movies: Post Colonial Portraits of a Lady," *The Henry James Review* 18, no. 2 (1997): 186.

34. James, *Portrait of a Lady,* 7.

35. Ibid.

36. Millicent Bell, "Isabel Archer and the Affronting of Plot," in ibid., 748–83.

37. Dana Polan, *Jane Campion* (London: British Film Institute, 2001), 128.

38. Kathleen Murphy discusses Isabel's narcissistic search for a "loyal mirror" in "Jane Campion's Shining Portrait," 29.

39. Gordon, "Portraits Perversely Framed," 17.

40. Laura Jones, *The Portrait of a Lady: Screenplay Based on the Novel by Henry James* (New York: Penguin Books, 1996), 1.

41. Virginia Wright Wexman discusses the similarities between Ada and Isabel in "The Portrait of a Body," *The Henry James Review* 18, no. 2 (1997): 184. She stresses Campion's overall emphasis on physicality in her films.

42. Robert Sklar, "A Novel Approach to Movie Making: Reinventing *The Portrait of a Lady," The Chronicle of Higher Education* 43, no. 23 (1997): B7.

43. Vivian Sobchack, *Carnal Thoughts: Embodiment and Moving Image Culture* (Berkeley: University of California Press, 2004), 59.

44. James, *Portrait of a Lady,* 10–11.

45. David Bordwell, "The Art Cinema as a Mode of Film Practice," in Wexman, *Film and Authorship,* 45.

Part III
Jane Campion's "Geographies"

Isabel, a young American woman in the Old World. Courtesy of the Academy of Motion Picture Arts and Sciences.

Jane Campion and the International Theme

From *The Portrait of a Lady* to *An Angel at My Table*

The defining character of Jane Campion's films can be described in two con-trasting ways. One can view the series of movies from *Sweetie* to *In the Cut* as reflecting the subject's predicament in mirrors of varying dimensions. In *Holy Smoke,* this reflection provides an image of the heroine's interior psychic state as well as an image of her isolation in open space, while in *In the Cut,* the heroine is shown undergoing a kind of sexual confinement. Alternatively, one can view the same series of films as embodying a progressive movement toward a more universal form of filmmaking. The advantage of invoking such a distinction is that it makes it possible to identify several different tendencies in Campion's practices as a filmmaker. On one hand, she seeks to reveal the heroine's sense of her world from a subjective perspective; on the other, she attempts to objectify that world. Because of these contradictory impulses, one encounters a certain heterogeneity in these movies that makes it difficult for the spectator to link them interpretively into a continuous, coherent sequence.

Irrespective of which frame of reference is chosen to account for Campi-on's evolution as a filmmaker, nobody can ignore the presence of a reflexive movement that constitutes the predominant characteristic of each movie, as well as of the series of movies as a whole. Awareness of this principle of reflexivity removes the need for any spectator to be disconcerted by what might appear to be contradictions in Campion's movies. For example, the representation of Maori in *The Piano* as clownish and childlike should not be viewed as incompatible with a denunciation of the colonial situation. Simi-larly, even though their themes are quite different, there is no clearly estab-lished opposition between the national point of view presented in *An Angel at My Table* and the explicitly international argument of *Holy Smoke.* The reflexive movement that informs Campion's movies enables her to construct her characters and represent actions and places in a way that allows them to complement one another. In this way, she makes characters, actions, and places correspond to one another at the same time as they show contrasts.

While there are many manifestations of this reflexive movement that could be discussed, for the purposes of this essay I propose to focus upon just one of them: the international theme. Four reasons justify this choice. First, the international theme is self-evidently present in many of the movies, and is also explicit in the literary source of *The Portrait of a Lady.* Second, it accounts for the diversity to be found in Campion's films, while at the same time delineating a constant structure that makes it possible for local and universal representations to coexist within a common frame of reference: simply to point to a contrast between national (New Zealand) and international elements does not get one very far. Third, it justifies a paradoxical interpretation of the series of movies as simultaneously embodying a movement in two contradictory directions—progressive and regressive. Fourth, it allows one to describe the reflexive stand as a means of evaluating the subject's condition from both a present-day perspective and also a historical point of view. These four justifications for focusing on the international theme are equally applicable to the three movies that gained Campion worldwide fame—*An Angel at My Table, The Piano,* and *The Portrait of a Lady.*

The International Theme from Henry James to Jane Campion

The international theme that has been identified by scholars studying American literature—that is, the complex relationships between naive Americans and cosmopolitan Europeans—is very obviously present in these three films by Campion.[1] In literary studies, the notion of an international theme was first suggested with reference to the novels of Henry James. Inevitably, it can also be found in Campion's *The Portrait of a Lady,* since the movie adapts James's novel. *An Angel at My Table* similarly offers a substantial depiction of Janet Frame's stay in London and shorter representations of her time in Paris and Ibiza. *The Piano,* too, narrates the story of a woman who moves from Scotland to New Zealand. These movements from the United States to Europe, from New Zealand to Europe, and from Europe to New Zealand indicate the presence of a distinct international theme in Campion's works—one that invests them with an internal coherence.

In James's novels, the international theme provides the basis for cultural comparisons and definitions of historical discontinuities (the old and the new), as well as a means of setting up oppositions and mutual transpositions between opposites, to depict the effect of cultural differences and historical discontinuities upon the characters. James's international characters transfer cultural identities from one place to another, translating one cultural identity into another with which it is contrasted. Consequently, their actions display the effects of these "translations," which also promote a personal development that arises as a response to the oppositions they bring into being. On one hand, the international character synthesizes cultural data and differences in a singular way that constitutes his or her specific story. On the other hand, whatever cultural data and places are presented and specific stories and arguments narrated, the international character is always a transfer character, the one who exhibits cultural differences. This dual function makes it possible for the international character to be either a kind of blank (one needs only to recall the lead character in *The Wings of the Dove* to underline this point) or else wholly defined by their encounter with cultural difference. *The Portrait of a Lady* (that is, the novel) offers clear examples of both kinds of interplay between cultures: two American characters, Osmond and Madame Merle, end up being identified with a kind of European character that defines them as opposite to an American one, while Isabel Archer experiences both kinds of identities, ultimately appearing to be their sum.

I am invoking James's international theme here to suggest that Campion adhered to its structure and function in her adaptation of *The Portrait of a Lady* and also that the same structure and function can be found in *An Angel at My Table* and *The Piano*. I would go further to suggest that awareness of the interplay generated by cultural contrasts and transfers is an important determinant of Campion's vision and that not only are the works she selects for adaptation chosen because they revolve around this interplay but also her original screenplays are developed to embody it. These observations allow one to read the three movies, *An Angel at My Table, The Piano,* and *The Portrait of a Lady,* in a reverse chronological order.

Since the transfer character is a woman character, the cultural contrasts and transfers are inevitably associated with a feminine perspective. While this feminine perspective exists in its own right, it is also supported and enriched by the international theme. The feminine gaze serves not only to subject the male—the other—to scrutiny but also to highlight the contrasts and distinctions brought to light by the international theme. Moreover, the range and diversity of the cultural references in the movies prevent the observation of contrasts and differences from being restricted to a feminine perspective. This point can be formulated more specifically: with James, the feminine perspective and the human perspective are to be equated. This equation does not render the feminine perspective indeterminate—Isabel Archer remains an American woman, in the same way that the female lead characters of *An Angel at My Table* and *The Piano* also retain their identities. Rather, it allows images to be conveyed from a feminine point of view of subjects who are able to experience personal growth and model relationships to their communities that do not entail a conflict with their selves. By associating the feminine gaze and the international theme, Campion's movies are able to undertake an evaluation of the cultural and ethical conditions of anybody's life. The association allows historical points of view to be opened up so that evocations of the past can serve as lessons for the present as far as the status of women is concerned, even though the distance between past and present is stressed. The integration of the feminine perspective and the international theme also gives added justification for descriptions of places attached to the international theme, by inviting the reader to view them as places that exemplify the double bind in which the woman character finds herself: on one hand, she can attain fulfillment, or completion, in these places; on the other hand, she recognizes the gap between what she aspires to and the reality she encounters in these places.

The International Theme versus Contract: Jane Campion's Films and Stories of Completion

As I have suggested, the international theme depends upon ideas of transfer and translation that allow for the opposing identities to remain discrete, even though they are linked and integrated. The international theme, conceptualized in this way, should be contrasted with another theme that Campion's three films exemplify: the contract.[2] In *The Portrait of a Lady*, this theme is evident in the contract that allows Isabel Archer to inherit a part of Daniel Touchett's money; in *The Piano*, it resides in the marriage contract that binds a mute woman to a man she does not know; and in *An Angel at My Table*, it occurs in the contract that binds Janet to her training school for teachers. Each of these contracts is a means of binding opposites together, or entails such a binding: Isabel and Osmond, Ada and her husband, Janet and the New Zealand state or society. Each of these contracts also presupposes that the individuals or entities who are parties to it are unchanged and not mutually translatable. Moreover, each contract involves a degree of ignorance on the woman's part: Isabel does not know about the contract; Ada does not know her husband; Janet does not know the future that will ensue for her as a result of her teacher training. These contracts are blind contracts. This blindness is the main cause for the women characters' misfortune, and, furthermore, it provides a specific example of patriarchy: each contract may arise from a good intention—to make a woman free, to allow a widow to start a new life, to make a young woman able to study beyond secondary school—but it also undermines the very self-determination and self-image of the subject because it does not allow for any negotiation between differences or for any mutual translation of these differences.

In contrast, the international theme does allow for negotiation and translation. Isabel Archer is finally free to reject Osmond, to return to Garden Court, to be at Ralph's deathbed, and not to enter Daniel Touchett's mansion. She can do so because she has experienced and synthesized a variety of different cultural and personal conditions. In *The Piano,* Ada leaves her husband after three contracts have been breached—the one concerning her marriage, the one about the piano, the one about the land—after she has crossed cultural borders. In London, Janet frees herself from her own past, is able to confront what she does not know (British culture), and finds she can live on her own once she devotes herself exclusively to her vocation. In highlighting the notions of negotiation and translation, I wish to emphasize the way in which a cultural interchange, which includes sexual experience, makes the character able to recognize the three causes that motivate her actions and reactions: one attached to her birth and past life, one attached to the foreign place, and one that results from her recognition of these two other attachments.

In a way that is deeply paradoxical, both negotiation and translation are practiced by characters who are powerless: Isabel, at first, does not know about the money she has inherited, nor what Osmond's behavior will turn out to be; Ada is mute; Janet, following her diagnosis, is trapped within the confines of assumptions about schizophrenia. To be powerless does not imply blindness or any inability to understand, nor does it deprive the character concerned of the potential for signification. It is appropriate at this point to invoke a formulation borrowed from Gilles Deleuze: Isabel, Ada, and Janet are characters rich with an *exprimé* (an "expressed") that waits for an "expression."[3] Or, put in the critical discourse of the sixties, each of them is a signified that needs to receive a signifier.[4] Jane Campion exposes this duality in a thematic way: Isabel Archer is finally forbidden to express herself by Osmond; Ada is mute; Janet writes but is identified as schizophrenic. This duality is also revealed through recurrent and obsessive close-up shots of the women's faces—whose expressions convey the image of an *exprimé* waiting for an "expression." The processes of negotiation and translation that they undergo finally endow each of the characters with an expression that is her own, being attuned with their identities and others' identities so that both kinds of identity become their "expressions." At the end of the movie, Isabel can choose not to enter Garden Court and to face Goodwood; Ada can play the piano again and live with George Baines; Janet can return home and be a New Zealand writer who is recognized abroad.

The international theme reverses the terms of the original contract: the character is free to act because an "expression" has met with an *exprimé,* and because a knowledge of various cultural conditions and identities has become available that does not contradict the identities that the women characters have acquired. There is no contradiction because the knowledge that has been obtained, being a consequence of the transfer and "translation," applies to a range of conditions and identities. The translation is shown in various ways: Isabel Archer deciphers Osmond according to her own expectations; Ada does the same with her husband and George Baines; Janet reads and experiences the other in a similar fashion. Such acts of translation show that both the subject and the other have to be mutually completed. Ada's husband provides the most remarkable example of this translation process: he is able to listen to, understand, and reconstruct the words that she cannot pronounce.

Translation is a form of interrelation that contradicts two other kinds of explicit interrelation: one is predation; the other is exchange. Predation— when one character seeks to exploit another—is exemplified by the husband's behavior in *The Piano* and by Bernard, the "Americano," in *An Angel at My Table.* It makes the other prey. It may be preceded by a kind of exchange— what is transferred from one person to another and entails a giving back—or by a transmission of goods or money, which makes the receiver dependent upon the donor. By contrast, translation involves a kind of sharing: it makes what is translated the shared belonging of both the translator and the one who owns or represents what is translated. To illustrate the difference between translation and predation, one might recall the final understanding of Ada voiced by her husband, Alisdair Stewart: "Understand me. I am here for her. . . . I love her. But what is the use? She doesn't care for me." In contradistinction, we can define Isabel Archer as a character who is able to belong to America, England, and Italy and to make these places her own. She is a sharing figure, who contrasts not only with Osmond, the predator, but also with Daniel Touchett, the donor, and with Ralph Touchett, who suggests the legacy—both of whom, father and son, set up a kind of dependence. We should view Ada as a character who is able to join her own identity and the other's identity and who seizes the initiative to drop the contract made about the piano and her own body and to oppose her husband's attempt to make the marriage contract an opportunity for predation. We can characterize Janet Frame in the same way—her literary vocation allows her to "express" New Zealand and England and to offer mutually illuminating perspectives upon New Zealand and England—after she has emerged from her earlier dependency on the normative experiences and images she acquired in her native country. It is apparent that mere exchange does not succeed in Campion's universe, because the reciprocity it implies is compulsory. That is the way Goodwood and the young Rosier understand any love relationship. Isabel Archer rejects both of them because she refuses to recognize any compulsory reciprocity. In contrast to the assumptions underlying exchange, translation allows for a recognition on the part of the subject that without the presence of the other—that is, of his or her identity and his or her point of view—the subject would remain incomplete and that, conversely, without the presence of the subject's identity and point of view, the other would remain incomplete. Some characters experience this completion: Isabel Archer and Ralph Touchett; Ada; Janet Frame.

At the start of this essay, I stressed that the international theme and the feminine perspective could not be disassociated. This remark is confirmed by the stories and arguments of the three movies: the lead woman character is the one who crosses borders. More precisely, in *An Angel at My Table* and *The Piano,* the female character is the only one who does so, which makes her border-crossing exemplary.[5] In *The Portrait of a Lady,* a number of characters are displaced—which requires us to delve deeper into the relationship of the international theme with the feminine perspective. Defined as a translation that opposes predation, exchange, and transmission, the international theme allows for a feminine correction of them. The predators, the characters who are ready to exchange and to practice transmission, are male. They do recognize their counterpart—the female character—and that they would be incomplete without her. However, this recognition is limited. First, it reflects an acknowledgment that without the woman's body and her perspective on the male character, he would be incomplete. Second, it carries with it an implicit refusal to allow the woman a comparable right to be completed by the other—the male. The male character wishes the completion for himself only. This male wish is demonstrated in many ways. Janet stops her relationship with Bernard because he is afraid to have a child with her—that is, afraid to have his own identity shared by Janet through a child. In *The Portrait of a Lady,* Osmond's daughter is accorded the right to marry but only to the extent that this right conforms to her father's will. She is denied the reciprocity of completion; consequently, she is the perfect mirror of Isabel's misfortune. This function of the daughter character in *The Portrait of a Lady* finds both a parallel and a contrast in the function of Ada's daughter in *The Piano:* Ada's daughter witnesses, on the one hand, the denial of completion reciprocity and, on the other hand, its acceptance and practice. By joining the international theme and the feminine perspective, and by denying any contract and the rules it imposes, Campion aims at redefining the collective ethos found in James. In her view, this ethos should be defined by a rejection of any opposition between identities and by a refusal to make any kind of hybrid the symbol of completion. It is worth reiterating that each lead woman character retains her own cultural identity. Campion's final suggestion, therefore, should be read as follows: whatever influence different cultures appear to exert on our identity, we nevertheless share the same human inner world—the one that expects mutual completion. Cultural and sexual differences are unchangeable, and trigger this expectation. The international theme supports Campion's argument about completion and broadens its relevance: it demonstrates that completion should bind not only bodies but also cultures.

The seduction scenes in Campion's films confirm this interpretation. Female characters strongly contrast with male characters by allowing reciprocity in completion. The seduction scene in *The Portrait of a Lady* involving Isabel and Osmond proceeds as if a symbolic circle is being drawn, and develops in the way that a merry-go-round turns upon itself. The circle is a symbolic figure of completion. Because this figure is partly a fantasy—as any seduction experience is a fantasy—the completion has to be practiced and proved; the proof will not be offered. In *An Angel at My Table*, Bernard and Janet never say they fall in love. They react to their mutual attraction that makes the seduction possible. But the extent to which there is any reciprocity of completion is left questioned. In *The Piano*, the mutual seduction of Ada and George Baines is a seduction in progress, because in order for it to be accomplished, the contract involving the piano needs to be dropped. It is the dropping of the contract that opens up the path to completion reciprocity.

Unquestionably, all these seduction scenes are shown from the feminine perspective. In two cases—*The Portrait of a Lady* and *An Angel at My Table*—the woman character recognizes the male refusal of completion reciprocity. In one case—*The Piano*—she finally sees that this reciprocity is possible. The extent to which the woman character can or cannot be lucid regarding this matter is not dependent upon the kind of story Campion narrates. To the contrary, the female character is wholly identified with an expectation of mutual completion, is the measure of any male completion expectation, and finally becomes aware of the imperfection of the male in terms of his unwillingness or inability to provide it. At the same time, because of her international situation, her own completion expectation comes to be read as applying to cultural identities as well. *The Portrait of a Lady* exemplifies this observation by offering a scene that has no counterpart in James's novel and that has often been commented upon: Isabel's erotic dream of her three suitors, just after she has sent Goodwood away. This dream provides a contrast with the previous scenes related to these suitors and presents a contradictory image of them. It does not express any kind of love for these suitors on Isabel's part. Rather, it shows that Isabel is waiting for a completion experience and that any completion experience that does not negate reciprocity is a primary feminine expectation. Because this dream is inserted into a movie that refers to cultural identities and in which the suitors represent two national identities—American and British—it also signals that Isabel Archer is a character who is able to reconcile various cultures into a mutual completion, just as Ada does in *An Angel at My Table*. This translation, which is attached to the international theme, is the cultural equivalent of the mutual completion that is to be associated with sexual love.

By offering this interpretation of the seduction scenes and the international theme, I am attempting to highlight the main divergence between Campion and James as far as the handling of the international theme is concerned. In the conventional interpretation of the novel, Isabel Archer experiences evil, and it is this experience that makes her human and accomplishes her female completion. No critic neglects the split with Osmond, but many critics assume that Isabel is essentially touched by evil.[6] This routine interpretation presumes a further supposition: that at the beginning of the novel, Isabel is innocent. Her story is the European story of the entrapment into evil. I will not elaborate upon these assumptions but use them as a means of highlighting the distinctiveness of Campion's point of view. Doubtless, there are many symbolic figures of entrapment in the movie—the seduction scene takes place in a closed room; Isabel constantly moves from one closed place to another. The existence of these figures merely shows that Campion is aware of the implications that the novel invites the reader to recognize. That does not prove that her own vision is aligned with them. Campion does not define Isabel Archer in terms of any kind of innocence. Isabel Archer's ability to reject the various suitors attests not only to her feminine self-consciousness but also to the fact that she is not ignorant of innocence and evil; consequently, she does not experience any ethical fall. Her story is not about ethical issues related to the international theme; it is about symbolic completion, which is attached to sexuality and cultures. Ralph Touchett wants Isabel to be free—this is one of James's themes. Campion converts Isabel's story to her own purposes by using it to bring together various cultural and personal experiences to form a completion story. The same argument can be made with respect to *The Piano* and *An Angel at My Table*.

The International Theme: Time and Places

In James's novels, the international theme qualifies not only characters and cultures but also historical identities and places. That means that historical and local differences are explicitly exhibited. James does not merely aim to evoke a *couleur locale*: he stresses these differences. The same is true of Campion's *The Portrait of a Lady*, since it is an adaptation of James's novel. A similar concern to emphasize differences can be seen in the two other movies by Campion that I have been discussing. In *An Angel at My Table*, New Zealand history, places, and landscapes are contrasted with British ones. Although *The Piano* focuses on a single country, it shows contrasted places and local histories. What makes sense is the contrast. In *An Angel at My Table*, there is a gap between Great Britain and New Zealand; the sea voyage constitutes a caesura, which figures it. In *The Piano*, the same gap prevails between Alisdair Stewart's world and George Baines's and is figured by the intricate path that leads from the first to the second. The contrast brings together historical and spatial identities and consequently makes the question of the function of their paradoxical proximity.

This paradoxical proximity—especially the one involving American and European history—has an explicit function in James's novels. The historical oppositions between the Old World and the New World should not be read in a literal way only. Such a reading would simply repeat the opposition between European and American identities. A better reading should assume that these oppositions show a discontinuity between America and Europe, that is to say, a historical gap, and that this gap serves to suggest the continuous evolution from monarchic societies to a democratic society.[7] Change cannot be pictured; it can be only designated by its start and by its end. By its very nature, therefore, the international theme is inherently a historical theme, although it does narrate the change from monarchy to democracy. We should add that any representation of time and history is always archeological, to a certain degree. James's international novels should be considered historical novels, although they do not picture change—or should we say, because they do not.

To visit the past and make it contemporaneous to the present always involves contriving a fable that implies a time leap, and one that bears an explicit message: any time sequence can be read backward and forward; not to show the change from yesterday to today, while both times are referred to, does stress how the lesson of the past should be recognized as being relevant today. That is one suggestion arising out of James's international theme. Frame invokes it in her approach to the representation of the status of a woman, confirming that the issue she addresses is the definition of a new ethos—involving mutual completion—that cannot be identified with any past or current conditions. Campion complies with this characteristic of the international theme by offering two period movies that exemplify a double time leap. The spectator is able to view these films as linked to our present, although Campion does not translate them into contemporary terms or data.

In *The Portrait of a Lady*, the first presentation of the time leap is attached to the characters—on the one hand, the American ones, on the other hand, the European ones, and in between, an American woman who remains American (Isabel Archer) and an American man who turns a kind of European (Osmond). The differences between characters approximates to the gap between a democracy and monarchies. The final split between Isabel Archer and Osmond, which is Campion's invention, proves that the historical distance between Europe and America is to be permanent. The second presentation of a time leap resides in the contrast between the prologue and the rest of the movie. The prologue has been often commented upon. It should be viewed as epitomizing a basic play of discontinuity and continuity. *Discontinuity:* it stresses that the movie is a period movie by contrasting its shots with the subsequent ones. It sets up two obvious discrepancies with the movie itself. First, it makes a group of young women of today visible—no men are shown. The subsequent scenes do not offer any equivalent presentation. Second, this group moves and draws circles, which are shown from above. It is the only presentation of this kind. *Continuity:* the prologue is an explicit thematic introduction. As commentators have noted, the voices that can be heard are talking about kisses, which announces the erotic theme of the movie. The group of young women also provides a figure of a kind of feminine perfection—the circle that is attached to the representation of completion. These two observations may be merged into a single formulation: these young women are free to love and to experience mutual completion. The prologue defines the women's self-determination and identity as immediate, while the movie itself shows the long path Isabel Archer needed to traverse in order to accomplish her self-determination and her ability to experience completion. By incorporating an explicit time leap from the present to the past, Campion shows the evolution that has taken place in the status of women—which justifies the play upon discontinuity. However, the account of the prologue offered here is not the final word on it. The absence of any male figure in the prologue seems designed to suggest that the perfection of the women's world contains an implicit warning to men, who should not be deceived into thinking that they can expect to participate in a completion experience with those women who inhabit it. Put in other words, we could say that Isabel Archer's predicament, which is represented in terms of a period movie, may be the future of today's women, even though there is no comparison between their status and recognition and that of women in Isabel Archer's day—which justifies the play upon continuity. The two presentations of the time leap and the play upon discontinuity and continuity thus constitute a complete argument: progress has been made in raising the status of women; it can be only be identified through identifying the gap between the condition of women in the past and those in the present; however, such progress cannot prevent a regressive move—which is exemplified by Osmond from an ethical and cultural point of view and by Isabel Archer in James's novel when she returns to her husband's home.

A similar reading may be offered for *The Piano.* The film does not show how George Baines becomes a nineteenth-century bourgeois. It imposes a time leap between Baines's life with the Maori and the final picture of the character. The time leap is attuned to the symbolic rebirth that Ada undergoes—she is immersed into the sea and reappears. The conclusion of the movie—showing the bourgeois life of the couple—has often been commented upon and interpreted as conventional. Let us be more specific: it could be described as conventional according to our present standards but far less conventional according to nineteenth-century ones. The conclusion can be viewed simultaneously in terms of its continuity within the movie as a whole—that is, as a constituent part within the homogeneity of the period movie—and in terms of an implied reference to our present. This implied reference activates a second time leap: by playing upon the past and our present, it recalls the obstacles that had to be surmounted to make our present standards possible and that these obstacles may still pertain to our days—*mutatis mutandis.*

These observations about the time leap attached to the international theme reinforce the logic that I suggested at the outset of reading the three movies, *An Angel at My Table, The Piano,* and *The Portrait of a Lady* in a reverse chronological order. More specifically, from *An Angel at My Table* to *The Piano* and *The Portrait of a Lady,* a time leap prevails. The last two movies investigate the archeology of Janet's predicament and show that her misfortune and liberation should be viewed within a broader context. Put in other words, *An Angel at My Table* might be read as a prologue to the subsequent two movies, and these movies might be characterized as kinds of post-texts to *An Angel at My Table.* The dual structure of *The Portrait of a Lady*—prologue and movie—is a *mise en abîme* of the syntagmatic structure that constitutes the three-movie-series.

The paradoxical contrasts and proximities that qualify the times and moments of the movies apply also to the representation of places in the three movies. Locations, countries, and space at large are presented according to some constant structures and oppositions: open space versus closed space, itineraries versus immobility, ancient places versus recent or new ones, rich buildings versus poor ones, rural locations versus urban locations, village versus city, outdoor versus indoor, earth versus sky and water. Each of these items can be divided into opposites that relate to the spatial play of the international theme through a kind of *mise en abîme*. This level of reference cannot be disassociated from the territory and border themes, which apply to international or national territories. *The Piano* and *The Portrait of a Lady* exemplify these dualities in specific ways. *The Piano* exhibits a duality of the sea and the seashore, of the forest, homeland of George Baines, and its intricate paths. *The Portrait of Lady* shows a duality of the closed places and of the multiple walks in the cities, woods and parks, and so on. *An Angel at My Table* epitomizes the play upon the local and the figures of open space. Through her treatment of New Zealand landscapes, Campion demonstrates that to limit the identification of a location to circumscribed areas of land—these areas of land are many—does not do justice in terms of capturing what could be seen as natural settings foreign to us in order to objectify them through representation. The identification actually associates a familiar space with a universe—the universe of nature—that can be easily viewed but not easily possessed. The perfect image of this duality is the one of the train shown on the background of the horizon.

The specific ways in which Campion handles the international theme means that any place is defined as limited and connected to a broader space. The translation function we have identified in the international theme should be read as informing the representation of space. That makes the local convertible into the global, while also making the local appear quite distant from the global. The duality of discontinuity and continuity, which time exemplifies, applies to spatial representations. The female character in Campion's movies experiences the spatial dualities because she is displaced. That does not mean that she is a kind of go-between who interrelates spatial opposites but rather that she is made into their potential sum. In the course of traversing a number of territories, she makes the experience of them accessible in a way that can be shared at a universal human level, rather than limiting them to any specific territory, legacy, and exchange. In Campion's movies, this experience is represented in a highly symbolic manner. Isabel Archer does not enter Garden Court at the end of *The Portrait of a Lady*, turning instead to face the open space although she has received a part of Daniel Touchett's legacy. Ada, who, at the beginning of *The Piano,* came out of the sea, is finally immersed into the sea after having experienced a world of mud and slush and undergoes a symbolic rebirth into open space after she has been freed from the symbol of the past—the piano. At the end of *An Angel at My Table,* upon returning to her parents' place, Janet finds that nothing much is really left, moving her to turn to the open space of New Zealand. Locations, countries, and space at large are designed to translate the completion theme into the spatial one and to picture the woman character as capable of encompassing any multiplicity. Such identifications turn the female character into a kind of symbol: the one that figures an alliance between the human being and the world that ensues from the completion that the female character experiences. Nevertheless, a gap remains between the character and the open space to which she turns— Janet Frame is ultimately defined by the place where she writes; the final image of Ada locates her at home; Isabel Archer faces the wood surrounding the Touchett's mansion, and does not walk into it. As the time leap recalls the archaeology of the women's progress, the space gap still shows the distance remaining between society and nature—from possession to completion.

Romanticism Again

Through this reworking of the international theme, Jane Campion confirms the reflexive argument of her movies and, paradoxically, invokes an ethos that is characteristic of European Romanticism. (I use "ethos" as a rhetorical term that designates the ethical self-image and identity of a character and implies that both self-image and identity have to be extended to a community, since "ethos" necessitates that the relationship between the individual and his or her community is made obvious.) The reflexive argument is to be observed in the play upon past and present, continuity and discontinuity, and in the use of the typical woman's story for the realization of a completion fable, which is independent neither from the evaluation of men's universe nor from an agreement with contemporary society (for as long as the woman character remains, metaphorically speaking, distant from "open space"). This return to a kind of romantic ethos is paradoxical because James's international theme is most often considered to be related to a literary development of American realism, which means that we cannot assign it a romantic archaeology. Nevertheless, the presence of romanticism in Campion's films has been emphasized in the book about her by Dana Polan.[8] The paradox can be mastered if we probe deeper into the notion of a romantic ethos. For the sake of exemplification, let us again refer to James. About thirty-five years ago, an American commentator, Quentin Anderson, asserted that James's international characters—in particular, his main women characters—should be described as "imperial selves," that is, personalities who are able to encompass the world (i.e., nature and society) and to maintain the appearance of being rigorously "singular."[9] While the word "singular" predominantly means "distinct," it can also imply a kind of minor status. This characterization applies to Isabel Archer: she is defined by a story that is uniquely her own and by her ability to epitomize cultural and ethical issues. We can detect here the ideal conception of the subject in a democratic society, which Alexis de Tocqueville described, as exemplified in the United States.[10] To put it another way, this type of character (the best models of which, in James's international novels, are the women characters) symbolically manifests the reversible relationship of subjectivity and objectivity and offers it as a device for measuring the state of a community, a society. Such an ethos is "romantic" because it is associated with the character's self-expression, without showing any contradiction between being committed to the world on one hand and questioning society, norms, and social communications on the other. These remarks are just as applicable to Isabel Archer in Campion's *The Portrait of a Lady,* Ada in *The Piano,* and Janet in *An Angel at My Table* (in which the young female writer often refers to romantic and postromantic British poets). To express oneself, as Janet does, does not mean an outpouring of subjectivity but rather an initiation of the difficult effort to link subjectivity to objectivity to allow an association between the subject and what is strange to her to be formed—with the end result that she finally defines her self-image as one manifesting the imperial self. One can see in *The Piano* the same story that one finds in *The Portrait of a Lady.* Moreover, because the story in the former film is not a writer's story, it is all the more convincing. By identifying female subjectivity with an imperial self, Campion achieves a congruency between the typical completion story and the reflexive movement of her films. And she does more: she designates the new ethos that is to come—one that will be able to be shared anywhere in the world, without requiring particular cultural and gender identities to be relinquished. Through its association with the reflexive move and imperial self, the international theme, which is a play upon local and global, national and transnational, allows the presentation of an image of women characters who are both singular and universal—outside of alterity, exoticism, and hybridity, while nonetheless displaying clear cultural identifications.

Notes

1. See, e.g., *American Literature, an Anthology and Critical Survey,* ed. Joe Lee Davis, John T. Frederick, and Frank Luther Mott (New York: C. Scribner's Sons,

1948–49); John Halperin, "Trollope, James, and the International Theme," *The Year-book of English Studies* 7 (1977): 141–47; and Michael E. Connaughton, "American English and the International Theme in *The Portrait of a Lady,*" *Midwest Quarterly: A Journal of Contemporary Thought* 22, no. 2 (1981): 137–46.

2. For the importance of the contract theme in Campion's Jamesian source and its origins in American literary realism, see Jennifer C. Black, "Contractual Fictions," *Novel: A Forum on Fiction* 32, no. 2 (1999): 290–91.

3. Gilles Deleuze, in *Logique du sens* (Paris: Les Editions de Minuit, 1969), writes:

> Expression is grounded on the event as an entity deriving from what is capable of being expressed, or of what has been expressed. The event is what makes language possible, as long as it is confused neither with the proposition that expresses it, nor with the condition of the person who pronounces it, nor with the state of things that is designated by the proposition. . . . The event results from bodies—from their inter-actions, their actions, and their passions. But it differs in nature from that which produces it. Thus, it is also to be attributed to bodies, to the state of things, but in no way as a physical quality: only as a very special attribute that is dialectical, or rather noematic, incorporeal. In other words, this attribute has no existence outside the proposition that expresses it.

> L'expression se fonde sur l'événement comme entité de l'exprimable ou de l'exprimé. Ce qui rend le langage possible, c'est l'événement, en tant qu'il ne se confond ni avec la proposition qui l'exprime, ni avec l'état de celui qui la prononce, ni avec l'état de choses désigné par la proposition. . . . L'événement résulte des corps, de leurs mélanges, de leurs actions et passions. Mais il diffère en nature de ce dont il résulte. Aussi s'attribue-t-il aux corps, aux états de choses, mais non pas du tout comme une qualité physique: seulement comme un attribut très spécial, dialectique ou plutôt noématique, incorporel. Cet attribut n'existe pas hors de la proposition qui l'exprime. (212–13; translation by Alistair Fox)

4. See Ferdinand de Saussure, *Course in General Linguistics,* ed. Charles Bally and Albert Sechehaye in collaboration with Albert Riedlinger, trans. Wade Baskin (New York: McGraw-Hill, 1959), 102–3: "The linguistic entity exists only through the associating of the signifier with the signified. Whenever only one element is retained, the entity vanishes; instead of a concrete object we are faced with a mere abstraction."

5. In *The Piano,* Georges Baines also crosses a border by falling in love with Ada and by moving to the city—he does so, however, because he is triggered by Ada.

6. See, e.g., Leon Edel, *Henry James: A Life* (New York: Harper and Row, 1985), 261.

7. For a detailed exposition of this idea, see Mona Ozouf, *La Muse démocratique: Henry James ou les pouvoirs du roman* (Paris: Calmann-Lévy, 1998).

8. Dana Polan, *Jane Campion* (London: British Film Institute, 2001).

9. Quentin Anderson, *The Imperial Self: An Essay in American Literary and Cultural History* (New York: Vintage Books, 1972).

10. Alexis de Tocqueville, *De la démocratie en Amérique* (1835, 1840; Paris: Gallimard, 1992).

The ironically named suburb of Sans Souci ("without a care") in *Holy Smoke*.

CHAPTER TEN

The Suburb in Jane Campion's Films

Many of Jane Campion's films are located in a suburban milieu. Viewed collectively, they reveal a fascination with the peculiarities of suburban culture, a culture that is often inextricably linked to family relationships. Although Campion generally presents the suburbs in a critical light—especially in those films where she is preoccupied with suburban family life—she does reveal some interest in recording the everyday life of the suburbs and in using suburban environments to explore the local, in a way that suggests she is also intrigued by aspects of Australian cultural identity.

Because for the last twenty-five years Campion has lived in Australia, which is where she trained and made most of her films, I have couched my discussion in terms of the suburb in Australian cinema. That is not to deny that Australian and New Zealand suburbs have much in common, or that there is a high rate of suburbanization in both countries. However, the cinematic representation of this subject in Australia and New Zealand is tantalizingly different. Whereas the depiction of the suburb is central to contemporary Australian cinema, rural and small-town settings prevail in New Zealand cinema, which portrays natural landscape far more frequently than any other kind of locale. Very few New Zealand films take the suburb as their subject and even fewer celebrate suburban life.

In town planning terms, the concept of the suburb derives from Ebenezer Howard's *Garden Cities of Tomorrow* (1902), in which he proposed a pattern of settlement that would combine the best urban and rural elements. The modern suburb is often said to be an American invention, and, as Robert Beuka has noted, America is now a largely suburban nation, since many more people live in suburbs than in the city or the country.[1] In their history of Australia, Donald Denoon and Philippa Mein-Smith discuss how Australia's identity as a suburban nation facilitated American influence in that country and how the post–World War II baby boom led to the growth of the suburbs. During this period of economic uncertainty, "the state fostered reassertions of identity based on family and domesticity. The house with . . . the Australian backyard and barbeque spoke of privacy and leisure" and "the goal became 'to own the dream.'"[2]

Given the extent to which the suburb has shaped the development of twentieth-century American life, it is appropriate that in the United States, the cinema—that quintessentially modern art form—should play a dominant role in depicting suburban culture. Beuka indicates some of the polarities associated with the suburb. He sees it being neither country nor city, and as being associated with both place and placelessness and with utopian and dystopian views. Indeed, he refers to the "persistence of a reductive, two-dimensional vision of suburbia" in the United States, which "reflects both an idealized image of middle-class life and specific cultural anxieties about the very elements of society that threaten this image."[3] Thus, the utopian and the dystopian can be seen as two sides of the same coin. Beuka also associates the suburb with the 1950s, the American dream, the nuclear family, rigid gender identities, and cultural homogenization.

Despite this tendency to see the suburb as quintessentially American, some have argued that it is also crucial to definitions of Australian identity. Sarah Ferber, Chris Healy, and Chris McAuliffe examine the suburb from a cultural studies perspective, which informs their desire to seek significance in everyday cultural and social practices. For Healy, "Suburbia can allude to a barbeque or a lifestyle, to the Hill's hoist or the national ethos. Like 'culture,' the terms 'suburb' and 'suburbia' have functioned as imagined spaces onto which a vast array of fears, desires, insecurities, obsessions and yearnings have been projected and displaced."[4] Both Beuka and Healy distinguish between "suburb," which is commonly used to refer to an actual place, and "suburbia," a state of mind. Rose Lucas claims that "in this land of huge urban concentration and suburban sprawl, films which situate their narratives within the geographical and/or ideological milieu of the suburbs inevitably continue [an] inquiry into the origins and aspects of Australian cultural identity."[5] Lucas also examines how visual representations of the suburb hold personal and public significance for those working- and middle-class Australians who have grown up in postwar suburban environments.

Not only do most Australians live in suburbs, but also the suburb is frequently portrayed in Australian cinema, to the extent that quirky suburban comedy has been seen as the dominant way of presenting the Australian way of life in the feature films of the 1990s. In the best known of these—P. J. Hogan's *Muriel's Wedding* (1994) and Rob Stich's *The Castle* (1997)— lower-middle-class and working-class suburban life is largely displayed in an unflattering light, in that it is shown to be parochial and tasteless, but these films are still feel-good comedies that ultimately celebrate their central characters.[6] McKenzie Wark writes of *The Castle* that "regardless of the degree of irony with which we might be invited to read the Kerrigan's taste, there is little doubt that the emotional pull of [the film] is toward extending our sympathy to the Kerrigans."[7] Thus, in these films, any criticism of the suburbs is offset by a tendency to champion their underdog inhabitants.

If, as Beuka claims, images of the suburb in American film are typically either utopian or dystopian and there is a dearth of films that present a more inflected view, Campion's depictions tend to be similarly polarized, and those that depict family environments are dominated by negative images, as I shall argue in this chapter. There is really only one film by Campion that depicts the suburb in an affirmative way, and it is anomalous for this and other reasons. *Passionless Moments* (1983), which was made while Campion was still at art school, is a nine-minute collaborative project between Campion and Gerard Lee, who is listed as scriptwriter and ex-director. *Passionless Moments* bears the traces of somebody else's work, in that it has a lighter tone than is characteristic of the films we associate with Campion. Even the other contemporaneous short student films that Campion made on her own are more intense than this.

Positive treatments of the suburb in Campion's work tend to value the everyday and the local, and *Passionless Moments* proves no exception. The film consists of ten short narratives that present fleeting moments of insight. Although these episodes are characteristically ironic and throwaway, they collectively record and even celebrate the quotidian details of suburban life. The settings of these episodes, which include brick bungalows, a corner shop, a clothesline, a car in a driveway, a messy bedroom, a living room hung with freshly ironed shirts, a refrigerator, and a toy-strewn bedroom, are resolutely commonplace. There is a disjunction between the moments of insight, which contain a sense of possibility, however small, and the banal routines from which they arise, which serves to undermine any real passion. There is also a gap between the official tone of the voiceover narration and the trivial nature of the events being described. These include such incidents as two neighbors mistakenly waving to one another and a man mulling over song lyrics as he washes his jeans in the bath.

Besides demonstrating an interest in the ordinary, this film explores that which is momentary and short lived. At the end of *Passionless Moments*, we are told, "There are one million moments in your neighborhood, but, as the filmmakers discovered, each has a fragile presence which fades almost as it forms." The episode that shows a man idly watching particles of dust and

An early depiction of life in the suburbs: Julie Fry in *Passionless Moments*. Courtesy of the National Film and Sound Archive of Australia.

remembering how his mother told him they were angels signals this interest in evanescence. The statement "recorded in Sydney, Australia, Sunday October 2nd" indicates that such transient details of daily life are considered worth recording. By highlighting Australian suburban content in this way, Campion and Lee suggest the value of the local cultural and social practices, and, by implication, this choice of subject resists hegemonic Hollywood influences. Thus, although *Passionless Moments* employs ironic humor to create a sense of the ridiculous, any criticism is affectionate and its portrayal of the suburb is largely positive.

The same could not be said for *A Girl's Own Story* (1984), which explores adolescent crushes and sexual relationships within a troubled family setting and treats its suburban backdrop in dystopian terms. (There is some justification for considering this a portrayal of girlhood in 1960s Australasia, since there are no obvious Australian references in this film and Campion herself was living in Wellington when she was growing up.)[8] As its name suggests, *A Girl's Own Story* provides a strongly gendered perspective on its subject. This suburban nuclear family is divided by sibling rivalry, adultery, and possible molestation, and Pam's friend experiences incest and teenage pregnancy.

Gender roles are not just rigid, but downright imprisoning. Indeed, Adrian Martin has described women's experience of confinement as the dominant characteristic of Campion's cinema.[9] As both Frieda Freiberg and Gina Hausknecht indicate, the exuberant, exploratory attitude toward sexuality that the girls exhibit at the beginning of the film is replaced by a suppression of desire.[10] Verina Glaessner has described how these social and sexual restrictions are represented by Sally Bongers's cinematography, in that "Campion's figures inhabit the frame with the same sense of psychic awkwardness as [Diane] Arbus' subjects, their very ungainliness suggestive of extreme discomfort within the 'feminine' space allotted to them, almost as a protest against it."[11] There is some affection for 1960s paraphernalia, such as Beatle boots, and in this sense the negative depiction of the film's setting is modified by nostalgia for this definitively teen era. There is also some pleasure provided by the itemization of girlish clutter in Pam's bedroom. Yet, as the camera pans across a row of seminaked Barbie dolls displayed in provocative poses, their grotesqueness is more in keeping with the disturbing aspects of this film, which Freiberg characterizes as "the bizarre in the banal."[12] *A Girl's Own Story* ends with scenes of isolation and iciness, as the girls, who are wearing diaphanous white dresses and have projected images of skaters superimposed upon their bodies, huddle around one-bar heaters singing "Feel the Cold."

Although it came out in 1989, Campion's first feature film, *Sweetie*, incorporates some of the typical features of 1990s Australian cinema, according to Tom O'Regan. What is particularly pertinent to depictions of the suburb is the way that *Sweetie* marks a departure from realism. O'Regan writes:

In *Sweetie* and films like *Strictly Ballroom*, *Muriel's Wedding* and *Adventures of Priscilla Queen of the Desert* a space is created for celebrated "quirkiness," "eccentricity," and "individuality." In these the banality and richness of contemporary, usually urban settings and culture, are foregrounded and turned away from their usual moorings in realist social problem filmmaking.[13]

In the same essay, he describes how Peter Castaldi praises *Strictly Ballroom* for the manner in which it "liberates the suburban from the grip of the realists and lets fantasy run free."[14]

In *Sweetie,* Bongers's cinematography has done a great deal to contribute to the film's antirealist visual features. She enlists a range of expressionist film techniques to reflect the disturbed state of Kay's psyche. For example, she uses exaggerated camera angles to show that things are out of balance after Kay has observed physical intimacy between her sister and her father. We see Kay in bed with the covers drawn up to her chin; canted framing makes the composition seem misaligned. Likewise, following the breakdown in their relationship, Kay and Louis are photographed using a fisheye lens, which creates a distorted effect. Stylized framing is used to similar ends: Bongers frequently focuses on the ceiling or the floor in her startlingly decentered compositions, and she employs very low or very high camera angles to make figures loom or recede. These techniques have an emotional effect upon the viewer. For instance, Anneke Smelik identifies an excessive visual style in *Sweetie,* which subverts narrative structures and privileges the image. She states that *Sweetie's* visual elements create a subtle sense of *Verfremdung,* in which a "bizarre style converges with the irrational behavior of the characters, creating a psychical reality that remains far removed from psychological realism" and that makes domestic surroundings appear *unheimlich* and hostile.[15]

In *Sweetie,* as in *A Girl's Own Story,* the hostile nature of these suburban settings is related to their confining nature, in that women's bodies often appear uncomfortable in space. For example, in *Sweetie,* Kay is surrounded by menacing foliage, encroaching shadows, overpowering patterns, and discordant shapes, which collectively work to create a claustrophobic atmosphere. Not only do these elements of the mise-en-scène elicit an almost visceral response, causing us to recoil from this oppressive environment, but they also evoke the entrapment of the suburban gothic genre.[16] According to Anna Johnson, Campion's gothic mode is distinguished by its "insidious detail," and it is dominated by domestic interiors, which for Johnson contain the sort of visual excesses that prompted Robin Boyd's "explosion of aesthetic spite and cultural outrage" in his antisuburban polemic *The Australian Ugliness* (1960).[17] Interestingly, Johnson compares the "psychological oppression" of *Sweetie* with that of Janet Frame's novels.[18] Thus, *Sweetie's* depiction of suburban domestic environments is far removed from most notions of realism.

Yet, despite its many antirealist features, *Sweetie's* setting has elements of the Kitchen Sink genre, which is synonymous with a certain kind of realism in British films of the 1950s and 1960s. Campion has depicted a lower-middle-class 1970s milieu, as can be seen from Kay's pink-collar job, the worn furnishings, the shabby backyard, and the blighted streetscape. The film also deals with social issues, such as incest, yet, while it might be argued that Campion provides a feminist critique of the situation she describes, she does not provide a coherent critique of the class system, as is typical of British Kitchen Sink films (for example, Jack Clayton's *Room at the Top* [1957]). Campion seems to be more concerned with creating the appearance of lower-middle-class Australian suburban life than with drawing any inferences from it. Regarding viewers' ambivalence to *Sweetie,* Ann Hardy writes that "perhaps some of the unease about the film comes from a feeling that it is slightly condescending to its characters, who are placed socially as working class by the extraordinary kitsch of their suburban surroundings but arise from an abstract, unexamined, world of work."[19]

Critical portrayals of the suburb often borrow American tropes, and *Sweetie* is no exception. Resemblances between *Sweetie* and David Lynch's film *Blue Velvet* (1986) are to be expected, given that Campion describes Lynch as one of her "modern film heroes."[20] *Blue Velvet* parodies suburban life and alludes to sinister forces lurking behind its brightly painted façade. The opening sequence of *Blue Velvet* provides a striking instance of this. The camera cuts from a shot of red roses growing in front of a white picket fence to a scene showing white weatherboard houses on an orderly suburban street, along which a shiny red fire engine travels. The fireman on the running board smiles fixedly and waves at the camera. The scene then shifts to shots of yellow tulips, of children crossing a road, and of a man watering a well-tended lawn outside a prosperous, middle-class house. The previous images have all had an unreal quality about them, created by the use of very bright colors, the robotic movements of the fireman, and the idealized portrayal of family and community. Yet the idyll is interrupted when the man who is watering his lawn collapses from a stroke. The felled man holds the garden hose erect so that it resembles a spraying penis, thus making Lynch's implied satire overt. The camera then zooms in on individual blades of grass and travels under the earth, to reveal an extreme close-up of insects battling one another in the dark undergrowth: a magnified roaring on the soundtrack seems to symbolize hidden, elemental forces. Since the film depicts a nice boy's attempt to delve beneath the surface of his own suburban neighborhood, by investigating the sex and violence that is conducted underground, as it were, this opening sequence functions as a metaphor for the whole narrative of *Blue Velvet.*

Sweetie could be said to resemble *Blue Velvet* in its satiric treatment of suburban domestic life, since it employs a similar metaphor to that used in Lynch's film. *Sweetie* has a sequence in which a camera lens zooms in on a hole in the ground, within which a sapling has been planted, in order to mark the anniversary of Kay and Louis's relationship. After cutting to a scene that shows Kay lying in bed at night worrying whether the sapling will die, we are given a cross-section of the earth, in which time-lapse photography reveals roots rupturing the surface of the ground. These black-and-white nightmare images represent Kay's neurotic fear of trees, which she believes have hidden powers. For Kay, the planting of a yellow-leafed baby elder foreshadows the demise of her relationship with Louis. In both *Blue Velvet* and *Sweetie,* subterranean footage appears to symbolize unconscious forces and hidden fears. That these buried emotions threaten to disrupt the norms of suburban life by exposing the perverse and destructive passions that lie beneath its surface is in keeping with the kind of satire I perceive in *Blue Velvet.* Of course, that which lies beneath the surface in *Sweetie* is Dawn's incestuous relationship with her father, Gordon, which damages all the relationships within the family.

If *Sweetie* borrows *Blue Velvet*'s suburban metaphor, the film's visual images suggest comparisons with Lynch's *Eraserhead* (1977), in their use of dreamlike black-and-white footage and in their grotesque, surrealistic and horror references. In both films the propensity to focus on empty space, or on insignificant or ugly aspects of the environment, creates a sense of blankness, alienation, and oppression. Lynch's depiction of decaying urban landscape may also be relevant to *Sweetie,* since Lynch himself was familiar with the painting and writing of Robert Henri, a member of the Ash Can School, which took everyday city life as its subject.[21]

As an aside, I would like to allude briefly to *The Piano,* because, although the period setting of *The Piano* (1993) predates the suburb, *Blue Velvet*–style visual suburban references are used to undermine the ending, in which Ada and her settler family reside in a colonial wooden villa in Nelson, in what appears to be domestic bliss: we see Baines kissing Ada and Flora turning somersaults. However, this apparently peaceful domestic scene has some menacing features that undercut the happy ending: the contrast between Ada, the melancholy, Brontësque, black-clad heroine, with her slightly sinister finger and hood, and her surroundings in the sunshine capital of New Zealand (with white weatherboard house instead of white picket fence) seems more parodic than literal.

Campion's film *Holy Smoke* (1999) contrasts an artificial suburban environment with "authentic" spiritual and emotional life in New Delhi, as Sue Gillett indicates.[22] Indeed, suburbia is satirized in *Holy Smoke.* The grid pattern of streets in San Souci, Sydney, suggests conformity. This suburban environment is also shown to be ludicrous (the miniature gate) and synthetic (animals are groomed and nature is represented by a cheap print of a waterfall). When Ruth Barron's father, Gilbert, tries to stop her running away from a deprogrammer he has hired to undo the brainwashing her parents believe she has undergone in India, he pulls on her sari, thus unraveling her newly assumed identity. Ruth retaliates by pulling off his toupee; she then proceeds to destroy the façade of respectability he has constructed by revealing that he has had an illegitimate child by his secretary. If Ruth's revelation challenges the suburban model of the nuclear family and her obsession with marrying an Indian guru confronts the cultural homogenization of the suburb, then her brother, Tim, opposes heteronormative gender identities through his gayness. Suburban characters are explored in varying degrees of depth, from the sympathetic treatment of Ruth's sweetly muddled mother, Miriam, to the one-dimensional depiction of Ruth's shallow sister-in-law, Yvonne. (Yvonne's cartoonlike quality is enhanced by the fact that she is played by Sophie Lee, who acted in two iconic 1990s feel-good suburban comedies, *Muriel's Wedding* and *The Castle*.)

Although the suburb is satirized in *Holy Smoke*, it is treated less negatively than in *Sweetie*, because the distancing and distorting effects of *Sweetie's* visual style make its environment seem particularly hostile, as was suggested earlier. In *Holy Smoke*, Ruth's bedroom in Sans Souci, which a subtitle ironically designates as "home," is festooned with teenage bric-à-brac, including soft toys, butterfly decorations, frilly pillows, floral wallpaper, makeup, and youthful drawings. This feminine, girlish room is one that Ruth has demonstrably outgrown; the behavior of Ruth's giggling girlfriends is in keeping with this bedroom, even while it is out of step with the enlightenment she has undergone in India. While Ruth's teenage bedroom has some features in common with Pam's, the sharply critical tone of *A Girl's Own Story*, which is evident in the disquieting frieze of Barbie dolls, has no real equivalent in *Holy Smoke*, partly because the visual imagery of the later film is more realistic, aside from two lurid images of spiritual and sexual visions. Nevertheless, we are left with the impression that Ruth's suburban background is confining, even if *Holy Smoke* uses a different visual vocabulary than *A Girl's Own Story* and *Sweetie* to convey its effects.

More than Campion's other films, *Holy Smoke* relies on stock imagery in its criticism of the suburb, as can be seen in the use of a grid to connote conformity. It could therefore be said to reflect the sort of "reductive, two-dimensional view of suburbia" of which Buerka writes. It could also be seen as treating suburbia as a state of mind. But the notion of the suburb as a place need not stand in apposition to suburbia as a state of mind, as Healy suggests, since *Holy Smoke* displays some interest in exploring cultural and social practices that are specific to the country of Australia (or to Australasia), if not to a particular geographic locale. While San Souci is the dominant suburban setting in *Holy Smoke*, Ruth's Aunt Puss's house is strongly evocative of Australian domestic suburban culture, despite being situated at an emu farm in Wee Waa. For instance, Puss's backyard contains many common suburban objects, such as a rotary clothesline, a laundry basket, and a trellis. Like Miriam, Puss is portrayed sympathetically, and her surroundings reflect the warmth with which she is depicted. Thus, although *Holy Smoke* is more critical than celebratory in its attitude toward the suburbs, the film also records the quotidian features of suburban life. While *Holy Smoke* does not endorse suburban culture to the degree that *Passionless Moments* does, it nevertheless reveals some interest in recording it.

Overall, Campion's treatment of the suburb emphasizes both its menacing and its everyday aspects. However, if Australian feature films of the 1990s are dominated by quirky suburban comedy, then Campion's films oppose this trend in that they are more likely to provide disturbing than lighthearted depictions of suburbia. In Campion's works, apart from *Passionless Moments*, the suburb is the locus of family life, and her portraits of family dynamics tend to be critical rather than amusing. Those aspects of the suburb that are treated affectionately are tempered by dark or disquieting elements.[23]

Notes

1. Robert Beuka, *SuburbiaNation: Reading Suburban Landscape in Twentieth-Century American Fiction and Film* (New York: Palgrave, 2004), 2.

2. Donald Denoon and Philippa Mein-Smith, with Marvic Wyndham, *A History of Australia, New Zealand and the Pacific* (Malden, MA: Blackwell, 2000), 355.

3. Beuka, *SuburbiaNation*, 4–7.

4. Sarah Ferber, Chris Healy, and Chris McAuliffe, eds., *Beasts of Suburbia: Reinterpreting Cultures in Australian Suburbs* (Melbourne: Melbourne University Press, 1994), xiii.

5. Rose Lucas, "'Round the Block': Back to the Suburb in *Return Home*," in ibid., 112.

6. There is a tradition of such suburban representations. In his discussion of cultural critics' dismissal of the suburb, Kim Ian Michasiw writes of how, for some, the postwar American suburb was the "domain of a lower-middle-class kitsch." See Michasiw, "Some Stations of Suburban Gothic," in *American Gothic: New Interventions in a National Narrative*, ed. Robert K. Martin and Eric Savoy (Iowa City: University of Iowa Press, 1998), 242.

7. McKenzie Wark, "Screening Suburbia," http://www.ludiccrew.org/wark/ccc/06_screening_suburbia.html (accessed 7 March 2007).

8. In *A Girl's Own Story* there is nothing as self-consciously Australian as the t-shirt decorated with a Vegemite label that hangs on the clothesline in Kay's backyard in *Sweetie*. But this example demonstrates the difficulty in distinguishing between Australian and New Zealand cultural practices, because Vegemite is apparently more

often eaten in New Zealand than in Australia, and it is listed as a cultural icon in Stephen Barnett and Richard Wolfe's book on Kiwiana, although arguably it is not as much a national symbol here as it is in Australia, whence it derived. See Barnett and Wolfe, *New Zealand! New Zealand! In Praise of Kiwiana* (Auckland: Hodder and Stoughton, 1989), 73–74.

9. Adrian Martin, "Losing the Way: The Decline of Jane Campion," *Landfall* 200 (2000): 94.

10. Frieda Freiberg, "The Bizarre in the Banal: Notes on the Films of Jane Campion," in *Don't Shoot Darling: Women's Independent Filmmaking in Australia,* ed. Annette Blonski, Barbara Creed, and Freda Freiberg (Richmond: Greenhouse Publications, 1987), 328–33; Gina Hausknecht, "Self-Possession, Dolls, Beatlemania, Loss: Telling the Girl's Own Story," in *The Girl: Constructions of the Girl in Contemporary Fiction by Women,* ed. Ruth O. Saxton (New York: St Martin's Press, 1998), 21–24.

11. Verina Glaessner, "A Girl's Own Story," *Monthly Film Bulletin* 57, no. 678 (1990): 209.

12. Freiberg, "Bizarre in the Banal," 328.

13. Tom O'Regan, "Beyond 'Australian Film'? Australian Cinema in the 1990s," Murdoch University, http://www.mcc.murdoch.edu.au/ReadingRoom/film/1990s .html (accessed 7 March 2007).

14. Ibid.

15. Anneke Smelik, "Forces of Subversion: On the Excess of the Image," in *And the Mirror Cracked: Feminist Cinema and Film Theory* (Basingstoke: Macmillan, 1998), 140.

16. There have been some efforts to define the gothic/suburban modes in an Australian context. Gerry Turcotte's "Australian Gothic," in *The Handbook to Gothic Literature,* ed. M. Mulvey Roberts (Basingstoke: Macmillan, 1998), 10, defined the gothic in the antipodes, which he sees as "a world of reversals, the dark subconscious of Britain." More recently, Jonathan Rayner describes urban, but not suburban, gothic in his survey *Contemporary Australian Cinema: An Introduction* (Manchester: Manchester University Press, 2000), 43–56. However, Romana Ashton's PhD thesis, "Antipodean Gothic Cinema: A Study of the (Postmodern) Gothic in Australian and New Zealand Film since the 1970s" (Brisbane, Central Queensland University, 2005), examines the suburban gothic in relation to two specific Australian and New Zealand films, *The Night Prowler* and *Heavenly Creatures.*

17. Anna Johnson, "The Root of Evil: Suburban Imagery in Jane Campion's *Sweetie* and Bill Henson's Series *Untitled* 1985/6," in *Binocular, Focusing, Writing, Vision,* ed. E. McDonald and J. Engberg (Sydney: Moet and Chandon, 1991), 132–239.

18. Ibid. While Frame's suburban gothic has been commented upon by critics, such as Mark Williams, "Janet Frame's Suburban Gothic," in *Leaving the Highway: Six Contemporary New Zealand Novelists* (Auckland: Auckland University Press, 1990), there is no visual equivalent to these gothic aspects in Campion's adaptation of Frame's second volume of her autobiography, *An Autobiography: An Angel at My Table; Volume Two* (Auckland: Random Century, 1989), for which the cinematographer Stuart Dry-brugh employed an understated realist style. This is not surprising, since Frame does

not really refer to the suburbs in her autobiography, besides describing how she stayed with her sister in Northcote, which caused the writer Frank Sargeson to aver: "It's no good your living in suburbia among the nappies and bourgeois life." See Frame, *Autobiography*, 245. Sargeson's line is included in Campion's film in a slightly altered form. Yet, if the depiction of the suburb in *Sweetie* is more negative than positive, Campion chooses to end *An Angel at My Table* on an affirmative note, by concluding the film with a sequence that shows Janet contentedly typing a novel in a caravan parked outside her sister's new, architect-designed suburban house.

19. Ann Hardy, "Sweetie: A Song in the Desert," *Illusions* 15 (1990): 11.

20. Miro Bilbrough, "Different Complexions: Jane Campion, An Interview," in *Film in Aotearoa New Zealand,* ed. Jonathan Dennis and Jan Bieringa (Wellington: Victoria University Press, 1992), 101. In a question session following the screening of *Sweetie* during the Campion colloquium, Sally Bongers described how she and Jane Campion saw *Blue Velvet* together and were very excited by the film. She also noted how the scene in which Dawn handles a garden hose makes reference to the hose sequence in Lynch's film.

21. Kenneth C. Kaleta, *David Lynch* (New York: Twayne, 1993), 3.

22. Sue Gillett, *Views from Beyond the Mirror: The Films of Jane Campion* (Melbourne: Australian Teachers of Media, 2004), 72–74.

23. I would like to thank Peter Kuch for his discussions of the Australian suburb and him and Cathy Fowler for their responses to this essay.

Carnivalesque figures silhouetted against the sky in *The Piano*.

From Antipodean Cinema to
International Art Cinema

In one of the first articles about Jane Campion in France, on the occasion of the presentation of *Sweetie* at the Cannes Festival in 1989, Marie Colmant describes the filmmaker as "une jeune épicière en films fins" (a young owner of a delicatessen's shop for specialty films): "she likes to compare herself to a small-time delicatessen owner specializing in refined or exotic produce that surprises her customers with 'little perfect objects', rather than 'a sort of mega-supermarket like Hollywood films.'"[1] Without wishing to privilege this definition of Campion's filmmaking, I have nevertheless been struck by the richness of the specialty delicatessen metaphor and its pertinence for describing her cinema.

A specialized *épicerie* is a small shop on which the owner imposes her style by selecting the products that she displays and sells, in contrast to a supermarket chain that offers the same range of produce everywhere, displayed in a fairly similar manner. The claiming of an "identity" is thus at the heart of the metaphor: it can be read as resistance against globalization, homogenization, and "gigantism" (the desire to augment in scale and magnitude)—three characteristics now associated with Hollywood cinema—but it can also be understood as the affirmation of an individual distinctiveness, that of an auteur. Furthermore, all sorts of different products are gathered together in a specialized delicatessen's shop. This heterogeneity, in my opinion, is also characteristic of Campion's cinema. Such heterogeneity is evident in the course of almost every one of her films in the form of visual and aesthetic ruptures, such as the insertion of dream or fantasy sequences in *Sweetie* (1989), *The Portrait of a Lady* (1996), and even *In the Cut* (2003). Finally, just as in a delicatessen's shop products originating in different countries are presented together in the same place, on the same shelves, the

189

films of Campion offer a complex exoticism, given that the representations they articulate contain elements that are culturally heterogeneous.

The metaphor of the specialized delicatessen's shop, then, suggests an auteurist position, evident from Campion's first feature film onward, in addition to a transnational dimension. If we consider further that the owner of the delicatessen's shop is a woman ("*une* épicière"), this metaphor also reminds us of Campion's distinctiveness as a woman filmmaker in a profession dominated by men—a distinctiveness that is even more obvious in the sphere of international art cinema, to which Campion's oeuvre belongs. Finally, if one recalls that Australia and New Zealand are remote and largely unfamiliar countries for international audiences, especially European ones, the exoticism of Campion's films also inheres in references to, and images of, what I (along with many other French speakers) call the Antipodes.

That is why it strikes me as interesting to analyze how, in the first part of Campion's career—encompassing *Sweetie, An Angel at My Table* (1990), and *The Piano* (1993)—these different identifying characteristics (auteur, woman, New Zealander, representative of a postnational era) are variously superimposed, combined, or brought into conflict with one another to create the signature "Jane Campion," which has become identified and recognized by international art cinema audiences. To pursue this analysis, I first briefly consider the current status of the "international auteur" to demonstrate how the articulation of the local (whether national or regional) and the global ("the universal occidental") is a distinctive feature of contemporary art cinema. In my view, it is not a question of denying the uniqueness of Campion but of showing that the trajectory of her career and her cinema are also representative of a strong tendency evident in the cinematic landscape at the end of the twentieth century. Following that, basing the discussion on several examples, I explore how this "local/global" hybridity is inscribed in an idiosyncratic manner in Campion's first three feature films.

The articulation of the local, the national, and the international is one of the significant traits of contemporary international art cinema. As Alan Williams remarks, the landscape of contemporary cinema is organized into three large groupings that are determined, in economic terms, by the size of the budget they have and the different audiences that they target.[2]

The first grouping, "the capital-intensive, increasingly faceless 'global' cinema," includes large-budget films. The most characteristic productions are the "blockbusters," often made in Hollywood, and, in general, related to different subgenres of the action film. This cinema, which corresponds to what French scholars have designated since the end of the 1980s as the *cinéma-monde,* or what Toby Miller calls "Global Hollywood," is characterized by the erasure of the local, the identificatory, and the national.[3]

The second grouping comprises middle-budget films. Generally, these involve national productions, aimed at national audiences. If these films are successful, their success tends to be limited, if not to national audiences, at the very least by geographic confines (e.g., Belgium and Québec for French films). In addition, the forms and representations offered by these films are too culturally encoded and too nationally specific to enjoy real success in foreign markets. Popular national cinemas are readily identifiable as belonging to this second type, most notably in the form of comedies. However, certain types of films with more elevated artistic ambitions can also fall into this category, such as what is referred to as "le jeune cinéma français."[4]

The third grouping in Williams's typology comprises "the low-budget, film festival oriented 'art,' 'independent' or 'auteur' cinema." This sector may be properly termed "international." The difference between global and international is crucial in today's marketplace: on the film festival and the art house/independent cable channel circuit, a visible national origin is de rigueur, almost as important as a visible author/director. A double identity, local and international, is therefore one of the conditions of the production and the promotion of auteur films. In the case of Campion, this fact is accentuated from the beginning by the background of the director, as well as the manner in which she defines her identity in interviews, sometimes emphasizing her New Zealand origins (especially in relation to those films that are set in New Zealand), and sometimes her film-training and life in Australia. *Sweetie* was presented at Cannes in 1989 as an Australian film, filmed in Australia by a director whom the French press sometimes identified as a New Zealander and sometimes as an Australian. *An Angel at My Table,* on the other hand, which is a film adaptation of the autobiography of the New Zealand writer Janet Frame that is filmed mostly in New Zealand, is almost always presented as a New Zealand film, directed by a New Zealander. The international dimension of auteur films was also enhanced as the 1980s moved into the 1990s by changes to the film market that encouraged producers and distributors to bring auteur cinema out of the ghetto of art cinema, both for financial reasons and reasons of prestige.[5]

This change is manifest in an internationalization of productions, a phenomenon that particularly benefited auteurs who had been noticed in festivals, meaning that they could enjoy greater financial backing and a more significant international distribution. For example, following the public triumph of *Mujeres al Borde de un Ataque de Nervios* (Women on the verge of a nervous breakdown) at the Venice Film Festival and the Berlin Film Festival in 1988 and its popular and critical success in France—events that marked the recognition of Almodóvar as an auteur—CiBy 2000, the prestige subsidiary of the French company Bouygues, provided Almodóvar with a level of financial and strategic backing that his small company, *El Deseo,* could not offer him.[6] This support coincides with the beginning of what Almodóvar specialists consider the second part of his career. CiBy 2000, often viewed in France as a "Palme d'Or machine," is also the producer of the Iranian Kiarostami's *A Taste of Cherry* (1997) and, as is well known, *The Piano.* This film, which established Campion on the international scene, also marks the internationalization of her cinema. It was produced in large part by a French company with Australian participation, which gave it the label "Australian Film" at the Cannes festival; the film was shot in New Zealand but gives top billing to two American actors; it called upon the British composer Michael Nyman for the soundtrack, and was distributed by Miramax as "a work of uplifting prestige, [an] important film that a general cultured public should see rather than as modest little experimental works."[7] After *The Piano,* the internationalization of the cinema of Campion was extended. Campion abandons antipodean settings in *The Portrait of a Lady* and *In the Cut,* and uses American actors (Harvey Keitel, Meg Ryan, John Malkovich), or—and here one can detect an oscillation between the local and the global—Hollywood stars whose persona combines identifying aspects that have regional associations. Nicole Kidman was born in Honolulu but grew up in Australia and has dual citizenship, American and Australian. Kate Winslet, before being the star of James Cameron's *Titanic,* began her career in Peter Jackson's *Heavenly Creatures* (1994), a New Zealand drama based on a shocking crime that stunned New Zealand during the 1950s.

For Campion, as for other contemporary filmmakers, national or regional branding is not restricted to a statement of their national origins, or to the national label attributed to the film in festivals. In fact, admission to the status of international auteur always begins with the perception of a difference that is manifest in various ways, especially in the form of cultural and national differences (to which, in Campion's case, should be added a gender difference). In other words, films by international auteurs often (in a conscious and reflective manner) take a national and cultural tradition as their starting point, whether they work with or against it. This is not the case for national genre cinemas, which are "naturally" inscribed in their national historical, cultural, and cinematic landscape. International art cinema productions are thus marked by a tension between "self" and "other"—a tension that one can easily observe, for example, in the cinemas of Pedro Almodóvar and Aki Kaurismaki.[8]

Even though the image of Campion is strongly associated with Australia or New Zealand, a grounding in the national and the regional does not constitute a continuous sign in her cinema—if only because two of her films (*The Portrait of a Lady* and *In the Cut*) contain almost no references to the antipodes. In one sense, the geographic locations and the diverse periods brought to the screen could be viewed as merely the vehicle, the pretext for Campion to explore variations on a single subject: the struggle of a woman searching for psychic autonomy in the quest for her subjectivity. Similarly, without wishing to succumb to a reductive notion of auteurism, I would suggest that certain stylistic characteristics are much more instrumental in imparting a general cohesiveness to the work of Campion the auteur. These include a certain fragmentation and heterogeneity in the story that I have already mentioned; the intermittent use of a female voiceover that is difficult to locate; and open endings, the traditional and canonical recognition sign for auteur cinema (e.g., the shot of the feet of Kay and Louis suggesting, without insisting upon, the possibility of a romantic and erotic reconciliation between the two characters at the end of *Sweetie;* the decision to depart from James's novel by ending *The Portrait of a Lady* with the ambivalent image of Isabel having her hand on the knob of the door at Garden Court; the door of the apartment closing on Frannie, who has enfolded herself in the arms of Malloy, still handcuffed to the radiator, at the end of *In the Cut*).

Nevertheless, even though national or regional labeling does not in itself impart unity to the work of Campion—to the extent that Dana Polan and others view her as an exemplary postnational figure—it seems to me that the first part of her feature film work, up to and including *The Piano,* testifies to a balanced blend of Australasian specificity and the personal exploration of more universal themes and figures. My hypothesis is that this blend assists the recognition and emergence of Campion as an international auteur. The subject of *Sweetie,* the dysfunctional family, is, in fact, a fairly universal theme (or at least familiar to contemporary Occidental audiences), of which the film might appear to be a specific exemplification. There is little emphasis on the iconic aspects of Australia in the major part of the film: all of the urban spaces, the work places, the housing suburbs, and the beach (which contrasts starkly with the stereotyped international image of "the Australian beach") are spaces that are characteristic of modernity and could be almost anywhere. One should note, however, that French critics at the time of the film's release perceived this absence of Australian clichés as marking an authentic representation of Australia: "Let us make no mistake: Australia is not only a country of surfers and kangaroos. And Sweetie has none of the qualities of a lolly. . . . Imagine the setting: a grassy suburb that reeks of neglect, beaches devoured by industrialization, a middle class in the process of disintegration."[9]

Similarly, Jean-Pierre Lenôtre expresses delight that *Sweetie* is not like *Crocodile Dundee,* clearly identifying the double local/universal dimension of the film:

As far as its setting is concerned, this is Australia. Not a window opening on to the southern miracle, rather a suburb of global expansion. Stretches of earth cracked by the sun, cheaply-built houses that lack planning and elegance. Practical, comfortable, and ugly like Anglo-Saxon interiors know how to be right to the world's end. Judging by the ambiance, one could be anywhere: the cramped families have no country, and have nothing to look forward to but shriveled destinies, petty love affairs and pathetic jobs. It's there that Kay and Sweetie have grown up.[10]

Nonetheless, when Gordon, Louis, and Kay manage to elude Sweetie's vigilance and rejoin Flo, the mother, outside the city, the film offers other images—of the outback and of jackaroos—that clearly refer to a more local reality. These sequences in the country represent a parenthesis in the story, an island of recovered happiness without Sweetie, but they retain the same visual style that is often referred to as "quirky," the same play of editing and framing that, paradoxically, simultaneously enhances and undermines the picturesque quality of the scene. We see this clearly, for example, in the swimming sequence at the river, particularly in the last shot, strangely filmed at the edge of the surface of the water, where the arrival in the foreground of Kay's face comes to interrupt the viewer's contemplation of this idyllic natural scene.

It is worth noting how the quirky style of *Sweetie* serves both to establish Campion as an auteur, and also to reinforce the geographic exoticism of the film.[11] As Tom O'Regan notes, "The prospect of quirky, eccentric cinema [is] a means of establishing international attractiveness. In *Sweetie, Strictly Ballroom, Muriel's Wedding,* and *The Adventures of Priscilla, Queen of the Desert* a space is created for what has become an international expectation of Australian "quirkyness," "eccentricity," and "individuality.""[12] Given that the other films cited by O'Regan chronologically follow *Sweetie,* it is not inconceivable that Sweetie inaugurated this association between Australia and the eccentric.

An Angel at My Table is linked more strongly to a distinctive geographical, historical, and culturally specific world, being an adaptation and the story of the life of a New Zealand writer. Although nominated for a Nobel

The swimming sequence in *Sweetie.*

Prize, Janet Frame remains relatively unknown in France, as is evidenced by numerous articles appearing at the time of the film's release that draw parallels between the life and travels of Campion and of Frame, and even speak of the "twins" or the "New Zealand sisters." The film, however, because it is both the biography of an artist and the story of a woman who struggles with her alienation and her "madness," is easily identified as belonging to an international genre—the *biopic* (even if the film fragments the form)—and as dealing with general themes. From the beginning of the film, the emphasis is placed much more clearly on Janet's "madness" and her failure to adapt than is the case in Frame's own autobiography. Campion and Laura Jones select childhood scenes from *To the Is-land* that suggest malaise—choosing to omit, for example, those chapters in which Frame warmly depicts her family or the intensity of her discovery of words. Moreover, at the beginning of the film, the train stops at Seacliff Station during the shift of the Frame family to their new home, and reference is made to its psychiatric hospital—a reference that does not appear in Frame's autobiography until the beginning of the second volume, *An Angel at My Table.* In moving this scene to the beginning of the film, Campion activates the threat of madness for her heroine. The New Zealand landscape is very much present in the first part of the film (the greenness of the fields made a big impression on French critics), but whether it is natural or architectural, it is always minimally invoked. As Barbara Cairns and Helen Martin remark, "Jane Campion shoots

195

in a very tight style, showing characters with only as much background as is necessary. When she does shoot in wide shot, such as when the young Janet stands alone on an empty metal road, . . . the images are of immense power and resonance."[13] Because the setting, though extremely specific, is never shown gratuitously, little information is given to us about the places, and, most of the time, Campion eliminates even the transition shots during the different "voyages" made by Janet across the country. This is so that the film can concentrate, claustrophobically, on what is happening inside the character, or around her. The ordinary landscape is not truly highlighted except when it is a matter of expressing a particular emotion of the characters—for example, the moment of happiness when Janet and her sisters sing on the cliff, or the progress of Janet in her relations with others, and her persisting awkwardness when, at the end of the film, she places herself on a bank at the request of local reporters.

I would like to consider at greater length the second sequence of the film, the shots of little Janet on the road that gave the film its poster. This series of shots serves to give us a strong impression of the countryside, the wide-open space, the green of the fields, which enables the film to establish clearly its New Zealand context, even for the least informed spectator. The framing, the perspective delineated by the road, cannot fail to recall the road movie, a genre developed to portray a country but also a genre that has become one of the preferred vehicles for young auteurs. But, as the little girl approaches, the camera lowers slightly, and at the end of the shot the landscape is almost hidden by the body and the face of the little girl, who looks steadily at the camera, which is always a bit discomforting for the spectator, and introduces a distancing effect that comes to shatter the "contemplative status" of the landscape. The use of color in the film then takes on another, symbolic, meaning—through the contrast between Janet's thick, red hair and the green of what remains visible of the fields around her. The intervention of the voiceover and the close-up inserts of Janet's hand that nervously touches her clothing completes the displacement of the spectator's attention and announces from the beginning that the story will focus on the emotion of the individual, not the context. It is thus more the flight of the little girl (who turns her back and runs, because she is afraid of our look) that is the striking element at the end of the sequence, when we return to the initial framing.

Inscription in the category of "international art cinema" increases with *The Piano,* not only because of its financing, its casting, and, of course, retrospectively, its success, but also, and above all, because of its generic anchoring in the "heritage cinema"—a prestige genre in the 1990s that could assure international success for an independent or average production. Many heri-

Little Janet intercepts the spectator's gaze in *An Angel at My Table.* Courtesy of Photofest.

tage films are British films, from adaptations of Jane Austen to those of E. M. Forster by Ivory, or French (such as *Cyrano de Bergerac* [1990] or *Le Hussard sur le toit* [The horseman on the roof, 1995]). Such films have proven that the genre can compete with Hollywood in the field of the spectacular, at least outside America. Generally, these films borrow from a heritage (literary, cultural, architectural, and historical) that is strongly anchored in national identity, while at the same time having international aspirations. In contrast to costume films from earlier periods, they offer a meticulous reconstruction of interiors and costumes, producing an effect of authenticity (an aesthetic sometimes referred to as "museum pieces"). In addition, they emphasize a symbolic and emotional interaction between the characters and the landscape, and they align the pleasure of the story with a pleasure in aesthetic contemplation.[14] Finally, the genre accords a large place to women, gays, and lesbians, often invoking a progressive discourse. This becomes apparent when one considers the authors (both of the films and the original literary works that are adapted) as well as the representations themselves and the targeted audiences.

While none of the earlier Campion films are firmly tied to a particular genre (even though they can be likened, in terms of certain features or their narrative structure, to one genre or another), Campion inscribes *The Piano* unequivocally and explicitly in the genre of the heritage film by situating her story during the Victorian period—which is, along with the Edwardian period in Anglophone fiction, the preferred period for this genre. The director's decision to make a period film is not surprising, not only because of the interest in heritage film as a vehicle for addressing issues of gender, but also because it gives her an internationally recognized framework for exploring the figure of the heroine. A part of the film's originality derives from its New Zealand location and its evocation of colonization, very rarely addressed in my experience by the heritage film, whose historical interests remain largely European. In addition, while the heritage films that evoke a non-European elsewhere offer utopian and romantic visions of ships leaving the Old World for a new life (as in *Persuasion* or *Maurice*), Ada's journey to New Zealand is not voluntary but something to which she reluctantly resigns herself. The shots of her arrival evoke an experience of violence (the dark forms of the hands of the men, backlit in silhouette under a menacing sky, who strain themselves to disembark Ada, Flora, and their goods) and solitude (the fragile silhouette of Ada at the end of the sequence of the deserted beach). The fleeting evocation of Ada's life in Scotland before her departure seems to me to fulfill several functions: first, it immediately situates the female character in a relationship of domination, and in the historical patriarchal and colonial world in which women, like the lands of the Maori, are sold, bought, and exchanged; then it attaches the film to a European referent, in the accustomed manner of the international formula for the genre, which the narrative later abandons for faraway countries that are also exotic from a generic point of view. This strategy for managing the tension between the local New Zealand referent and the international heritage formula is also expressed in comments by Campion, and in reviews of *The Piano* by French critics, who seek to account for the exoticism of the film by regularly citing Emily Brontë and the atmosphere of *Wuthering Heights*.

In keeping with the aesthetic of the genre, *The Piano* derives a large part of its visual impression from the local and historical "reality" of the country. Campion draws upon it to create unusual images (such as the piano on the beach, reproduced on the film's posters) and also, as in an *Angel at My Table*, images that have a more symbolic function—for example, Ada's numerous excursions in the bush and the mud visually suggest the traps in which the heroine struggles (not only her marriage, but also the blackmail by Baines). The shots of the devastated bush around the homes of the colonists suggest

A Maori man mimicking Alisdair Stewart in *The Piano*.

the violence of colonization in a film that valorizes primitive nature, which is here associated with the Maori. A double vision of New Zealand's past emerges from the film, which aptly illustrates the ambiguity of the relationship that contemporary authors have with their country: on the one hand, the violent, exploitative, puritan, and often ridiculous world of the colonists and, on the other, a Maori society, situated on the periphery of the story, but peaceful, with the Maori being guardians of authentic values, attached to the land in a mystical, genuine manner. Ultimately, the character of Baines offers a reconciliatory and reassuring synthesis of the two worlds, both because of his closeness to the Maori—represented by the tattoos on his face—which makes him a "good colonist," and also by his sensuality, which ends up making him a "good husband" for Ada.

To conclude this brief account of *The Piano,* I would like to discuss the scene of the first contact between Ada and her new companions, on the beach. The very first shot of the sequence, in which the dark silhouettes of the men stand out against the sky and the seas, is striking in its carnivalesque dimension. The backlighting and the tonality of the music of Michael Nyman produces an unreal and burlesque effect that erases the local and referential dimension of the shot, in a way that might just as well remind one of a Fellini-esque troupe (see the frontispiece to this chapter). The treatment of the Maori, present in the background during the rest of the sequence, is interesting as much from the perspective of genre as from a consideration of the characteristic thematic preoccupations of the film (voyeurism, the illicit look). In this sequence (as in the entire film) the Maori fulfill a somewhat decorative, picturesque function that allows Campion to resolve one of the difficulties posed by the New Zealand location of her period film: how does one actualize a museum aesthetic in a new country? The Maori are, in a sense, the equivalent of the authentic objects and interiors of European heritage films. They constitute the indispensable historical background on which the heritage film inscribes the emotions of the primary characters, which explains the negative reactions generated by *The Piano* in this regard.[15] Here, the logic of the genre competes with (and even overpowers) any desire to denounce the colonial situation, or to draw a parallel between masculine domination and colonial domination. However, although the camera never adopts their point of view, the Maori are also portrayed as ironic observers of the white characters. Stewart and Ada are both doubled, in the background, by Maori who imitate their gestures. Starting from a specific colonial situation, Campion's film thus distinguishes itself from the heritage genre, just as a few years later Robert Altman's *Gosford Park* (2001) would do, by having servants observe and comment on the actions of the masters.

The second part of Campion's oeuvre, which I will not address in this essay, is marked by a lessening of the regional or national dimension. It is significant, for example, that *Holy Smoke,* which is set mainly in Australia, sends its two heroes back to the United States and India in its epilogue, where each appears to have found his or her way. This contrasts with *An Angel at My Table,* which ended with the return of Janet, showing clearly that thenceforth she would assume both her identity as a writer and also her national identity—signaled in the shots that show the heroine sliding her foot into the shoes of her father, participating in an interview conducted by the local press, and writing in a caravan parked next to the house of her sister.

There are two reasons, I suggest, for this shift toward a transnational discourse (*Holy Smoke*) and toward essentially international filmic forms (a European heritage film, *The Portrait of a Lady,* and an American thriller, *In the Cut*). First, it is a consequence of the worldwide success of *The Piano,* and of Campion's subsequent elevation to the status of an international auteur. Following these twin events, she had new resources at her disposal, pursued her career as a filmmaker in a different cinematic milieu that necessarily informed her cinema, and saw recognition of the personal signature she had achieved transcend geographic specificity. It is significant that French critics, even though they continue to mention Campion's nationality, cease making references to the antipodes from the time of *The Portrait of a Lady* onward.

Such references had been common with regard to her first films, even at times being used for the titles of articles, such as "Antipodean. Sweetie no longer lives here."[16] When *The Piano* received the Palme d'Or in Cannes, the magazine *Positif*, which had supported Campion's career since the time of her first film, published an enthusiastic editorial that simultaneously praises the talent of the author of *The Piano* and the authenticity of antipodean filmmakers:

After the Australian George Miller (*Lorenzo*), here on the cover (and for the third time!) is the New Zealander Jane Campion and her third film, *The Piano*. What is it that makes us feel so close to these Antipodean filmmakers? Perhaps it is because they possess, unquestionably, that which was formerly the prerogative of their Anglo-Saxon cousins in the United States: the spirit of adventure, a faith in emotions, a love of storytelling. At a time, our own, which is caught up in postmodernism, Jane Campion prefers modernity, and for the *mise en abîme*, the abyss of the passions.[17]

Second, Campion's evolution to a more transnational discourse expresses another tendency in international art cinema that is ignored by Alan Williams, whose study is centered on the relations between cinema and nation. Contemporary auteurs, once their signature is established, work to varying degrees on a range of memories, forms, and cinematographic practices to imprint their personal "brand," rather than on a single memory, identity, or local culture. This is what Thomas Elsaesser calls the creation of a tour de force: "Authority and authenticity lie nowadays in the way film-makers use the cinema's resources, which is to say in their command of the generic, the expressive, the excessive, the visual, and the visceral. From David Lynch to Jane Campion, from Jonathan Demme to Stephen Frears, from Luc Besson to Dario Argento—all are auteurs and all are valued for their capacity to concentrate on a tour de force."[18]

The Portrait of a Lady and *In the Cut* thus replace local/international hybridity with an alteration in generic functioning, produced essentially by the insertion of the "feminine voice." Alterity and exoticism are no longer linked to geographic referents, even for symbolic purposes, but to the intrusion of fantasy scenes that do not belong to the conventions of the genre. The young women that we encounter at the beginning of *The Portrait of a Lady* refer more to a contemporary feminine discourse—thereby establishing a link between the twentieth century and the story of Isabel that undermines the illusion of romance—than to anything specifically Australian in this discourse. If it is the case, given the film's lack of success, that members of the international audience did not find there "their Jane Campion," neither did the French critics. To echo the words used by *Positif* with respect to *The Piano* (and quoted earlier), it seems as if critics found a postmodern Campion in the place of their modern Campion. *Cahiers du cinema* describes *The Portrait of a Lady* as "decorative machinery," and sees in *In the Cut* an "arty varnish," a cinema "de relookeuse."[19] Predictably, *Holy Smoke,* which was not successful in France, received largely good reviews, being a film that is not generically coded. Critics emphasized the performance of the actors, in particular Kate Winslet, to whom Campion offered the opportunity for rebirth after *Titanic* (1997). They also detected in this film the eccentric dimension of the first films by Jane Campion (whether or not they approved of it) and a reinvigorating freshness after *The Portrait of a Lady.* As several articles written at different points in Campion's career show—including not only the review from *Positif* that I cite earlier but also a series of reviews noting that Campion "n'a pas de culture cinéphilique" (doesn't have the background of a cinephile)—the French associate this freshness, the capacity to tell stories and reinvigorate cinematic discourse, with Jane Campion the individual, and also with a mythic construction of the antipodes as an exotic and somewhat primitive location in which the cinema of the Old World might once again find its lost innocence and vitality.

Notes

Translated from the French by Hilary Radner and Alistair Fox.

1. Marie Colmant, "Une jeune épicière en films fins," *Libération,* 17 May 1989.
2. Alan Williams, ed., *Film and Nationalism* (New Brunswick: Rutgers University Press, 2002), 18–19.
3. See Charles-Albert Michalet, *Le Drôle de drame du cinéma mondial* (Paris: La Découverte, 1987); Claude Forest, *Économies contemporaines du cinéma en Europe. L'improbable industrie* (Paris: CNRS Éditions, 2001); and Toby Miller, Nitin Govil, John McMurria, and Richard Maxwell, *Global Hollywood* (London: British Film Institute, 2001).
4. "Le jeune cinéma français" in French film criticism refers to a group of films and filmmakers that have appeared since the beginning of the 1990s, which are considered to have renewed French cinema. This group, although fairly diverse in terms of style and genre, gathers together films by auteurs, and by young auteurs (in many instances their first film), as varied as Cédric Klapisch's *Un air de famille* (Family resemblances) (1996), Olivier Assayas' *Les Destinées sentimentales* (Sentimental destinies) (2000), Mathieu Kassovitz' *La Haine* (Hate) (1995), Olivier Ducastel and Jacques Martineau's *Jeanne et le garçon formidable* (Jeanne and the perfect guy) (1998), Patricia Mazuy's *Saint-Cyr* (The king's daughters) (2000), and so on. According to critics, the emergence of "le jeune cinéma français" has been viewed either positively (as a kind of

new "nouvelle vague," a testimony to the vitality of French cinema) or negatively (as a minor auteur-cinema, mediocre and without any real ambition). See Marie-Claude Trémois, *Les Enfants de la liberté. Le jeune cinéma français des années 1990* (Paris: Le Seuil, 1997); Michel Marie, ed., *Le Jeune Cinéma Français* (Paris: Nathan, 1998); and René Prédal, *Le Jeune Cinéma Français* (Paris: Nathan, 2002).

5. This change occurred not only in Hollywood but also on a global scale. On this subject, see Michael Allen, *Contemporary U.S. Cinema* (Essex: Longman/Pierson Education, 2003), 86–88.

6. Bouygues dominates the construction sector in France and owns the powerful television channel TF1, the epitome in France of mediocre commercial television, considered as *télé poubelle* (trash TV). For this company, then, CiBy 2000 is a dancing girl that costs a great deal but reguilds its crest.

7. Dana Polan, *Jane Campion* (London: British Film Institute, 2001), 16.

8. To take only the case of the former, the localism that is a significant trait of his Hispanic identity is expressed in an attachment to settings in modern Madrid, to settings in mythic, ancestral villages, in an abundance of picturesque and stereotypical details, in the recollections of Franco's Spain in *Carne trémula* (Live flesh, 1997) or *La mala educación* (Bad education, 2004), and in references to popular or learned Spanish practices and cultures. Nevertheless, Almodóvar also repeatedly introduces references to American cinema and procedures for distancing and subverting the spectator from the representation. These involve details presented in an ironic manner—an innocent gazpacho becomes an offensive weapon in *Mujeres al Borde de un Ataque de Nervios* (Women on the verge of a nervous breakdown)—or that contribute to a radical deconstruction of masculine identity, in which deviant and marginal figures relegate bourgeois normality to the periphery of the story and impose, in an empathic manner, their alterity on the heart of a Spain that is reinvented by the filmmaker. Obviously, the national dimension occupies a place that is different for all filmmakers, and one that is perhaps susceptible to interrogation: is it a formative part of their oeuvre and central in their cinema (which is the case with Almodóvar, who always remained in Spain, but does not seem, to me, to be true of Jane Campion)? Is it essential to the construction of their world and filmic representations, or is its function simply to provide local color in order to provide the added value of authenticity and exoticism to the film to gratify a global audience?

9. "Évitons les malentendus: l'Australie n'est pas seulement le pays des surfeurs et des kangourous. Et Sweetie n'a rien d'un bonbon. . . . Imaginez le décor: une banlieue herbeuse qui pue l'abandon, des plages bouffées par l'industrialisation, une middle class en décomposition." M.D., "Cette garce de Sweetie" (That bitch Sweetie), *L'Express,* 29 December 1989.

10. "Côté décor, c'est l'Australie. Pas la vitrine du miracle austral, plutôt une banlieue de l'expansion. Des étendues de terre écrasées par le soleil, des maisons construites à l'économie, sans recherché ni grâce. Pratiques, confortables et laides comme savent l'être les intérieurs anglo-saxons, même au bout du monde. Côté ambiance, on pourrait être n'importe où: les familles étriquées n'ont pas de patrie, les destins racornis, les petites amours et les boulots minable non plus. C'est là que Kay et Sweetie ont grandi." Jean-Pierre Lenôtre, "Contes de la névrose ordinaire," *Le Figaro,* 17 May 1989.

11. In part, this style can probably be ascribed to Campion's collaboration with the cinematographer of *Sweetie,* Sally Bongers. Nevertheless, it is found again several years later in *Holy Smoke* (1999), occurring in a more kitsch form.

12. Tom O'Regan, "Australian Cinema as a National Cinema," in Willams, *Film and Nationalism,* 102.

13. Barbara Cairns and Helen Martin, *Shadows on the Wall: A Study of Seven New Zealand Feature Films* (Auckland: Longman Paul, 1994), 198.

14. See in particular Ginette Vincendeau, *Film/Literature/Heritage* (London: British Film Institute, 2001); and Julianne Pidduck, *Contemporary Costume Film* (London: British Film Institute, 2004).

15. See Leonie Pihama, "Ebony and Ivory: Constructions of Maori in *The Piano,*" in *Jane Campion's* The Piano, ed. Harriet Margolis (Cambridge: Cambridge University Press, 2000), 114–34.

16. "Antipodique. Sweetie n'habite plus ici" was the title of the review by Louis Skorecki, *Libération,* 3 January 1990, 28–29.

17. "Après l'Australien Georges Miller (Lorenzo), voici en couverture (et pour la troisième fois!) la Néo-Zélandaise Jane Campion et son troisième film, *La Leçon de piano.* Qu'est-ce qui nous rend si proches ces cinéastes des antipodes? Qu'ils possèdent sans doute, ce qui était jadis l'apanage de leurs cousins anglo-saxons des États-Unis: l'esprit d'aventure, la confiance dans les sentiments, l'amour du recit. À une époque, la nôtre, éprise de postmodernisme, Jane Campion préfère la modernité, et à la mise en abîme, l'abîme des passions." Editorial in *Positif* 388 (1993): 3.

18. Thomas Elsaesser, "Putting on a Show: The European Art Movie," *Sight and Sound* 4, no. 4 (1994): 24.

19. Jean-Marc Lalanne, review of *The Portrait of a Lady, Cahiers du cinéma* 508 (1996): 78–79; Stéphane Delorme, review of *In the Cut, Cahiers du cinéma* 585 (2003): 37–38.

Part IV
Viewers Respond to Jane Campion

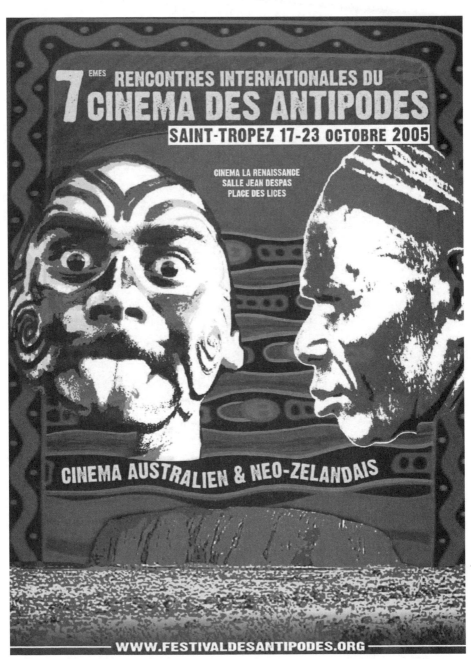

Poster advertising the seventh Festival du Cinema des Antipodes held in Saint-Tropez. Courtesy of Bernard Bories.

"Comme une invitation au voyage"

French Reception of Jane Campion,
An Angel at My Table, and *The Piano*

Responses to an overseas film can tell us much about the film culture—and indeed the surrounding culture—from which they emerge. This is particularly the case when the films function as a powerful emotional catalyst. Reviews of Jane Campion's *An Angel at My Table* (1990) and *The Piano* (1993) bear witness to the strength of French interest in mise-en-scène and the concept of auteur, and more generally to the aesthetics of surrealism and to ideas of the South Pacific (including New Zealand) as an exotic, primitive location. These concepts interact in various ways, with reviewers fascinated by the novelty of a female auteur and convinced that the primitive energies of the South Pacific help to explain the strength of her authorship. Viewed in these terms, Campion and her films hold a huge resonance for French cinephiles.

Discourses on film unfold within national cultural frameworks that include perceptions about the place of films and the cinema in society and the symbolic role that images have in the cultural imaginary. In this case the images have an immediate iconographic value because of the long history of exploration and commerce that France has conducted with the islands of the South Pacific. Although negligible as a material resource, the Pacific islands have had "an intellectual influence out of all proportion to their physical size."[1] When the Europeans discovered Tahiti in the 1760s, for example, this encounter was briefly salutary as they conceded "for the first and only time in their experience [that] a group of people . . . might be living a life better than their own."[2] Tahiti seemed to offer living proof that the myth of the noble savage was no myth at all. As Richard Lansdown writes, "Nothing Europeans had seen in Asia, Africa, and America had a remotely similar effect."[3] Such was the power of the Southern Seas that French fascination with it has not ceased, and New Zealand has sufficient links with the smaller islands of the region to invite the same mythology.

An article written by John Ellis for *Screen* initially inspired the methodology I employ here.[4] Ellis analyzed the "discourse of those film critics who used and promoted the conception of the 'quality' British film between 1942 and 1949."[5] He describes his textual practice as "a kind of attentive listening, trying to transcribe the various random comments and remarks of different individuals into the complete systematization that they were never given."[6] In listening to the terms used by the French film reviewers, I have detected two principal concepts: first, a critical consensus about "what matters most" in journalistic film criticism, parts of which are internal to the cinema, for example, the use of mise-en-scène in constructing and conveying powerful cognitive and emotive meanings, and, second, broader ideological systems, for example, ideas about the antipodes that have evolved over time. Ellis considers the sampled utterances "a discourse" because they constitute "an object (the 'quality film') which can be identified across particular practices."[7] Similarly, the French film critics writing in the reputable cultural press constitute their "objects" as "New Zealand" and "Jane Campion." The discourse across the French film reviews is not homogenous, but there is enough regularity for us to recognize some underlying mythologies.

For this study, film reviews of *An Angel at My Table* and *The Piano* have been taken from the following dailies and weeklies: *l'Humanité, Libération, le Monde, le Nouvel Observateur, le Quotidien de Paris, les Echos, le Journal du dimanche, la Croix, l'Express, France-soir, le Figaro, Globe Hebdo,* and *Télérama.* The critics associated with these media institutions are Marie Colmant, Annie Coppermann, Véronique Philipponnat, Jean-Luc Macia, Domique de Saint Pern, Anne de Gasperi, Claude Sartirano, Jean Roy, Philippe Vecchi, Olivier Séguret, Bénédicte Mathieu, Danièle Heymann, Bernard Géniès, Aurélien Ferenczi, François Jonquet, Phillipe Plazzo, Isabelle Danel, Alain Riou, Serge Rémy, Jean-Pierre Leonardini, Claire Devarrieux, Monique Pantel, Richard Gianorio, and Claude Baignères.[8]

Imagining the Antipodes—"à l'écart du monde" (removed from the world)[9]

La Leçon de piano est, avant tout, un film qui resonne comme une invitation au voyage.

(*The Piano* is, first and foremost, a film that resonates as an invitation to travel.)

—Philippe Plazzo, "Questions pour un Campion"

What resonates here is the title of Baudelaire's famous poem, the dream of escaping to a paradise in some exotic region of the world. Part of Campion's attraction for the film critic in *Télérama* was the way both she and the film bore the alluring marks of familiarity and alterity: "To go and see her film has become a gentle obligation akin to a friendly visit to someone fascinating. Fascinating because of being both familiar and distant. Just like the film."[10] Another critic noted that the New Zealand landscapes "add to the intimate strangeness of this exceptional film" ("ajoutent à l'étrangeté familière de ce film exceptionnel").[11]

Being both familiar *and* distant is a potent amalgam that keeps desire alive and suggests that New Zealand as an imaginary signifier resonates powerfully in the French imagination. It is simultaneously an actual location and a screen for emotional projection (to use a term relevant to film). These preconceptions have a long history. An unknown space, such as Terra Australis was once, offers few obstacles to mythmakers and projections of various desires; although the gradual filling in of the world map by eighteenth-century voyages gradually destroyed the habitat of the narratives of imaginary voyages, the reduction of the vast southern continent (Terra Australis) to the actual coastlines of Australia and New Zealand did not completely do away with an implicit desire to preserve elements of them for the imagination. It might be useful to summarize the European origins of this narrative, which stretch back several hundred years. This will frame their contemporary reemergence when vestiges, or mutations, of this discourse are heard in the texts written about Campion's films and, indeed, about Campion herself.

The first aspect of the historical European imagining of "Austral lands" concerns a utopian desire for an elsewhere where life is markedly better, and the second describes an inclination to primitivism. A long time ago, the equator was the great dividing line where the known world slid into the unknown. Below this divide were "elected lands of alterity (even though the relationship that one is tempted to establish between *austral* and *other* [autre] is etymologically false)," which meant that "the Austral lands are therefore naturally fated to utopia."[12] In 1756, Charles de Brosse published his *Histoire des navigations aux Terres australes.* The author attempts to define linguistically—for seafarers and scientists had not yet conducted explorations—the still unknown vast southern continent believed, since antiquity, to symmetrically counterbalance the northern, physically and morally. De Brosse's text takes shape as a mosaic of other texts, absorbing and transforming them. He envisages new forms of commerce (this was also a colonial project) and bright new physical specimens of great moral virtue.

A contemporary echo of that yearning for physical and moral health imagined to exist in the South can be heard in a description of Campion published in the weekly *l'Express:* "She has a radiant smile. Expresses herself warmly. Nourished with cornflakes, made athletic from tennis, and bronzed by the golden rays of the Australian sun, Jane Campion is nothing like the inhibited or unhinged characters who implode in her films."[13] Campion is textually constructed as a strong, healthy, simple (and therefore honest) descendant of the mythical "noble savage" that took shape in the minds of Europeans following the tales told by travelers.

The myth of "le bon sauvage" seemed no myth at all once Tahiti was discovered. Denis Diderot's *Supplément au Voyage de Bougainville* (1773 and 1774) gave a romantically utopian coloration to life in Tahiti after Louis-Antoine de Bougainville's original description of his voyage had appeared two years earlier in 1771.[14] The main aim of Diderot's text was to contrast Tahiti and France, and to show how and why Tahitians were better and happier than the French, principally through closer contact with, and observation of, nature and its laws: "Life in the wild is so simple, and our societies are such complicated machines! The Tahitian is at the world's beginning, and the European at its old age."[15] As with any colonial endeavor, and de Brosse's text was also designed to stimulate such ventures, the "native" question must also be considered. Who are the autochthones and how should they be treated? Sometimes written off as savages leading brutal lives that might yet be raised to the condition of civilization, which often justified the colonization, they could also be the surviving witnesses of mankind's original Edenic state before the Fall and its attendant sins corrupted human nature. There is, thus, the possibility to depict the indigenous inhabitants of these far-flung isles, these preeminently utopian spaces, as either noble or ignoble. For Diderot, they were distinctly the former: "Look at these men; see how honest, sound, and sturdy they are. Look at these women; see how honest, sound, fresh, and beautiful they are."[16]

The Piano strongly raised such issues for French critics, in terms both of the Maori and the Pakeha characters. The settler played by Harvey Keitel has grown so close to the indigenous inhabitants that he is almost one of them. The *Figaro*'s review of *The Piano* describes the civilizing process that leads to the transfiguration of this character. Ada's piano playing "exerts a magical power over he alone who knows how to listen; it instills purity, discretion, energy, and calm in his heart and soul. Civilization thus manages to overcome the brutality of human nature. By their sensual and spiritual authenticity, his metamorphosis and colorful ascension from semisavagery toward human perfection make for an exciting demonstration."[17]

Film critics also pragmatically contrasted the putatively anemic state of French narrative cinema in the late 1980s and early 1990s with Campion's more robust fictions, and symbolically replenished New Zealand's utopian predilection in the process—this new film industry in a raw country could reinvigorate the cinema. One review tried to penetrate Campion's "secret" for success: "And her secret, perhaps, is to believe intensely—in contradistinction to many of her contemporaries—that one can still tell stories."[18] Campion's ability to believe deeply in the capacity to tell stories, as a child might, distinguished her from the crop of European postmodern film fabulists who doubted too much to create compelling cinematic fictions. Another review noted Campion's renewal of basic narrative principles whose force had diminished in France: "This good old principle became obsolete here, one that required from a film-maker at least one idea per shot, which means that *The Piano* abounds in events and surprises."[19]

There is evidence, then, of a contemporary French desire to evoke a persistent "primitivism" within the antipodean experience for the French cultural imaginary. This is consonant with an older European symbolic order that constructed the southern hemisphere as an imagined space of initially crude and absolute alterity to life in the northern hemisphere; this is a primeval space, as this passage about New Zealand landscape from a review of *The Piano* in *le Figaro* makes explicit: "A furious rain rules over there—the vegetative and liquid mud of the world's beginnings."[20] From such a primal soup, new life can emerge. Further evidence that the autochthonous exotic exerts a powerfully contemporary fascination in France is provided in the striking visual layout of a poster for the seventh Cinema des Antipodes held in Saint-Tropez (see the frontispiece to this chapter). Traces of this discourse are evident in French film critics' writing of New Zealand, as will become clear.

It needs to be noted that, as a general observation, references to New Zealand society—its historical, political, economic, and cultural condition and evolution—are few and far between in the daily and weekly reviews of Campion's films. One of the rare occasions when a critic leaves the diegetic world of the film for the historical New Zealand occurs in a review of *An Angel at My Table* where the cultural condition of life in the 1930s is described as being uncongenial to intellectual or imaginative endeavor: "'To the Is-Lands [*sic*]' depicts the childhood of a writer who, despite wild and unflattering appearances, reveals a gifted temperament, an intellectual identity in exile in its primitive and natural setting."[21] The direct association of "primitive" with "natural" also places New Zealand in a rustic condition that contrasts strongly with cosmopolitan Paris.

211

One reviewer's ignorance of the country was expressed thus: "Here we are, then, following Janet Frame in the '30s, in the heart of this country shaped like a question mark."[22] This surely expresses the critic's own sincere puzzlement; I have not seen anyone else conflate New Zealand's topography into a question mark. Given the formal constraints—space, semantics, paragraphs—involved in writing for these media institutions, such lacunae are in many respects unremarkable and understandable, so it is not necessary to rebuke them for the relative absence of such historical and realist anchoring.[23] However, such lacks can *also* be intriguing; they suggest that New Zealand as a physical space located in historical time does not satisfy the requirements of a French symbolic order more used to inscribing the country within imaginary boundaries of its own fabrication. The cultural and physical distances that separate France and New Zealand facilitate such a practice.

These distances also dilute a traditional French critical preoccupation with realism. A critical consensus about what matters most in film criticism in France has, since André Bazin in the late 1940s, made extensive use of a realist discourse that seeks to link the film's narrative and mise-en-scène to a variety of pre-filmic subjects and concerns, such as history, politics, culture, and identity.[24] The importance of social and psychological realism in French critical and theoretical writing about the cinema cannot be overstated; Bazin's legacy is strong and endures. For him, the cinema is the next step in the Western world's "obsession with realism"—an ever increasing perfection in mimesis, which he sees as a structuring device in the history of the arts: increasing fidelity in representing the observable world. Moreover, in the influential essays he wrote, later collected together under the title *What is Cinema?* there is a clear need to identify the intrinsic properties of the new medium—its specificity—and to show how these are best served when film seeks to reveal or redeem the real.[25] But as in the case of *The Piano,* these conscious concerns can be overruled by the emotional priorities of an older mythology.

Me Tarzan, You Jane

The story of Campion's "discovery" by the French is worth recounting for at least two reasons: first, to highlight the cultural importance of festivals (such as Cannes) in discovering and then nurturing talented filmmakers and, second, to reveal the modern French cultural explorers' captivating sense of mission "down under." The linguistic parallel with earlier French cultural and scientific voyages in the Pacific is deliberate. Each expedition returned laden with new knowledge, having a variety of epistemological, political, and commercial returns. Although the "product" that is now invited to appear in the French symbolic order has changed, the premise—the allure of the antipodes—endures and provides many of the benefits that Bougainville's discovery of the Tahitians occasioned for Diderot in his *Supplément au voyage de Bougainville,* notably an ability to contrast aspects of the present French social order with another, imagined as superior in various respects.

The story has it that Gilles Jacob, then director of the Cannes Film Festival, sent Pierre Rissient, described as "un voyageur français" (a French traveler) and "un bon connaisseur de l'hémisphère austral" (an expert on the southern hemisphere), out into the world to enlarge, where possible, the material available for selection.[26] It is important to understand that as one of the most prestigious international film festivals, Cannes has both a cultural mission and a critical reputation to maintain and defend, whence the need to continually explore beyond the confines of the known. Regular transfusions are needed for the ongoing legitimacy and vitality of film festival culture.

Rissient reportedly arranged for the entire Australian feature length film production for that year to be screened and, finding nothing that met Cannes' rigorous selection criteria, had a large number of short films screened too. It was during this process that his eyes opened more widely as Campion's short film *Peel* flickered onto his retina. The film's unusual tone and style had aroused his interest. Campion's film went on to win the short film prize at Cannes in 1986, where it was shown with two other shorts by the film-maker—*A Girl's Own Story* and *Passionless Moments.*

French film critics frequently included the story of this cinematic "discovery" in their reviews as they explained Campion's perfect trajectory from cinematic nursery (short film selection) to main event status and the much-coveted Palme d'Or. This is a tale of revelation and predestination in which the incipient traces of an auteur were detected, heralded, nurtured, and celebrated by film festival scouts and alert journalists. Campion's subsequent films merely confirmed the initial critical judgment of her obvious talent. Gilles Jacob saw her as an exemplary model of Cannes' cultural program in recognizing the originality of her singular vision. *Télérama* expressed the opinion that *The Piano's* success feted the arrival of a major new author.[27] Campion herself acknowledged the importance of Rissient's invitation to Cannes and the attention that came with winning the short film prize in 1986. She was reported as having said that since winning that prize she had never stopped making films, and had never had to wait in some sort of cinematic limbo for new projects to appear.[28] Her felicitous naivety may have flattered the French sense of mission when she confessed her total ignorance of Cannes: "I had no idea what Cannes represented and as I'd just finished a television film there was only one thing I wanted: holidays. Rissient was very insistent: that was my good luck."[29]

Rissient's role as godfather figure facilitating Campion's career was next evidenced in his suggestion that she contact CiBy 2000, a French production company, after he had read the script for *The Piano,* as he was convinced that it was the type of project they would support, which indeed they did, and on strikingly generous terms, as Campion herself recollected: "CiBy is a sort of showcase company, and they want to help certain independent directors . . . it's unbelievable but they gave us 100 per cent creative control and 100 per cent of the money—with a generous share of the profits."[30] French adoption or "ownership" of Campion was thus also material as well as symbolic, the adoption process deriving from her construction as a particular kind of cinéaste in France.

Campion as Author

For journalists of the French dailies and weeklies, Campion's films are first and foremost formidable expressions of cinematic *art* that allow viewers to appreciate essentially two things: the central role of the individual female figure in the film's diegesis and the singular vision (and personality) of the director reflected both through her mise-en-scène and her many interviews: "For *The Piano,* like the film-maker's other films, recounts the birth of a woman who has thus far lived within herself, quasi autistically, and who wakes up to the world."[31] Given the centrality of the auteur in both the French film canon and writing about film, this demonstrates a certain conception (or code) of the content that weekly newspaper and magazine film reviewing in France should address, distinct from the obvious and necessary narrative detail, plot synopsis, and actors' performance. This concern for thematic relevance across the films is an obvious sign of Campion's authorship, a marker of which is the way she pursues a relatively small number of central issues, variations of which are discernible in each film. This thematic coherence, not necessarily consciously fashioned by the filmmaker, in which case the critic as exegete will reveal it, designates an emergent oeuvre. Careful textual analysis will permit the critic to apprehend and delineate the distinctive contours of the creator's personality and vision through Campion's mise-en-scène; analysis of the latter was extensive, hardly surprising given the historical importance (and continuing relevance) of this concept in French film reviews.

For French reviewers, a film's mise-en-scène is *the* way into a filmmaker's specifically cinematic construction of meaning through such things as camera movement, shot size and angle, the tightness or looseness of the frame, the relationship of objects in the frame, the use of lighting and color, and so on. The fullness of these and other expressive strategies can only be understood through the mise en-scène, not the story's arc and trajectory, however important these are for good dramatic spectacle or narrative satisfaction. Most of the longer newspaper reviews dedicate as much time to Campion's stylistic *treatment* of story or subject as they do to providing readers with an understanding of the narrative, setting, decor, and acting. Typically, we also learn a bit about her place of birth, parents' professions, schooling, hobbies, university studies, and relationships.

In this attention to the language of Campion's mise-en-scène, we can hear a distant Rivettian echo from a time when the struggle to establish *Cahiers'* critical approach was more strident (because it was unfolding). Jacque Rivette's method may be understood through his assessment of Mizoguchi as an auteur whose Japanese nationality and cultural context were evacuated and replaced by mise-en-scène alone: "His films, totally foreign, speak to us in a familiar tongue. Which one? The only one that an auteur in the cinema must lay claim to: that of mise-en-scène. If music is a universal idiom, the mise-en-scène is one, too; it's the latter, and not Japanese, that one must learn to understand Mizoguchi."[32]

André Bazin, in his study of the Hitchcock-Hawksian (that is, auteurist) tendency within *Cahiers du cinéma,* wrote: "They value mise-en-scène so highly because they see in it the very material of film itself, an organisation of beings and things which is its own meaning, both moral and aesthetic."[33]

Campion's use of color and light as expressive strategies drew frequent commentary. One critic quite deliberately describes her use of color as painterly. Although such an association was not new, having been made in the 1920s and 1930s as critics sought to have film taken seriously as art, its re-emergence at this time was strategic: a perception that the cinema needed to be defended from audiovisual predation at a time when a commercially driven proliferation and flow of images (a greater number of television channels, advertising becoming more prominent) in France threatened to absorb the cinema into its vortex, flatten medium specific distinctions, and eliminate the spectator's critical capacity to engage with the cinema's systems of representations.[34] The strategy sought to alert viewers to the cinema's important associations with high art rather than with lowbrow televised distractions, with the latter believed to prevent viewers from establishing a connection with the world, with real people, and with oneself as a member of that real world.

In the texts of critics developing a more conventionally formalist analysis, Campion's film is described in other terms: "If the sea is blue, the mountain is, too. The green pastures exult as the colorful patchwork of the girls' dresses dances. And yet, it's ginger that dominates. Or, rather, it's around ginger that Jane Campion composes almost each of her shots with the boldness and control of a painter aware of the unsurpassable fullness of a finished painting—the savant play of lights, the secret harmony of colors."[35]

Another notes, on a narrative level, the affinities that *An Angel at My Table* has with Charles Dickens's novels and uses this association to lambaste television's contagious narratives: "This is an accomplished narration on the model of Dickens, which distinguishes it immediately from the basically anecdotal realism usually generated by the televised image, which has so contaminated cinema."[36]

Another critic extols the emotional truthfulness of the film and briefly alludes to the New Zealand landscape as a pre-filmic space, but this concession to the nondiegetic world is quickly transformed through astonishing mise-en-scène: "There's no slight of hand involved here. Just the real. Only the real. And a talent able to shake the birds of dark screens. Jane Campion has just invented a new cinema: one that uses reduced means to make you believe in a super production. Her landscapes are superb (should we thank New Zealand? That would be too simple. Campion invents trees, clouds, lights)."[37]

Un cinema d'auteur also invites the critic to read the film autobiographically, seeking parallels between the figure of the director and characters in the film. This is evoked in a review that recognizes the familiar female figure in Campion's work as an alter ego with existential difficulties: "If one likes auteur cinema, one must go and see this Angel, a much more seductive avatar—after the very disturbing Sweetie—of a character central to all of Jane Campion's films: a solitary woman, timid, emotional, on the edges of a madness that in this instance, and this is admirable, she tames, overcomes and finally ends via creation. Like the director?"[38]

In Campion's work the principal figures are heterosexual women who struggle to assert their subjectivity in trying circumstances. This was clearly noted in her burgeoning oeuvre: "The director persists with what is, for the moment, her main subject, one that runs through her four short films, her film for television, and her two films for the cinema: the intimate portrait of young women whose seduction emanates from their unflattering appearance, their aching body, and their inaptitude to life."[39]

As an auteur, it is crucial that Campion's "main subject" be read across her several film texts: "All Jane Campion's films speak of the pain of living, of relationship difficulties, of the thin line between abnormality and normality, of the vertigo that takes hold of you to suddenly plunge into death."[40]

Given the paucity of women making feature length films at that time, however, some reviews emphasized the treatment of the female figure by a *female* director: "There's also an idea going around that a film by a woman is almost guaranteed to be honest, the inevitably personal vision of an auteur."[41] Campion as auteur envisaged, and engaged with, an emancipation of the feminine from retrograde masculine stereotypes. Her films, most notably *The Piano,* were also strongly supported by developments within feminist film criticism that "wanted to regain a true feminine subjectivity and deconstruct the formative masculine model of representation used in education and art."[42]

Quickly recognized as those of an auteur, Campion's distinctive voice and singular vision added a layer of authenticity *and* art to feminine desire, a desire that was no longer in fealty to the masculine. As central and in some ways pioneering as this was, however, some critics pointed out that the fact that Campion was a woman representing other woman was not sufficient in and of itself to warrant the purchase of a ticket, which may indicate an anti-essentialist stance, or a relatively inoffensive expression of a pervasive misogyny.[43] (There are, moreover, male directors whose female protagonists carry the narrative, such as George Cukor.) But in the late 1980s and early 1990s, Campion's gender in a creative role dominated by men was sufficiently novel to merit comment, as a review in *France-soir* noted: "Jane Campion is the first female director to awaken the sexist world of the cinema" ("Jane Campion est la première réalisatrice réveillant l'univers sexiste du cinema").[44]

Considerably weakening the anti-essentialist stance, however, Campion's gender authenticated her ability to speak of the female figure, of the feminine, and, perhaps more important, if only numerically, of heterosexual feminine desire fairly conventionally understood and insufficiently represented in film. Although the gender role reversal in the following extract is intriguing, it is not shockingly subversive, it is unlikely to repel viewers, and it acts to encourage the "cross-over" appeal of Campion's audience demographic. As Danièle Heyman writes, "There's a very beautiful scene where Holly Hunter caresses a man's bare back, she caresses it with the back of her hand, not the palm, which is extremely unsettling. For once, feminine desire is filmed at very close quarters."[45]

Induction into Culture

Along with this French sense of cinematic discovery and subsequent critical ownership of Campion as an auteur whose position in the cinematic pantheon of "greats" was assured, there is also a desire to see in Campion someone who bears the lineaments of French high culture, albeit unconsciously and through some strange alchemical process. This may be a quite frequent journalistic device: to connect a talented outsider with outstanding national examples in order to alert one's readership to exemplary cultural parallels, or it may be a more distinctively French cultural trait—an instance of either ecumenical Republicanism or Catholicism. In either case, Campion was adopted by the French critical establishment as "one of us" and located within a widely understood and solidly established cultural hierarchy that included some of the great pillars of French film and literature, both past and present. The desire to adopt Campion and to make her more familiar to French publics, whose knowledge of her was for the most part constructed by the media, could be astute.

The following took advantage of a British linkage where the reviewer made a linguistic association with Jane Birkin, a well-known English actress and singer whose career was initially made in France in the late 1960s through her intimate relationship with a prominent male, the popular singer-songwriter Serge Gainsbourg. The reviewer makes a deliberate play on words that many French readers would have been alert to, as they had first been used in a song of Birkin: "Physical description: Jane C., female, New Zealander, pale complexion, aquiline nose. . . . Gainsbourg would have sung her marvelously" ("Signalement: Jane C., de sexe féminin, néo-zélandaise, teint pale, le nez aquilin. . . . Gainsbourg l'aurait chantée à merveille").[46] More commonly, Campion was associated with French high culture largely as a marker of continuity and replenishment rather than revolt and rupture, a strategy that appealed strongly to French heritage values; this may also be linked to the heritage film genre that her French-financed New Zealand film, *The Piano,* in various ways belongs to.

One reviewer saw Campion as fulfilling a vision of "absolute art" that the young poet Rimbaud had foreseen: "That it is a woman who revives the flame [of the cinema as total art] is not indifferent. Rimbaud had prophesied that this would occur, and that on the day when they reached the poetic continent, we would see what there was to see. It's all been seen."[47] This connection with late-nineteenth-century French poetry was preceded (in the same review) by an early-twentieth-century surrealist linkage that saw one image in *The Piano* (Ada underwater through the deliberate entanglement of her foot in the rope around the sinking piano) as an instance of the "sublime precipitate" of surrealist imagery ("un sublime précipité de l'imagerie surréaliste"). This reminded the critic of Charles Laughton's *The Night of the Hunter* (1955) and Max Ernst's graphic novel *La Semaine de la bonté* (1934). The review in *Globe Hebdo* that appeared the following day reinforced the surrealist thread with the subtitle, "Le retour d'un authentique surréalisme" (The return of a genuine surrealism), and went on to exclaim that Campion

had rediscovered "by her poetic inspiration the grandness of a genuinely surrealist cinema, where the real and the imaginary, the tale and the fable join
up with one another."[48]

The most cinematically nationalistic of the cultural comparisons is one
where Campion is linked with two illustrious cinematic auteurs: Bresson and
Resnais. "But it is the paradox that fascinates and makes this long portrait a
model of exploration that one could consider a continuation of Robert Bresson's last works, if the exuberant delight of the colorist did not counterbalance
the asceticism. Moreover, faithful to the fragmentary work of memory, Jane
Campion films and reconstructs the destiny of her heroine in snippets and
incomplete sketches, in the same way that Alain Resnais was interested in
truncated images of the past."[49]

Associations were also made with authors belonging to the Anglo-
American literary canon, such as the Brontë sisters, Emily Dickinson, Katherine Mansfield, D. H. Lawrence, and Nathaniel Hawthorne.[50]

"Plus 'barbare' qu'esthète"[51]

Although the critic has taken care to bracket "barbarian" when using it as
part of his subtitle, the notion that some of Campion's cinematic strength
is linked to "primitive" intuitions, and the telluric forces of a primeval land,
is inescapable in the French texts. In their desire to describe Campion's cinema, cinematic primitivism is one concept frequently foregrounded. Others
wonder at her ability to reconcile the seemingly irreconcilable, which leads
us to the concept of utopian romance. Her films are cultural artifacts whose
hybridity is enabled because of the antipodal space in which they are made,
and the individual she has become through having grown up in an environment where "making do" with disparate physical and symbolic objects is
an integral part of the country's fairly recent pioneering past and mythology.[52] These antipodal conditions lead to couplings that would be untenable
in France, where boundaries of various types (cultural, political, social) are
more firmly demarcated and policed.

Campion is thus frequently represented as being more like a cinematic
"barbarian" than a sophisticated auteur whose aesthetic is informed by wide
and deep knowledge of film tradition. Although she has eminent affinities
with French high culture, she has a naive access to it. The suspicion that it is
her identity as a New Zealander and, by association, her status as a cultural *bri-
coleuse* that accounts for her ability to make use of preexisting film forms and
narrative is strong. As one critic wrote, "Jane Campion reconciles opposites:
the baroque and modernity, violence and tenderness, gloom and optimism"

("Jane Campion réconcilie les contraires: le baroque et la modernité, la violence et la tendresse, la noirceur et l'optimisme").[53] Another cultural coupling of high and low, distant and familiar was subtitled "The cinema lesson from a noncinephile: The return of a genuine surrealism" ("La leçon de cinema d'une non-cinéphile: le retour d'un authentique surréalisme").[54]

Many critics commented on Campion's cinematic "lack"—a lack of what the French would consider a "veritable" film culture, a form of which implies an extensive knowledge of world film history through its central, that is, canonical, film texts. This is the cinematic version of conspicuous high cultural consumption; a practice that continues to play a central role in contemporary French society in the maintenance of social class distinctions, the recruitment of political elites, and success in the educational system.[55] The journalist from *Globe Hebdo* observes this lack, but not derisively, and celebrates Campion's naive cinematographic art: "Jane Campion, so little a film-buff, admits to never having seen either *Atalante* [1934] or *The Night of the Hunter* [1955], in which women are immersed in water."[56] Note that neither of the two films cited by the reviewer has a director's name or production date attached; this is because they are considered such staples of film culture's canon of great films that such information is deemed superfluous for an educated French readership.

In Campion, a utopian reconciliation and creative recombination of both elite and popular cultures, the naive and the erudite are effected in the French imaginary. Campion is not burdened by the "dead" weight of her forbears. She has an "innocence" that allows her to refresh traditional forms of film language for narrative purposes. This clearly suggests the cinematic reinvigorating of the "Old World" by the "New" and is a view that Campion herself subscribes to in some of her interviews: "Being born in New Zealand has certain advantages. We ignore the weight of the past over there. I do things as they please me, without asking myself a lot of questions. Filmmakers in Europe seem to me to be crushed by the baggage of earlier generations, which requires an entire life to come to terms with."[57] The same lengthy review/interview also noted: "But Jane Campion's greatest merit is probably to have forgotten that many people made films before her, thereby reinventing a cinema language that is both traditional and new."[58]

One of the reasons for this is that Campion is not film literate in the sense the French understand and revere. This is obviously not to say that she had no "film culture" at all. Indeed, from a New Zealand point of view, quite the opposite could be claimed. Jane's parents were prominent members of the theater community, and one of their neighbors and close family friends was the pioneering filmmaker, producer, and longstanding Wellington Film

Society member John O'Shea, who held quite regular private film screenings for his and other children, including the Campions—Jacque Tati's *Jour de fête* (1949) and Albert Lamorisse's *Crin-blanc* (1952) enjoyed frequent repeat screenings.[59] Jane's mother even took her to see films by Buñuel (e.g., *Belle de jour*) when she was but thirteen or fourteen years old.[60] Her initiation into film culture was therefore precocious and deliberate, in the sense that O'Shea was an astute and cultured connoisseur of film—a cinéphile. The French, however, were ignorant of this, and it must have suited them to symbolically position her as a creatively energetic "barbarian" from the antipodes.

Another of Campion's strengths was in her attention to surface details, a close, indeed clinical, observation of the immediately apparent behaviors of her characters. This rigorous attention to appearance eschewed psychological probing of the "depths" as a means to understand character. Is she thus a modern-day Homeric narrator? In any case, she is not bogged down in tortured self-examination, and her art is described as being unrefined, crude, primitive:

As a director who refuses to alter her characters' perception by constructing them, notably, from their psychological attributes (first noted in *Sweetie*), Jane Campion sails against the current of cinema to rediscover an art brut, primitive, trusting only in attitudes, behaviours, and body language. Of Janet Frame's presence in the world, the director only wants to consider her physical appearance and density. As if the rest was merely . . . literature. O paradox![61]

A review in *Libération* enthuses over Campion's ability to avoid the cloying traps that other filmmakers have fallen into when seeking to represent cinematically the grand themes of literary biography: childhood, poetry, love, nature. Campion's treatment of these compulsory life stages restores "their singular palpitation, their pure incandescence" ("leur palpitation singulière, leur pure incandescence").[62] The same review waxes eloquently over Campion's formal audacity, whose power is found in simplicity of an almost primal and unfathomable kind:

An Angel at My Table stuns by its audacious simplicity, the obviousness of its images, and their unrivaled honesty. One would like to cite all those vertiginous shots, those moments of intense splendor that Jane Campion distills without trickery. . . . One would also like to describe those devastating ellipses, the unseen color range, this way of recollecting the plastic dimension of cinema, and this perfect use of the large grain that comes from using 16mm filmstock. One would like to reveal all, but one can't: success at this level is beyond words. It can only be understood through Jane Campion's moral rigor, her way of apprehending the cinema, which mixes naturalness with intense sophistication.[63]

Clearly, a good part of the appeal that Campion, the individual, and Campion as cinéaste have for the French is located in her ability to conduct sophisticated transactions naively; she has an urbane primitivism, which may be why a lengthy interview in *le Monde* ended with her recalling the significance of an image she had often contemplated when convalescing in her mother's bed: "Now I remember that in fact the founding image of this film comes from a painting . . . a canvas by Douanier-Rousseau, *Woman in the Jungle*. . . . I wondered why this woman was there, why she'd been left there. This image of mystery, of a primitive situation, of a woman in the jungle, never left me."[64]

Romancing Jane

The freedom and Otherness of Campion and the antipodes is evoked at the end of another rapturous article: "Jane Campion has no chains, no master, she comes from a vast country, an elsewhere that she gives to us; she is free, her cinema is, too."[65] The romance of the South Seas—storms, shipwrecks, castaways, and island sanctuaries—is suggested in two other articles that speak to the literary constructions of comparable spaces by earlier generations of romantic travel writers, such as Chateaubriand (*Atala,* 1801, and *René,* 1802), who gave prominence to the theme of savage nobility, and Daniel Defoe (*Robinson Crusoe,* 1719), who spoke of island refuges. Visual documents added to the emerging myth when Louis de Sainson's illustrations reached the French public upon the completion of Jules Dumont d'Urville's celebrated scientific expedition to the Pacific aboard the *Astrolabe* (1826–29); a warrior-led form of aristocracy was found in the Maoris of New Zealand (and other Polynesian peoples) that fueled the European revival of a mythical chivalric past.[66]

Commenting on the *The Piano,* one reviewer explicitly mentions parallels with *Robinson Crusoe* in that a shipwreck acts as a trigger for the narratives, "or more exactly a landing on a quasi virgin, hostile, and grandiose island that has all the moral allure of a shipwreck" ("ou plus exactement par un débarquement qui a toutes les allures morales d'un naufrage vers une île quasi vierge, hostile, grandiose")—an "almost virgin" land where a new beginning may be made.[67] The second review quite clearly confuses Ada's deliberate arrival with a disaster brought on by a storm. After describing the land as a primal soup, "a vegetative and liquid chaos of the world's beginning" ("un chaos vegetal et liquide des commencements du monde"), the writer goes on to say that Campion "imagined grafting onto this context the story of a young mute woman that the storm dumps on the beach with her young daughter and her piano" ("a imaginé de greffer sur ce contexte l'histoire d'une jeune femme muette que la tempête dépose sur la grève avec sa petite fille et son piano").[68] Clearly, the Austral lands have aroused the exotic and adventurous imagination here, for it is hard to conceive of a tempest, unless it be Shakespearian, deposing a piano on one of Auckland's west coast beaches intact.[69]

Traditionally, the narrative ploy of a storm serves to realistically explain how travelers have been swept from the normal seafaring routes and come ashore to an island "elsewhere" in which normal standards of behavior no longer apply. Storms also function symbolically—all is awhirl, direction has been lost, and various trials will need to be met before another "perfect order" can be established.[70]

A more direct romance of Campion can be read in the many texts that give succinct descriptions of both her character and physique. Marivaux might have written of her as "La Paysanne parvenue," the antipodean colonial who seeks success in the metropolis. Campion is "blond, round, pink, and smooth, this young woman of provincial charm in no way resembles a porcelain doll" ("Blonde, ronde, rose, et lisse, cette jeune femme au charme provincial n'a rien d'une poupée de porcelaine").[71] Her social origins are also of significance. A contrast favorably evoked concerns Campion's beauty, distinguished appearance, and upper-middle-class culture (Shakespeare, horse riding, a university education, parents with an independent income) and her down-to-earth humor: "Jane Campion has a distinguished air, but she films like someone rude and indecent" ("Jane Campion a une allure distinguée, mais filme comme un charretier").[72] Her candor and good humor are also noted: "Seven and a half months pregnant, Jane Campion answers all questions without embarrassment or subterfuge" ("Enceinte de sept mois et demi, rieuse et détendue, Jane la championne répond sans rosir et sans détour à toutes les questions").[73] Although described as "romantic," Campion is not cloyingly so, nor does her more robust passion prevent her from being "une déconneuse."[74]

Let us recall the effect of her charm and rude health: "She has a radiant smile. Expresses herself warmly. Nourished with cornflakes, made athletic from tennis, and bronzed by the golden rays of the Australian sun."[75] Such a magnificent specimen of the New World sounds like advertising for immigration—the imagery for which a latter-day Gauguin might have been commissioned to provide. The last of these descriptions sees Campion's "soul" conflated with the Pacific Ocean: "Jane Campion's soul is like the Pacific Ocean, smooth on the surface but shaken in the deep by dreadful storms that rise, bellow, roar, and suddenly die down as they break onto the sand's softness."[76]

Oceania—the Dusky Maiden in the French imaginary. Courtesy of Jaz Coleman.

To Conclude

The Eurocentric designation of New Zealand's place vis-à-vis France has undergone various phases since its development several hundred years ago, and the more anthropologically fantastic elements of it, such as that people living in Terra Australis walked upside down or that they had only one foot, gradually withered in the light of actual voyages; but the many islands and their inhabitants in the southern hemisphere continue to function imaginatively in an inverted and often utopian relationship to Europe, and the Rousseauesque figures of noble and ignoble "savages" accompanied by "dusky maidens" still populate the French (and European) imagination. The cover art for a recent music CD, *Oceania* (1999), is offered here to illustrate its enduring appeal.[77]

An earlier mythology continued to provide a convenient cultural toolkit with which to assess the continuing relevance of Campion's work. Such a "repertoire of evaluation" made strong linkages with utopianism and primitivism. Seemingly contradictory elements in the narratives and in Campion's character could be resolved in the French imaginary because of her location in the New World, a more fluid space that allowed of admixtures the Old World could not admit. As one critic put it, the force of *The Piano* resides "in an ideal where the most diverse, even contrary, aspirations meet up."[78]

For the French symbolic order, the name Jane Campion was associated with the austral imagination; invoking it meant invoking the Other—a European fiction whose narrative resolved opposites: the baroque and modernity, violence and tenderness, darkness and optimism. Such fantastic reconciliation did little to advance French understanding of New Zealand, but this seems not to have been the point; responses to *An Angel at My Table* and *The Piano* show French film critics construing New Zealand as a symbolically important space populated by an Otherness both pleasing and necessary to the French cultural imaginary. As a consequence, the attributes they foreground in their appraisal of Jane Campion as a filmmaker are those that constitute, from the French perspective, an "art brut."

Notes

All translations are mine unless otherwise indicated.

1. Richard Lansdown, ed., *Strangers in the South Seas: The Idea of the Pacific in Western Thought* (Honolulu: University of Hawai'i Press, 2006), 18.

2. Ibid.

3. Ibid.

4. John Ellis, "Art, Culture, and Quality: Terms for a Cinema in the Forties and Seventies," *Screen* 19, no. 3 (1978): 9–49.

5. Ibid., 10.

6. Ibid., 18.

7. Ibid., 17.

8. The reviews were drawn from the *Bibliothèque du Film*'s press review collection in Paris.

9. Jean-Luc Macia, "L'ange et ses démons," *la Croix,* 25 April 1991.

10. "Aller voir son film s'est imposé en douce comme une visite sentimentale à quelqu'un de fascinant. Fascinant parce qu'à la fois familier et lointain. Exactement comme le film lui-même." *Télérama* is a weekly cultural magazine that carries radio and television listings—New Zealand's equivalent would be the *Listener* minus the Catholicism.

11. Annie Coppermann, "La poésie contre l'angoisse," *Les Echos,* 24 April 1991.

12. Jean-Michel Racault, "Résonances utopiques de l'*Histoire des navigations aux Terres australes* du président de Brosses," in *Mythes et géographies des mers du sud,* ed. Sylviane Leoni and Réal Ouellet (Dijon: Editions Universitaires de Dijon, 2006), 44–45.

13. "Elle vous coule des sourires lumineux. S'exprime avec chaleur. Nourrie aux corn flakes, musclée par le tennis, d'orée à l'or fin du soleil australien, Jane Campion n'a rien à voir avec les personnages inhibés ou déjantés qui implosent dans ses films." Dominique de Saint Pern, "Le sceau de l'Ange," *l'Express,* 25 April 1991.

14. Louis-Antoine de Bougainville, *Voyage autour du monde par la frégate du Roi "La Boudeuse" et la flute "L'Etoile,"* in Peter Jimack, *Diderot: Supplément au Voyage de Bougainville* (London: Grant and Cutler, 1988), 31.

15. "La vie sauvage est si simple, et nos sociétés sont des machines si compliquées! Le Tahitien touche à l'origine du monde, et l'Européen touche à sa vieillesse." Denis Diderot, "Supplément au Voyage de Bougainville," http://www.gutenberg.org/dirs/etext04/8spvb10.txt (accessed 21 October 2008).

16. "Regarde ces hommes; vois comme ils sont droits, sains et robustes. Regarde ces femmes; vois comme elles sont droites, saines, fraîches et belles. " Diderot, "Supplément au Voyage de Bougainville."

17. "Exerce un pouvoir magique sur celui-là seul qui sait l'entendre, il insinue dans son coeur et son âme pureté, réserve, énergie, calme. Ainsi la civilisation finit-elle par vaincre la brutalité de la nature des hommes. Sa métamorphose, son ascension chromatique de la demi-sauvagerie vers une perfection humaine constituent par son authenticité sensuelle et spirituelle une enthousiasmante démonstration." Claude Baignères, "De la musique avant toute chose," *le Figaro,* 18 May 1993.

18. "Et son secret est peut-être de croire intensément—à la différence de tant de ses contemporains—que l'on peut encore raconter des histoires." M. C., "La leçon de cinema d'une non-cinéphile," *Globe Hebdo,* 19 May 1993.

19. "Ce bon vieux principe tombé en désuétude chez nous, et qui exigeait d'un metteur en scène au moins une idée par plan, ce qui fait du *Piano* un fourmillement d'événements et de surprises." Alain Riou, *le Nouvel Observateur,* 13 May 1993.

20. "Là-bas règnent la pluie furieuse, la boue végétale et liquide des commencements du monde." Baignères, "De la musique avant toute chose."

21. "'To the Is-Lands' dépeint l'enfance de l'écrivain qui, sous des apparences farouches et peu flatteuses, montre un tempérament surdoué, une identité intellectuelle en exil dans son cadre primitif et naturel." Anne de Gasperi, "Rousseur de vivre," *le Quotidien de Paris,* 25 April 1991.

22. "Nous voilà donc sur les traces de Janet Frame, dans les années 30, au coeur de ce pays en forme de point d'interrogation." Olivier Séguret, "Jane Campion, manifeste pour un Ange," *Libération,* 24 April 1991.

23. Supercilious comments, however, do warrant rebuke. *Le Quotidien de Paris* was responsible for the following flippancy: "Janet Frame est rondouillarde, rouquine et a les dents gâtés. Pour arranger le tout . . . elle grandit dans une famille néo-zélandaise (aïe!)." Aurélien Ferenczi and François Jonquet, "Rousse, ronde, moche et folle," 24 April 1991. The presumption that growing up in a New Zealand family is particularly calamitous for plump redheads with rotten teeth is not an obvious one.

24. France has a long history of influential national cultural politics and the highly centralized education system provides strong grounds for consensus around national "repertoires of evaluation" that legitimate certain types of ideas about art.

25. This commitment to social realism has also worked to prevent the emergence of a genuinely indigenous genre of fantastic or horror film, with George Franju's *Les Yeux sans visage* (Eyes without a face) (1959) and *Judex* (1963) being exceptions that demonstrate the rule; films long misunderstood by the French critical establishment whose dominant paradigm valorised (perhaps excessively) the auteur and *le cinema d'art et d'essai,* the personal expression of a filmmaking artist. An article by Catherine Wheatley in *Senses of Cinema,* titled "Les Yeux sans visage," gives a good overview of the critical reception given to Franju's film. Wheatley, "Les Yeux sans visage," *Senses of Cinema,* http://www.sensesofcinema.com/contents/cteq/07/42/yeux-sans-visage .html (accessed 21 October 2008).

An economic argument is also used to partially explain the contemporary absence in France of a flourishing genre cinema: "De l'avis des professionnels, cette pauvreté serait le fait, en partie du moins, des structures de marché. 'Le cinéma de genre en général, et les films d'horreur en particulier, ne fleurissent que sur les territoires où il existe un marché vidéo très fort, à savoir les pays anglo-saxons,' explique Vincent Maraval, directeur des ventes internationales chez *Wild Bunch.*" Jean-François Rauger and Isabelle Regnier, "Emergence de l'horreur à la française," *le Monde,* 12 June 2007. More recent examples of French genre cinema, such as *À l'intérieur* (Inside, 2007), by Julien Maury and Alexandre Bustillo, still serve to highlight their exceptional nature in France, where social and psychological realism are the preferred generic modes.

26. Riou, *le Nouvel Observateur,* 13 May 1993, 21.

27. Plazzo, "Questions pour un Campion."

28. Riou, *le Nouvel Observateur,* 13 May 1993.

29. "Je n'avais pas la plus petite idée de ce que représentait le Festival de Cannes, et comme je venais de terminer un film pour la télévision, je n'avais qu'un désir: des vacances. Rissient a beaucoup insisté: ce fut ma chance." Ibid.

30. Andrew L. Urban, "Piano's Good Companions," in *Jane Campion Interviews,* ed. Virginia Wright Wexman (Jackson: University Press of Mississippi, 1999), 147.

31. "*Car la Leçon de piano,* comme les autres films du metteur en scène, nous raconte la naissance d'une femme, jusque-là repliée sur elle-même, quasi autiste, qui va s'éveiller au monde." M. C., "La leçon de cinema."

32. "Ses films, totalement étrangers, nous parlent un langage familier. Lequel? Le seul auquel doive prétendre un auteur du cinema: celui de la mise en scène. Si la musique est idiome universel, la mise en scène aussi: c'est celui-ci et non le japonais, qu'il faut apprendre pour comprendre 'le Mizoguchi'." Antoine de Baecque, *Histoire d'une revue,* vol. 1, *Les Cahiers à l'assaut du cinéma* (Paris: Cahiers du cinéma, 1991), 158.

33. "Ils prisent à ce point la mise en scène parce qu'ils y discernent dans une large mesure la matière même du film, une organisation des êtres et des choses qui est à elle-même son sens, aussi bien moral qu'esthétique." Ibid., 157.

34. For certain influential French film critics, such as Michel Frodon (*le Monde* and *les Cahiers du cinéma*), the cinema, as the preeminent art form of industrial

capitalism, has a historic role, which is to create a singular space by way of its system of representation that allows for individuals to participate in a critical debate whose purpose is to articulate a relationship between the real and the imaginary, the collective and the singular. Questioning the specificity of the medium of the cinema in its relationship with multiple realities is, for Frodon, of great importance. It is specifically because the cinema is an art that individuals are enabled in this way to engage in what for Frodon are urgent debates concerning citizenship in contemporary postindustrial capitalist societies. See Michel Frodon, *Horizon cinéma: l'art du cinéma dans le monde contemporain à l'âge du numérique et de la mondialisation* (Paris: Cahiers du cinéma, 2006), a text that seeks to redefine the place that cinematographic art occupies in the new audiovisual landscape created by digitization and globalization.

35. "Si la mer est bleue, la montagne aussi. Le vert des pâturages exulte alors que danse le vif patchwork des robes des fillettes. Pourtant, c'est le roux qui domine. Ou, plutôt, c'est autour du roux que Jane Campion compose presque chacun de ses plans avec la hardiesse et toute la maîtrise d'un peintre qui sait la plénitude indépassable d'un tableau fini, le jeu savant des lumières, l'harmonie secrète des couleurs." Claude Sartirano, "Les Trois paysages intérieurs," *l'Humanité,* 25 April 1991.

36. "C'est une narration accomplie sur le modèle d'un roman de Dickens. Ce qui la distingue immédiatement du réalisme essentiellement anecdotique généralement généré par l'image télévisée qui a tellement contaminée le cinéma." Anne de Gasperi, "Et qui sait, à celle du jury," *le Quotidien de Paris,* 15 September 1990.

37. "Aucun trucage là-dedans. Du vrai. Rien que du vrai. Et un talent à faire frémir tous les oiseaux des écrans noirs. Jane Campion vient d'inventer un nouveau cinéma: celui des moyens réduits qui vous font croire à la superproduction. Ses paysages sont superbes (merci la Nouvelle-Zélande? ce serait trop simple. Campion invente les arbres, les nuages, les lumières)." Bernard Génies, "La folie à l'horizon," *le Nouvel Observateur,* 2 May 1991. The critic's metaphorical use of birds and dark screens in his description of Campion's talent and invention may reference Vincent Van Gogh's expressive representations of nature, e.g., *Wheat Field with Crows.*

38. "Il faut, si l'on aime le cinéma d'auteur, aller voir cet Ange, avatar beaucoup plus séduisant, après le très perturbante Sweetie, d'un personnage au coeur de tous les films de Jane Campion: la solitaire, timide, émotive, aux frontières d'une folie qu'ici, c'est très beau, elle apprivoise, dompte et finalement jugule par la création. Comme la réalisatrice?" Coppermann, "La Poésie contre l'angoisse."

39. "La réalisatrice persiste, dans ce qui est, pour le moment, son grand sujet, celui qui traverse ses quatre courts métrages, son film de télévision et ses deux films de cinéma, le portrait intime de jeunes femmes dont la séduction vient précisément de leur physique ingrat, de leurs corps douloureux, et de leur inadaptation à la vie." J. R., "La Chaleur sous la glace," *l'Humanité,* 15 September 1990.

40. "Tous les films de Jane Campion parlent de la douleur de vivre, de la difficulté des rapports humains, de la frontière tenue entre l'anormalité et la normalité, du vertige qui vous prend soudain de plonger dans la mort." Isabelle Danel, "La Leçon de piano," *Télérama,* 19 May 1993.

41. "L'idée circule aussi qu'un film de femme, c'est presque une garantie d'honnêteté, la vision forcement personnelle d'un auteur." Plazzo, "Questions pour un Campion."

42. "La nouvelle critique anglo-saxonne voulait reconquérir une véritable subjectivité féminine et déconstruire le modèle de représentation et de formation masculine utilisé dans l'éducation et dans l'art." Steven Bernas, *L'auteur au cinéma* (Paris: L'Harmattan, 2002), 18–19.

43. Plazzo, "Questions pour un Campion."

44. Monique Pantel and Richard Gianorio, "Jane la championne brise les tabous sexuels," *France-soir,* 18 May 1993.

45. "Il y a cette scène très belle où Holly Hunter caresse le dos nu d'un homme, elle le caresse du dos de la main, pas de la paume, c'est extrêmement troublant. Pour une fois le désir féminin est filmé, de très près." Danièle Heyman, "Passion: mode d'emploi," *le Monde,* 13 May 1993.

46. Véronique Philipponnat, "Le vol de l'ange noir qui a bouleversé Venise," *le Journal de Dimanche,* 21 April 1991. Gainsbourg's song "Janc B." was in their first collaborative album, titled simply *Jane Birkin & Serge Gainsbourg* (1969). Some of the lyrics were "Signalement yeux bleus / cheveux châtains / Jane B. / Anglaise / De sexe féminin / Âge: entre vingt et vingt et un / Apprends le dessin / Domiciliée chez ses parents."

47. "Il n'est pas indifférent que ce soit une femme qui . . . ranime la flamme [du cinéma comme art absolu]. Rimbaud avait prophétisé qu'il en serait ainsi et qu'au jour où elles aborderaient au continent poétique, vous allez voir ce que vous allez voir. C'est tout vu." Jean-Pierre Leonardini, "Elle est Campion toutes catégories," *l'Humanité,* 18 May 1993.

48. "Par son inspiration poétique la grandeur d'un cinéma authentiquement surréaliste, où se rejoignent le réel et l'imaginaire, le récit et la fable." M.C., "La leçon de cinema."

49. "Mais c'est ce paradoxe qui fascine et fait de ce long portrait un modèle d'exploration que l'on pourrait situer, si la suavité exubérante de la coloriste n'en contrebalançait pas l'ascétisme, dans le prolongement des derniers travaux de Robert Bresson. En outre, fidèle à la fonction fragmentaire de la mémoire, Jane Campion filme et recompose par bribes, par saynètes incomplètes le destin de son héroïne, comme ses images tronquées du passé auxquelles s'est intéressé également Alain Resnais." Sartirano, "Les Trois paysages intérieurs."

50. Jean-Pierre Leonardini, "Elle est Campion toutes categories," *l'Humanité,* 18 May 1993; Claire Devarrieux, "Pulsion, Passion et Piano Forte", *Libération,* 18 May 1993; and M. C., "La leçon de cinema d'une non-cinéphile", *Globe Hebdo,* 19 May 1993.

51. Thomas Bourguignon and Michel Ciment, "Entretien avec Jane Campion: Plus 'barbare' qu'esthète," *Positif* 383 (1993): 6–11.

52. See Nick Perry's essay "Antipodean Camp" for a more extensive analysis of this cultural phenomenon, in his *Hyperreality and Global Culture* (London: Routledge, 1998), 4–23.

53. Danel, "La Leçon de piano."

54. M. C., "La leçon de cinema."

55. Daniel Weber, "Culture or Commerce in Publishing," in *Rethinking Comparative Sociology: Repertoires of Evaluation in France and the United States,* eds. Michèle Lamont and Laurent Thévenot (Cambridge: Cambridge University Press, 2000), 142.

56. "Jane Campion, si peu cinéphile, avoue n'avoir vu . . . ni *l'Atalante* [1933] ni *La Nuit du chasseur* [1955], où des femmes sont englouties dans les eaux." M. C., "La leçon de cinema."

57. "Il y a certains avantages à être née en Nouvelle-Zélande, confesse Jane Campion. Là-bas, nous ignorons le poids du passé. Nous n'y pensons jamais. Je fais les choses comme elles me viennent, sans me poser de questions. En Europe, les cinéastes me paraissent écrasés par le bagage hérité des générations précédentes, qu'il faut une vie entière pour aborder." Riou, *le Nouvel Observateur,* 13 May 1993.

58. "Mais le plus grand mérite de Jane Campion est probablement d'avoir oublié que bien des gens ont filmé avant elle, réinventant un langage de cinéma à la fois traditionnel et neuf." Ibid.

59. Jane Campion, "A Memoir of John O'Shea," in John O'Shea, *Don't Let It Get You: Memories—Documents* (Wellington: Victoria University Press, 1999), 7–9.

60. Rachel Abramovitz, "Jane Campion," in Wexman, *Jane Campion,* 189.

61. "En cinéaste, on l'a vu avec *Sweetie,* qui refuse d'altérer la perception de ses personnages en les construisant, notamment, avec leurs caractéristiques psychologiques, Jane Campion remonte en fait le courant du cinéma pour retrouver un art brut, primitif, ne se fiant qu'aux attitudes, au comportement, à la gestuelle des corps. De la presence au monde de Janet Frame, la réalisatrice ne veut prendre en compte que l'apparence physique, sa densité. Comme si le reste n'était que . . . littérature. Ô paradoxe!" Sartirano, "Les Trois paysages intérieurs."

62. Séguret, "Jane Campion."

63. "*Un Ange à ma table* stupéfie par la simplicité de ses audaces, l'évidence de ses images, leur insondable probité. On aimerait citer tous ces plans vertigineux, ces moments d'intenses splendeurs que Jane Campion distille sans effet de manche . . . On voudrait aussi décrire ces ellipses foudroyantes, ce chromatisme jamais vu, cette manière de rappeler la dimension plastique du cinéma, et cette utilisation parfaite du gros grain inhérent au format 16 mm. On voudrait tout dire, mais on ne le peut pas: la réussite à ce stade, se passe de mots. Elle ne s'explique que par la rigueur morale de Jane Campion, sa manière d'appréhender le cinéma qui mélange le naturel et l'intense sophistication." Ibid.

Campion's "perfect use" of 16-millimeter filmstock was a consequence of two things: budget and audience. *An Angel at My Table* was originally made for television—its three-part structure is a reflection of that. Moreover, she was initially opposed to its release in cinemas because both the visual style and the viewing conditions were designed for the small rather than the big screen.

64. "Maintenant je me rappelle que, en fait, l'image fondatrice de ce film provient d'un tableau . . . une toile du Dounaier-Rousseau, *Femme dans la forêt* . . . je me demandais pourquoi cette femme était là, pourquoi l'avait-on laissée là. Cette image de mystère, de situation primitive, de femme dans une forêt ne m'as jamais quittée." Heyman, "Passion."

65. "Jane Campion n'a pas d'entraves, pas de maître, elle vient d'une vaste contrée, d'un ailleurs qu'elle nous donne, elle est libre, son cinéma aussi." "Un Ange à ma table," *le Monde,* 15 September 1990.

66. Harry Liebersohn, "Images of Monarchy: Kamehameha I and the Art of Louis Choris," in *Double Vision: Art Histories and Colonial Histories in the Pacific,* ed. Nicholas Thomas and Diane Losche (Cambridge: Cambridge University Press, 1999), 45.

67. Riou, *le Nouvel Observateur,* 13 May 1993.

68. Baignères, "De la musique avant toute chose."

69. Karekare Beach, west of Auckland, was the location for the beach scenes in *The Piano.*

70. Jean Garagnon, "French Imaginary Voyages to the Austral Lands in the Seventeenth and Eighteenth Centuries," in *Australia and the European Imagination,* ed. Ian Donaldson (Humanities Research Council, Canberra: Australian National University, 1982).

71. Pantel and Gianorio, "Jane la championne brise les tabous sexuels."

72. Literally, a cart driver ("charretier"). Philipponnat, "Le vol de l'ange noir qui a bouleversé Venise."

73. Pantel and Gianorio, "Jane la championne brise les tabous sexuels."

74. Someone who enjoys clowning around. Marie Colmant, "Jane Campion: 'Ça vous fouette les sangs,'" *Libération,* 18 May 1993.

75. de Saint Pern, "Le sceau de l'Ange."

76. "L'âme de Jane Campion est semblable à l'océan Pacifique, lisse en surface mais secoué dans les fonds de terribles tempêtes qui surgissent, mugissent, rugissent et s'apaisent soudain, en venant se briser dans la douceur du sable." Riou, *le Nouvel Observateur,* 13 May 1993.

77. English expatriate composer Jaz Coleman and New Zealand singer Hinewehi Mohi collaborated on this 1999 album. Mohi's sense of Maori cultural identity is firmly announced on the back page of the liner notes, perhaps to mitigate the exploitive potential of the imagery.

78. "Sa force est bien là: dans un idéal où les aspirations les plus diverses, voire contraires, se retrouvent." Plazzo, "Questions pour un Campion."

Flora and Ada on the beach in *The Piano*. Courtesy of Photofest.

"The piano is mine. It's *mine*."
My (Free Association with) Jane Campion, or, the Child in the Spectator

Perhaps because I haven't actually been bruised or scarred myself in the process of being in a family I'm not protecting myself when I discuss it. I think I can enter into the imaginary world of family conflict fairly confidently.

      —Jane Campion

CHILD: I told you not to talk to that man.
MOTHER: But he's my friend. And you know, you don't own me.
CHILD: Well, what if I cut you up into bits. *Then* you'd be mine. I'd eat all the pieces—your arms, legs, head, body—and you'd be inside me.

    —Conversation with my seven-year-old son

I have always been fascinated by the profound emotional affects generated by Jane Campion's films. My monograph *Views from Beyond the Mirror: The Films of Jane Campion* explored this interest largely through an inquiry into her films' distinctive address to female spectators, and in particular to myself as a woman. In this essay I press further into the affective dimension of spectatorial response through a personal sensitivity to the ways in which the child aspect of the adult viewer is acknowledged and stimulated, especially in *Sweetie, The Piano,* and *In the Cut.*

Campion's films are acutely aware of how little actual power children have in societies governed by adults who see their guardianship roles in terms of discipline, regulation, and control. All of her films evince this interest in children's preoccupation with power and their vulnerability before the abuses of adult power. But what is most impressive is the capacity these films have to unsettle the viewer's adult subjectivity, to initiate a regression, fragmentation, and reconstruction of the adult subject.

The methodology employed in this essay could be called ficto-critical—or perhaps autobio-critical: it consists of a hybrid form of writing that deliberately upsets the hierarchical splitting and ordering of knowledge into objective and subjective modes and challenges the critic's presumption of authorial authority. The "analysis" proceeds by a simulation of the psychoanalytic method of free association, where the films, to some extent, are given the position of the analyst who provides the material—or prompts—to which the critic associates. The aim is less to offer *interpretations* of the films than to stage the *undoing* and *reconstitution* of the academic critic-spectator and explore the tensions and conflicts within her as she experiences her inner responses and performs her public readings. My way into the analysis proceeds from a meditation/confession regarding my participation, as audience member and discussant, in the Jane Campion Symposium in Dunedin. During those three days I re-viewed and reconsidered the entire corpus of Campion's filmmaking, in the company of other spectator-critics who were equally attentive and immersed. It was a remarkable and humbling experience. In noticing the ebb and flow of my feelings during the screenings and the various presentations by delegates, I began to ask myself questions about the nature of my investments in "Jane."

The Possessive Critic: Retrospective

There are many experts here, a whole community of us from around the globe, gathered together to share what we have seen and understood. I feel compelled to be among them, to be included.[1] We speak in a variety of accents and languages, we focus our attention from different sites, through different framings, but our object is the same: the films of Jane Campion. I expect that it is our shared love for this object that has brought us together; it is of this love and this object that we will speak and listen. This happens. Together we extend our understanding of what we have seen and experienced and the processes involved in effecting our responses. I am excited, expectant, greedy. It feels like Christmas! I am inward, cautious, afraid. I don't know what I want.

There is something in the private communion between the object and myself that I am both reluctant and eager to share, reluctant and eager to hear. I don't quite want the public discourse. I do, I don't. I've been snuggling in her petticoat. I'm not sure about those men. Ambivalence fractures my concentration.

Jealousy flares. The possibility of loss hangs in the air. Like the truest of lovers I assert that my love has no equal, and the fact that so many others are here confirms the worthiness of my choice. But I have rivals (not really. *Really!*): endless siblings claiming equal privilege, access, and importance. More than equal. Have they seen what I have seen? Have they also been entered, pierced, held, filled with longing? And if so, where does that leave me? Has my love object chosen others over me? Have I got it wrong? Is the door now shut against me? Am I reduced to peeping through the cracks at superior lovers as they tongue the secret folds I'd foolishly cherished as mine alone? Alone, undistinguished among the many, I chafe against the knowledge that, in linking me with another, separates me from her. I spiral inward down the years, watching from doorways, supplanted, burning inside with violent hatred. She and he, a cozy pair, while I'm a big girl now. No consolation. I am sending bolts of fire from the deepest blackness of my stormy fantasy to incinerate them both. No, I'll take her tongue but let her live. My skin tingles, prickles, with suppressed aggression.

I am no longer special and flickering, no longer wheeling in the softly golden borderland prior to prying eyes. Elusive memory! Instead I am divided against myself, forced in this communion to recognize my kinship with the exiled and the ordinary. Flora stamps her foot, clenches her fists, rages, and curses: "Bloody, bloody bugger her." Sweetie throws a tantrum: "I'm really going to do something now." Kay whines plaintively: "I'm sick of it, Mum." At other times she feigns indifference, moves on to other objects, plans to have her hair cut: "You know I'm seriously thinking about getting this chopped." Even Clayton, with his toy cars lined up for sale and no customers willing to play, offers an impulsive solution: he takes out his temper on the merchandise, renouncing ownership in favor of a gesture of repudiation, turning gold into shit with one quick kick.[2] But I know how to compose myself in public. I'm not a child anymore. I am a teacher, a writer, a speaker. I work to tame the flames of hatred and envy. I listen and learn. All the time I am stepping further along the ascending paths of grown-up land. I am on the move, always walking away.

Sometimes looking back.

Oral Desires

MILK (Kate Llewellyn[3])

We found you
like a shell on a beach
and brought you home
and put you into bed

with your mother
every morning you are there
between them
singing with milk
before you sing
you swim with milk
lying at her breast
taking milk like history
three drops fall
and again as a shell drinks
the ocean
you drink milk
and then you kick

FRIDGE DOOR

My friends have two young children. On their fridge door, written in magnetic words, is a short poem, written by the younger daughter. It reads:

`eat` `mama` `and` `papa`
`healthy` `yummy`

OYSTER DREAM

In my sleep I dream of oysters, a plate of oysters, and my refusal to share them. "They are mine!" I command. I am an aggressive, hoarding hostess, turning away the uninvited couple who try to sample my silky delicacies at this gathering of peers. My selfish defiance is rewarded with disgrace and expulsion. My kind friend turns her back to me and directs her welcoming gaze toward my thieves. From the edge of the party I watch as my evacuated place is occupied by the freeloaders. My soundless, choking tears elicit no pity from the outraged group nor remorse from the dreamer. Meanwhile, the rescued oysters are safely stored in the freezer.

Family, food, sexuality. The group, the triangle, the couple, the one. I slide dreamward through the social order into frigidity and abjection. Oysters on ice. Slippery territory on which to skate. At what cost is desire preserved? At what cost do I refuse to share my plate with the couple?

On waking I think of shame and guilt; the child's struggle to lay claim to her precious, erotic organ, her access to arousal, in defiance of punishment, the daughter's prohibition against the couple's unwelcome, intrusive appetites. I think of parents and daughters. I see fridges and freezers, ice and milk, mouths and tongues. I recall the plates of food Flo prepares for her husband, Gordon, to tide him over when she leaves him. "What, no freezer?" he laments, incredulous, as he unpacks the cling-wrapped meals at daughter Kay's house (the mother's food feeding the father's appetite at the daughter's table); Sweetie, choking on her sister's china horses and spitting them out with blood (Kay's precious "food," resurrected from childhood, being stolen and incorporated by the favored daughter);[4] Pauline, picking morsels from a plate in the fridge and licking her fingers as she recounts her latest episode of promiscuous indulgence with the married doctor; Frannie, unlikely milkmaid, pouring milk for a white cat that laps at the saucer, innocent, babyish; the same cat scavenging for scraps, opportunist, streetwise; Frannie, watching others stuffing their mouths, licking and tasting, while her lips stay closed; Frannie, sitting slumped in a drunken, grief-stricken stupor against the open door of her almost empty refrigerator, dreaming of her mother's engagement story; the young woman, maiden, fiancée, skating on ice, a pretty ballerina, spinning, spinning, going nowhere, falling— chop!—legs of frozen sausage sliced right through by a daughter's dream of a lethal, would-be husband, a serially romantic father. Red meat on white ice. Rodriguez, negative figure of the law, uses body parts for fish bait and invites Frannie to a meal of calamari. Octopus, fish, oysters. Delectable fishy women. Cold, bloodless corpses. Frannie declines.[5] So do I. I will keep my expensive oysters until the time—and the company—are right.

Triangles, pairs, appetite, horror. I remember the pubescent girls—Stella, Pam, Gloria—who feel the cold, who are left out in the cold. They sit on a cold, bare floor, in singlets and cottontails, worshipping radiators, attempting to thaw and warm. Spotlight on Gloria, playing a game of cats with her brother, showing him how to drink like a cat. She purrs. Laps. Cozies up to the radiator's glow. He snarls, insists on the tomcat grossness of feline animality. Girl's game over.[6]

We are hungry. But for what?

Look at Me

On my fridge door is a list headed, "The Seven Point Mind Training by Lama Atisha"—my daily mantra. Points 1 and 7 advise:

Consider all phenomena to be dreams.
Don't expect a standing ovation.

The seventh point makes me laugh. When I first read this list I thought it was an impossible task to give up the expectation of applause. In the context of this retrospective of Campion's films, Sweetie bursts into the frame, desperately performing her childhood tricks, licks, and curtsies for her father and his heirs; Louie, more quietly, follows suit when he asks Flo to watch him do a handstand in the backyard; Pauline, fantasizing about her successful seduction of the married doctor she has been stalking, imagines that when he sees her in court—"he will look at me and realize he loves me." I think of my young son, always calling to me "Mum, watch me, Mum, watch this. Are you watching?" To be looked at, to be seen—to be loved. Every day I meditate on letting go, freeing my mind from attachment, especially to itself, but the clever, subtle ego is always looking for ways to grab the limelight.

Yes, I am showing off. Posturing. Doing ballet on the beach. Tap dancing on the table. Preparing my smile for the mirror. Hogging the attention. Trying to steal the show. Undeniably. And yet, this is too simple, and partial. Something else is happening—I hope. It's not all about me—not completely. Dad is a fucking arse-hole. A cunt. He's kept me captive, a psychotic princess. He's sold me in marriage. Touched my sister. Killed my mother. Left me for dead. His leather-gloved fist is clenched. He's made me love him. He's laid on my bed and entered my dreams. I sing to him, a song from my grave—"love me with all your heart as I love you." I've been his number one girl, such a clever little thing. But now I'm going too far, right out on a limb, way over the top. I'm breaking into the script, unloosing my tongue. I might say anything! He's in the circle of my head, with his knife. He scores a blood-soaked curve around my throat. I choke, vomit, disarticulate. My head falls in the basin. Splat. My hair is such a mess.

Behind the wish for admiration and congratulation (which proves itself to be so empty when realized) hides a deeper, incurable loss that constantly nags and gnaws: more analysand than analyst, I will try to work my way down and back to it. Sweetie crashes. Ada drowns. Pauline is beheaded. Kay moves on. Janet writes. Isabel looks to the future. In my performance, self-indulgent as it is, I'm retracing the fall of falling women. These films have made me fall to pieces, *sick with longing*. In the end I come together again, broken parts salvaged and glued like Kay's treasured china horses, not perfect but whole enough. I am a patchwork of screen-colored images, luminous scraps of character and narrative intermingled with dreams and recollections.

A Love There Is No Cure For

The lights are dimmed. Excerpts from *The Piano* appear on the screen.[7] Amniotic fingers, webbed in bleary, blood-colored light; a small girl's feet in cumbersome roller skates; the girl herself, aloft a reluctant pony who strains against the reins as the father tugs and tugs, trying to force a forward step; shadowy form of . . . a mother? . . . at the edge of a frame. I have no trouble seeing these snippets as the images of a dream. I know this language, as unconsciously scripted, as remote, fleeting, tantalizing, and familiar as any I have really dreamed while tossing in my bed.

Now a longer segment. We sit in darkness. . . .

Ada's skirt billows around her sinking body—beauty in abjection—the lush, unbearable, silky collapse. Aesthetic tenderness around the swoon into acceptance, the sublime, the absoluteness of the cut, the cushioned blow, nothing will ever be the same again; there can be no going back—but possibly also no going forward. The dress billows again under water, in her dreams, an ever-present moment of death-in-life—epiphanous, subterranean, siren. I hold my breath as she succumbs to the sinking; my body is filled with air held in as if it will never again be released, suspended in this plenitude of nowhere, everywhere, in-between, not yet born, not yet dead, close to coming, close to expiring, densely floating, consciously dreaming, falling and resisting in the same instant. Who am I? Perhaps I am on the brink of knowing as I enter the drift of unknowing, the surrender to those mortal limits, face to face with the inevitable real. The sob swells in my chest, and my throat aches with unshed tears.

But I am on duty here, academic. The lights will be on soon, and I struggle against the undisciplined, intimate impulse that wishes only to merge, claim, cling, own. I resist, but listen, as another voice—the analyst's—guides me through the scene, interprets the powerful latency that I have lived but lacked the words and distance for. That night I cry and cry and cry until I am sufficiently released of the dark energy to pick up my pen again. The words flow in ecstatic abandon, riding on the crest of death. The child will not be repudiated. She rises and clamors, so young and unformed I have no memory of her, only this uncanny feeling, in the pores of my skin, of having known her struggle for air.

She kicks off her shoe, slips free of the cord, separates body from piano, flesh from music, and pushes her face against the membrane of sea, breaks into bubbling light, color, and sound, her dreamy mermaid existence impossible, too real, barely imaginable, poetic.

Life pulls at one arm, death at the other, and I long to split along the fault line of my psychic life. This sublime divide. I am falling into the gap: into love; toward death; into myself. I am yearning for that exchange of the ineffable. Love. Kisses. The desire to kiss, be kissed, inwardly tasted, surrendered. To be completed? No. To be self-sufficient, wholly torn apart and lost within an immense, borderless fluidity. Words loop back into themselves as I struggle for legibility.

Seaweed somersaults and wraps itself around, around. We are back to mirrors and mothers, the holding gaze that simply is and does not mean, perfect circular exchange of glances, mirror bliss. Prior to the otherness of self. Prior to narcissism. I look into the mirror as if it is him (or do I mean her?), willing it to be that Other, whom I love, looking at me; feeling the tug of loss and impossibility in the recognition of my reflection. To say "my" is already to have been halved into singularity. My love. Our eyes meet. The old cliché. The perfect circle. There we have it. The rapture of the mutual gaze. We are all so young, so small, so all encompassing, remembering, in thrall to the original entrancement, listening for that ancient echo of the ancient love where sight and sound and touch and taste and skin outside and in were indistinguishable. When looking and holding were inseparable. The grief, always close to the surface, at knowing and denying the truth of the cut that has endowed us with the name of "me" and not "you." The grief at knowing and denying that the best that adult love can offer is a temporary island of deluded mirror satisfaction; small snatches of infinity in the larger daily-ness of ego-boundaried life.

The Mother's Shelter

THE CHILD'S PATH

> The route to individuality that leads through identificatory love of the father is a difficult one for women to follow. The difficulty lies in the fact that the power of the liberator-father is used to defend against the engulfing mother. . . . Curiously enough, psychoanalysis has not found this split, with its devaluation of the maternal, to be a problem.
>
> —Jessica Benjamin, *The Bonds of Love*

I am also mother. Childless before, I saw and felt only as daughter.[8] Severed only as daughter from mother and not yet as mother from child, I relived that first cut, the deepest as they say. As daughter I was Ada only, strange as that may sound, fully expressive and inarticulate, singular and self-absorbed, in the lead, aloof, perversely omnipotent. All, and nothing. As mother I am guide and guardian, holder of young hands, patient follower of my child's steps. As a watchful mother I can be/see Flora, my speech can be more alert to mimesis and relatively stabilized in its flexibility. As I walk along the beach I see her smaller footprints hurrying to join mine, making a thickly corded umbilical track. My duty is to let her find or make a path that neither simply doubles (faithful only to the original number—one—which it marries) nor divides (in spite and self-mutilation, a path that divorces and kills): a third path? Parallel?

240

Journeying with my son, Tristan.

I am returning to The Piano, *taking another spin.*

Flora, like all children, is a mimic, and her mother is the original. She mimics Ada's facial expressions, the tilt of her head, her hand gestures, and even her kisses. The intimate attachment between mother and daughter is visually choreographed. They are twin figures in their matching bonnets, tight bodices, and full skirts. Both wear their hair parted in the center and tightly pulled back into braided buns. Together they inhabit an idyllic, private world, a space defined as feminine and maternal. On the beach, after their arrival in New Zealand, they shelter together inside a tent made from Ada's hooped undergarment. The warm golden light that surrounds this inner space contrasts strongly with the cold blue outside. The same golden light illuminates their resting, nesting bodies when they share a bed in Stewart's house. They form a duet, where Ada plays the piano and Flora dances, sings, and accompanies. When they walk through the swampy woods near Stewart's house, Ada leads and Flora follows. One after the other their shoes sink to the ankle in mud. The physical caresses that pass between mother and daughter are enhanced by the fact that they share a tactile language that no one else understands: Flora is the privileged interpreter of her mother's hand signs, which also means that she is often at the interface between her mother and others. And it is here that the trouble begins.

Against the idyll of her union with her daughter are the struggles Ada encounters in her dealings with two men: her "husband," Stewart, and the man she "bargains" with, Baines. The harmonious unity between mother and daughter is able to hold fast as long as Ada stays aloof from the men, each of whom offers Ada a "relationship" based on a different version of patriarchal economics: her father has given her to Stewart in marriage, and he appraises her in the same terms as he might appraise a stock animal; Baines, on the other hand, offers to let her buy back her piano from him in exchange for sexual favors. Because of the nature of the piano lessons Ada is giving Baines, Flora is made to stay outside his hut while the lesson is in progress. As a direct consequence of the contract between Ada and Baines, the first explicit, tangible barrier separating child from mother is inserted between them. In shifting into the zone of heterosexual commerce, Ada simultaneously excludes Flora. Where Flora had once been under her mother's skirt, now it is Baines who is being let in (literally). Flora is furious. She protests. She swears. She begins to argue against her mother instead of for her and to pass on messages that are not maternally authorized. When Stewart once asks where Ada is going, Flora, in a rage, yells, "To hell!" Where she had been proud to act as her mother's voice, she now begins to echo Stewart, repeating his wishes and orders to her disobedient mother, referring to him as Papa, and striving to enforce his authority to make Ada stay at home. The protective interface she had been between Ada and all others becomes allied to the other side, the side of paternal law. This shift is to have catastrophic consequences.

I want to think about the meaning of the crucial shifting of alliances that Flora makes. The obvious explanation arises that this is Flora's classical Oedipal moment: as she steps onto the path that will take her to Stewart, in defiance of her mother's command, she enters into the stage of taking the father as her replacement love. Her previous stubborn refusal to acknowledge the father has finally given way to active courting of his attention.

Where the bonnet was the most potent visual symbol of her exclusive attachment to Ada in the first half of the film, the angel wings in the second half are a sign of Flora's entrance into a world that is more than just Ada, as well as outside of her: this is a world of public performance, common understandings, shareable meanings; a world that contains traditional folktales, like the horror story of Bluebeard that the local European community are staging and that also clearly parallels the nuclear, authoritarian Victorian family Ada and Flora are now captive to. In the critical scene where Flora takes her mother's message to Stewart instead of Baines, the child is dressed in her angel costume. The figure of the cherubic child was a staple of Victorian domestic imagery, but it is the meaning of angel as messenger, and not its sentimental association with purity, innocence, and holiness, that *The Piano*'s climactic events exploit.

Ada has written a message of love on a piano key and instructs Flora to deliver it to Baines. She dare not go herself because Stewart has previously imprisoned her for infidelity, so his prohibition is weighty. Reluctantly, and after argument and anger, Flora takes the key. A large "V" pattern divides the screen; each leg is composed of wooden planks placed upon mud and leading away from the house, into the forest. We have seen the planks before, but not from this angle, where they assume such a striking symbolic shape. Flora starts down the left path, towards Baines's hut as directed. But she hesitates, turns back, and decides on the right fork, the one that leads to Stewart, the (step)father. The power Flora exercises here still falls within the limits of her child-messenger role. The only form of autonomous agency she has is to make a choice between two paths, neither of which has been of her own devising. She still delivers her mother's message, albeit, by choice, to the wrong man. The consequence of this expression of rebellion is that Flora will suddenly find herself in service as Bluebeard's messenger. Completely and ruthlessly shocked back into powerless servitude, the traumatized and hysterical little girl will be forced to carry her mother's severed finger, chopped off by her father in his jealous rage, to her mother's lover.

According to Freud, the price boys and girls must pay for their successful transition into the social-symbolic order where they may take their place in the organized transactions of adult commerce, is their intimate connection with the mother. In the Freudian schema a child's "progress" toward adulthood is distinctly gendered: the mother represents the disordered, undifferentiated, claustrophobic space of infantile fusion—the pre-Oedipal—and the father represents the expansive sphere occupied by the autonomous, individuated, social subject. Unfortunately for the girl child, again according to Freud, her sameness to her penis-lacking mother presents her with consequences unlike those faced by her brother. As Danielle Bergeron writes, "Freud suggests that for the girl it is the castration complex, through 'penis envy,' that causes her to enter into the Oedipus complex. But as her relation to *jouissance* is not centered on an organ subject to castration, the girl will have a weak superego that responds solely to external pressure such as education and the threat of loss of love, and that compromises her social participation and moral values."[9]

The Piano overtly refers to this Freudian story, not only through the "castrated" finger, but more especially in its positioning of Flora, literally and explicitly, at the intersection between the mother's desire and the (step)father's law. However, the film also makes significant challenges to the classical "feminine" Oedipal scenario, and it does so by revisiting it with a vengeance—and a difference.

Re-viewing the Primal Scene

A child's demands for love are immoderate, they make exclusive claims and tolerate no sharing.

—Sigmund Freud, "Femininity"

After Ada and Baines have become lovers, the excluded Flora becomes voyeur: pressing her eye to a hole in the wall of the hut, she sees her mother's naked body with the man's lying down beside her. What does it mean to have a child, a daughter, in this most unusual position, the position traditionally ascribed in cinema to a male sexual predator, a peeping Tom, a Norman Bates? Flora's understanding of the complex import of the event is limited. A deliberate juxtaposition is established (for the spectator's eyes only) between Flora at the peephole and Stewart, a few scenes later, in the same place, seeing a similar performance of intimacy. This parallel voyeuristic activity allows the spectator to recognize the (unconscious) contest between Flora's and Stewart's perspectives on the scene of Ada's infidelity.

The symbolism of bifurcating paths and castrating axe tempts us to read the daughter's choice of path in terms of the Oedipal plot. However, I want to argue that Flora's strategy in choosing the path to the father results from a wish to retain the mother for herself. It is her rage at having lost her privileged place in relation to her mother's body (having been shifted from the inside to the outside of her mother's boundaries, having been usurped) that motivates Flora's assertion of independence, and revenge, in refusing to act as her mother's interpreter. Flora's eventual betrayal of Ada is related to her lack of power, as a mere child, and her fantasy of revenge. She adapts the resources she already has as a child in such a way that she can direct the power of another.

Flora is observant enough to deduce that her own anger at Ada would be mirrored in Stewart and that he would have the actual power to prevent Ada from leaving, whereas she, Flora, is relatively impotent. Flora manipulates what she understands of the patriarchal division of authority within marriage toward her own ends. It is not the father's desire this daughter is after—he, after all, is parallel to her in being cuckolded and excluded—but the mother's. Stewart is merely a pawn in her possessive fantasy. Flora is not taking him as her replacement love object, a la Freud; rather, she is using him as her agent in an impulsive decision to thwart her mother's desire for another. What is most chilling about the events that follow is that Flora cannot, in fact, harness Stewart's power to her own motives and wishes. His agenda and his passion are not symmetrical with her own. Under the pressure of a husband's claim to ownership of his wife's body, Stewart's authority asserts itself as overwhelming brutality.

Freud insists that the daughter's anger at her mother, and her motivation to reject and separate from her, is fueled by penis envy and humiliation at the discovery of her mother's, and hence her own, castration. But, as Bergeron writes, "To equate femininity with feminine sexuality on the strength of reproductive function, and to reduce it to the object of masculine fantasy, is to attempt to limit excess in femininity by circumscribing it entirely within the field of the phallus."[10] "The field of the phallus" is suggested in *The Piano,* only to be rejected as an adequate explanation of the girl's psychic processes. In contrast to the Freudian Oedipal account of female psychic development (and Freud remained notoriously and tantalizingly mystified by the depths of the mother-daughter relationship), *The Piano* suggests that the girl is angry with her mother because she is too powerful, too active in the pursuit of her own desire, a desire that is neither phallic nor maternal. That Stewart is moved to chop off her finger demonstrates that Ada is not castrated but that he endeavors to make her so.

The Child's Sadism
"The axe falls. Ada's face buckles in pain. Blood squirts on to Flora's white pinafore, her angel wings are splattered in mud. . . . She [Ada] watches Flora, concerned and confused. Uncontrollably, her whole body begins to shake and as if by reflex Ada begins to walk. Flora trots parallel to her."[11]

I am being literal—and conscious. Realist. Resistant. Thinking through the plot, Flora's plot, I see that she attempts to take control of the action, but that her characters are simultaneously struggling for their own control.

245

Here is the surface drama. Through it all I am protective of Flora, and I want to excuse her. She didn't *really* want to hurt her mother. Did she? No . . . and . . . yes.[12]

Flora's key roles are messenger and witness. Being a conduit for events, a vehicle for their relay, she links the plot pieces and directs our gaze. She delivers the fateful piano key, and she witnesses the horrific consequences. Next she delivers her mother's finger to Baines, accompanied by her own words: "He chopped it off, he chopped it off!" The key, via the axe, has become a finger. Ada's initial instruction—to take the message to Baines—has been accomplished, but a vital, vengeful twist has been inserted. Flora had destroyed her mother at least once before, when she invented the story of her mother and father's powerful, all-consuming love. The film gives graphic, cartoon expression to the climactic conclusion to this story, where a flash of sudden lightning sets fire to Ada's unfortunate lover, killing him and leaving Ada mute. The comic, cartoon rendering of this image of fiery death alerts us to the imaginary nature of Flora's story but also suggests the film's willingness to lend the support of its visual resources to her fantasy (without, however, supporting the veracity, or literalness, of her version of events). One way, among others, of seeing Stewart's punishing axe is in relation to this earlier fantasy of lightning. It is swift, shocking, tragic—a second blow! As the traumatized witness of the scene, and the one who reports the story (to the public as it were), the visual narrative can be interpreted as Flora's own sadistic fantasy projected onto and enacted by her substitute—the (step)father.

Perhaps Melanie Klein's concept of projective identification brings us closer than does Freud's castrating Oedipal father to an understanding of Flora's psychic drama. Freud noticed that the primal scene (the child's perception or fantasy of the parental intercourse) is always felt by the child as a sadistic one, but he gives no explanation why this should be so. Klein shows that the combined figure is imbued with such sadism because of the hatred with which the child experiences it: "[She uses the] concept of projective identification . . . to account for the hated figure being perceived as a hating one. . . . She came to view anxiety as a fear of persecutory attack by parents who have themselves been attacked by the child in phantasy, particularly in relation to the primal scene."[13]

According to a Kleinian perspective Flora could be said to attack her mother's body in fantasy, then fear that her mother will be completely destroyed. "He says you're not to see her or he'll chop her up," she screams at Baines. But Ada is eventually repaired, in the manner of the fairy tale heroine described by the title "The Handless Maiden."[14] The final scenes show her wearing a specially crafted silver finger that taps distinctively on the piano keys. In the final frames Ada and Baines are together on the veranda, contented, domestic, affectionate, "married"; Flora is cartwheeling nearby, but robustly occupying her own frame—within eyeshot but separated by an edit (which replaces the tangible wall that previously cut off Ada—with George—from Flora). It would seem that she has accepted her mother and father as a couple and found a comfortable place within the triangle they form.

The scene of Ada's mutilation is deeply traumatic and hard to watch, even after repeated viewings across a decade of years. The realism is impressive and engrossing. But if we are willing to enter and depart as if this is indeed a dreamscape (and of course it is!), we will also be impressed by Ada's survival, George's loving goodness, and Flora's integration. The wound inflicted by the daughter's fantasy has left its mark—both visible and audible—but, as with a well-healed scar, it is not incapacitating. Instead, it remains as a permanent sign of history on the material of the body. It is significant that this scar is located on the *mother's* body, that it registers the daughter's struggle with that body, and that it heralds the beginning of a new stage of life. If it has been in Flora's fantasy that Ada lost her voice and then her finger, it is also within the power of her fantasy to recuperate those losses. Her mother's will is strong and can withstand these efforts toward abjection. Flora's spinning body is as graceful in conclusion as it was before the axe fell.

A Return Journey

In my worst dreams, my feet are stuck, numb, paralyzed. I can't run from danger. I can't reach the elusive haven—can't even glimpse it. In my nightmares I have heavy legs, so thick with heaviness that my will is useless in the struggle to shift this weight of self. As if my boots were made of lead. As if I had been drugged. As if quicksand sucked at my calves. Still, I try to walk. All I can think of is my feet and the steps I must take. I don't know where I'm going. I know I'm trying to leave something behind. I know I have a lot further to travel. I despair that I will ever get there. I pull against the irresistible force of gravity, anticipating release on the other side of resistance.

All the time, I say, I am stepping out and beyond, lifting one foot after the other, leaving my footprints on tracks that we grown-ups have established. I am on the move, watching my shoes as they tiptoe, pace, stride, or dance through space. I make my way to the airport, climb into the plane, and now I am airborne, in another dream altogether, gliding through the sky on borrowed cybernetic wings. I return home and put my feet up.

I sleep. I wake. I sleep again. It does not end, neither the dreaming, nor the fleeing from the dream. It goes on.

Notes

"The piano is mine. It's *mine*." These words, including the vehement emphasis on "mine," are written by Ada after her husband, Stewart, has announced that he has sold her piano to their neighbor, Baines.

1. I write "I," a bold yet featureless standing figure, interchangeable with all the other I's who would thrust their heads above the crowd.

2. These examples are from *Sweetie* (1989).

3. Kate Llewellyn, "Milk," in *Figs* (Hawthorn: Hudson Publishing, 1990), 57.

4. Scenes and characters from *Sweetie*.

5. Scenes and characters from *In the Cut* (2003).

6. Scenes and characters from *A Girl's Own Story* (1984).

7. The presentation I am referring to here, and in what follows, was by Richard O'Neill-Dean, a psychoanalyst, in which he invited us to consider *The Piano* as a dream. I am also grateful to Richard for his conversations with me about Melanie Klein and the significance of oral fantasies in Campion's films. It was a pleasure to discover the similarities in our responses to and thoughts about Jane Campion's films, especially *The Piano*.

8. I am referring to my response to *The Piano* when I first saw the film in 1993. I subsequently wrote about this in "Lips and Fingers: Jane Campion's *The Piano*," *Screen* 36, no. 3 (1995): 277–87.

9. Danielle Bergeron, "Femininity," in *Feminism and Psychoanalysis: A Critical Dictionary*, ed. Elizabeth Wright (Oxford: Blackwell, 1992), 95.

10. Bergeron, "Femininity," 97.

11. Jane Campion, *The Piano* [screenplay] (London: Bloomsbury, 1993), 97.

12. Although sections of this chapter were written before the symposium, the line of thinking that I develop here was again influenced by Richard O'Neill-Dean's presentation and our subsequent discussions.

13. Hanna Segal, *Klein* (Brighton: Harvester Press, 1979), 63.

14. Jane Campion has described *The Piano* as "a project that comes close to the spirit and atmosphere of a Grimm's fairy tale." Interview with Michel Ciment, reprinted in Kathleen McHugh, *Jane Campion* (Urbana: University of Illinois Press, 2007), 151.

"Campion's use of styles of excess is not traditionally associated with 'genuine' spirituality in Western films." Kate Winslet (Ruth) in *Holy Smoke*.

Jane Campion and the Moral Occult

Published interviews with Jane Campion make it clear that a spiritual approach to life is of personal significance to her and that the embodiment of questions about the best way to live—questions she sees as spiritual in nature—are important motivations for her activity as a filmmaker. There is also explicit reference in some films to eclectic spiritual practices, especially in a pair of features—*Sweetie* and *Holy Smoke*—based on her original story ideas. Like most Western filmmakers born mid-twentieth century, Campion has the religious cultural knowledge of someone educated in a society imbued with Christian traditions and values, yet her personal sympathies appear to be not so much with organized, Christian religiosity as with Eastern-influenced spiritual technologies such as the practice of meditation. It is ironic, therefore, that it is Christian critics who are most comfortable making religious or spiritual readings of her work, while that tendency in her filmmaking is rarely commented on in a sustained or appreciative manner in the main streams of Campion criticism. This essay speculates about the reasons for that lack of attention.

In considering why there has been little critical foregrounding thus far of spiritual issues in Campion's work, one needs to look to three related areas of analysis: to the characteristics of the wider Western social context that shapes matters of representation in general, and the representation of spirituality in particular; to fashions shaping commentary on Campion's films; and thirdly, to matters of style, tone, and emphasis in the films themselves.

As cultural workers and audience members we have been living in an age that, until recently, with the resurgence of fundamentalist, evangelical forms of religion, was presumed to be irreversibly post-Christian and postreligious. The era in which that process of secularization is presumed to have begun varies among scholars, but Peter Brooks, whose work on the melodramatic imagination informs this essay, chooses the French Revolution of the 1790s as "the epistemological moment . . . that symbolically, and really, marks the final liquidation of the traditional Sacred and its representative institutions (Church and Monarch), the shattering of the myth of Christendom, the dissolution of an organic and hierarchically cohesive society."[1]

The overthrow of venerable systems of governance understood as secured by divine power has had diverse societal consequences, including the gradual development of democratized systems of political control, but Brooks is most concerned with the downstream effects of secularization on forms of artistic representation. Tragedy and the comedy of manners, the literary forms that depended on a concept of divinely ordained hierarchical society for their effect, were invalidated by this rupture, claims Brooks—and in their place, what he calls the "melodramatic imagination" gradually permeated the theater and the novel (and by extension, the cinema). This development is not a mere matter of a change in entertainment fashions; it is crucial to modern society, argues Brooks, because of the role that such artistic representations play in reflecting and shaping our moral and ethical conscience. Melodrama, he asserts, "does not simply represent a 'fall' from tragedy, but a response to the loss of the tragic vision. It comes into being in a world where the traditional imperatives of truth and ethics have been violently thrown into question, yet where the promulgation of truth and ethics, their instauration as a way of life, is of immediate, daily, political concern."[2] The key assumption shaping the melodramatic mode is that there is no divine power transcendent of earthly social arrangements yet capable of authorizing them. In order to maintain a sense of order, human beings are therefore left to struggle, or cooperate, with one another and their material circumstances. Spiritual—that is, nonmaterial—longings, speculations, and internalized injunctions as to appropriate moral behavior, do still occur; indeed, they seem to be an indivisible part of the package of human consciousness, but under this new model there was no longer certainty as to where the satisfaction of those longings might be found. In elaborating on this inherent need for spiritual forms of understanding, Brooks postulates the Romantic movement as an almost immediate reaction to the apprehension of desacralization. In his opinion it testified to human beings' need for a sense of the sacred at the same time as the varied artistic testimonies to that need "offered further proof of the irremediable loss of the Sacred in its traditional, categorical, unifying form."[3]

In practice religion itself has not disappeared to the extent that a sense of the sacred has been irredeemably lost. Mainstream religious traditions, although in decline, continue to guide their adherents, but that adherence is often a matter of cultural identity rather than passionate belief.[4] For the majority, a relationship to religion has arguably dwindled away or has become more personalized and contingent, often drawing, for example, on the psychological self-development techniques that are the means by which many people nowadays seek to reconcile personal spirituality and social context.[5] Rather than automatically being able to shelter under the umbrella of a unifying religious myth, each person has become potentially responsible for his or her voluntary adoption of an ethical or spiritual code. Brooks's description of the change in the locus of spiritual authority is also, therefore, the narrative of change endorsed by most contemporary sociologists of religion:

Mythmaking could now only be individual, personal; and the promulgation of ethical imperatives had to depend on an individual act of self-understanding that would then—by an imaginative or even terroristic leap—be offered as the foundation of a general ethics. In fact the entity making the strongest claim to sacred status tends more and more to be personality itself. . . . [T]he individual ego declares its central and overriding value, its demand to be the measure of all things.[6]

This search for personal belief that could serve the individual as a basis for ethical living in a secularized world is expressed in art, according to Brooks's model, by means of melodramatic form: the restless, emotive, emblematic, extreme, structural, and aesthetic system that refuses "to content itself with the repressions, the tonings-down, the half-articulations, the accommodations, and the disappointments of the real."[7] According to commentator Maria Gillespie, certain shared features are visible across a range of media that use the melodramatic form. These include

the making visible of the everyday lives of "ordinary people"; the exploration of the most private and intimate realms of human experience; the representation of heightened emotions brought about by human suffering; the concern with the rupturing and restoration of an underlying social and moral order; the interlinking of private selves and public citizens; the emphasis on the role of fate, chance and circumstance in intervening in and destroying the hopes and dreams of individuals.[8]

If this melodramatic orientation is the prevailing focus of contemporary cultural production, there are, nevertheless, certain texts in which the use of a melodramatic aesthetic is particularly overt and intense. These texts are likely to be marked by "the indulgence of strong emotionalism; . . . extreme states of being, situations, actions; overt villainy, persecution of the good, and final reward of virtue; inflated and extravagant expression; dark plottings, suspense, breathtaking peripety."[9] While taking as its material the lives of ordinary people, the melodramatic aesthetic, therefore, is itself neither ordinary nor subdued. It often substitutes metaphor for the more dreary techniques of surface realism, since, again in Brooks's words, "it is tensed toward an exploitation of expression beyond. It insists that the ordinary may be the place for the instauration of significance. It tells us that in the right mirror, with the right degree of convexivity, our lives matter."[10]

The model of the melodramatic imagination is itself also constructed through metaphor. The everyday world is one of surfaces, roles, and repressions: the real drama is to be found either "below" those surfaces or, in a more complex metaphor, "within" them. Here is located what Brooks calls the "moral occult," the domain of operative spiritual values that is both indicated within and masked by the surface of reality, and labeled "occult" because it is customarily hidden from consciousness. The moral occult, where our most basic desires and interdictions lie, is not, he says, "a metaphysical system; it is rather the repository of the fragmentary and desacralized remains of sacred myth . . . whereby the melodramatic mode in large measure exists to locate and articulate the moral occult."[11] This realm of "meaning and value," while likely drawing on communal themes and representations, is also individualized in the sense that it is "inward and personal."[12]

Brooks saw the concerns of spirituality, psychoanalysis, and melodrama as intertwined, with psychoanalysis gradually taking over as the most publicly talkative of these discursive regimes. For him, they converge in the figure of the hystericized body, usually a female body, which also becomes a site of metaphorical representation, because "it is a body pre-eminently invested with meaning—a body that has become the place for the inscription of highly emotional messages that cannot be written elsewhere and cannot be articulated verbally."[13]

This argument for the relevance of melodrama has been powerful in its effects of creating critical interest in the mode, and in tracing its operation across popular modern genres, especially those directed at female audiences. Furthermore, in terms of my own interests in religion and media, I find Brooks's model of the melodramatic imagination persuasive in accounting for the paradoxical situation that many contemporary films and television programs contain discernible religious content but seem to offer little purchase on a sense of the sacred for audiences or critics who tend, instead, to prefer other discursive frameworks for their interpretations.[14] This is a fate, as will be demonstrated, that has befallen, in particular, the most explicitly religious of Campion's films, *Holy Smoke*. However, Brooks's contention that the development of melodrama reflects a change in the location and expression of religious or spiritual consciousness rather than its extinguishment—a contention that leaves room for ideas about religion to be active even in a melodramatic text—is typically stated briefly in works that use his approach and then put it to one side. Few critics have worked with the implications of Brooks's statements about religion and melodrama, although a recent book on Indian cinema by Rachel Dwyer makes moves in this direction, and Tom Gunning has also proposed that deeper consideration of this set of implications in Brooks's work would be profitable.[15] In the meantime it is likely that restricted critical knowledge of the nature of religiosity in contemporary cultures has implications for the manner in which the application of the melodramatic mode to cinema is discussed, or, more often, is overlooked. A filmmaker such as Campion who works within the framework of the melodramatic imagination and in some films draws overtly on elements of a melodramatic aesthetic, thereby almost ensures that her negotiations with spirituality and the moral occult will struggle to find an appreciative audience.

While a range of motivations attend the production of any film, it appears that Campion, in part, creates films as a means both of constellating her own search for ways of living that emerge out of the inchoate but deeply felt values of the moral occult and, if her published statements are to be believed, of modeling for others, especially women, which areas of life may yield similar ethical or spiritual grounding for them. It is argued, therefore, that three of Campion's films in particular—*Sweetie, The Piano,* and *Holy Smoke*—are typical of their times both by virtue of their interest in spiritual and ethical issues and by the ambivalent, coded nature of their dealings with those issues. Explorations of spirituality involving a personal search for moral grounding are often tentatively produced in the first place, and are then readily reclassified by public interpreters within a psychological framework, as examinations of affect, desire, and psychic unrest—especially when they are narratives that also traverse the life experiences of female characters, as is the case with Campion's films.

Furthermore, in the history of cinema studies there are some modes of filmic address that are more readily acknowledged as carrying potential spiritual or religious significance than others, and it is proposed that Campion's work, in utilizing the techniques of Brooks's "melodramatic imagination," has left itself open to charges that its references to spiritual issues are shallow and inconsequential.

This inquiry proceeds predominantly through a study of secondary sources since examining what commentators have said about Campion's filmmaking, and what the filmmaker herself is on record as saying, makes evident emphases and elisions in discussion of her work thus far. Before returning to discussion of the melodramatic aspects of her films, however, it is necessary to establish that dealing with Campion's work within a religious or spiritual framework is as justifiable as using other interpretive approaches.

Theological Criticism and The Piano

Of the strands of inquiry that constitute the now substantial body of work known as Campion studies, one of the least well known is a small strand in a field that spans both theology and film. Writing in this field is typically the output of religious people—academics in schools of divinity or theology and clergy and laypeople enculturated into and passionate about the world of film—who wish to use discussion of the movies to confirm and reinvigorate the relevance of a Christian worldview. In general this is a group who would find little to please them in Brooks's theorizing: since they need film to support the proposition that there is a transcendent deity, traces of whose presence can be found in the material world. As David John Graham puts it in a chapter titled "The Uses of Film in Theology,"

Religious encounter, will not then, be limited to sacred buildings, religious symbols or architecture, or even writings which are religious or theological in character. The notion of God-in-everything (however God may be conceived) then operates. . . . What we are discussing here is not the view that God is to be found in everything (sometimes called pantheism), but the idea that the experience of God can be transmitted through anything.[16]

In practice, however, it is not quite "everything" that is considered suitable material for prompting a "religious encounter" through the medium of cinema, since there is a preference in this field for films that are either the work of art-cinema auteurs or are clearly metaphysical or philosophical in their content. Therefore, analyses of the same titles circulate through a number of volumes in film and theology.[17] For instance, the films of a group of male auteurs including Bresson, Tarkovsky, Scorsese, and Kieślowski possess the explicit references to religious themes and the gravity of tone, coupled with copious significatory ambiguity, that makes space for such encounters to constellate themselves—or at least for scholars to be able to argue that they do. These directors may personally be in a troubled or skeptical relationship with faith, but by employing modernist modes of representation their work exhibits a dignity and sense of serious purpose that conditions audiences to read the works as significantly spiritual. Individual films such as *Babette's Feast, Jesus of Montreal, Groundhog Day,* and *Ghost* also regularly receive theological readings since they work with the concepts of guilt, self-sacrifice, and redemption that commentators consider to be the hallmarks of the significantly religious or spiritual film.

When Campion's work is co-opted in this project of pursuing religious encounter, it is inevitably and only *The Piano* that is used as the object of study. This film, which has been called "a major point of reference for our contemporaneity" by Polan, and which Barbara Klinger notes has taken up "sustained residence" in the imaginations and emotions of its fans, has rapidly achieved the high-cultural status necessary for inclusion in the canon of auteur works.[18] Despite the fact that it exhibits few explicit signs of religiosity, it is popular as an inspirational text in the film and theology field. This may be partially because of considerations of demographic balance, since it provides a rare example of a women's film by an antipodean female auteur. Its theological interpreters are also predominantly female, and the intersection with religiosity is usually framed around issues of gendered power, a point on which Christianity is vulnerable to criticism.

Diane Apostolos-Cappadona, for example, discoursing on the topic of "The Image of Woman in Contemporary (Religious) Film," praises *The Piano* for the way in which the character of Ada can be understood as resolving a corrosive dichotomy between images of femininity in Christian culture:

For Campion . . . that classical pattern of interpreting woman through the image of virgin or whore is no longer appropriate inasmuch as Ada reflects the fundamental ambiguity and fullness of the female experience within one identifiable person. . . . She has created a feminist (religious) film, but not because she is a woman director who had a woman scriptwriter. Rather this Australian director brings to visual reality through Ada a single and complete figure who encompasses the totality of female character—she is both Eve and the Virgin and, more than that, she is fully human.[19]

Margaret Miles, professor of historical theology at Harvard Divinity School, analyzed *The Piano* alongside *Thelma and Louise* as a feminist film about love in *Seeing and Believing*, her 1996 study of "religion and value in the movies." The theological basis for her argument is that the movies are bidding to supplant religion in "its traditional capacity to define and encourage love," love being seen as a divinely originated quality.[20] Miles admires the way that *The Piano* ventures an unconventional view of heterosexual relationships: although she is ultimately disappointed in the ending of the film since conventional patterns of heterosexual socialization regain ascendancy. A third example is from the Clive Marsh and Gaye Ortiz volume *Explorations in Theology and Film,* in which David Rhoads and Sandra Roberts describe as "an experiment in intertextuality" a process whereby two unrelated works, in this case *The Piano* and the New Testament's Gospel of Mark, are transposed "as a means to understand each work more fully."[21] The link that makes this transposition possible is posited as a theme of proper and improper uses of power. In the world of *The Piano,* it is the two European males, Stewart and Baines, who are scrutinized in terms of the ways in which they use their power over others, where the former is evaluated as arrogant, inflexible, and controlling to the point that his inflexibility thwarts his own desire for love and connection, while Baines is lauded as the character "who chooses to let go of his power to control and therefore saves himself and Ada."[22] The theme of the proper use of power is also illuminated, assert Rhoads and Roberts, in the Gospel of Mark, when, for example, Jesus urges his disciples to become the servants of those less powerful than themselves.

In this intertextual encounter the Gospel of Mark is judged by Rhoads and Roberts to be the more compelling because it asks more of its audience, urging them to "embrace its story as their way of life."[23] *The Piano's* utility, by contrast, lies in its ability to be interpreted as an updating and reinforcement of this message; it provides, they say, "a modern, extended illustration of the dynamics of the rule of God as applied to individuals: the transforming power of mutual service in contrast to the futility of coercive domination."[24]

By secular screen studies standards, the analytical methods employed in these theological interpretations are inadequate to deal with the complex construction of *The Piano* and the additional complexities of its historical and cultural positioning. The interpretations themselves, due to their teleological tendencies, are reductive, foreclosing on the ambiguity that has made the film such a productive property in other spheres of inquiry. Nevertheless, despite their restricted focus, these theological interactions with *The Piano* do highlight the degree to which some of Campion's thematic preoccupations can be understood as impinging on territory in which religion has traditionally been authoritative and for which religious interpretations would have been preferred in earlier epochs.

Spirituality—Hiding in Plain Sight

Indeed, there are many occasions on which Campion has herself offered explanations of her work by drawing on discursive resources from a spectrum of constructions of religiosity, although she is more in tune with elements from what British theorists Linda Woodhead and Paul Heelas call the "spiritualities of life" end of the spectrum than she is with what they describe as "religions of difference," that is, traditional and highly codified forms of religiosity.[25] In 1986, for example, Campion remarked that she was fascinated by Zen Buddhism, and by 1989 she was speaking about a consistent practice of meditation, which she saw both as a personal benefit and as placing herself within a wider social movement of development of spiritual consciousness.[26] As Campion professed to Michel Ciment, "I think that my generation is drawn to the spiritual and desires less to participate in the ways of the world. I myself have meditated for five years. It helps me to moderate myself. I'm more conscious too of my inner feelings. Often we are led to do things out of pure excitement when they don't correspond to our profound selves."[27]

According to statements Campion has made about *Sweetie,* she envisaged that film, in the preproduction phase at least, as being an effort to take the spiritual temperature of her environment. Even at this early stage in her filmmaking career, she links love and penetrating through delusion as key concerns: "*Sweetie* is me trying to work out what's going on in the '80s, and in a way it's about new age spirituality, love and delusions . . . and occasional moments of reality and how these are precious."[28] The depictions of the characters Kay and Louis meditating and of Kay consulting a clairvoyant in *Sweetie* are therefore not merely tacked-on exhibitions of the bizarre; they are mediated representations of the texture of Campion's world at the time—albeit framed in a light-hearted, equivocal manner:

I thought it would be good to have it that people meditate, not as an unusual thing but as a matter of course—part of the fabric of life. I'd been involved with meditation and workshops and I found it was prevalent although people didn't admit it. So many of my friends were searching for some depth in their life, trying this and trying that and it always seemed incredibly humorous when we looked at it. That's what it started with but it's not so heavily in there now.[29]

The superstition that Kay displays, falling in love with a man because one of his curls forms the shape of a question mark, for instance, while obviously represented whimsically, is therefore "just the normal level of superstition that many people have," says Campion, and she also remarks knowledgeably: "You often find that in clairvoyants: contrary to what one thinks they are very down-to-earth."[30] These comments suggest an orientation toward the eclectic practices of personal development and efforts at control of one's environment through "magical" techniques that were known in the 1980s and early 1990s as "New Age spirituality."[31] The New Age label had pejorative connotations that have since diminished as "spirituality" has become accepted in general discourse as referring to a variety of personal, informal systems of belief, but it is not surprising that comments Campion made on the subject in the 1980s should have had an ambivalent tone, poised between advocacy and disavowal.

Unproduced "Spiritual" Projects

During the next decade, over the period when she was directing *An Angel at My Table, The Piano,* and *The Portrait of a Lady,* Campion also developed two other projects that would have brought her interests in spirituality to the foreground had they been produced. In an interview in 1993, she described a project named *Ebb* about a coastal nation where the sea retreats because of the spiritual errors of its population. Subsequently, one of the community's members develops his spiritual consciousness and the sea returns in order to claim him. From the brief description provided, it sounds as if this project, rather like *The Piano,* presented powers of vision and blocked powers of speech as indexes of spiritual health and was also concerned with the sacrificial engulfment of the individual as necessary to the survival of a larger community.

A second unmade project deepens considerably understanding of elements of *Holy Smoke,* in particular. In an interview with Thomas Bourguinon and Michel Ciment, Campion twice mentions a script in development from Christopher Isherwood's autobiographical text *My Guru and His Disciple,* which was being developed for the backers of *The Piano,* CiBy 2000.[32] She was working on it again in 1994 in the period after the success of *The Piano,* but by 1997 the project seemed to have faded, replaced by discussion of *In the Cut* and the script that she was writing with her sister Anna that would become *Holy Smoke.*

My Guru and His Disciple is an account of the writer Isherwood's spiritual friendship with a Hindu Vedantic swami named Prabhavanandra, whom Isherwood met in Los Angeles in 1939. It tells of the struggle between Isherwood's attraction to a life of spiritual study and meditation, which demanded celibacy, and his desire to find sexual pleasure and love with a series of male partners. One can see why the project was attractive to Campion: like her filmmaking, Isherwood's writing is intelligent, compassionate, and frank; the effort to understand one's own motivations and to see through self-delusion, even when the results of self-reflection are unflattering or challenge social taboos, is of primary importance.

At times Isherwood put great effort into spiritual practice, to the extent that, in the mid-1940s, he was on the verge of becoming a monk. However, his failure to live up to his own ideals is treated with humor that undercuts pretension at the same time as it contributes to the richness of the world he describes: again, this is a serio-comic approach that also distinguishes several of Campion's films, especially *Sweetie* and *Holy Smoke*. The implication is not that the subject matter or the author's attitude to it is inconsequential because it is framed as a subject for laughter or mockery; rather, this degree of "convexity," as Brooks puts it, is one way of drawing attention to the gaps between surfaces and depths, where the extreme and the emblematic point to the difficulty of expressing emotions and desires that do not meet the repressive standards of everyday custom.

Isherwood's longing to find a form of spiritual truth through an ascetic attempt to transcend the physical world is constantly undermined by incursions from the realm of the moral occult, which insist that "transgressive" desire should not be denied, that opting for one side or other of an ascetic/erotic divide would be a false victory. A similar tension also marks Campion's films, although with the erotic emphasis primarily on heterosexual interactions, the impetus toward transgression manifests itself differently. The sexual desires of the female protagonists are complicated by a series of indirectly glimpsed familial attractions and antagonisms, giving rise to the fury, for instance, with which Ruth and P. J. confront each other at times *in Holy Smoke* or the contrasting lasciviousness and frigidity of the two sisters in *Sweetie*. This Oedipal murkiness is, however, just one component of the force with which the issue of gender relationships presents itself to and through Campion. The larger focus is on reconciling the need for sensuality and connection with the need to stay self-contained enough to function effectively in the realms of intellectual and creative endeavor: to stay one's own woman.

In speaking to Michel Ciment in 1996 about the characterization of Isabel in *The Portrait of a Lady*, Campion expressed that dichotomy in this way: "Personally, I feel in myself, among other things, two principal forces that guide me: the excitement of discovering the truth of things and beings, where it's found, and the desire to be loved. They are two companions that are difficult to reconcile."[33] Again, that same year, in an interview with Rachel Abramowitz, she stressed her concern about finding a way to live ethically between those two sets of forces: "I think it is a really important issue for women today, or men and women today; [to realize] that life is not made up of career choices. One of the most important things is to participate in relationships and friendships and particularly in the mythology of love. I have a deep need for intimacy. Almost every human being has it, and how you reconcile that with everything else in your life is a problem that comes up."[34]

It is therefore possible to discern in *Holy Smoke* several concerns that are similar or adjacent to those in *My Guru and His Disciple* and that, while being partially amenable to rational discussion in subsequent commentaries, are expressed in the films themselves in the restless, emblematic manner that indicates the presence of unconscious as well as conscious components. These elements, which I argue involve Campion trying to locate and articulate the contents of a moral occult with which she can identify, cluster around the apparent conflicts between the pursuit of truth and of sensuality, between personal satisfaction and genuine acknowledgment of the existence of others, between seeking wisdom and being taught; for in *Holy Smoke* Ruth and the cult-"exiter," P. J., are each other's antagonists but also each other's teachers, as P. J.'s vision of Ruth as a goddess makes explicit. The ethical resolution of these conflicts is often expressed in images of physicality, of the body in action. For instance, Isherwood cites one of the key points of wisdom given to him by his teacher Prabhavananda: "Christopher," he said, "always dance." This injunction combines seriousness and play in a manner that is also often found in Campion's films: to take the metaphor literally, in *Holy Smoke* there are several key scenes exploring dance as an expression of a spiritual state of fully inhabiting the moment, even when the layers of complexity underlying that moment are far from reconciled.

Without herself commenting on the links between the two projects, Campion has asserted that she wanted the film to encourage audiences to think about religiosity in the contemporary world:

Holy Smoke is quite religious in the big, broadminded sense, in the big grownup sense . . . the way I think the big Christian mind really works: completely unafraid, not dogmatic, rigorous, always questioning and reconfirming faith. A fun but very painful process. I'm hoping that now, just at the turn of the millennium, the film will open up a line of inquiry about ways of western thinking and questions about layers of commitment and illusion in the spiritual life. I tried very hard to tell a story that doesn't talk about this in a simple way, doesn't tell you solutions.[35]

Campion's hopes for the film's reception were ambitious but also contain an indication of why those hopes may have not been realized: there has been an attempt to tell the story in a manner that is unexpected, that is ambiguous, that is not "simple." The director does not specify the "way" or style that she did use, but in practice she has not drawn on one of the modes filmmakers customarily employ when they wish a film to exude spiritual or religious gravity.

Contemplative, Mythological, and Transcendental Styles

The debate around which style is most suitable for representing spiritual or religious experience circles around four major positions, only one of which hints at any space for the melodramatic. These positions variously privilege an aesthetic of contemplation, mythological form, the logic of the parable, and a celebration of abundance and grace.

In advocacy for a contemplative, observational style of filmmaking, for instance, Siegfried Kracauer praised the ability of the cinematic apparatus to provide an enhanced form of perception that could revive an appreciation of the spiritual dimension of existence by rendering visible what could not ordinarily be seen. The Catholic critic André Bazin also favored a pared-back, noninterventional filming style, with long takes, deep focus, and minimal editing if one were to achieve what he called "ontological realism," which can offer "a re-presentation of the world [bearing] witness to the miracle of creation."[36]

Mythological style is more concerned with the preferred meanings generated by narrative structure than it is with individual moments of vision. In this context, myths are stories powerful enough to underpin and guide the behavior of groups and, indeed, whole societies of people. Myths are resonant, appealing stories that are also essentially conservative in that their (re)telling maintains diverse peoples as one community of belief and thereby helps to reinforce existing societal forms of organization.

Parables, by contrast, are also stories that may be told in a religious context, but they are accounts of going beyond mythical conditioning to a state as close as possible to original vision: seeing afresh, thinking newly, connecting with a universal source of creative power rather than dealing with mediations of that power.[37] The paradox is, of course, that as soon as one tries to describe that experience it enters mediation and is dissipated. This dilemma is evoked in *Holy Smoke* by the depiction of Ruth's experience of meeting the guru at the beginning of the film. The experience is life-changing for her, but its strength and nature cannot readily be shared with anyone else. Her inarticulateness on this matter puts her in a weak position with her family, and only through utmost exertion does she manage to trigger a parallel experience in her tormentor, P. J., at the end of the film and thus cause him to make his peace with her. The filmmaker, Campion, is caught in a similar bind: the iconography she uses to depict this experience is both oddly placed in narrative terms (positioned at the beginning of the film so we understand it as precursor, not central event) and, because it reproduces Hindu visual style, is coded as kitsch rather than numinous in a western context of reception (see the frontispiece to this chapter).

Films about religion structured on the pattern of myth are the default setting in the mainstream cinema industry, since they pleasurably rehearse familiar stories.[38] Commentators are divided on their merits, however: many theological critics, for instance, find mythological style the most amenable to their project of reinforcing belief in a particular religious system. However there is a stronger preference among modernist auteurs and critics for the minimalism and difficulty of the parable form as an attempt to see beyond the banalities of narrative to some manifestation of the real.

The most developed of these nonmythological models is Paul Schrader's theory of "transcendental style."[39] Transcendental style, he writes, "can reliably bring man as close to the ineffable, invisible and unknowable as words, images and ideas can take him."[40] This style is more calculated, shaped, than that advocated by Kracaeur or Bazin: it proceeds from representation of a normal cinematic level of complexity, what Schrader calls "abundance," through the confrontation of the human being with forces he or she can neither control nor avoid, to a state and style of representation that is increasingly stark and reified, or "sparse." When the characters are finally forced up against the limits of their knowledge, it is in this place of unknowing, where previous forms of perception and understanding no longer function, that space is created for an intuition of the Transcendent itself to occur.

While Campion's films do typically contain a harsh encounter with life that challenges the protagonist's knowledge and reshapes her identity, it is obvious that they do not operate with an aesthetic that is consistently contemplative, mythological, or sparse. Instead, as critics have noted, her films have a tendency toward stylistic excess, whether that is excessive aesthetic self-reflexivity as in *Sweetie,* a maximum romantic expressiveness in *The Piano,* or an excessive hybridity of style and characterization in *Holy Smoke.* It is this deliberate inclusion of excess in films other than *The Piano* that disbars Campion from full-time membership of the club of modernist (male) spiritual auteurs.

Campion's work is therefore implicated in debates about the validity of styles of excess in representing religion and spirituality. Whereas aesthetic techniques of distance, repression, and self-control have been advocated by male directors and critics as suitable for engendering a sense of spirituality, styles of excess, styles that emphasize emotion, vivacity, and affirmation, have been associated with subaltern spiritualities such as those of black and working class communities.[41] In generating a serious spiritual intention for her work, yet using abundant, melodramatic style to create it, Campion is venturing into territory that connoisseurs of art cinema are unlikely either to recognize or to value, and where aspects of her achievement are likely to go unrecognized.

Receiving a Different Message: Spiritual and Nonspiritual Decodings of Campion's Work

Noting that Campion sometimes speaks of her own filmmaking in spiritual terms and that theological critics have been drawn to the thematics of *The*

Piano is not sufficient, therefore, to ensure that readings of her films from this angle are in easy circulation. Her feature films have polarized commentators, receiving negative as well as appreciative reviews, although it has tended to be the positive reviews that have circulated in Campion studies. As a recent reconsideration of the reception of *The Piano* by Klinger indicates, this is likely to be because of the strong initial reactions to the film by female commentators, many of whom report being surprised, even physically affected by, the way the film reflected back to them their own, often only half-acknowledged, yearnings and frustrations.[42] Evaluation by female critics has therefore circled around a number of theoretical frameworks affiliated to feminist, postfeminist, and psychoanalytic approaches. While reaction to Campion's films is not neatly divided along gender lines, it is fair to say that some male critics, including Dana Polan and Adrian Martin, whose negative evaluations of *Sweetie* and *Holy Smoke* I will now consider, experience the films as operating at a greater distance from their own psychic concerns and are therefore attracted to more broadly applicable, "cooler" frameworks of analysis, and perhaps to less appreciative readings overall.

Polan's book-length analysis of Campion's films aims to deconstruct her status as an auteur by pointing out disjunctures across her body of work. He uses the method of genre classification to pursue this goal, demonstrating how each film has contact points with a number of genres, including, for instance, quirky art film, female Gothic, reverse female Gothic, romance, screwball comedy, and melodrama. The term "melodrama" is used with particular reference to *The Piano*—which, for Polan, as for most critics, is outstanding among Campion's oeuvre—but is narrowly defined and rejected as the dominant framework for considering the film. This is because Polan understands a melodramatic film to be focused on female desire, whereby the heroines of such films risk falling into fatalism and madness.[43] While this temptation is indeed present for most of Campion's female protagonists, in choosing the female-stalker movie *Fatal Attraction* (1987) as paradigmatic of this type of film, Polan moves the boundaries to embrace an extreme territory Campion rarely explores. Rather, Polan decides that the more specific term "female romance" best identifies *The Piano's* generic ambitions, romance being defined "not only as a longing for a specific thing—a person, an object like a piano—but for a promise of spirituality or radiant uplift that unity with the thing ostensibly will provide" and that "hints at an ineffable reward beyond the merely physical."[44] Polan, therefore, makes the common assumption that if a text references a positive sense of spirituality it cannot also be melodramatic. If, however, the purview of melodrama is reenlarged along Brooks's lines to include the various subgenres Polan identifies, this reading does point to the melodramatic mode as the aesthetic and ideological container of the film's dealings with spirituality. This particular inflection of response is even more evident in the book's introduction, when Polan activates the language of mysticism and transcendence to foreshadow his subsequent assessment of *The Piano.* The film, he writes, is "an expression of mystery and even of the mystical that implies deeper secrets to the universe. . . . [I]t offers an intimation that we can enter into a mythic realm in which 'normal' physical laws of being are to be suspended; a sense of life's deeper meaning as radiating through forms of affect (the music, the dance) rather than through rationality alone."[45] While the first half of that quotation uses language that references the kind of "deep" religiosity the films of the modernist "theological" directors can provide, its second half, with its emphasis on the expression of emotion and immersion in the sensate, is close to a description of aspects of melodramatic method.

However, it is not *The Piano*–event I am identifying as pointing to a critical blindspot in the treatment of Campion's films, since there was clearly an alchemical marriage of content, style, and reception on that occasion that made spiritually inflected language the appropriate register of discourse for many who viewed the film. Rather, I am interested in why so many critics note briefly, especially in relation to *Holy Smoke,* that the film operates in the realm of spiritualized meaning but move on to undertake substantive analysis from some other perspective.

For instance, in discussing *Sweetie,* Polan commits himself to the framework of "quirkiness" as an apt description for the results of the early career collaborations between Campion as writer/director and Sally Bongers as cinematographer. "Quirky" is normally a reviewer's shorthand for movies displaying a lighthearted, calculated originality in terms of content, narrative structure, and/or mise-en-scène. There is, Polan writes, a mise-en-scène "of systematic strangeness," whereby the Campion/Bongers enterprise "deform[s] norms in strikingly evident patterns," and *Sweetie*'s presiding tone is one of "intense visual and narrative strangeness."[46] Consequently, the pyrotechnics of these games with form impress themselves on the consciousness of the viewer more powerfully than aspects of content: "The early films do at times deal with serious issues (madness, sexual exploitation, incest, family strife) that resonate for spectators, but frequently a surreal style turns attention away from subject matter to the films' status as quirky efforts at visual experimentation through distortion."[47] When the thematic implications of the film's content are evaluated, this is done using secular and psychological concepts of gendered, distorted power relations that involve repression, narcissism, fear, and self-assertion. The elements of narrative that I would consider as pointing to a search for transcendence of these neurotic relationships—the scenes of meditation, the recourse to a clairvoyant, the reliance on intuitive logic and superstitious ritual—are interpreted by Polan as merely examples of the "quirky randomness of life" in this claustrophobic diegetic world. The only sequence not evaluated as claustrophobic is where the family escapes to the country without its most challenging member, Sweetie. This event indeed is seen in terms of a fleeting spiritual release from restriction, since it is described as evincing "exhilaration and openness" and as containing "effusive and affirmative expressions of personal joy."[48]

When it comes to considering *Holy Smoke,* Polan is even less in sympathy with Campion's opinion that it undertakes an undogmatic exploration of spirituality, which inevitably for her also involves the exploration of intimate relationships. Instead, he echoes other reviewers who frame reactions to the film in terms of an *either* spiritual *or* gender framework, and prefer the latter:

It is quite possible to feel that *Holy Smoke* in no evident, easy or inevitable way offers its viewers the means to judge whether or not this or that "way of living . . . makes better sense." . . . Ruth's commitment to the spiritual life is no more thought out, nor more secure, no more profound, than her mother's own hesitant engagement with the world around her. For many viewers *Holy Smoke* is only minimally a serious investigation of spiritual quest. Indeed many critics of the film focused on the ways the film quickly leaves its Indian origins to become a battle of the sexes.[49]

Polan accuses the film of "lightness and insubstantiality": it has, he says, none of the profundity and "depth" that moved him in regard to *The Piano.*

The critical framework Adrian Martin applies to Campion's filmmaking is auteurism. In a damning review essay in the New Zealand literary journal *Landfall,* Martin posits an initial rise and later fall in the director's alignment with the public imagination. He evaluates *Holy Smoke* as "superficial" before deciding that the problem is more deep-seated and that Campion is actually a flawed storyteller, whose career has rightly lapsed into incoherence "frozen, like Isabel Archer at the end of *Portrait,* between the twin magnetic poles of love and confinement."[50]

Many of the points that Polan and Martin make in evaluating *Holy Smoke* as unsuccessful are relevant and persuasive. For instance, both note an oscillation of tone between serious and kitsch sequences of the narrative, which means it is often difficult to discern the ground the film stands on. For instance, the broadly drawn comic performances of Ruth's family draw attention to themselves to the extent that their supposed concern about Ruth's psychological well-being lacks credibility. In particular, the logic behind the representation of the cult deprogrammer, P. J., played by Harvey Keitel, is hard to fathom. Initially, he is introduced in a mock-heroic style that renders him simultaneously small and over-inflated. One forms the impression that he is a fool, only to find that we are supposed to see him as a worthy, equal opponent for Ruth in later sections of the film.

It is a step too far, however, for Polan to take this admittedly hybrid mix of attributes and to categorize the film as a "screwball comedy" on the grounds that "the screwball hero and heroine are both figures adept at the little games and stratagems of the battle of the sexes."[51] That interpretation overlooks the manner in which the narrative moves away from comedy and into the register of harsh psychic confrontation in its last third as the characters increasingly assault each other's moral integrity and conceptions of self-identity. Polan's final critical maneuver is to propose that the film also be interpreted as a narrative about a globalized, postnational world, where characters associated with different locations in that world must inevitably separate. While this approach is interesting, it occasions a further dismissive pronouncement on the film's shortcomings in relation to spirituality: "Here again the film's modesty of ambition becomes part of its subject: there is no transcendental spirit here, no ultimate uplift and the film can hold out no permanent values (whether of religious devotion or romantic fulfillment)."[52] There is little sense, therefore, that either Polan's or Martin's assessments of *Holy Smoke* recognize the possibility that the film and its director might be involved an effort to locate or make visible the moral occult in a manner marked particularly by female experience. In desiring to prove that Campion's directorial project is marked by thematic and aesthetic disjunctures, they see no value, for instance, in further exploring the melodramatic or "romance" mode that Polan acknowledged as crucial to explaining the absorbing "spiritual" tone of sections of *The Piano*. Coherence and consistency are privileged as guarantees of auteurship, rather than, for instance, playfulness, ambivalence, or risk-taking, while, in Polan's case, profundity and the assertion of "permanent values" are seen as necessary for the treatment of spiritual issues to have significance. This latter preference arises from a more traditional paradigm of religiosity, however, than Brooks's assertion that the moral occult is nowadays not so much a complete metaphysical system; that is, it is not something that can offer an extensive and permanent set of values, as it is an unconscious realm functioning as the "repository of the fragmentary and desacralized remains of sacred myth."[53] It is perhaps appropriate, then, that Campion's film about, in her words, "layers of commitment and illusion in the spiritual life" should offer a number of moments, fragments,

"In *Holy Smoke* Campion decisively, if ironically, triggers the markers of melodrama." Harvey Keitel (P. J.) in *Holy Smoke.*

or gestures around spiritual issues that are difficult to resolve into a unity through the lens of logic but that may have considerable emotional coherence, especially for some female viewers.

Holy Smoke *as Melodramatic and Spiritual Text*

It remains, therefore, to demonstrate that *Holy Smoke* is a film that pursues an apprehension of the moral occult, where the moral occult represents a realm of operative spiritual values: an earthbound spirituality that seeks but fails to go beyond the limitations of human existence. And, moreover, that it is a film that seeks to locate the moral occult through the application of melodramatic technique, as well as through the activation of a melodramatic vision. This vision is, in my opinion, a constant shaping force in Campion's work, but her use of melodramatic techniques is more evident in some films than others.

In relocating the action of *Holy Smoke* away from India to the Australian suburb and desert habitat she had previously used in *Sweetie,* and also by shifting the guru-disciple relationship into the domain of heterosexual power relationships, Campion more decisively triggers the markers of melodrama. These include, in a set of surprisingly literal correspondences, most of the elements from Brooks's list of characteristics cited earlier. A laconic, almost stunned, state of dissociation from the world may be the habitual emotional setting of Ruth's family, but the "indulgence of strong emotionalism" and the depiction of "extreme states of being, situations, actions" is evident in the majority of Ruth's reactions both to them and to her enforced intimacy with P. J., whom she gradually draws out of his stale, "persona" routine and over the edge into her realm of passionate intensity. As a "good" creature, one who has done no harm, except to see things in a way that separates her from her culture of birth, Ruth, attired in a white sari, is restrained and persecuted by acts of "overt villainy" and "dark plottings," when she is lured back from India by a lie, imprisoned by her family, and then interrogated on their behalf by black-clad, mustachioed P. J. Her virtue, the virtue of a modern melodramatic heroine, consists in her commitment to honesty: initially to her understanding of the transformative vision of the guru, but later, when that fails her, to her sense of vulnerability and despair, and also to the expression of her sexual power. For this commitment she is finally rewarded: she is given her freedom again, but she also gains the prize of P. J.'s conversion and submission so that, as the coda of the film demonstrates, he becomes someone with whom she will always be connected.

It is also apposite that the tensions in the film, which are substantially conflicts around the location and nature of the moral occult for each of the two main characters, are played out in terms precisely of their effect on the body: the hysterical body that Brooks saw as pivotal to the expression of the melodramatic imagination. "Melodrama reminds us," Brooks wrote in 1994, "of the psychoanalytic concept of 'acting-out'; the use of the body itself, its actions, gestures, its sites of irritation and excitation, to represent meanings that might otherwise be unavailable to representation because they are somehow under the bar of repression."[54]

This hysterical female body, unable at times to speak and then only fluent in an extravagant form of physical expression, but still in pursuit of its own form of truth, is one of the constants of Campion's melodramatic aesthetic. It is found in the sister in *Peel,* in both Kay and Sweetie in her second feature, in the response of Janet to psychic stress in *An Angel at My Table,* in Ada in *The Piano,* and again in the representation of Ruth. At one point Ruth says to the inquisitorial P. J. that, try as she might, she cannot verbalize to him what he wants to know, what really matters to her—for that he would have to look inside her heart. Then, as the pressure on her grows and the beliefs that have formed her own understanding of the moral occult to that point become untenable, the stresses on her sense of self become visible in her body. In a scene of confrontational intimacy she emerges naked from the darkness and confesses her sense of confusion and fragmentation. When P. J. turns to walk away from her, her body speaks, as it were, by voiding urine down her legs: she also begins to weep. In a visual rhyme on her earlier comments, she shows him, rather than tells him, what is inside her, what she feels.

Similarly and unusually, the male body, P. J.'s body, is also changed by the encounter in that both direction and performance are concentrated on making evident on the body what is in P. J.'s "soul" at this time. As Ruth's passion for truth assails his self-image, he loses the lineaments of kitsch villainy and lets her remake him as a travesty of the feminine. Anecdotal responses suggest that this is a section of the film that repelled many viewers, but there is a link here also to melodramatic technique where Brooks notes that the villain is branded as evil, or rather in this case, branded physically as perverse, and driven from the social realm, to be relegated to an off-stage space, here identified as the desert. These, then, are some of the explicit signs of melodrama; these are some of the motifs and actions that tell the viewer they are watching a struggle between "the most fundamental psychic relations and cosmic ethical forces," where melodrama "seeks constantly to express these forces and imperatives, to bring them to striking revelation, to impose their evidence."[55]

It may seem that this is too literal a reading of the texture of *Holy Smoke* and that there is actually less of a moral distinction between the characters—between Ruth and P. J., between virtue and villainy—than I have proposed. Indeed, on this point I would have to agree. There was one element of Brooks's list of melodramatic characteristics that I omitted from the initial list because prima facie it appeared not to apply to Campion's films: that was the phrase "moral schematization and polarization." The phrase was omitted because the nature and tendency of emotions and motivations are not always clear in Campion's moral universe: aspects of villainy and virtue are shared between the characters in the central relationships—dyads and triads—in her films. It has been suggested that eroticized interactions typically condition access to the moral occult for Campion's characters. The power of the erotic often obfuscates the location of the moral occult for the female protagonist for much of the time, but ultimately it also triggers the apprehension of the moral occult for that individual. However, the range of ways in which Campion customarily treats the central relationships in her films entails a subversion of the dichotomous moral schematization associated with both the melodramatic imagination and the melodramatic aesthetic.

For instance, Brooks states that conflict in melodrama involves "the polarization of good and evil [and] works toward revealing their presence and operation as real forces in the world. Their conflict suggests the need to recognize and confront evil, to combat and expel it, to purge the social order."[56] The identification of evil and the intention of purging the social order were certainly features of *Sweetie* in the sense that the family could only achieve peace once Dawn, or "Sweetie," was dead. However, in the subsequent films the desire to denounce and to purge begins to fade (although it makes a bloody resurgence in *In The Cut*). In *An Angel at My Table* Janet is the disruptive element the community tries to isolate, but she survives and is partially reincorporated into the collective. Alasdair Stewart is expelled from the world of Ada, Flora, and Baines, but the manner of his leaving does not match the viciousness of the violence he expended on Ada: there is an element of mercy in his dispatch. Isabel in *The Portrait of a Lady* may or may not go back to Osmond, but Ruth in *Holy Smoke* ends up in the back of a truck, cradling the bloodied but still living body of the adversary she had previously tried to abandon in the desert. This is a reconciliation of opposing forces that proposes neither of them should be perceived as occupying a simple position of good or evil.

An articulation of this aspect of Campion's own moral philosophy is provided in an interview broadcast on the ABC radio program *The Religion Report* in December 1999. In response to a question about how much of *Holy Smoke's* depiction of spirituality comes from her own experience, she talks again about her strong need to gain some understanding of the point of life and the wish to share that understanding both with people around her and through film, with those she does not personally know. She agrees with the interviewer that both "New Age flakiness and institutional churchiness" benefit from the kind of criticism her intermittently ironic treatment of them can provide but nevertheless takes a stand on a preferred moral meaning for *Holy Smoke:* "I think the film is trying to say that no matter what they say, it's how they walk the talk that makes the difference, and learning that and learning compassion really, and that finally, in whatever language you speak, is really the language of the heart and of love and religion."[57] In other words, it is the message that P. J. writes on Ruth's forehead near the end of the film and that she stares at in the mirror—"be kind"—that condenses all those three areas of reference, the heart, erotic love, and religion, into a phrase that represents a summation of the results, up to that point, of Campion's spiritual enquiries through film. Framed as an apprehension of the moral occult on behalf of both the characters but specifically addressed to Ruth and writ large on her body, it is, despite Campion's stated reluctance to speak in simple ways, or to offer solutions to others, a minimalist, fragmentary, and temporary recommendation on how best to live, with or without a guru.

Literature in the field of the sociology of religion suggests there was a sea change in understandings of the direction of the development of modern

"Eroticized interactions [typically] condition access to the moral occult for Campion's characters." Kate Winslet (Ruth) and Harvey Keitel (P. J.) in *Holy Smoke.*

religiosity that began in the mid 1990s, about the time that Brooks wrote the preface for the 1995 edition of his book. This change in mood continues today, gathering force after events at the millennium, and is sometimes associated with an apocalyptic view of religious prophecy. Religion and spirituality have become important topics for discussion once more, but within an aesthetic and ideological milieu that still thinks of itself as formed by the secularizing consciousness that Brooks employed as his framework for the investigation of melodrama. It may be, therefore, that filmmakers who are personally interested in religion or spirituality continue to see their audiences as predominantly secular in orientation and are likely to shape their works in order to suggest an interest in religion or spirituality but, simultaneously, to refrain from unambiguous commitment to that interest.

The tensions inherent in using melodramatic techniques to represent issues of religious belief in a new era where they are once more the object of collective interest are only just becoming apparent. However, Campion's work is an excellent site to see these tensions in operation. For those who do not wish to return to either the partisanship of religious myth used as the basis, for instance, for narratives of national destiny or to the gendered elitism of transcendental style, her films can yield the apprehension of a female-centered, abundant spirituality that takes human passion and desire seriously but also treats them with a sense of humor and a willingness to see any solutions offered as contingent rather than magisterial. These qualities are what makes this aspect of Campion's work attractive, as well as limiting the range of audiences it can reach.

Notes

1. Peter Brooks, *The Melodramatic Imagination: Balzac, Henry James, Melodrama, and the Mode of Excess* (1st ed., 1976) (New Haven: Yale University Press, 1995), 15.

2. Ibid.

3. Ibid., 16.

4. E.g., in New Zealand, with census results in 2006 showing that just under 52 percent of the population would call themselves Christian but where less than 10 percent of the population actually attend church, there is debate as to whether the country can still justify being described as a "Christian" nation.

5. For an explanation of the complex nature of contemporary religiosity, including its subjectivization, psychologization, and privatization, see Linda Woodhead and Paul Heelas, eds., *Religion in Modern Times: An Interpretive Anthology* (Oxford: Blackwell, 2000).

6. Brooks, *Melodramatic Imagination,* 16.

7. Ibid., ix.

8. Maria Gillespie, "Melodrama and Modern Subjectivity," in *Media Audiences,* ed. Gillespie (Maidenhead: Open University Press, 2005), 150.

9. Brooks, *Melodramatic Imagination,* 12.

10. Ibid., ix.

11. Ibid., 5.

12. Ibid., 6.

13. Ibid., xi.

14. My own PhD research, e.g., found that magazine and newspaper reviewers writing about texts with explicit religious content tended to prioritize the expectations of their imagined audiences, especially in relation to genre and tone, rather than specific aspects of content. Ann Hardy, "Sites of Value? Discourses of Religion and Spirituality in the Production of a New Zealand Film and Television Series" (PhD diss., Waikato University, 2003).

15. Rachel Dwyer, *Filming the Gods: Religion and Indian Cinema* (London: Routledge, 2006); Tom Gunning, "The Horror of Opacity: The Melodrama of Sensation in the Plays of André de Lorde," in *Melodrama, Stage, Picture, Screen,* ed. Jacky Bratton, Jim Cook, and Christine Gledhill (London: British Film Institute, 1994), 59.

16. David John Graham, "The Uses of Film in Theology," in *Explorations in Theology and Film,* ed. Clive Marsh and Gaye Ortiz (Oxford: Blackwell, 1997), 37.

17. See, e.g., John May, ed., *The New Image of Religious Film* (Kansas City: Sheed and Ward, 1997); Marsh and Ortiz, *Explorations in Theology and Film*; and Mary Lea Bandy and Antonio Monda, eds., *The Hidden God: Film and Faith* (New York: Museum of Modern Art, 2003).

18. Dana Polan, *Jane Campion* (London: British Film Institute, 2001), 2; and Barbara Klinger, "The Art Film, Affect, and the Female Viewer: *The Piano* Revisited," *Screen* 47, no. 1 (2006): 19.

19. Diane Apostolos-Cappadona, "From Eve to the Virgin and Back Again: The Image of Woman in Contemporary (Religious) Film," in May, *New Image of Religious Film,* 126.

20. Margaret Miles, *Seeing and Believing: Religion and Values in the Movies* (Boston: Beacon Press, 1996), 156.

21. David Rhoads and Sandra Roberts, "From Domination to Mutuality in *The Piano* and in the Gospel of Mark," in Marsh and Ortiz, *Explorations in Theology and Film,* 47.

22. Ibid.

23. Ibid., 57.

24. Ibid., 55.

25. Woodhead and Heelas, *Religion in Modern Times.*

26. Andrew L. Urban, "The Contradictions of Jane Campion, Cannes Winner," in *Jane Campion: Interviews,* ed. Virginia Wright Wexman (Jackson: University Press of Mississippi, 1999), 15.

27. Michel Ciment, "Two Interviews with Jane Campion," in Wexman, *Jane Campion,* 44.

28. Andrew L. Urban, "Campion: Cannes She Do it?" in Wexman, *Jane Campion,* 18.

29. Philippa Hawker, "Jane Campion," in Wexman, *Jane Campion,* 21.

30. Ibid.; Michel Ciment, "Two Interviews," 41.

31. For a comprehensive account of the origin and characteristics of the New Age Movement, see Paul Heelas, *The New Age Movement* (Cambridge: Blackwell, 1996).

32. Thomas Bourguinon and Michel Ciment, "Interview with Jane Campion: More Barbarian than Aesthete," in Wexman, *Jane Campion,* 112.

33. Michel Ciment, "A Voyage to Discover Herself," in Wexman, *Jane Campion,* 179.

34. Rachel Abramowitz, "Jane Campion," in Wexman, *Jane Campion,* 187.

35. Kathleen Murphy, "Jane Campion's Passage to India," *Film Comment* 36, no. 1 (2000): 30.

36. André Bazin, *Bazin at Work: Major Essays and Reviews of the Forties,* ed. Bert Cardullo, trans. Alain Piette and Bert Cardullo (New York: Routledge, 1997), xii.

37. See John Dominic Crossan, *The Dark Interval: Towards a Theology of Story* (Sonoma: Polebridge, 1988), for an exposition of the characteristics of the parable.

38. They range from explicitly religious narratives such as Dreamworks' animated retelling of Exodus, *The Prince of Eygpt,* and Mel Gibson's *Passion of the Christ* (although that production's hyperbolic presentation of violence all but takes it out of a comfortable mythological realm) through stories about angels, demons, and humans who exhibit saintly levels of self-sacrifice when challenged.

39. Paul Schrader, *Transcendental Style in Film: Ozu, Bresson and Dreyer* (Berkeley: University of California Press, 1972).

40. Ibid., 8.

41. Terry Lindvall, W. O. Williams, and Artie Terry, "Spectacular Transcendence: Abundant Means in the Cinematic Representation of African-American Christianity," *The Howard Journal of Communications* 7 (1996): 205–20.

42. Klinger, "Art Film, Affect," 19–41.

43. Polan, *Jane Campion,* 34.

44. Ibid., 33.

45. Ibid., 3.

46. Ibid., 57–60.

47. Ibid., 60.

48. Ibid., 100–101.

49. Ibid., 142.

50. Adrian Martin, "Losing the Way: The Decline of Jane Campion," *Landfall* 200 (November 2000): 101.

51. Polan, *Jane Campion,* 152.

52. Ibid., 155.

53. Brooks, *Melodramatic Imagination,* 5.

54. Peter Brooks, "Melodrama, Body, Revolution," in Bratton, Cook, and Gledhill, *Melodrama, Stage, Picture, Screen,* 19.

55. Brooks, *Melodramatic Imagination,* 13.

56. Ibid.

57. John Cleary, "*Holy Smoke:* A Conversation with Jane Campion," *The Religion Report,* Radio National Australia, 22 December 1999.

A backyard in un-iconic Australia: cracked concrete, rusty corrugated-iron fence, and uprooted rotary clothesline (from *Sweetie*).

On Viewing Jane Campion as an Antipodean

Being Antipodean

The quality of being antipodean attaches itself to Jane Campion's films and to herself. She has described herself in this way, and interviewers frequently comment on her accent, her laugh, her expletives, and her manner as having a quality they identify as New Zealand, Australian, or a mix of both. Certain elements of this identity, those that look different, are apparent to North Americans or Europeans, but other elements of that identity are more visible to New Zealanders or Australians. In this essay, I consider how to view Campion and her films as antipodean, that is, to see the director and the films, or most of them, as connected to the *quality* of being antipodean, but also to see them from the *perspective* of being antipodean (and in my case, a New Zealander). This question has quite a bit to do with Campion as a woman and as a woman director.

I address this question first by considering the larger question of being female in New Zealand and Australia, and then by addressing the trajectory of a series of Campion's heroines as they cross the boundaries of Old World and New. Here I focus specifically on *The Piano* and *The Portrait of a Lady* (a more antipodean film than it might at first appear), and ask if we can detect an antipodean feminine in these films. I then rehearse the truism that an identity category will always fracture on closer examination, and specifically that while "antipodean" might be defined against Europe, New Zealand is also defined against Australia and vice versa. This difference, a difference not of but within the antipodes, is also evident in Campion's public persona and in her films. Here I consider particularly *Sweetie, An Angel at My Table, The Piano,* and *Holy Smoke.* I suggest that in making the "Australian" films Campion has taken up a productive position of marginality and that in turning her gaze back on New Zealand she does so as an expatriate. Though Campion has expressed her liking for the country, her cinematic eye has been a sharp one when she has turned it on Australia. Her representations of New Zealand have been, if hardly sentimental, a great deal more seductive. While the key difference here is geographical, there is also a temporal element at play, and the "pastness" of New Zealand for Campion works itself out in at least two different ways.

Women, the Antipodes, and Filmmaking

New Zealand and Australia have been good places to grow up a white woman. "If you're going to be born a woman," the retiring female director of New Zealand's largest company said recently, "be born in New Zealand." The self-definition of both countries, but perhaps especially New Zealand, as "advanced" in the opportunities they offered white women emerged during the period of European colonization, which for these, the last of Britain's colonies, occurred at a time when industrialization was disrupting gender relations in the Old World. An unsettling of the gender regime was always part of the emergent identities of these new settler societies. For white settlers in Australia and New Zealand, these were circumstances of extraordinary possibility: in societies that were only just forming, that were far from having established long-standing traditions, and that demanded versatility above all from their new citizens, the possibilities for gender change were now greater even than in older New World societies such as the United States.[1] The early achievement of the universal female franchise in New Zealand (1893) and the Australian states (between 1894 and 1908) signaled an element of antipodean identity that came to occupy a central place in the cultural nationalism of these countries, even if the forms of masculinity that emerged simultaneously also worked to curtail their utopian potential.[2]

The character of the feminine as it appears in a number of articulations of antipodean identity occurs in Jane Mander's novel *The Story of a New Zealand River* (1920), in which the character Asia, born in Australia and brought up in the New Zealand bush, is overtly and at times flamboyantly cast as a New World New Woman characterized by physical energy and confidence:

A small sailing-boat . . . came zigzagging down the river . . . with reckless daring, it tacked across the steamer's bows, cut through the water on the left, and came round on the wind at her stern with a flourish, and so alongside.

"It's a girl!" exclaimed Lynne, in amazement. . . . The breeze flapped her skirt about her bare legs. Her clear skin, painted by the swish of the wind, told of the simple life, strong nerves and beauty sleep, and in her eyes there glowed the joyous spirit of the wood nymph and the water sprite.[3]

At eighteen, Asia departs alone to make a career in the city, and knowingly forms a relationship with a man she cannot marry, a relationship founded on intellectual sympathies as well as sexual attraction. The New World has created her a different kind of woman from her Old World mother, whose course is constrained by a more conventional morality. Mander's fictional landscape is drawn according to the progressive political vision of politician and historian William Pember Reeves's "social laboratory": "New Zealand," writes Mander, "even more than any other part of the world, seethed with the atmosphere of social and moral experiments."[4] The character of Asia, and the potential inherent in the colonial environment for women in particular, concentrates the sense of experiment and possibility in the social laboratory. A generation earlier, Australian feminist Miles Franklin had written a similar narrative of feminine defiance with her witty semi-autobiographical novel *My Brilliant Career* (1901), in which heroine Sybylla Melvyn spurns marriage to handsome, charming, wealthy Harry Beecham so that she can pursue an artistic career.

These are narratives of first-wave feminism and are not unique to Australia and New Zealand. But the settler histories of gender in both of these countries have offered unusual opportunities to women, who have taken up education, the arts, sports, careers, and politics in large numbers even while matriarchal domesticity has remained a powerful tradition; and the idea of an independent womanhood has continued to operate as a defining element of social organization. In the context of a relatively permeable class structure and a prevailing egalitarian ethos, what Campion describes as the "can-do" attitude of antipodeans abroad undoubtedly describes a key element of national identity as it relates to antipodean women in particular.

This is not to say that these societies have not confronted women with difficulties: indeed, Campion's early *A Girl's Own Story* concentrates a feature film's worth of female difficulty into twenty-seven minutes. Both countries were mired in cultural conservatism in the postwar period, from which Australia emerged first. Like many other young New Zealanders in the 1970s, Campion headed for Australia's greater wealth and larger cities. She began art school (which she loved) in Sydney in 1977 and film school in 1981. Campion has criticized the Australian Film, Television, and Radio School (AFTRS) for its conservatism, but she has also observed that it paradoxically allowed her to do what she wanted to do in part because her work was not taken seriously: "My talent wasn't the kind they were ever going to understand, which was one of the luckiest things for me. . . . [T]hey tend to wreck the people they think are talented."[5] She also happened on Australia at a significant moment of possibility in the cultural politics of gender. She has commented more than once on the effect that seeing Gillian Armstrong's film version of *My Brilliant Career* (1979) had on her:

I think particularly seeing Gill Armstrong make *My Brilliant Career,* it was just like "God they're going to let girls do it too." . . . [W]e all know women make movies now but at that time really there was hardly anyone, especially in Australia, nobody, and it was rumoured that the guys gave you such a hard time that it would never be worth while. . . . [J]ust seeing that they were going to let Gill do it gave me the idea, it just opened up that door in my mind that maybe it would be possible for me too.[6]

My Brilliant Career has been widely recognized as an important event in filmmaking by Australian women. As Jocelyn Robson and Beverly Zalcock note, six of its eight principal credits are women, and it is "a feminist film rooted in Australian cultural politics. It is, in fact, the first Australian feminist film."[7] That Campion recalls the making of *My Brilliant Career* as such a revelatory moment alerts us to an identity—that of female antipodean auteur—that was becoming available to her but also to the character of industry politics at the time.

Although the emergent feature film industry in both countries was supported by tax concessions (for a period) and the establishment of film commissions and government funding bodies, these structures did not eliminate the particular difficulties faced by women. The Women's Film Fund in Australia, established in the mid-1970s, was an attempt to address this. In the 1980s and early 1990s opportunities were increasing. Campion noted, "I don't know enough of what happens in America, but there's something not happening there that is happening in Australia."[8] Indeed, Campion's work immediately after film school coincided with a very particular and enabling moment for women in the growing film industry in Australia. Australian arts bureaucracies were then still supported by a Labor government that was, she notes, "terrified of the feminists" and very concerned to demonstrate equal opportunity.[9] The Women's Film Unit, for which Campion made a film about workplace harassment (*After Hours*), was a product of this effort. She does not like that film because of the unit's directive that it take a specific feminist position.[10] But she acknowledges that "all the same, the unit did address a major inequality. Also, there was a radical feminist group, filmmakers and activists, who had a huge impact on the Australian Film Commission. They were astonishing in their ability to intimidate the bureaucracy into supporting more women."[11]

In the tradition established by some of her predecessors and followed by women filmmakers both in Australia and New Zealand, a remarkable number of Campion's collaborations have been with other women who also emerged in that period: Sally Bongers shot *Peel, A Girl's Own Story,* and *Sweetie,* thereby becoming the first woman to shoot a feature film in Australia and one of the few female cinematographers internationally at that time. Campion's longest-standing collaborative relationships have been with producer Jan Chapman, editor Veronika Jenet, and writer Laura Jones. Although she disavows a specifically feminist perspective, then, Campion credits the changes in gender politics since the 1970s with providing the conditions in which it has been possible for her both to make films and to make the films that she has wished to make; and she has elected to work with many women collaborators. And, of course, she has made films that are mostly about women, and she has declared that they are made from a woman's point of view.

Campion has been conscious, then, of the context in which she became a woman director in Australia. She has also spoken on a number of occasions about being antipodean in England and Europe. She follows a long antipodean tradition in registering discomfort with English society: "I couldn't take the look of the place or the style of friendship. I need more intimacy from people than is considered O.K. there, and I felt that my personality and my enthusiasms weren't understood. I had to put a big lid on myself."[12] In defining antipodean difference in terms of class, opportunity, and identity, she expresses a common response of Australians and New Zealanders to England in particular:

All my egalitarian spirit really sent me into a fury every time I heard those sort of dandy voices with nooooo ability to feel emotional or feel for anybody else. It was only recently that I can hear that kind of voice and suddenly recognize it not so much as my enemy as a sort of weird antiquated cultural design. What's most sad is the resignation amongst English people about their opportunities in life. Where they begin is where they end. We colonials have a different spirit—like anybody can have a go.[13]

She has also spoken of living in Venice and trying to go to art school there but being defeated by misery and alienation. That alienation was replayed when *Sweetie* was nominated for the Palme d'Or in 1989 but met with hostility from many in the Cannes audience: "We were all very excited about participating in the competition. It was my first feature film, a minor film. So we were all the more surprised by the ensuing clamour. We found it totally stupid to consider this film shocking. We were staying in these incredibly expensive hotel suites. We were crying and asking ourselves why we were here among these bastards. They hated us and we hated them."[14]

Campion was sufficiently hurt by this reception that she would not initially allow *An Angel at My Table* theatrical release and restricted it to a television version. She was eventually persuaded by Lindsay Shelton, who marketed it, and she received a rapturous standing ovation and the Grand Jury Special Prize at the Venice Film Festival in 1990.[15] This sense of difference—of defining herself as other to England and Europe—that she has articulated in interviews can also be traced through her films.

In a sequence of Campion's films—from *An Angel at My Table* to *Holy Smoke*—a series of young women travel between the Old World and the New, and the crossing of that boundary constitutes the ground of their adventure. Janet Frame leaves New Zealand for England and Europe, embarking awkward and unknowing on a bleak and unwelcoming Old World. Ada journeys from Scotland to a wild New Zealand shore unlike anything she has encountered before: the opening sequences of the film mark the transition with the moments of departure and arrival. She enters a strange, microcosmic caricature of Old World society set in the remote antipodean bush. In this setting, threatening, lonely, and dangerous as it is, she effects a transition in her own capacity to act upon the world and upon herself. Isabel Archer, a New Englander, blows a New World wind through the English and European society she encounters: but she too is transformed by the encounter. And Ruth Barron, in flight from the spiritual poverty of her New World, seeks enlightenment in India and returns in possession of a power to be reckoned with. In the next section, I look at elements of these border crossings in two of these films: first, I consider how Ada's reworking of the "exchange of women" in *The Piano* (1993) marks her process of becoming an antipodean woman in the sense I have suggested, and second, I contend that in Campion's adaptation of *The Portrait of a Lady* (1996), an antipodean feminine can also be detected.

The Piano: *Reworking Exchange*

Whether or not *The Piano* constitutes an adaptation (probably not), Campion had read Mander's *The Story of a New Zealand River* before she wrote the screenplay, and the film and novel share several core elements: the woman arriving in a remote bush area of New Zealand with a daughter of unknown paternity; her marriage to one man but love for another; and the piano through which she expresses her passion. In Mander's tale, the mother, Alice, does not follow her own desire while her husband is alive: she remains obedient to what is named as the "puritanism" of the country she had left. The antipodean woman of this story is her daughter Asia, the strong-minded "wood nymph and the water sprite." In Mander's novel, the New World has made her a different kind of woman from her Old World mother. In *The Piano,* however, the self-refashioning into an antipodean is not left to the daughter but is made by Ada, the immigrant, herself.

Jane Campion gained a degree in anthropology in the 1970s, a time when Mauss and Lévi-Strauss occupied pride of place on reading lists—perhaps she even read Gayle Rubin's groundbreaking article "The Traffic in Women," which developed Lévi-Strauss's structuralist contention that women can only be the object, not subject, of exchange.[16] As a number of critics have remarked, the themes of gift and exchange are central to the elaborate structure of *The Piano* (but not to *The Story of a New Zealand River*). One of the first things we learn about Ada is that she has been passed from the hands of one man (her father) to another (Stewart): "Today he married me to a man I've not yet met."[17] Then the piano she has brought across the world is sold by her husband, who now legally owns her possessions, to Baines in exchange for a piece of land. Her labor is sold along with it: she is contracted to give Baines piano lessons as part of the bargain. She protests strongly at the sale of both piano and labor but must take her place as object of exchange. Thus far the story proceeds according to structural anthropology: women cannot undertake exchange; they can only be exchanged. But Baines, marked as a New World man by his moko and his close relations with Maori, now offers to deal privately not with Stewart but with Ada herself. To regain the piano—her voice but also the vehicle of her *jouissance*—she has nothing to exchange but her body.[18] That is the commodity in which Baines, a New World man but not yet a New Man, wishes to deal: "Do you know how to bargain? There's a way you can have your piano back."

Ada's intervention—her own shift into a new order of gender relations—is to begin to define the terms of exchange: to drive increasingly hard bargains, to take the risk of higher stakes, and to transact her body but retain her feeling. In the economy of the New World, where trading is all, she too becomes a proficient trader, at which point, of course, she has trumped Baines by forcing him to recognize their deal *as* trade: "The arrangement is making you a whore and me wretched," he must now confess. Lest we miss the shift that takes place when Baines returns the piano, Stewart visits Baines to ask whether he will want the land back:

Stewart: And what does this do to our bargain? I cannot afford the piano if you
     mean me to pay.
Baines: No, no payment. I have given it back. I don't want it.

Stewart: Well, I doubt I want it very much myself.
Baines: It was more to your wife that I gave it.[19]

Correcting Stewart's assumption, Baines explains that this time it is not an exchange but a gift without expectation of reciprocity, and a gift to Ada in her own right, not to Stewart as owner of Ada and all her goods. Ada has effected two transitions: the return of the piano to herself, rather than to her husband, marks her as an independent economic actor, and it transfers her sexual relationship with Baines out of the economy of exchange. Hilary Neroni argues that Ada's *jouissant* piano playing "makes it painfully clear that Stewart can never own her, that no one—and especially no social rule—can lay claim to the experience she has while playing the piano."[20] It is this autonomy that Baines, in returning the piano to her without payment, concedes. Baines's desire, he finds, is for a woman free to give her love, or none at all—a New Man after all.

Independence, then, is a critical element in the arrival of Ada in the New World, and it defines the process by which she takes up a life in New Zealand. Her adoption of a new nation also involves the adoption of a new practice of independent femininity. In the country that was, some decades later, to be the first to accord women political agency, the fact that she resumes the use of her voice is surely not coincidental. (And she does so in Nelson, the town from which Mary Ann Müller began writing the letters that began New Zealand's campaign for women's suffrage.)

The Brilliant Career of The Portrait of a Lady

Campion herself alerts us to the fact that in creating an Isabel Archer for our time, she has made a narrative more antipodean than American:

Portrait, Campion said, is one of her favorite books, partly because she herself feels "so Isabel Archerish. I think that coming from Australia or New Zealand now makes one more like Americans going to Europe were then than Americans going to Europe are now. They're much more sophisticated, whereas we have more of a colonial attitude about ourselves, a more can-do, anything's-possible attitude. I felt so much like Isabel as a young woman, a sense of having extraordinary potential without knowing what the hell to do with it."[21]

Campion has explicitly acknowledged Gillian Armstrong and the other Australian women filmmakers of that time in interviews.[22] Robson and Zalcock have pointed to the significance of *My Brilliant Career* for a number of women filmmakers, suggesting that "it is Sybylla who in a sense represents the starting point, prototype and role model for many of the strong female representations that were to follow [in Australasian women's cinema]. It could be argued that the recurrent visual motif of Sybylla at the piano finds its apotheosis much later in the film *The Piano,* Jane Campion's stunning study of female determination."[23] I wish to suggest that another specific, encoded acknowledgment of Campion's debt to Armstrong is traceable in her adaptation of *The Portrait of a Lady* (1996).

The Portrait of a Lady references *My Brilliant Career* in a number of respects. Nicole Kidman's Isabel Archer, particularly in the first half of the film when she is a "free" woman, strikingly recalls Judy Davis as Sybylla Melvyn. Isabel's pre-Osmond frizzy red hair mimics Sybylla's divided, loose style (and this style returns when Isabel leaves Rome and Osmond). Campion's adaptation selects and enhances Isabel's un-English independence, recalling Sybylla's frequently noted propensity for flouting etiquette: Isabel's incredulity that she cannot go to London chaperoned only by Henrietta prompts the question (not in the novel) "Isn't anything proper here?" Campion also adds the scene in which Isabel and Henrietta repeatedly touch the effigies in the Victoria and Albert, to the echo of repeated admonitory whistles from the guards on duty. Campion has pointed out that she has redrawn James's Isabel for the late twentieth century, particularly with regard to her fantasy of sexual encounter. But her Isabel is frankly physical in other ways too, sniffing her boots to see if they smell, kicking the door shut with a bang after Mr. Goodwood, leaning far out over the balustrade at Gardencourt to see what is going on downstairs—Nicole Kidman's height is exploited extensively in developing Isabel's energetic physical vigor, which defines the character so strongly in the first half of the film. In the film's opening sequence her subsequent entrapment is signaled and predicted by her still, seated position; but immediately after Lord Warburton leaves her, she rushes in a burst of released energy and tension and, appropriating a moment from a different position in the scene, picks up Ralph's dog to give it an affectionate but very energetic shake. Lord Warburton's disconcerted sisters sit in immobile English counterpoint at the tea table on the lawn. In this energy too Kidman's performance is reminiscent of Davis's Sybylla, another remarkable runner (and dancer, fighter, and retriever of cows from mud) of an order that is not at all common in the women of heritage cinema, eloquent feminists though they may sometimes be.

Both characters defend their unmarried independence against ardent suitors, and a similar symbolism of entrapment connotes the threat posed by marriage in each film. The birdcage that arches over and around Sybylla as

"I think particularly seeing Gill Armstrong make *My Brilliant Career*, it was just like 'God they're going to let girls do it too.'" Nicole Kidman's Isabel Archer bears the trace of Judy Davis's Sybylla Melvyn. Courtesy of Photofest.

she contemplates marriage to Sam Neill's Harry anticipates the visual symbolism of bars, grids, and cages in Campion's *Portrait*. The significant narrative difference—that Sybylla does not marry and Isabel does—is marked by the parasol that Campion borrows from Armstrong. Sybylla never yields hers: she herself commands the parasol, deploying it flirtatiously as she prepares to upset the boat and tip both Harry and herself out of the (potentially premarital and certainly conventional) punt and into the pond. But Osmond has taken Isabel's and made it the hypnotic, seductive device by which he precipitates her fall.

If the spirit of Sybylla Melvyn hovers like a beam of hope around Isabel, a broader sense of an antipodean feminine also infuses James's New Yorker in the translation to film. Kathleen McHugh remarks that when the young women who direct their gaze at the camera and speak about falling in love and kissing dispose themselves in a circle on the ground, they constitute the portal through which she looks, linking the nineteenth-century story to the late twentieth century.[24] Their voices locate them in place as well as in time: they are Australians. The casting of Kidman as Isabel confirms it: the film declares itself an antipodean woman's take on *Portrait*. Indeed, odd as it seems, there is a sense in which *Portrait* is Campion's most extensive elaboration of antipodean femininity.

Campion has said that *The Portrait of a Lady* was one of her favorite novels as a young woman, and it is worth speculating on why. In James's novel, Isabel Archer is first characterized, in her aunt's enigmatic telegram from America, as "quite independent." That phrase alone, puzzled over by Ralph and Lord Warburton, describes her until her arrival at Gardencourt.[25] It is her defining characteristic, and as the complexities of the novel unfold, the forms of her independence—intellectual, economic, and moral—move into and out of alignment with each other. Her identity as a New World figure, a young East Coast American woman with a post–Seneca Falls sensibility, precipitates the action both of the novel and of Campion's adaptation. That is, independence is as much a national and political condition as a personal trait even in James's Isabel. It is set against the restrictions, dependencies, and various kinds of incapacity for action of the English, European, and Europeanized characters, of the "sterile dilettante," the Italianate Gilbert Osmond whose two talents are taste and control, but also, for example, Ralph, brought up in England and never quite able to "do" anything, and Pansy, whose "education," her father explains, is "for this—that when such a case should come up she should do what I prefer" and who in Campion's *Portrait* is confined to a sequence of barred and darkened spaces, unable, in a strikingly resonant little scene altered from the novel but entirely consistent with

James's Pansy, to walk into the sunlight without her father's permission.[26] When Madame Merle calls herself a "compatriot" of Isabel's, this might as well be yet another of her deceptions: she too is a confirmed European. Only the "true" New World characters—Mr. and Mrs. Touchett, Caspar Good-wood, Henrietta Stackpole—share Isabel's quality of independence.

It is not surprising, however, that Isabel's ability to contend with Os-mond and to seek a way out—perhaps—of her marriage plot is a point on which Campion's adaptation most carefully works with and against James's novel, as a number of commentators have observed.[27] It is entirely consis-tent with Campion's fascination with determined, independent women for whom independence, even at a price, pays off. I am not the first to point out that Campion ends the film before the end of James's narrative, and whether or not Isabel returns to Osmond remains uncertain. It is worth looking closely, however, at the moment in the novel that becomes the final shot of the film.

Here is James's version of the end of this scene:

There were lights in the windows of the house; they shone far across the lawn. In an extraordinarily short time—for the distance was considerable—she had moved through the darkness (for she saw nothing) and reached the door. Here only she paused. *She looked all about her; she listened a little; then she put her hand on the latch.* She had not known where to turn; but she knew now. There was a very straight path.[28]

James makes that "straight path" explicit: it is a path back to Rome and to controlling, abusive Osmond. Campion ends her film here, with Isabel's hand on the door: we might read this as another retrospective "gift" to Isabel. Just as we register the bars of the framing on the door, repeating the film's visual theme of bars and cages, Campion's Isabel turns and looks back, look-ing at neither the warm but entrapping interior nor the ardent but insistent lover. In this long final frame Kidman's posture and her look are critical, and Campion's version reverses the order of James's sentence. With her hand on the door, Kidman turns, then straightens, and her gaze lengthens. The frame conveys trepidation and then possibility, a possibility that Campion leaves undefined. This posture and this look do not plainly anticipate a "straight path" back to Rome, nor do they suggest a return to the confined interior. Campion's *Portrait* differs from James's primarily in the openness of Isabel's future. Perhaps here too we can detect the trace of Sybylla, but perhaps we can also detect conditions of possibility that are part of Campion's own iden-tification as Antipodean.[29]

Here is one sense, then, in which Campion figures herself and her films as antipodean: she inherits, occupies, and rearticulates, in her films and in her public persona, a particular narrative of gender politics that sets itself against the constraints and certainties of Old World femininity. Participating in broader New World narratives of freedom and adventure, it asserts that to be an antipodean woman is a condition of possibility, enabling an independence of spirit and an ability to act upon the world.

Being a New Zealander/Being an Australian

To the extent that "antipodean" may be an identity claimed in Campion's self-fashioning for northern hemisphere audiences, however, it is also a category undone in many of her other performances. As often as "antipodean" is defined against "Europe" or "America," New Zealand and Australia are defined against each other; and Campion herself has taken on the identity of each country at different points in her career. Speaking to Yves Alion in 1991, she explained, "I currently live in Sydney. I left New Zealand many years ago. It's a country that is really too provincial, where it's not easy for a director to work, first because the structures of production are truly insufficient; and also because the New Zealand mentality is still a bit cramped. If you say you want to make movies, they say to you: 'But who do you think you are? Why you?' It's true in effect, why me?"[30]

Of course, as any antipodean knows, Campion did not say exactly that. (Perhaps only in translation from the French is "provincial" used in just this way, and this interview has been translated into French and back into English.) Nevertheless, what was being articulated to a French readership here was the difference not *of* the antipodes but differences *within* the antipodes.

It is perhaps not at all surprising that Campion's citizenship has sometimes been a matter of uncertainty. She is described as an Australian director or a New Zealand director; she lives in Sydney, Australia, describing it even as "my home town," but grew up in Wellington, New Zealand, and now has a house in the shadow of the Southern Alps in Central Otago, New Zealand. Much of Campion's filmmaking career has seen her track back and forth across the Tasman. She made the short film *Peel* at film school in Sydney and went on to make *Passionless Moments, A Girl's Own Story,* and *Sweetie,* all made and set in Australia with Australian collaborators, crew, and actors. But then she looked back and made *An Angel at My Table* and *The Piano,* both set in New Zealand and both historical; then later, *Holy Smoke* returned emphatically to an Australian setting. She has worked with Australian producers, a New Zealand producer based in Sydney, and Australian and New

Zealand directors of photography. She has worked with Australian and New Zealand actors as well as international casts and collaborators. Predictably, both countries rushed to claim her when *The Piano* began to reap awards. She has been marketed strategically as one or the other. Lindsay Shelton writes, "One of my challenges in launching *An Angel At My Table* had been to reposition the director as a New Zealander, because her previous films had been made in Australia. This, I said repeatedly, was a New Zealand film by a New Zealand film-maker."[31]

On a number of occasions, Campion has registered both her identity and her discomfort with New Zealand and in the process sums up some of the differences between the cultures of the two countries:[32]

Going back there made me realize what an influence the country had on me. . . . It's quite a Presbyterian work ethic country. Thinking that you're better than anyone is a cardinal sin. . . . New Zealanders believe in modesty at all times and we all thought Australians were vulgar and coarse. But I enjoy the way Australians are.[33]

I like Australia. It's warm, the people are relaxed and quite informal. I like this renunciation of formalities. There is a general openness to cultural things because nobody knows exactly where the next good thing will be coming from.[34]

New Zealanders are very, you know, watching, cautious, suspicious, and delving, you know.[35]

Historically, New Zealanders have characterized Australia, and especially Sydney, as brash, robustly over-confident, hedonistic: United States to our Canada, Sweetie to our Kay. New Zealand viewed from Australia looks darker, more introverted: Australian novelist Patrick White, reading Janet Frame's *Edge of the Alphabet* in 1963, reflected on what he saw as "despair and confusion under the simple, uncomplicated New Zealand surface. I shouldn't be surprised if any New Zealander took a gun to his neighbour."[36] New Zealand cinema has sometimes seemed set on enacting this dark vision, with films such as *Bad Blood* (Mike Newell, 1981), which told the story of Stanley Graham's killing of police and flight into the bush. Peter Wells, four years older than Campion, grew up in suburban Auckland in the 1950s and 1960s and writes of it as a place where you waited until your real life could begin. He casts Auckland and Sydney as opposites—repressed Auckland and seductive Sydney: "I've always thought Sydney played Paris to our prosaic London. . . . Sydney was the place you went *to sin*."[37] The differences play out in the comic register too, with each country the frequent butt of jokes about the other. When Australian comedian Barry Humphries played his signature character, the grotesque, self-promoting, and over-jeweled Dame Edna Everage, his "New Zealand bridesmaid, Madge," would sometimes play fall-gal: she was mute, sour, small, and cardiganed, and we knew what she meant. Here "antipodean" splits into a divided identity. Campion's rendition of the differences is not so extreme, but in her interviews it falls into the pattern of Australia as warm, relaxed, open, and informal, and New Zealand as darker, more introverted and repressed. It is all the more curious, then, that in her films the representations of Australia tend toward the dystopic and those of New Zealand often evoke nostalgia. It is not quite so simple as this, but in the rest of this chapter I explore this paradox.

The Early Films: Un-iconic Australia

Peel, the short film made at AFTRS and so disliked by Campion's teachers, is a study in boredom and irritation, startling in its "Australian" familiarity and the detailed attention to ordinary dysfunction. The landscape through which the family drives is anything but iconic: fields that are decidedly ordinary, with a bit of industry on the skyline, and a scrubby roadside with cars and trucks roaring by. It sets the pattern for a rendition of Australianness in Campion's work as modern, dystopic, and urbanized. *A Girl's Own Story* presents a much more threatening world but one that is clearly continuous with that of *Peel.* Here, however, despite the Australian accents of the characters, the convent setting of Gloria's confinement, and the emphatically vernacular quality of the sets and costumes, the location has as much to do with time as with place.[38] The time is the cusp between the sexual regimes of postwar societies and the sexual revolution (the final dedication is "to the spirit of the 60s in which she grew up"), and the film's subject is the way in which adolescent girls were thrown into this confused and confusing era. The claustrophobic interiors and confined exteriors, the cold of the black-and-white, entrap and chill these girls struggling to enter a hostile world. "Feel the cold," sing the girls bleakly at the end, as skates cut into ice—hardly the warmth and relaxation with which Campion characterizes Australians.

Passionless Moments, co-written with Australian Gerard Lee, is the gentlest and most affectionate of the early films that deal with the Australian suburb, but like all of them, it adopts an ironic outsider position, as it narrates its series of everyday strangenesses and alienation. Estrangement marks all these stories of Australia. As Rochelle Simmons argues at greater length in this volume, they are all contemporary or near-contemporary, all to some degree suburban, all to greater or lesser degree dystopic.

Sweetie, Campion's first feature, is also a film marked by a vernacular Australian setting, especially in its use of hyper-ordinary suburban ugliness, and the working-class Sydney characterization.[39] As *Holy Smoke* would do later in Campion's career, *Sweetie* participates in the Australian cultural legacy of contrast between the city and the desert heart. But *Sweetie's* emphasis is on the suburb: a suburb presented with an extreme degree of estrangement, with Sally Bongers's skewed angles and the enactment of surreally ordinary events in scruffy suburban backyards studded with "Australian" detail (the bare concrete in Kay and Louis's backyard, the loungers, the paddling pool, the shed with the rusting corrugated iron roof in the neighbors' yard, the rotary washing lines, of which there are three—one is uprooted in favor of the baby alder, another appears in the neighbors' yard, and a third skews over the heads of Kay, Gordon, and Flo as the dying Sweetie looks up at them).[40]

Yet in another sense *Sweetie* might be read as playing differences within the antipodes through the two main characters. Sweetie herself is excessive, uncontrolled, and self-indulgent; Kay dreams dark dreams of all that lurks beneath, anxiously fearing and over-interpreting, intense and asexual for much of the film. The dream of the tree's roots, running out of control beneath the paved but cracking surface of the backyard in Kay's dream, defines Kay in terms of the intensity of her fears. For Kay, what lies beneath may erupt at any moment and must at all costs be contained. The trace of incest snakes in and out of the interstices of the film, hovering in Kay's, and our, peripheral vision. Out comes the threatening tree, and into the cupboard it goes, poorly hidden and awaiting its inevitable discovery. Asked to reflect on her relationship to her characters, Campion once said, "Kay is the closest to what I was."[41] I have sometimes thought this might be a New Zealand joke (sly, low-key, self-deprecatory), but it is certainly one way in which we might map the divide between Australianness and New Zealandness in Campion's work. More than any of Campion's other films, *Sweetie* enacts something that we could read as a parodic rendition of differences within the antipodes: excess versus restraint, noise versus quiet, lots of sex versus no sex, madness as acting out versus madness as bottling up.[42]

Looking Back across the Tasman, Looking Back in Time

When Janet Frame's autobiographies began to be published, they achieved a broad New Zealand readership that quickly outstripped that of her novels. Probably the most important element in that popularity was nostalgia. Frame's ability to use significant detail and word choice to conjure readers' memories and to recreate a familiar past with unusual immediacy gave these books a wide appeal. For a generation they stood for a New Zealand still remembered but now gone. The nostalgic appeal was enhanced as the later volumes retold, from Frame's point of view this time, the accepted cultural narrative of the "birth" of a distinctively New Zealand literature, centering on writer Frank Sargeson and the literary scene associated with him on Auckland's North Shore in the 1950s.

In Campion's turn to a New Zealand setting in *An Angel at My Table* (1990), a distinctive emotional geography can be detected. The past of this film is not a sentimental past but is nevertheless infused with a depth of desirability, with lustrous, intense "period" color, something absent in any of Campion's films up to this time. No doubt some of this can be chalked up to a change of cinematographer, as New Zealander Stuart Dryburgh's images replace the angular, skewed photography of Australian Sally Bongers. But Campion chose her directors of photography and worked very closely with them. When Campion began to look back in *Angel*, she did so on three levels: she looked back in time, to the period of Frame's childhood and youth; she looked back across the Tasman to New Zealand; and she looked back visually, using a deeper, richer palette and more chiaroscuro. From bright, hard, modern Australia (*Peel*, *Sweetie*), New Zealand begins to look like the past and—despite the story of *Angel*—to elicit a nostalgic response. Despite its facility with the awkward and the uncomfortable, there is intense longing for the past in this film, in the visual style but also, for example, in the tender filming of Janet as a child, in the slow motion shots of Myrtle dancing away poignantly to her death, in Janet stepping into her father's boots and willing him back with her mimicry. In the documentary *The Grass Is Greener* Campion describes her own response to reading Frame's autobiographies: "What I found was happening was I was discovering my own childhood again and realizing the specialness of that childhood through Janet's book."[43]

Stuart Dryburgh also shot *The Piano*. The spectacular filming of beach and forest recalls an often-quoted line from the letters of another well-known expatriate, Katherine Mansfield, who as she embarked on her own series of New Zealand stories wrote of wanting "to make our undiscovered country leap into the eyes of the Old World."[44] Dryburgh's lush cinematography emerges from what was by the time of *The Piano* a substantial tradition of the filming of New Zealand wilderness as landscape, as a fitting object of a romantic cinematic gaze.[45] Despite the famous mud, *The Piano*'s treatment of landscape sits clearly within the Romantic tradition: in its pristine beauty, the spectacular scale of forest and wild coast, and of course the accompanying presence of the soundtrack, which would in another context seem extravagant. Genre provides the context for the sublime and compounds the intensity of the viewing of landscape as extreme pleasure. In an interview with Thomas Bourguignon and Michel Ciment (another that bears the signs of translation into French and back again, and in which she clearly seeks to explain New Zealandness to Europeans), Campion talks about landscape in relation to her own childhood and her imagination:

I knew the atmosphere and the power of this scenery, having grown up there. I walked in the bush, spent nights there, which is a custom in New Zealand. . . . It's a landscape that is unsettling, claustrophobic, and mythic all at the same time. . . . It's scenery that troubled a lot of Europeans when they arrived, and since they didn't like it, they cleared a lot of it so that it looked more like Europe. I thought that this wild landscape was right for my story. Romanticism has been misunderstood in our era, especially in films. It has become something "pretty" or lovable. Its hardness, its dark side has been forgotten. I wanted to create a feeling of terror in the spectator when faced with the power of natural elements. That's, I think, the essence of Romanticism: this respect for a nature that is considered larger than you, your mind, or even humanity.[46]

For me, and for many New Zealanders, the relationship with very wild beaches, especially the black sands of the west coast beaches around Auckland and New Plymouth, and the very private, secretive and extraordinary world of the bush, is a kind of colonial equivalent to Emily Brontë's moors.[47]

Campion's comments here anticipate something of the debate that environmental critic Geoff Park has sparked in his recent writing about landscape and the picturesque as an element in Pakeha New Zealanders' relationships to their country. Park's discussion of the Claude glass—an encased mirror enabling the viewer to see, reflected, a framed landscape—as both an antecedent of the camera and a key element in the European envisioning of New Zealand, are pertinent here. Campion situates her own vision in relation to the Romantic sensibility of English wild places, yet asserts that Europeans cut down the New Zealand forest because they did not like it. Park, along with a number of art historians, contends that the Romantic sensibility was in fact much evident in eighteenth- and nineteenth-century envisioning of New Zealand. Registering the disenfranchisement that follows from imaging a land primarily understood as something to look at, Park is concerned to reimagine the human, and particularly Maori, occupation of this "wild" country.

Also nostalgic, and—for a different reason—also the mark of an expatriate, was *The Piano*'s handling of Maori. Campion has said that the genesis of the film occurred when she looked at nineteenth-century photographs of

Maori in the Turnbull Library, and was intrigued by their adoption of dress that was partly Maori, partly European.[48] This comment seems to suggest that the moment of cultural encounter for Maori might have become a central theme of the film. The major criticisms of *The Piano* in New Zealand, however, centered on the fact that Maori function only as a backdrop and counterpoint to the drama enacted by the European immigrants and that they are represented largely as ahistorical. In particular, the Maori characters are represented as enjoying an unfettered sexuality, in this way constituting a primitive Other against which the over-civilized European sexuality is given prominence and outline. Lynda Dyson identifies a series of points in the film in which "primitivist discourses . . . construct the Maori as 'outside culture,'" particularly in the way in which they appear "unable to distinguish between representations and the real."[49] While many international reviewers responded positively to the representation of colonial encounter, in New Zealand, critic after critic objected. David Eggleton refers to the Maori in the film as "Harpo Marxists"; Leonie Pihama complained that *The Piano*'s representation of Maori "left no stereotype stone unturned."[50] Reid Perkins summed up much of the critical disquiet:

So, while *The Piano*'s production notes might aver that "essential to the truth of the period was the inclusion of a Maori 'story,'" nothing that in fact merits this description actually manifests itself in the film. Maori are not given their own story but merely a cramped though prominent space on the edge of the Pakeha one; this they occupy in order to provide the necessary contrast for throwing the dilemmas of the European characters into an appropriate relief. The point here is not to criticize Campion for failing to meet the requirements of some kind of "cultural quota" in the distribution of her narrative, but rather to point out the discrepancy between the symbolic weight carried by Maori in the film and the slightness of their actual presence in the storyline; their importance as "signs" as against their negligibility as "characters"; their positioning as "objects" rather than "subjects." For the manner in which Campion has looked to this historical situation to tell a tale of passion and repression requires, as its corollary, a limiting of the meanings Maori are able to claim in the film to those along a single dimension: nature, innocence, wildness, authenticity.[51]

The Piano was made in the early 1990s, though Campion had worked on the screenplay for quite a few years. During the later stages of writing, she consulted Maori advisors and made some, though not all, of the changes they recommended. She told Vincent Ostria and Thierry Jousse that the Maori involved with the production thought that my first description of the Maori in the screenplay was bad. They spoke frankly about it and offered to fix it. I worked with Waihoroi Shortland who wrote the Maori dialogues. He wanted to help me represent the Maori universe in a convincing way. In his mind, it was the occasion to make them better known. But I explained to him that I didn't want to approach the question from a political angle. I wanted to find the reality and authenticity of Maori behaviour, of their way of speaking, without trying to impose a political point of view.[52]

This appears to have been a rather unsatisfactory relationship. By the time the film was complete, Campion had not lived in New Zealand for about sixteen years. Over this period, the country had undergone an enormous social, cultural, and economic upheaval that had effectively changed the cultural landscape and rewritten the narratives of national identity. A Maori Renaissance involving political activism, a concerted endeavor to save the Maori language, and a cultural revival was emerging from the 1970s but became more emphatic through the 1980s and 1990s. In 1981 the South African rugby team had accepted an invitation by the New Zealand Rugby Union to tour the country, invitation and acceptance both flouting international sporting boycotts of South Africa. The Tour, as it is still known, generated protest movements on a scale never seen before and divided the country on the issue of race. The most important of the downstream effects of the Tour in New Zealand were national debate about the significance of the Treaty of Waitangi, signed in 1840 between Maori and the British Crown, and an effective revolution in beliefs about the relationship between Maori and Pakeha. Maori were in the process of moving to occupy a more central—and less purely ceremonial—place in national identity. While *The Piano* sought to declare its sympathy for Maori dispossession, and the sympathies of the film affiliated it with the philo-Maori Baines as against the crudely colonialist Stewart, its representation of Maori as exotic backdrop for the over-civilized Europeans' sexual dilemmas had a distinctly unsophisticated air in the New Zealand of the early 1990s, marking its vision as an expatriate one. "Thus, arguably," wrote Bridget Orr, "*The Piano*'s feminocentric narrative seeks to recentre its female protagonist by writing her out of history into romance; to absolve her from settler guilt by linking her through an erotic metonymy to Maori, and to focus colonial culpability on the male pioneer's sexual and territorial possessiveness."[53] "Gender," she affirmed, "is not available as an alibi for participation in colonial history."[54] While "New Zealand" as *past* had operated evocatively in *Angel,* then, drawing Frame's and Campion's nostalgic desires into alignment and evoking similar longings in responsive audiences, the past of *The Piano* was more complex. The Romantic and the colonial could not quite cohere; and the temporal disjunction between Campion and her New Zealand critics now marked her as out of step with racial politics in New Zealand. Looking back at home, she had become an outsider.

Holy Smoke: *Modern and Ancient Australia*

After the nineteenth-century settings of *The Piano* and *The Portrait of a Lady*, *Holy Smoke* saw Campion return emphatically to another Australian present. Here there is a clear distinction drawn between spiritual and emotional depth on the one hand (India, the desert) and superficiality on the other (the red brick banality of the Sydney suburb). It is a strange present, this suburban exterior and interior, supposedly the home of a fairly well-off middle-class couple in the 1990s: its look references an Australian tradition of comedies in which "Australian culture" is rendered oxymoronic. The contrast between India and Sydney immediately determines our sympathy for Ruth's choice and situates her family's wish to reclaim her as ironic. The appeal to the audience is effected through a contrast in taste that, as Rochelle Simmons argues, has precise class connotations. India is "rich" in its light and color, and there is a sense of a deep past. Sans Souci is precisely that—without care—in its tacky, clichéd clutter that is not old but outdated.[55] Here we are returned to Australia as modern, urban, and dystopic—even the outback settings of Mt. Emu Farm, at least its interiors, and the Outback Inn, are continuous with this aesthetic.

But *Holy Smoke* distinguishes between two Australias: as we travel further into the desert, "Australia" deepens spiritually and emotionally. As Sue Gillett observes, the outback locations, "in contrast to Sans Souci, would seem to signify the real Australia. The history of representations of Australia is loaded with this equation of desert and heart or essence. It would also seem that the film has now moved our heroine from the superficiality of one environment to the depth and uniqueness of another, thus preparing the way for her real spiritual awakening."[56]

The colors and the light of the Halfway Hut interior and the outback exteriors are not the same colors as the Indian scenes, but they return us to the use of clear color and transcendent light: the clear orange, blue, and purple of ancient landscape, the intense orange of the sun, the softly lit ochre of the old-fashioned kitchen, the backlit stained glass in the hut define this as a setting in which, far from being returned to the "Australia" of her family, Ruth can pursue her experience of spirituality. This setting, unlike any of the Australian settings in Campion's previous films, is neither modern nor urban. Even its aridity is literal rather than visual. Its clarity of color and light, and its age, are reinforced for us by the interspersed scene in the pub, where the soft backlit stained glass of the Hut is countered by glittering neon, while the intense "truths" of the elemental war between Ruth and P. J. are parodied by the debauched call-and-response of band and crowd ("Am I ever gonna see your face again / Go 'way! Get fucked! Fuck off!"), and the complex back-and-forth of the play of power between them is replaced by a brief rape-culture narrative as two young men attempt to force Ruth to drink while removing her clothes.

For the first time in Campion's films, then, here is Australia with an ancient past: a setting that can accommodate experience of spiritual depth ("Something really did happen, didn't it?" writes Ruth to P. J. a year later). There are parallels here with the sense of the past and the power of landscape in the "New Zealand" films. It is striking, however, that unlike Sans Souci or the Outback Inn or Mt. Emu Farm or the pub, the spiritual and emotional possibilities inherent in the setting of the Hut and the surrounding landscape are contingent upon its lack of human habitation: except for the trace of past habitation that the Hut itself represents, "Australian culture" and spirituality remain mutually exclusive. Once again, the rupture between Campion's comfortable adoption of Australia as home and her representations of it is evident.

It is also curious—and I can only speculate here—that if the critiques of the representations of Maori in *The Piano* should lead us to look for the representations of indigenous Australians in *Holy Smoke,* what we find is that there are none. It may be that Campion was scared off by the response to *The Piano* and decided that this terrain was too difficult. Or perhaps, given the legacy of representations of Aboriginals in the outback, it may have seemed impossible to avoid falling into made-for-tourism cliché. Another possibility is that it did not occur to her to populate this landscape: that the conception of a *terra nullius* (which in recent decades has become such a hotly debated field in Australian legal history) was reproduced in film without particular thought, repeating the original erasure. Given Campion's public position on the Australian government's intervention in the Northern Territory, however, this last possibility seems unlikely.

"Everybody has a family and there's a legacy you carry from that. I was lucky to have good, encouraging parents, but it wasn't until my late 20s that I realised how similar I was getting to Mum," Campion said. "Suddenly you realise that you haven't left your family behind at all, that you've been carrying them with you."[57]

In this chapter I have attended not to a family legacy but to a regional and national one, but Campion's point here applies. I have suggested, first, that over a sequence of films, Campion drew on an inheritance of the antipodean and especially the antipodean feminine both in the adventure of her heroines and in the fashioning of her public persona. To the extent that this is the case, we can read her as producing a narrative that answers back to the Old World: to what antipodeans often understand as its constraints, its conventions, its lack of opportunity. Yet—second—once we begin to unpick the differences within "antipodean," this narrative of defiance unravels somewhat, and a more contingent, mobile, and at times problematic identity emerges. New Zealand now is defined against Australia, and vice versa, and each is less heroic, more mired in the complexities of a past that has produced postcolonial national identities. In shuttling between antipodean, New Zealand, and Australian identities—all of which themselves contain uncertainties and which are subject to change—Campion has participated in ambiguities that have been both fruitful and troubling.

Notes

This chapter was written after the colloquium Jane Campion: Cinema, Nation, Identity, and I am deeply indebted to the ideas and debates that took place at that event.

1. Patricia Grimshaw, "Women's Suffrage in New Zealand Revisited: Writing from the Margins," in *Suffrage and Beyond: International Feminist Perspectives,* ed. Caroline Daley and Melanie Nolan (Auckland: Auckland University Press, 1994), 25–41; see also Annabel Cooper, Erik Olssen, Kirsten Thomlinson, and Robin Law, "The Landscape of Gender Politics: Place, People, and Two Mobilisations," in *Sites of Gender: Women, Men and Modernity in Southern Dunedin, 1890–1939,* ed. Barbara Brookes, Annabel Cooper, and Robin Law (Auckland: Auckland University Press, 2003), 15–49.

2. See Grimshaw, "Women's Suffrage"; Raewyn Dalziel, "Presenting the Enfranchisement of New Zealand Women," in Daley and Nolan, *Suffrage and Beyond,* 42–64, and for the dates of the franchise, 349; Raewyn Dalziel, "An Experiment in the Social Laboratory? Suffrage, National Identity, and Mythologies of Race in New Zealand in the 1890s," in *Women's Suffrage in the British Empire: Citizenship, Nation, and Race,* ed. Ian Christopher Fletcher, Laura E. Nym Mayhall, and Philippa Levine (London: Routledge, 2000), 87–102; and Angela Woollacott, "Australian Women's Metropolitan Activism: From Suffrage, to Imperial Vanguard, to Commonwealth Feminism," in Fletcher, Mayhall, and Levine, *Women's Suffrage,* 207–23.

3. Jane Mander, *The Story of a New Zealand River* (1920; repr., Christchurch: Whitcombe and Tombs, 1973), 191.

4. Ibid., 51.

5. Kristin Williamson, "The New Filmmakers," *Cinema Papers,* December 1984; reprinted in *Jane Campion: Interviews,* ed. Virginia Wright Wexman (Jackson: University Press of Mississippi, 1999), 5.

6. *Conversations in World Cinema—Jane Campion,* produced by Scott Hopper, television program (New York: Sundance Channel, 2000).

7. Jocelyn Robson and Beverly Zalcock, *Girls' Own Stories: Australian and New Zealand Women's Films* (London: Scarlet Press, 1997), 10.

8. Carrie Rickey, "A Director Strikes an Intimate Chord," in Wexman, *Jane Campion,* 52.

9. *Conversations in World Cinema.*

10. In fact, it seldom appears in Campion filmographies.

11. *Conversations in World Cinema.*

12. Mary Cantwell, "Jane Campion's Lunatic Women," *New York Times Magazine,* 19 September 1993; reprinted in Wexman, *Jane Campion,* 156.

13. Jay Carr, "Jane Campion, the Classical Romantic," *The Boston Globe,* 14 November 1993; reprinted in Wexman, *Jane Campion,* 171.

14. Heike-Melba Fendal, "How Women Live Their Lives," *EPD Film,* April 1991; reprinted in Wexman, *Jane Campion,* 89.

15. Lindsay Shelton, *The Selling of New Zealand Movies* (Wellington: Awa Press, 2005), 107–13.

16. Campion has spoken of her interest in Lévi-Strauss: "My degree didn't really lead me anywhere but we had a fantastic professor, a Dutchman by the name of Power. He had studied with Lévi-Strauss—and we discussed structural anthropology and linguistic problems. . . . I believe, moreover, that I have an anthropological eye." Michel Ciment, "Two Interviews with Jane Campion," *Positif,* January 1990; reprinted in Wexman, *Jane Campion,* 31.

17. Jane Campion, *The Piano* [screenplay] (London: Bloomsbury, 1993), 9.

18. Hilary Neroni, "Jane Campion's Jouissance: *Holy Smoke* and Feminist Film Theory," in *Lacan and Contemporary Film,* ed. Todd McGowan and Sheila Kunkle (New York: Other Press, 2004), 209–32.

19. Campion, *The Piano,* 78.

20. Neroni, "Jane Campion's Jouissance," 214–15.

21. Cantwell, "Jane Campion's Lunatic Women," 162.

22. I develop the antipodean elements of *Portrait* further in Annabel Cooper, "'I Am Isabel, You Know?' The Antipodean Framing of Jane Campion's *Portrait of a Lady,*" *M/C: A Journal of Media and Culture* 11, no. 5 (2008).

23. Robson and Zalcock, *Girls' Own Stories,* 10.

24. Kathleen McHugh, this volume; and Priscilla L. Walton, "Jane and James Go to the Movies: Post Colonial Portraits of a Lady," *The Henry James Review* 18, no. 2 (1997): 187–90.

25. Henry James, *The Portrait of a Lady,* 2nd. ed. (1908), ed. Robert D. Bamberg (New York: Norton, 1975), 24.

26. Ibid., 315.

27. Including Irene Bessière, this volume.

28. James, *Portrait of a Lady,* 490 (my italics).

29. Note that Campion, unable to conclude with Frannie's murder, also changed the ending of *In the Cut*: her heroine emerges victorious.

30. Yves Alion, "Interview with Jane Campion: In the Country of the Hypersensitive," in Wexman, *Jane Campion*, 85.

31. Shelton, *Selling of New Zealand Movies*, 111.

32. In fact, these differences would now play out in somewhat altered ways than those described here, as both countries have undergone rather different processes of cultural and political change.

33. Katherine Tulich, "Jane's Film Career Takes Wing," *Daily Telegraph*, 23 September 1990; reprinted in Wexman, *Jane Campion*, 71–73.

34. Heike-Melba Fendel, "How Women Live Their Lives," *EPD Film*, April 1991; reprinted in Wexman, *Jane Campion*, 86–90.

35. *The Grass Is Greener: Interview with Jane Campion*, dir. Greg Stitt (New Zealand and Australia: Rhymer and Bayly Watson, 1990).

36. Patrick White, *Letters*, ed. David Marr (Sydney: Random House, 1994), 219.

37. Peter Wells, *Long Loop Home* (Auckland: Vintage, 2001), 221.

38. Irish Catholicism is particularly strong in New South Wales.

39. I wish to thank Sally Bongers for explaining just how much labor was involved in producing the suburban disarray of *Sweetie's* sets and Rochelle Simmons for our discussions about Australia, New Zealand, and suburbs.

40. Again, for a fuller discussion of this trope, see Rochelle Simmons's chapter in this volume. The rotary washing line is not unique to Australia and New Zealand, but it is such an omnipresent feature that it constitutes a defining mark of antipodean suburbia.

41. Thomas Bourgignon and Michel Ciment, "Interview with Jane Campion: More Barbarian Than Aesthete," *Positif*, June 1993; reprinted in Wexman, *Jane Campion*, 110.

42. Alistair Fox in this volume elaborates this theme in relation to *The Piano*.

43. Stitt, *The Grass Is Greener*.

44. C. K. Stead, ed., *The Letters and Journals of Katherine Mansfield: A Selection* (London: Allen Lane, 1977), 65.

45. Geoff Park, *Theatre Country: Essays on Whenua and Landscape* (Wellington: Victoria University Press, 2006), especially the title essay, 113–28.

46. Sandra Hall, "The Arts/Film," *The Bulletin*, 26 October 1993, reprinted in Wexman, *Jane Campion*, 167.

47. Miro Bilborough, "The Piano," *Cinema Papers*, May 1993, reprinted in Wexman, *Jane Campion*, 115.

48. The research library of the National Library of New Zealand, which has an extensive collection of historical photographs.

49. Lynda Dyson, "The Return of the Repressed? Whiteness, Femininity, and Colonialism in *The Piano*," in *Piano Lessons: Approaches to* The Piano, ed. Felicity Coombs and Suzanne Gemmell (Sydney: John Libbey, 1999), 117.

50. David Eggleton, "Grimm Fairytale of the South Seas," *Illusions* 23 (1994): 2–5; and Leonie Pihama, "Are Films Dangerous? A Maori Woman's Perspective on

The Piano," *Hecate* 20, no. 2 (1994): 239. See also Pihama's "Ebony and Ivory: Constructions of Maori in *The Piano,*" in *Jane Campion's* The Piano, ed. Harriet Margolis (Cambridge: Cambridge University Press, 2000), 114–34; and Anna Neill, "A Land without a Past: Dreamtime and Nation in *The Piano,*" in Coombs and Gemmell, *Piano Lessons,* 136–47.

51. Reid Perkins, "Imag(in)ing Our Colonial Past: Colonial New Zealand on Film from *The Birth of New Zealand* to *The Piano*—Part II," *Illusions* 26 (1997): 21. For another, much stranger, account that sees *The Piano* as consistent with New Zealand fantasies of colonial encounter, see Stephen Turner, "Once Were English," *Meanjin* 58, no. 2 (1999): 122–39. An exception to the international applause is Reshela DuPuis, "Romanticizing Colonialism: Power and Pleasure in Jane Campion's *Piano,*" *The Contemporary Pacific* 8, no. 1 (1996): 51–70; and more recently, Margaret Jolly, "Looking Back? Gender, Sexuality, and Race in *The Piano,*" *Australian Feminist Studies,* forthcoming.

52. Vincent Ostria and Thierry Jousse, "The Piano: Interview with Jane Campion," *Cahiers du Cinema,* May 1993; reprinted in Wexman, *Jane Campion,* 130–31.

53. Bridget Orr, "Birth of a Nation? From *Utu* to *The Piano,*" in Coombs and Gemmell, *Piano Lessons,* 149.

54. Ibid., 158.

55. The costuming and the interiors of this film are discussed more extensively by Rochelle Simmons in this volume.

56. Sue Gillett, *Views from Beyond the Mirror: The Films of Jane Campion* (Melbourne: Australian Teachers of Media, 2004), 74–75.

57. Ruth Hessey, "Campion Goes Out on a Limb—Again," *Sydney Morning Herald,* 5 July 1989; reprinted in Wexman, *Jane Campion,* 28.

Filmography

À l'intérieur (Inside, Alexandre Bustillo and Julien Maury, 2007, France)
The Adventures of Priscilla, Queen of the Desert (Stephan Elliott, 1994, Australia)
After Hours (Jane Campion, 1984, Australia)
Un Air de famille (Family resemblances, Cédric Klapish, 1996, France)
All That We Need (Barry Barclay, 1966, New Zealand)
An Angel at My Table (Jane Campion, 1990, United Kingdom/Australia/New Zealand)
L'Atalante (Jean Vigo, 1933, France)
The Audition (Anna Campion, 1989, Australia)
Babette's Feast (Gabriel Axel, 1987, Denmark)
Bad Blood (Mike Newell, 1981, New Zealand/United Kingdom)
Bad Lieutenant (Abel Ferraro, 1992, United States)
Bad Timing (Nicholas Roeg, 1980, United Kingdom)
Belle de jour (Beauty of the day, Luis Buñuel, 1967, France/Italy)
Blue Velvet (David Lynch, 1986, United States)
The Bodyguard (Mick Jackson, 1992, United States)
Broken Skin (Anna Campion, 1991, United Kingdom)
Carne trémula (Live Flesh, Pedro Almodóvar, 1997, France/Spain)
The Castle (Rob Sitch, 1997, Australia)
Chacun son cinéma (To each his cinema, Theodoros Angelopoulos and Olivier Assayas, 2007, France)
Chinatown (Roman Polanski, 1974, United States)
Clockers (Spike Lee, 1995, United States)
Clueless (Amy Heckerling, 1995, United States)
Conversations in World Cinema—Jane Campion (Scott Hopper, 2000, United States)
Crin blanc: le cheval sauvage (White mane, Albert Lamorisse, 1953, France)
Crocodile Dundee (Peter Faiman, 1986, Australia)
Cyrano de Bergerac (Jean-Paul Rappeneau, 1990, France)
Desperately Seeking Susan (Susan Seidelman, 1985, United States)
Les Destinées sentimentales (Sentimental Destinies, Olivier Assayas, 2000, France/Switzerland)
The Duellists (Ridley Scott, 1977, United Kingdom)

8 (Jane Campion, Gael Garcia Bernal, et al., 2008, France)

Emma (Douglas McGrath, 1996, United Kingdom/United States)

Eraserhead (David Lynch, 1977, United States)

Fatal Attraction (Adrian Lyne, 1987, United States)

Fingers (James Toback, 1978, United States)

Gaslight (George Cukor, 1944, United States)

Ghost (Jerry Zucker, 1990, United States)

A Girl's Own Story (Jane Campion, 1984, Australia)

Gosford Park (Robert Altman, 2001, United Kingdom/United States/Italy)

The Grass Is Greener: Interview with Jane Campion (Greg Stitt, 1990, New Zealand/ Australia)

Groundhog Day (Harold Ramis, 1993, United States)

La Haine (Hate, Mathieu Kassovitz, 1995, France)

Heavenly Creatures (Peter Jackson, 1994, United Kingdom/Germany/New Zealand)

Holy Smoke (Jane Campion, 1999, United States/Australia)

Howard's End (James Ivory, 1992, United Kingdom/Japan)

Le Hussard sur le toit (The horseman on the roof, Jean-Paul Rappeneau, 1995, France)

In the Cut (Jane Campion, 2003, Australia/United States/United Kingdom)

Jaws (Steven Spielberg, 1975, United States)

Jeanne Dielman, 23 Quai du commerce, 1080 Bruxelles (Chantal Akerman, 1976, Belgium/France)

Jeanne et le garcon formidable (Jeanne and the perfect guy, Olivier Ducastel and Jacques Martineau, 1998, France)

Jesus of Montreal (Denys Arcand, 1989, Canada/France)

Jour de fête (Holiday, Jacques Tati, 1949, France)

Judex (George Franju, 1963, France/Italy)

Klute (Alan J. Pakula, 1971, United States)

Loaded (Anna Campion, 1994, New Zealand/United Kingdom)

Looking for Mr. Goodbar (Richard Brooks, 1977, United States)

Lorenzo's Oil (George Miller, 1992, United States)

La Mala educatión (Bad Education, Pedro Almodóvar, 2004, Spain)

Mansfield Park (Patricia Rozema, 1999, United Kingdom)

Maurice (James Ivory, 1987, United Kingdom)

Mishaps: Seduction and Conquest (Jane Campion, 1981, Australia)

Mujeres al Borde de un Ataque de Nervios (Women on the verge of a nervous break-down, Pedro Almodóvar, 1988, Spain)

Muriel's Wedding (P. J. Hogan, 1994, Australia/France)

My Brilliant Career (Gillian Armstrong, 1979, Australia)

The Night of the Hunter (Charles Laughton, 1955, United States)

Orlando (Sally Potter, 1993, United Kingdom/Russia/France/Italy/Netherlands)

The Passion of the Christ (Mel Gibson, 2004, United States)

Passionless Moments (Jane Campion and Gerard Lee, 1983, Australia)

Peel: An Exercise in Discipline (Jane Campion, 1982, Australia)

Persuasion (Roger Michell, 1995, United Kingdom/France/United States)

The Piano (Jane Campion, 1993, Australia/New Zealand/France)

The Portrait of a Lady (Jane Campion, 1996, United Kingdom/United States)

Portrait: Jane Campion and The Portrait of a Lady (Kate Ellis and Peter Long, 1997, Australia)

The Prince of Eygpt (Brenda Chapman, Steve Hickner, and Simon Wells, 1998, United States)

Psycho (Alfred Hitchcock, 1960, United States)

Room at the Top (Jack Clayton, 1957, United Kingdom)

A Room with a View (James Ivory, 1985, United Kingdom)

Saint-Cyr (The King's Daughters, Patricia Mazuy, 2000, France/Germany/Belgium)

Sense and Sensibility (Ang Lee, 1995, United States/United Kingdom)

Smithereens (Susan Seidelman, 1982, United States)

Someone to Watch Over Me (Ridley Scott, 1987, United States)

La Souriante Madame Beudet (Germaine Dulac, 1923, France)

Strictly Ballroom (Baz Luhrmann, 1992, Australia)

Summertime (David Lean, 1955, United Kingdom/United States)

Sweetie (Jane Campion, 1989, Australia)

A Taste of Cherry (Abbas Kiarostami, 1997, France/Iran)

Taxi Driver (Martin Scorsese, 1976, United States)

Thelma and Louise (Ridley Scott, 1991, United States)

Titanic (James Cameron, 1997, United States)

Two Friends (Jane Campion, 1986, Australia)

The Two Jakes (Jack Nicholson, 1990, United States)

Who's That Knocking at My Door? (Martin Scorsese, 1968, United States)

The Wild Bunch (Sam Peckinpah, 1969, United States)

Les Yeux sans visage (Eyes without a face, George Franju, 1959, France/Italy)

Select Bibliography

Abramowitz, Rachel. "Jane Campion." In Wexman, *Jane Campion,* 186–91.

Adelman, Kim. *The Ultimate Guide to Chick Flicks: The Romance, the Glamour, the Tears, and More.* New York: Broadway Books, 2005.

Adler, Stella. *The Technique of Acting.* Toronto: Bantam Books, 1988.

Alion, Yves. "Interview with Jane Campion: In the Country of the Hypersensitive." In Wexman, *Jane Campion,* 83–85.

Allen, Michael. *Contemporary U.S. Cinema.* Essex: Longman/Pierson Education, 2003.

Alley, Elizabeth, ed. *The Inward Sun: Celebrating the Life and Works of Janet Frame.* Wellington: Daphne Brasell Associates Press, 1994.

———. "Janet Frame/Interviewed by Elizabeth Alley." In *In the Same Room: Conversations with New Zealand Writers,* ed. Elizabeth Alley and Mark Williams, 39–54. Auckland: Auckland University Press, 1992.

Altman, Rick. *Film/Genre.* London: British Film Institute, 1999.

Anderson, Quentin. *The Imperial Self: An Essay in American Literary and Cultural History.* New York: Vintage Books, 1972.

Apostolos-Cappadona, Diane. "From Eve to the Virgin and Back Again: The Image of Woman in Contemporary (Religious) Film." In *The New Image of Religious Film,* ed. John May, 111–27. Kansas City: Sheed and Ward, 1997.

Bandy, Mary Lea, and Antonio Monda, eds. *The Hidden God: Film and Faith.* New York: Museum of Modern Art, 2003.

Barber, Lynden. "Angel with an Eccentric Eye." In Wexman, *Jane Campion,* 57–61.

———. "Playing It Low-Key." In Wexman, *Jane Campion,* 142–45.

Barnett, Stephen, and Richard Wolfe. *New Zealand! New Zealand! In Praise of Kiwiana.* Auckland: Hodder and Stoughton, 1989.

Baron, Cynthia, Diane Carson, and Frank P. Tomasulo, eds. *More Than a Method.* Detroit: Wayne State University Press, 2004.

Basinger, Jeanine. *A Woman's View: How Hollywood Spoke to Women, 1930–1960.* New York: Knopf, 1993.

Bauer, Dale. "Jane Campion's Symbolic *Portrait.*" *The Henry James Review* 18, no. 2 (1997): 194–97.

Bell, Millicent. "Isabel Archer and the Affronting of Plot." In Henry James, *The Portrait of a Lady.* 2nd ed. New York: W. W. Norton, 1995. 748–83.

Benjamin, Jessica. *The Bonds of Love: Psychoanalysis, Feminism, and the Problem of Domination.* New York: Pantheon, 1988.

Bergson, Henri. *Durée et simultanéité.* Paris: Quadrige/Presses Universitaires de France, 1968.

———. *Matière et mémoire.* Paris: Presses Universitaires de France, 1939.

Bernard, Jami. *Chick Flicks: A Movie Lover's Guide to the Movies Women Love.* Secaucus, NJ: Carol Publishing Group, 1996.

Bernas, Steven. *L'auteur au cinéma.* Paris: L'Harmattan, 2002.

Berry, Jo, and Angie Errigo. *Chick Flicks: Movies Women Love.* London: Orion, 2004.

Beuka, Robert. *SuburbiaNation: Reading Suburban Landscape in Twentieth-Century American Fiction and Film.* New York: Palgrave, 2004.

Bilbrough, Miro. "Different Complexions: Jane Campion, An Interview." In *Film in Aotearoa New Zealand,* ed. Jonathan Dennis and Jan Bieringa, 92–104. Wellington: Victoria University Press, 1992.

———. "The Piano." In Wexman, *Jane Campion,* 113–24.

Bordwell, David. "The Art Cinema as a Mode of Film Practice." In *Film and Authorship,* ed. Virginia Wright Wexman, 42–49. New Brunswick: Rutgers University Press, 2003.

Bourguignon, Thomas, and Michel Ciment. "Interview with Jane Campion: More Barbarian Than Aesthete." In Wexman, *Jane Campion,* 101–12.

Boyd, Robin. *The Australian Ugliness.* Australia: Angus and Robertson, 1963.

Bratton, Jacky, Jim Cook, and Christine Gledhill, eds. *Melodrama, Stage, Picture, Screen.* London: British Film Institute, 1994.

Brooks, Peter. "Melodrama, Body, Revolution." In *Melodrama, Stage, Picture, Screen,* ed. Jacky Bratton, Jim Cook, and Christine Gledhill, 11–24. London: British Film Institute, 1994.

———. *The Melodramatic Imagination: Balzac, Henry James, Melodrama, and the Mode of Excess.* New Haven: Yale University Press, 1995.

Brunsdon, Charlotte, ed. *Films for Women.* London: British Film Institute, 1986.

Bruzzi, Stella. "Tempestuous Petticoats: Costume and Desire in *The Piano,*" *Screen* 36, no. 3 (Autumn 1995): 261. Reprinted in *Piano Lessons: Approaches to The Piano,* ed. Felicity Coombs and Suzanne Gemmell, 97–110. Sydney: John Libbey, 1999.

———. *Undressing Cinema: Clothing and Identity in the Movies.* London: Routledge, 1997.

Butler, Alison. *Women's Cinema: The Contested Screen.* Short Cuts 14. London: Wallflower, 2002.

Cairns, Barbara, and Helen Martin. *Shadows on the Wall: A Study of Seven New Zealand Feature Films.* Auckland: Longman Paul, 1994.

Campion, Edith. *The Chain.* In *Tandem.* Wellington: A. H. and A. W. Reed, 1979.

———. *A Place to Pass Through and Other Stories.* Wellington: A. H. and A. W. Reed, 1977.

Campion, Jane. *The Piano* [screenplay]. London: Bloomsbury, 1993.

Campion, Jane, and Kate Pullinger. *The Piano: A Novel.* London: Bloomsbury, 1994.

Cantwell, Mary. "Jane Campion's Lunatic Women." In Wexman, *Jane Campion,* 153–63.

———. "Jane Campion's Lunatic Women." *New York Times Magazine,* 19 September 1993, 40–41, 44, 51.

Cardullo, Bert, ed. *Bazin at Work: Major Essays and Reviews of the Forties.* London: Routledge, 1997.

Carnicke, Sharon. "Jane Campion, the Classical Romantic." In Wexman, *Jane Campion,* 168–72.

———. "The Material Poetry of Acting: 'Objects of Attention,' Performance Style, and Gender in *The Shining* and *Eyes Wide Shut.*" *Journal of Film and Video* 58, nos. 1–2 (2006): 21–30.

———. *Stanislavsky in Focus.* Amsterdam: Harwood Academic Publishers, 1998.

———. "Stanislavsky's System: Pathways for the Actor." In *Twentieth-Century Acting Training,* ed. Alison Hodge, 11–54. London: Routledge, 2000.

Carter, Alison. "Kerry's Janet Moves Cinema-goers to Tears." *New Zealand Women's Weekly,* 6 August 1990, 8–9.

Cheshire, Ellen. *The Pocket Essential Jane Campion.* Harpenden: Pocket Essentials, 2000.

Ciment, Michel. "The Red Wigs of Autobiography: Interview with Jane Campion." In Wexman, *Jane Campion,* 62–70.

———. "Two Interviews with Jane Campion." In Wexman, *Jane Campion,* 30–44.

———. "Two Interviews with Jane Campion." In *Second Take: Australian Film-Makers Talk,* ed. Raffaele Caputo and Geoff Burton, 47–61. Saint Leonards NSW, Australia: Allen and Unwin, 1999.

———. "A Voyage to Discover Herself." In Wexman, *Jane Campion,* 177–85.

Clement, Shelley. "Frame to Screen." *Onfilm* 6, no. 6 (1989): 13–14.

Connaughton, Michael E. "American English and the International Theme in *The Portrait of a Lady.*" *Midwest Quarterly: A Journal of Contemporary Thought* 22, no. 2 (1981): 137–46.

Conversations in World Cinema—Jane Campion. Produced by Scott Hopper. Television program. New York: Sundance Channel, 2000.

Cordaiy, Hunter. "Jane Campion Interviewed." In Wexman, *Jane Campion,* 74–82.

Crossan, John Dominic. *The Dark Interval: Towards a Theology of Story.* Sonoma: Polebridge, 1988.

Dalziel, Raewyn. "An Experiment in the Social Laboratory? Suffrage, National Identity, and Mythologies of Race in New Zealand in the 1890s." In *Women's Suffrage in the British Empire: Citizenship, Nation, and Race,* ed. Ian Christopher Fletcher, Laura E. Nym Mayhall, and Philippa Levine, 87–102. London: Routledge, 2000.

———. "Presenting the Enfranchisement of New Zealand Women." In *Suffrage and Beyond: International Feminist Perspectives,* ed. Caroline Daley and Melanie Nolan, 42–64. Auckland: Auckland University Press, 1994.

Davis, Joe Lee, John T. Frederick, and Frank Luther Mott, eds. *American Literature, an Anthology and Critical Survey.* New York: C. Scribner's Sons, 1948–49.

D'Cruz, Doreen. "Textual Enigmas and Disruptive Desires in Jane Campion's *Sweetie.*" *Australian Feminist Studies* 21, no. 49 (2006): 7–22.

de Baecque, Antoine. *Histoire d'une revue.* Vol. 1. *Les Cahiers à l'assaut du cinéma.* Paris: Cahiers du cinéma, 1991.

de Baecque, Antoine, and Serge Toubiana. *Truffaut.* New York: Knopf, 1999.

de Bougainville, Louis-Antoine. *Voyage autour du monde par la frégate du Roi "La Boudeuse" et la flute "L'Etoile."* In Peter Jimack, *Diderot: Supplément au Voyage de Bougainville.* London: Grant and Cutler, 1988.

de Gasperi, Anne. "Et qui sait, à celle du jury." *Le Quotidien de Paris,* 15 September 1990.

———. "Rousseur de vivre." *Le Quotidien de Paris,* 25 April 1991.

Deleuze, Gilles. *Différence et répétition.* Paris: PUF, 1968.

———. *L'image-temps.* Paris: Editions de Minuit, 1985.

Denoon, Donald, and Philippa Mein-Smith, with Marvic Wyndham. *A History of Australia, New Zealand, and the Pacific.* Malden, MA: Blackwell, 2000.

de Saint Pern, Dominique. "Le sceau de l'Ange." *l'Express,* 25 April 1991.

de Saussure, Ferdinand. *Course in General Linguistics,* ed. Charles Bally and Albert Sechehaye in collaboration with Albert Riedlinger, trans. Wade Baskin. New York: McGraw-Hill, 1959.

de Tocqueville, Alexis. *De la démocratie en Amérique.* 1835, 1840; Paris: Gallimard, 1992.

Dobson, Patricia. "Portrait of a Lady." *Screen International* 1075 (13 September 1996): 25.

Drucker, Elizabeth. "An Angel at My Table." *American Film: A Journal of the Film and Television Arts* 16, no. 7 (1991): 52–53.

DuPuis, Reshela. "Romanticizing Colonialism: Power and Pleasure in Jane Campion's *Piano.*" *The Contemporary Pacific* 8, no. 1 (1996): 51–70.

Dwyer, Rachel. *Filming the Gods: Religion and Indian Cinema.* London: Routledge, 2006.

Dyson, Lynda. "The Return of the Repressed? Whiteness, Femininity, and Colonialism in *The Piano.*" In *Piano Lessons: Approaches to The Piano,* ed. Felicity Coombs and Suzanne Gemmell, 267–76. Sydney: John Libbey, 1999.

Edel, Leon. *Henry James: A Life.* New York: Harper and Row, 1985.

Eggleton, David. "Grimm Fairytale of the South Seas." *Illusions* 23 (1994): 2–5.

Ellis, John. "Art, Culture, and Quality: Terms for a Cinema in the Forties and Seventies." *Screen* 19, no. 3 (1978): 9–49.

Elsaesser, Thomas. "Putting on a Show: The European Art Movie." *Sight and Sound* 4, no. 4 (1994): 24.

Evans, Patrick. "At the Edge of the Alphabet." In *The Ring of Fire: Essays on Janet Frame,* ed. Jeanne Delbaere, 82–91. Sydney: Dangaroo Press, 1992.

———. "Coat, Strides: A Happy Ride." *Islands* 7, no. 5 (1979): 555, 558–60.

Fendal, Heike-Melba. "How Women Live Their Lives." In Wexman, *Jane Campion,* 86–90.

Ferber, Sarah, Chris Healy, and Chris McAuliffe, eds. *Beasts of Suburbia: Reinterpreting Cultures in Australian Suburbs.* Melbourne: Melbourne University Press, 1994.

Fine, Marshall. *Harvey Keitel: The Art of Darkness.* New York: Fromm International, 1998.

Fischer, Lucy. *Cinematernity: Film, Motherhood, Genre.* Princeton: Princeton University Press, 1996.

Forest, Claude. *Économies contemporaines du cinéma en Europe. L'improbable industrie.* Paris: CNRS Éditions, 2001.

Frame, Janet. *An Autobiography.* Auckland: Vintage, 2004.

———. *An Autobiography: An Angel at My Table; Volume Two.* Auckland: Random Century, 1989.

———. *Faces in the Water* and *The Edge of the Alphabet.* Auckland: Vintage, 2005.

Franke, Lizzie. "Jane Campion Is Called the Best Female Director in the World. What's Female Got to Do with It?" In Wexman, *Jane Campion,* 205–10.

Freiberg, Frieda. "The Bizarre in the Banal: Notes on the Films of Jane Campion." In *Don't Shoot Darling: Women's Independent Filmmaking in Australia,* ed. Annette Blonski, Barbara Creed, and Freda Freiberg, 328–33. Richmond: Greenhouse Publications, 1987.

Freud, Sigmund. *New Introductory Lectures on Psychoanalysis Volume 2,* trans. James Strachey. Harmondsworth: Penguin, 1973.

Frey, Hillary. "The Purloined Piano?" *Lingua Franca* 10, no. 6 (2000): 8–10.

Frodon, Michel. *Horizon cinéma: l'art du cinéma dans le monde contemporain à l'âge du numérique et de la mondialisation.* Paris: Cahiers du cinéma, 2006.

Fuller, Graham. "Sex and Self-Danger." *Sight and Sound* 13, no. 11 (2003): 16–19.

Furler, Andreas. "Structure Is Essential/Absolutely Crucial/One of the Most Important Things." In Wexman, *Jane Campion,* 91–95.

Garagnon, Jean. "French Imaginary Voyages to the Austral Lands in the Seventeenth and Eighteenth Centuries." In *Australia and the European Imagination,* ed. Ian Donaldson. Humanities Research Council, Canberra: Australian National University, 1982.

Garrett, Roberta. *Postmodern Chick Flicks: The Return of the Woman's Film.* New York: Palgrave Macmillan, 2007.

Gelder, Ken. "Jane Campion and the Limits of Literary Cinema." In *Adaptations: From Text to Screen, Screen to Text,* ed. Deborah Cartmell and Imelda Whelehan, 157–71. London: Routledge, 1999.

Géniès, Bernard. "La folie à l'horizon." *Le Nouvel Observateur,* 2 May 1991.

Giddens, Anthony. *Modernity and Self-Identity: Self and Society in the Late Modern Age.* Cambridge: Polity Press, 1991.

Gilbert-Rolfe, Jeremy. *Beauty and the Contemporary Sublime.* New York: Allworth Communications, 1999.

Gillespie, Maria. "Melodrama and Modern Subjectivity." In *Media Audiences,* ed. Maria Gillespie, 149–51. Maidenhead: Open University Press, 2005.

Gillett, Sue. "Lips and Fingers: Jane Campion's *The Piano.*" *Screen* 36, no. 3 (1995): 277–87.

————. *Views from Beyond the Mirror: The Films of Jane Campion.* Melbourne: Australian Teachers of Media, 2004.

————. *Views from Beyond the Mirror: The Films of Jane Campion.* The Moving Image 7. St Kilda: ATOM, 2004.

————. "Views from Beyond the Mirror: The Films of Jane Campion." *The Moving Image* 7 (2004): 32–37.

Glaessner, Verina. "A Girl's Own Story." *Monthly Film Bulletin* 57, no. 678 (1990): 209.

Gordon, Rebecca. "Portraits Perversely Framed: Jane Campion and Henry James." *Film Quarterly* 56, no. 2 (2003): 14–24.

Graham, David John. "The Uses of Film in Theology." In *Explorations in Theology and Film,* ed. Clive Marsh and Gaye Ortiz, 35–46. Oxford: Blackwell, 1997.

Grimshaw, Patricia. "Women's Suffrage in New Zealand Revisited: Writing from the Margins." In *Suffrage and Beyond: International Feminist Perspectives,* ed. Caroline Daley and Melanie Nolan, 25–41. Auckland: Auckland University Press, 1994.

Hall, Sandra. "The Arts/Film." In Wexman, *Jane Campion,* 164–67.

Halperin, John. "Trollope, James, and the International Theme." *The Yearbook of English Studies* 7 (1977): 141–47.

Hardy, Ann. "The Last Patriarch." *Illusions* 23 (1994): 6–13.

————.*Sites of Value? Discourses of Religion and Spirituality in the Production of a New Zealand Film and Television Series.* PhD diss., Waikato University, 2003.

————. "Sweetie: A Song in the Desert." *Illusions* 15 (1990): 7–13.

Haskell, Molly. *From Reverence to Rape: The Treatment of Women in the Movies.* Baltimore: Penguin, 1974.

Hausknecht, Gina. "Self-Possession, Dolls, Beatlemania, Loss: Telling the Girl's Own Story." In *The Girl: Constructions of the Girl in Contemporary Fiction by Women,* ed. Ruth O. Saxton, 21–24. New York: St Martin's Press, 1998.

Hawker, Philippa. "Jane Campion." In Wexman, *Jane Campion,* 20–25.

Heelas, Paul. *The New Age Movement.* Cambridge: Blackwell, 1996.

Hessey, Ruth. "Campion Goes Out on a Limb—Again." In Wexman, *Jane Campion,* 26–29.

hooks, bell. *Black Looks: Race and Representation.* Boston: South End Press, 1992.

Howard, Ebenezer. *Garden Cities of Tomorrow,* ed. F. J. Osborn. London: Faber and Faber, 1946.

Isherwood, Christopher. *My Guru and His Disciple.* London: Eyre Methuen, 1980.

Jacobs, Carol. "Playing Jane Campion's Piano: Politically." *MLN* 109, no. 5 (1991): 757–85.

James, Henry. *The Portrait of a Lady.* 2nd ed. New York: Norton, 1995.

Jayamanne, Laleen. *Toward Cinema and Its Double: Cross-Cultural Mimesis.* Bloomington: Indiana University Press, 2001.

Johnson, Anna. "The Root of Evil: Suburban Imagery in Jane Campion's *Sweetie* and Bill Henson's Series *Untitled* 1985/6." In *Binocular, Focusing, Writing, Vision,* ed. E. McDonald and J. Engberg, 131–41. Sydney: Moet and Chandon, 1991.

Johnson, Brian D. "Rain Forest Rhapsody: *The Piano* Is a Work of Passion and Beauty." In Margolis, *Jane Campion's* The Piano, 172–74.

Jones, Laura. *An Angel at My Table: The Screenplay from the Three-Volume Autobiography of Janet Frame.* London: Pandora, 1990.

———. *The Portrait of a Lady: Screenplay Based on the Novel by Henry James.* New York: Penguin Books, 1996.

Jones, Lawrence. "Puritanism." In *The Oxford Companion to New Zealand Literature,* ed. Roger Robinson and Nelson Wattie, 455–56. Oxford: Oxford University Press, 1998.

Kagan World Media. "Film Review and Cost Estimate Report (FRCE)." Baseline. http://www.hollywood.com. *The Piano* (1993); *The Portrait of a Lady* (1996); *In the Cut* (2003).

Kaleta, Kenneth C. *David Lynch.* New York: Twayne, 1993.

Kapitanoff, Nancy. "Cult of Campion." *Pulse!* February 2000, 34–36.

Kaplan, E. Ann. *Motherhood and Representation: The Mother in Popular Culture and Melodrama.* London: Routledge, 1992.

Kauffmann, Stanley. "A Woman's Life." *The New Republic* 204, no. 22 (1991): 28–29.

King, Michael. *Wrestling with the Angel: A Life of Janet Frame.* Auckland: Viking, 2000.

Klinger, Barbara. "The Art Film, Affect, and the Female Viewer: *The Piano* Revisited." *Screen* 47, no. 1 (2006): 19–41.

Krasner, David. "Strasberg, Adler, and Meisner: Method Acting." In *Twentieth Century Actor Training,* ed. Alison Hodge, 129–50. London: Routledge, 2000.

Lalanne, Jean-Marc. Review of *The Portrait of a Lady. Cahiers du cinéma* 508 (1996): 78–79.

Lancioni, Judith. "Murder and Mayhem on Wisteria Lane: A Study of Genre and Cultural Context in *Desperate Housewives.*" In *Reading "Desperate Housewives": Beyond the White Picket Fence,* ed. Kim Akass and Janet McCabe, 129–43. New York: Palgrave Macmillan, 2006.

Lane, Christina. *Feminist Hollywood: From* Born in Flames *to* Point Break. Detroit: Wayne State University Press, 2000.

Lansdown, Richard, ed. *Strangers in the South Seas: The Idea of the Pacific in Western Thought.* Honolulu: University of Hawai'i Press, 2006.

Liebersohn, Harry. "Images of Monarchy: Kamehameha I and the Art of Louis Choris." In *Double Vision: Art Histories and Colonial Histories in the Pacific,* ed. Nicholas Thomas and Diane Losche, 44–64. Cambridge: Cambridge University Press, 1999.

Lindvall, Terry, W. O. Williams, and Artie Terry. "Spectacular Transcendence: Abundant Means in the Cinematic Representation of African-American Christianity." *The Howard Journal of Communications* 7 (1996): 205–20.

Long Hoeveler, Diane. "Silence, Sex, and Feminism: An Examination of *The Piano*'s Unacknowledged Sources." *Literature-Film Quarterly* 26, no. 2 (1998): 109–17.

Lovell, Alan, and Peter Krämer, eds. *Screen Acting.* New York: Routledge, 1999.

Lucas, Rose. "'Round the Block': Back to the Suburb in *Return Home.*" In Ferber, Healy, and McAuliffe, *Beasts of Suburbia,* 111–26.

MacCabe, Colin. *Tracking the Signifier: Theoretical Essays: Film, Linguistics, Literature.* Minneapolis: University of Minnesota Press, 1985.

MacFarlane, Brian. "The Portrait of a Lady." *Cinema Papers,* April 1997, 35–37.

Mander, Jane. *The Story of a New Zealand River.* Christchurch: Whitcombe and Tombs, 1973.

———. *The Story of a New Zealand River.* Auckland: Vintage, 1999.

Margolis, Harriet, ed. *Jane Campion's* The Piano. Cambridge: Cambridge University Press, 2000.

———. "'A Strange Heritage': From Colonization to Transformation?" In Margolis, *Jane Campion's* The Piano, 1–41.

Marie, Michel, ed. *Le Jeune Cinéma Français.* Paris: Nathan, 1998.

Marsh, Clive, and Gaye Ortiz, eds. *Explorations in Theology and Film.* Oxford: Blackwell, 1997.

Martin, Adrian. "Losing the Way: The Decline of Jane Campion." *Landfall* 200 (November 2000): 88–102.

Mason, Bruce. "Towards a Professional Theatre." *Landfall* 65 (1963): 70–77.

Mayne, Judith. *Contemporary Film Directors: Claire Denis.* Urbana: University of Illinois Press, 2005.

McDonald, Paul. "Film Acting." In *Oxford Guide to Film Studies,* ed. John Hill and Pamela Church Gibson, 30–35. New York: Oxford University Press, 1998.

———. "Why Study Film Acting? Some Opening Reflections." In Baron, Carson, and Tomasulo, *More Than a Method,* 23–41.

McEldowney, Dennis. "Short Stories." *Islands* 7, no. 3 (1979): 314–17.

McGill, David. *Up the Boohai Shooting Pukakas: A Dictionary of Kiwi Slang.* Lower Hutt, New Zealand: Mills Publications, 1988.

McGlothlin, Erin. "Speaking the 'Mind's Voice': Double Discursivity in Jane Campion's *The Piano.*" *Post Script* 23, no. 2 (2004): 19–32.

McGregor, Rae. *The Story of a New Zealand Writer: Jane Mander.* Dunedin: University of Otago Press, 1998.

McHugh, Kathleen A. *Jane Campion.* Urbana: University of Illinois Press, 2007.

Mellencamp, Patricia. *A Fine Romance: Five Ages of Film Feminism.* Philadelphia: Temple University Press, 1995.

Mercer, Gina. *Janet Frame: Subversive Fictions.* Dunedin: University of Otago Press, 1994.

Michalet, Charles-Albert. *Le Drôle de drame du cinéma mondial.* Paris: La Découverte, 1987.

Michasiw, Kim Ian. "Some Stations of Suburban Gothic." In *American Gothic: New Interventions in a National Narrative,* ed. Robert K. Martin and Eric Savoy, 237–57. Iowa City: University of Iowa Press, 1998.

Miles, Margaret. *Seeing and Believing: Religion and Values in the Movies.* Boston: Beacon Press, 1996.

Miller, Toby, Nitin Govil, John McMurria, and Richard Maxwell. *Global Hollywood.* London: British Film Institute, 2001.

Modleski, Tania. *Loving with a Vengeance: Mass Produced Fantasies for Women.* London: Routledge, 1994.

———. *Old Wives' Tales, and Other Women's Stories.* New York: New York University Press, 1998.

Moine, Raphaëlle. *Les genres du cinéma.* Paris: Nathan, 2002.

Moore, Susanna. *In the Cut.* New York: A. Knopf, 1995.

Mulvey, Laura. "Visual Pleasure and Narrative Cinema." In *Issues in Feminist Film Criticism,* ed. Patricia Erens, 28–40. Bloomington: Indiana University Press, 1990.

Murphy, Kathleen. "Jane Campion's Passage to India." *Film Comment* 36, no. 1 (2000): 30–37.

———. "Jane Campion's Shining Portrait of a Director." *Film Comment* 32, no. 6 (1996): 28–32.

Nadel, Alan. "The Search for Cinematic Identity and a Good Man: Jane Campion's Appropriation of James' *Portrait.*" *The Henry James Review* 18, no. 2 (1997): 180–83.

Naremore, James. *Acting in the Cinema.* Berkeley: University of California Press, 1988.

Neill, Anna. "A Land without a Past: Dreamtime and Nation in *The Piano.*" In *Piano Lessons: Approaches to* The Piano, ed. Felicity Coombs and Suzanne Gemmell, 136–47. Sydney: John Libbey, 1999.

Neroni, Hilary. "Jane Campion's Jouissance: *Holy Smoke* and Feminist Theory." In *Lacan and Contemporary Film Theory,* ed. Todd McGowan and Sheila Kunkle, 209–32. New York: Other Press, 2004.

O'Regan, Tom. "Australian Cinema as a National Cinema." In Williams, *Film and Nationalism,* 86–136.

Orr, Bridget. "Birth of a Nation? From *Utu* to *The Piano.*" In *Piano Lessons: Approaches to* The Piano, ed. Felicity Coombs and Suzanne Gemmell, 148–60. Sydney: John Libbey, 1999.

O'Shea, John. *Don't Let It Get You: Memories—Documents.* Wellington: Victoria University Press, 1999.

Ozouf, Mona. *La Muse démocratique: Henry James ou les pouvoirs du roman.* Paris: Calmann-Lévy, 1998.

Park, Geoff. *Theatre Country: Essays on Whenua and Landscape.* Wellington: Victoria University Press, 2006.

Paul, Mary. *Her Side of the Story: Readings of Mander, Mansfield, and Hyde.* Dunedin: University of Otago Press, 1999.

Pearson, Bill. "Fretful Sleepers: A Sketch of New Zealand Behaviour and Its Implications for the Artist." In *Great New Zealand Argument: Ideas about Ourselves,* ed. Russell Brown, 88–89. Auckland: Activity Press, 2005.

Perkins, Reid. "Imag(in)ing Our Colonial Past: Colonial New Zealand on Film from *The Birth of New Zealand* to *The Piano*—Part II." *Illusions* 26 (1997): 17–21.

Perry, Nick. "Antipodean Camp." In *Hyperreality and Global Culture.* London: Routledge, 1998.

Pihama, Leonie. "Are Films Dangerous? A Maori Woman's Perspective on *The Piano.*" *Hecate* 20, no. 2 (1994): 239–42.

———. "Ebony and Ivory: Constructions of Maori in *The Piano.*" In Margolis, *Jane Campion's* The Piano, 114–34.

Polan, Dana. *Jane Campion.* World Directors Series. London: British Film Institute, 2001.

Prédal, René. *Le Jeune Cinéma Français.* Paris: Nathan, 2002.

Racault, Jean-Michel. "Résonances utopiques de l'*Histoire des navigations aux Terres australes* du président de Brosses." In *Mythes et géographies des mers du sud,* ed. Sylviane Leoni and Réal Ouellet, 44–45. Dijon: Editions Universitaires de Dijon, 2006.

Rayner, Jonathan. *Contemporary Australian Cinema: An Introduction.* Manchester: Manchester University Press, 2000, 43–56.

Read, Herbert. *Le sens de l'art.* Paris: éditions Sylvie Messinger, 1984.

Redding, Judith M., and Victoria A. Brownworth. *Film Fatales: Independent Women Directors.* Seattle: Seal Press, 1997.

Reid, Mark. "A Few Black Keys and Mäori Tattoos: Re-Reading Jane Campion's *The Piano* in Post-Negritude Time." *Quarterly Review of Film and Video* 17, no. 2 (June 2000): 107–16.

Rhoads, David, and Sandra Roberts. "From Domination to Mutuality in *The Piano* and in the Gospel of Mark." In Marsh and Ortiz, *Explorations in Theology and Film,* 47–58.

Rickey, Carrie. "A Director Strikes an Intimate Chord." In Wexman, *Jane Campion,* 50–53.

Ricoeur, Paul. *Temps et récit, Tome III Le temps raconté.* Paris: Seuil, 1985.

Ritts, Herb. "The Gospel According to Harvey." *Vogue,* December 1993, 288–91, 329–30.

Robson, Jocelyn, and Beverly Zalcock. *Girls' Own Stories: Australian and New Zealand Women's Films.* London: Scarlet Press, 1997.

Rosen, Marjorie. *Popcorn Venus: Movies and the American Dream.* New York: Coward, 1973.

Rowe, Douglas. "Jane Campion Hides Her Passion." *Associated Press,* 17 January 1997.

Rueschmann, Eva. *Sisters on Screen: Siblings in Contemporary Cinema.* Philadelphia: Temple University Press, 2000.

Sargeson, Frank. "Review." *Landfall* 125 (1978): 90–91.

Schrader, Paul. *Transcendental Style in Film: Ozu, Bresson, and Dreyer.* Berkeley: University of California Press, 1972.

Segal, Hanna. *Klein.* Brighton: Harvester Press, 1979.

Shelton, Lindsay. *The Selling of New Zealand Movies.* Wellington: Awa Press, 2005.

Silverman, Kaja. "The Female Authorial Voice." In *Film and Authorship,* ed. Virginia Wright Wexman, 50–75. New Brunswick, NJ: Rutgers University Press, 2003.

Sklar, Robert. "A Novel Approach to Movie Making: Reinventing *The Portrait of a Lady.*" *The Chronicle of Higher Education* 43, no. 23 (1997): B7.

Sobchak, Vivian. *Carnal Thoughts: Embodiment and Moving Image Culture.* Berkeley: University of California Press, 2004.

Stiles, Mark. "Jane Campion." In Wexman, *Jane Campion,* 3–8.

Stitt, Greg. *The Grass Is Greener: Interview with Jane Campion.* Television program. New Zealand and Australia: Rhymer and Bayly Watson, 1990.

Tarr, Carrie, with Brigitte Rollet. *Cinema and the Second Sex—Women's Filmmaking in France in the 1980s and 1990s.* London: Continuum, 2001.

Thompson, David. "Harvey Keitel: Staying Power." *Sight and Sound* 3, no. 1 (1993): 22–25.

Thornham, Sue. *Passionate Detachments: An Introduction to Feminist Film Theory.* London: Arnold, 1997.

Tomlinson, Doug. "Harvey Keitel." In *Actors on Acting for the Screen,* ed. Doug Tomlinson. New York: Garland, 1994, 303–4.

Trémois, Marie-Claude. *Les Enfants de la liberté. Le jeune cinema français des années 1990.* Paris: Le Seuil, 1997.

Tulich, Katherine. "Jane's Film Career Takes Wing." In Wexman, *Jane Campion,* 71–73.

Turcotte, Gerry. "Australian Gothic." In *The Handbook to Gothic Literature,* ed. M. Mulvey Roberts, 10–19. Basingstoke: Macmillan, 1998.

Turner, Stephen. "Once Were English." *Meanjin* 58, no. 2 (1999): 122–39.

Urban, Andrew L. "Campion: Cannes She Do it?" In Wexman, *Jane Campion,* 16–19.

———. "The Contradictions of Jane Campion, Cannes Winner." In Wexman, *Jane Campion,* 14–15.

———. "Piano's Good Companions." In Wexman, *Jane Campion,* 146–49.

Vance, Carol, ed. *Pleasure and Danger.* Boston: Routledge/Kegan Paul, 1984.

Vieillard-Baron, Jean-Louis. *Bergson—la durée et la nature.* Paris: Presses Universitaires de France, 2004.

Vincendeau, Ginette. *Film/Literature/Heritage.* London: British Film Institute, 2001.

Walton, Priscilla L. "Jane and James Go to the Movies: Post Colonial Portraits of a Lady." *The Henry James Review* 18, no. 2 (1997): 187–90.

Weber, Daniel. "Culture or Commerce in Publishing." In *Rethinking Comparative Sociology: Repertoires of Evaluation in France and the United States,* ed. Michèle Lamont and Laurent Thévenot, 127–47. Cambridge: Cambridge University Press, 2000.

Wexman, Virginia Wright, ed. *Jane Campion: Interviews.* Conversations with Filmmakers Series. Jackson: University Press of Mississippi, 1999.

———. "The Portrait of a Body." *The Henry James Review* 18, no. 2 (1997): 184–86.

White, Patrick. *Letters,* ed. David Marr. Sydney: Random House, 1994.

Wiener, Evan. "The Rap on Harvey Keitel." *Detour,* May 2000, 72–75.

Wikse, Maria. *Materialisations of a Woman Writer: Investigating Janet Frame's Biographical Legend.* Oxford: Peter Laing, 2006.

Williams, Alan, ed. *Film and Nationalism.* New Brunswick: Rutgers University Press, 2002.

Williams, Mark. "Janet Frame's Suburban Gothic." In *Leaving the Highway: Six Contemporary New Zealand Novelists.* Auckland: Auckland University Press, 1990.

Williams, Sue. "A Light on the Dark Secrets of Depression." In Wexman, *Jane Campion,* 175–76.

Williamson, Kristin. "The New Filmmakers." In Wexman, *Jane Campion,* 9–10.

Wojcik, Pamela Robertson, ed. *Movie Acting: The Film Reader.* London: Routledge, 2004.

Woodhead, Linda, and Paul Heelas, eds. *Religion in Modern Times: An Interpretive Anthology.* Oxford: Blackwell, 2000.

Woollacott, Angela. "Australian Women's Metropolitan Activism: From Suffrage, to Imperial Vanguard, to Commonwealth Feminism." In *Women's Suffrage in the British Empire,* ed. Ian Fletcher, Laura E. Nym Mayhall, and Philippa Levine, 207–23.

Wright, Elizabeth, ed. *Feminism and Psychoanalysis: A Critical Dictionary.* Oxford: Blackwell, 1992.

Contributors

Muriel Andrin holds a PhD from the Université Libre de Bruxelles. She is the author of *Maléfiques: Le Mélodrame filmique américain et ses héroïnes, 1940–1953* (Peter Lang, 2005). She teaches at the Université Libre de Bruxelles, the Universiteit van Antwerpen, and lectures at the Cinémathèque Royale de Belgique in Brussels. She is the author of several articles on women's representation in melodramas and contemporary cinema as well as on women directors. She also works on the new forms of interactions between cinema and contemporary art.

Irène Bessière is director of Les Européens dans le cinéma américain: émigration et exil at the Fondation Maison des Sciences de l'Homme and codirector of Histoire du cinéma et histoire de l'art at the Institut national d'histoire de l'art. She is also the co-convenor of the research colloquium Jane Campion: Cinema, Nation, Identity.

Jean Bessière received his education at the Sorbonne and École Normale Supérieure (Paris). He has taught at Université Paris X, Indiana University, Stanford University, McGill University, and Université d'Amiens. He has acted as president of the International Comparative Literature Association. The following are a selection of the many publications he has authored: *Enigmaticité de la littérature* (1993), *La littérature et sa rhétorique* (1999), *Quel statut pour la littérature?* (2001), *Principes de la théorie littéraire* (2005), *Qu'est-il arrivé aux écrivains français? d'Alain Robbe-Grillet à Jonathan Littell* (2007). He coedited *Histoire des poétiques* (1987), and *Théorie littéraire* (1989). He is professor of comparative literature at the Université Paris 3–La Sorbonne nouvelle.

Annabel Cooper is head of the gender studies program in the Department of Anthropology, Sociology, and Gender Studies at the University of Otago. Her work on the gendered cultural history of New Zealand, and occasionally Australia, includes publications on nation, autobiography, and locality.

Alistair Fox is professor of English and director of the Centre for Research on National Identity at the University of Otago. He has written extensively on humanism, politics, and reform in early modern England and on postcolonial literature, gender studies, and the formation of New Zealand cultural identity. His books include *Thomas More: History and Providence* (Yale, 1982), *Utopia: An Elusive Vision* (Twayne, 1993), *Politics and Literature in the Reigns of Henry VII and Henry VIII* (Blackwell, 1989), *The English Renaissance: Identity and Representation in Elizabethan England* (Blackwell, 1997), and *The Ship of Dreams: Masculinity in Contemporary/New Zealand Fiction* (University of Otago Press, 2008). He is also, with Hilary Radner, the translator of Raphaëlle Moine's *Cinema Genres* (Blackwell, 2008).

Sue Gillett is senior lecturer in literature, film, and art at La Trobe University, Bendigo, Australia. She is the author of *Views from Beyond the Mirror: The Films of Jane Campion* (ATOM, 2004), and has published widely in Australia and internationally on women's filmmaking and on contemporary literature, particularly by women authors. In addition to her critical writings, she writes songs, poetry, and lots of nonsense to amuse her child. She is currently writing the libretto for a contemporary opera dealing with those eternal passions, love and war.

Ann Hardy is senior lecturer in the Department of Screen and Media Studies at Waikato University. Her research interests include religion and media and New Zealand media. She is the author of two previous essays on Jane Campion's work: "A Song in the Desert" (*Illusions* 15 [1990]) and "The Last Patriarch," in *Jane Campion's The Piano*, ed. Harriet Margolis (Cambridge University Press, 2000).

Chris Holmlund is professor of French, cinema studies, and women's studies at the University of Tennessee. Her areas of interest and scholarship include contemporary film and video, including documentary, avant-garde, independent and mainstream feature work produced in the United States, Canada, Europe, Latin America, and Francophone Africa. Her publications include *Contemporary American Independent Film: From the Margins to the Mainstream,* ed. Chris Holmlund and Justin Wyatt (2005); *Impossible Bodies: Femininity and Masculinity at the Movies* (2002); and *Between the Sheets, In the Streets: Queer, Lesbian, Gay Documentary,* ed. Chris Holmlund and Cynthia Fuchs (1997). Her latest edited volume, *American Cinema of the 1990s,* appeared in 2008. She is completing a book titled *Stars in Action* for BFI/Palgrave Macmillan.

Lawrence Jones is emeritus professor of English, University of Otago. The first academic critic to publish on Janet Frame's work (1970), he wrote the general introduction to the new Random House/Vintage edition of Frame's fiction, *The Janet Frame Collection,* and the special introduction to the fiftieth anniversary edition of her *Owls Do Cry,* and is a trustee of the Janet Frame Literary Trust. Jones is the author of the section "The Novel" in *The Oxford History of New Zealand Literature in English* (2nd ed., 1998) and *of Picking Up the Traces: The Making of a New Zealand Literary Culture 1932–1945* (Vicbooks, 2003). He is working on a history of New Zealand literary culture 1945–65 and on a jointly authored book on Maurice Gee.

Harriet Margolis, senior lecturer in film at Victoria University of Wellington, is the editor of *Jane Campion's* The Piano (Cambridge University Press, 2000) and the coauthor (with Janet Hughes) of "Jane Campion's *The Portrait of a Lady*" in *Nineteenth-Century American Fiction on Screen*, ed. R. Barton Palmer (Cambridge University Press, 2007). She is also co-editor of *Studying the Event Film: The Lord of the Rings* (Manchester University Press, 2008).

Kathleen McHugh is a professor in the Department of English and in the School of Film, Television and Digital Media at the University of California, Los Angeles. In *American Domesticity: From How-To Manual to Hollywood Melodrama* (Oxford, 1999), she reconsiders melodrama and the feminist commentary applied to it in relation to domestic labor and its representation in the United States. She has co-edited a collection of essays titled *South Korean Golden Age Melodrama: Gender, Genre, and National Cinema* (Wayne State University Press, 2005) and published articles on domesticity, feminism, melodrama, the avant-garde, and autobiography in such journals as *Cultural Studies, Jump Cut, Screen, South Atlantic Quarterly*, and *Velvet Light Trap*. Her book *Jane Campion* was published in March 2007 by the University of Illinois Press, and she is editing a book on collaborative autobiographies in the Americas.

Raphaëlle Moine is Professeure en études Cinématographiques at the Université de Paris 10–Nanterre. Her books include *France/Hollywood. Echanges cinématographiques et identités nationales* (co-edited with Martin Barnier, L'Harmattan, 2002), *Les Genres du cinéma* (Armand Colin, 2002, 2nd ed., 2005; published in English as *Cinema Genre*), *Le Cinéma français face aux genres* (AFRHC, 2005), and *Remakes: Les films français à Hollywood* (CNRS Editions, 2007).

Hilary Radner is the Foundation Professor of Film and Media Studies in the Department of Media, Film, and Communication Studies at the University of Otago. She is the author of *Shopping Around* (1995), co-editor of *Film Theory Goes to the Movies* (1993), *Constructing the New Consumer Society* (1997), *Swinging Single* (1999), and the special issue "Strange Localities: Utopias, Intellectuals, and National Identities in the 21st Century," *Portal: Journal of Multidisciplinary International Studies* (2005).

Simon Sigley is a graduate of the University of Auckland. His doctoral thesis was titled "Film Culture: Its Development in New Zealand, 1920s–1970s" (2004). He studied the cinema in France, where he lived for several years, and has the French equivalent of a master's degree in film studies. He has produced, directed, and edited video in both New Zealand and France and is a media studies lecturer at Massey University's Albany Campus (Auckland).

Rochelle Simmons studied English and art history at the University of Auckland and earned a PhD in English from the University of Toronto. She teaches courses on American literature, textuality and visuality, and Cubism in literature and film in the Department of English at the University of Otago. She maintains a research and teaching interest in New Zealand cinema, and has a chapter on *The Piano* in *24 Frames: Australian and New Zealand Cinema* from Wallflower Press, 2007. She is writing a book on John Berger's fiction, art criticism, and filmmaking.

Index